Harden's

CHAMPAGNE
MUMM
London Party Guide

© Harden's Guides, 1993

ISBN 1-873721-02-1

British Library Cataloguing-in-Publication data:
a catalogue record for this book is available from
the British Library.

Printed and bound in Finland by
Werner Söderström Osakeyhtiö.

Harden's Guides
PO Box 1500
London SW5 0DX

The views expressed in this book are solely
those of Harden's Guides.

The contents of this book are believed correct at
the time of printing. Nevertheless the publishers
can accept no responsibility for errors or changes in
or omissions from the details given.

No part of this publication may be reproduced or
transmitted in any form or by any means, electronically
or mechanically, including photocopying, recording or
any information storage or retrieval system, without
prior permission in writing from the publishers.

Contents

Page

Introductory section
    How to use
    Mumm tasting notes
    Checklist
    Introduction
    Costs

Private venues 18

Moving venues 124

Action venues 128

Paint the town rouge 132

Party services
    Food and wine 148
    Party planners 157
    Entertainments 160
    Marquees 168
    Decoration 169
    Equipment 172
    Transport 174
    Dress 175
    Party shops 177
    Photography etc 178
    Miscellaneous 181

Indexes
    Private venues
        By type 184
        Outside area/Marquee site 192
        Capacities
            Standing 194
            Seated 207
            Dinner dance 219
    Alphabetical 224

How to use

Price bands

The price bands indicate, in the most general terms, the overall minimum level of expenditure per head you are likely to incur in giving a party at a particular venue

£B – Budget: It should be possible to organise a drinks party for about the same cost per head as an evening in a wine bar or a party with food and drink for the about the same cost as eating in a modestly priced restaurant.

£M – Medium: The costs of a party with wine and food will generally run at or a little above those of providing similar catering in a medium to high class restaurant. Drinks parties will probably cost as much per head as a meal in a modestly priced restaurant.

£E – Expensive: Outside the budget of most private individuals and mainly, therefore, used for corporate events.

Where two levels are shown (eg £B-M), the likely range of expenditure straddles two bands.

Capacities – eg (85,150)

The total normal capacity of the whole venue is given in bold at the beginning of each entry.

Individual room capacities are given in the smaller print. This list of rooms may not be exhaustive – details are given only of the more important or interesting rooms, or, in some cases, rooms which are representative of other similar rooms.

If a room or venue is particularly suited to a dinner-dance, three capacities are given:

(standing, seated, dinner-dance).

If a room or venue is not particularly suited to a dinner-dance, two capacities are given:

(standing, seated).

The fact that no dinner-dance capacity is indicated does not necessarily mean that it is not possible to dance.

Smoking, **Amplified music** and **Dancing** are permitted, unless otherwise indicated.

How to use

Restrictions on use
Any explicit restrictions upon hirers or types of function are noted. The absence of such a note does not, of course, mean that the venue may not be selective about the functions and hirers which it will accept.

Catering
Except in the cases of restaurants, hotels, wine bars and pubs, each venue's stipulations regarding catering arrangements are given:

"In-house caterer" – you must use the resident caterer.

"Xco catering" – the use of the specified caterer is obligatory.

"List of caterers" – one of a list of approved outside caterers must be used.

"Hirer's choice of caterer" indicates that you can, in principle, bring in the caterer of your choice (although some venues will wish to vet your decision). Note that there may also be a resident caterer (which will generally be cheaper than bringing in an outsider).

Finishing time
In the small print, the time (if any) is stated by which the venue likes guests to have left. Note however that, even if a time is given, it may either be applied with complete inflexibility or be open to negotiation. In some cases, the time given is subject to a licensing extension being obtained, but this will usually be dealt with by the venue.

Days and times available and Annual closures
Except as indicated (immediately after the finishing time, where applicable), venues are generally available daily throughout the year (except Christmas) for day and evening functions. Note that many of the more popular venues may need to be booked months or years ahead.

Telephone and Fax numbers
All numbers are "071-" numbers, except where preceded by "081-" or an STD code. Where relevant, fax numbers are given in brackets after the telephone number.

G.H. MUMM & CIE
REIMS - FRANCE

When asked why he drank champagne for breakfast every morning, Noel Coward responded in his inimitable manner, "Doesn't everyone?"

Few people can afford to be quite so cavalier in their attitude to champagne, but by the same token, very few people would not share Coward's appreciation of the finer points of one of France's most famous exports. For most of us, champagne retains its place as the drink for special occasions, the first choice for all celebrations and the epitome of the good life.

Throughout its long history champagne has kept only the best company, and since the Roaring Twenties Champagne Mumm, one of the leading Grandes Marques champagnes, has been enjoyed at all the most prestigious social occasions. Its origins can be traced back to March 1st, 1827, when the House was founded in Reims in the heartland of the champagne producing region.

The celebrated cuvée Cordon Rouge, bearing the red sash emblem of the French Légion d'Honneur, was first produced in 1875, and is now a symbol of true refinement and good taste.

Seven other cuvées now make up the full range of champagnes in the Mumm range; vintage and non-vintage Cordon Rouge brut, vintage Cordon Rosé, Cordon Vert, Mumm de Cramant, René Lalou and the pinnacle of perfection, Grand Cordon de Mumm.

Tradition, precision and true affection go into each and every bottle of Champagne Mumm. Perfect, subtle harmony on the nose and palate is achieved through careful blending, the creative art of the Cellar Master. At Mumm each champagne is made up of between twenty-five and forty crus, or growths, which are then blended to produce one single cuvée. Only when the Cellar Master is satisfied that he has achieved the finest blend, using the finest grape varieties will he permit a bottle of champagne to carry the name of the House of Mumm.

All fine words, but perhaps the most important thing to remember about champagne is that it is for drinking and for pleasure.

As Napoleon said of champagne, "In victory you deserve it, in defeat you need it!" After all, who really needs an excuse to enjoy one of the finer things in life?

TASTING NOTES
by the Cellar Master at Mumm!

CORDON ROUGE
Colour
Eager, exciting bubbles. Brilliant, full and laced with dreams. Golden on wheat straw background.
Nose
Ample, colourful and fruity. Redolent of smoking greengage jam.
Palate
A strong personality and decisive character... with velvet roundness. Chivalrous courtship of tastebuds. Transient touch of almond and peach. Lingering powerfully, charming and virile.
Tasting
A loyal, steady cuvée, the blend showing powerful body yet delicate form. Acts magnetically, for apéritif, and is a sprightly companion throughout a meal. A gem of a champagne, harmoniously combining many crus.

VINTAGE CORDON ROUGE
Colour
Delicate and harmonious bright tints. Light straw with a touch of mellow gold. Attractively eager yet gentle bubbles.
Nose
Earthy caress on a fresh spring morning. Aromas of healthy, fleshy yellow apples. Decisive, frank and full of go.
Palate
Reassuringly soft-angled robustness. Gallant and vivacious. A gentle touch on the tastebuds.

Tasting
A robust, lively wine eager to live long. It will enhance meat and poultry in the midst of a meal. A happy marriage of power and elegance and a smiling cuvée.

CORDON VERT
Colour
Mellow gold with amber tints. Bold confident bubbles.
Nose
Pulpy and fleshy. Penetratingly soothing. Velvet aromas of melting pear.
Palate
Heralding untold pleasures. Tastebuds under sugary spell. Top-bred glucose languorous and long.
Tasting
A symphony of many crus brought together in sweet alliance. A wine made from fully ripe selected grapes. An indispensable companion of refined desserts.

Vintage Cordon Rosé
Colour
Twirling, pink salmon. Subtle hints of gold and crimson. Springtime sprightliness and freshness.
Nose
Convincing and teasing. Aromas of cunningly-scented red fruit.
Palate
Generously firm, yet full of courteousness. Soothingly round, velvety and fresh. A fleetingly... lingering dream.
Tasting
Its youthful finesse is its hope and pride. The table's pleasures it sees as white meats and cheeses. It is at any time to be desired a symbol of love and happiness.

Grand Cordon
Colour
Laced with jade and gold. Roguishly gracious bubbles.
Nose
Floral and convincingly persuasive. Aromas of delicate earthy flavours. Ample, balanced and fruity.
Palate
Grace and charm, finesse and elegance, showing a smilingly personable presence. A discreet personality and a fine character.
Tasting
A fine, enchanting cuvée, caressingly and poetically evocative of pleasure. A champagne full of freshness and jollity, sweet at any time of the day, a byword for pleasure and love. An excellent apéritif, it is better still before meat, with starters and fish if the meal is to be champagne only.

René Lalou
Colour
Noble, eager bubbles. Stylish and proud in its bearing. Gold and jade form its colour.
Nose
Unctuous and enthralling. Aromas of blossoming hawthorn. Proud and fiery all along.
Palate
Strikes as frank and heady. Fruity, pressing, sweet and long. Generous, powerful, smiling and strong.
Tasting
A harmonious, pulpy, yet gracious wine. A desirable cuvée for the inquiring and informed palate. A champagne for all seasons, a noble wine to preside over a grand dinner.

Mumm de Cramant
Colour
A blend of jade and light. A light froth is to this champagne what delicate features are to a woman's face.
Nose
Full of freshness and youth. Noble wood seasoned with great spirits. Perky aromas of new-born vine-shoots.
Palate
Gentle, remarkably delicate impression. Lingering and caressingly voluptuous. Graceful, poetical finish.
Tasting
Fond of smiling lips, it will give joy and cheerfulness as an apéritif. Early in the meal, it will get on fine with fish, pastry and shellfish.

Checklist

This is a list for a ball – many of the same issues will arise for smaller parties.

Getting the ball rolling
Venue
Theme
Timetable for evening
Set-up schedule
Marquee
Loos
Furniture
Guest list
Seating plan
Invitations (and other information for guests)
Programme
Place cards
Menus
Inform police/neighbours

Food
Cooking facilities
Special food, eg cake
Snack food
Utensils
Crockery
Table linen/napkins
Catering for bands, performers and staff
Ashtrays

Drink
Cold storage
Glasses
Ice
Mixers and soft drinks
Fruit for cocktails, etc
Serving trays

Decoration
Balloons, streamers
Flower, fruit, or ice displays
Lighting

Entertainment
Dance-floor
Disco & DJ
Bands
Performers
Fireworks/laser
Diversions, eg Casino, funfair attractions
Retiring rooms for bands and performers

Transport
Parking space
Cars, buses, train, helicopter

Staff
Security
Car parking
Reception
Loos/Cloakroom
Waiters/waitresses
Toastmaster
Seamstress
Clearing up

Cleaning up
Brushes
Water/Buckets
Detergents
Cloths

Don't forget
Plan entry procedure
Insurance
Access for furniture/equipment
Photography
Power ('3 phase'?)

Icing on the cake
Gifts for guests
Accommodation for guests

Introduction

Palaces, pubs, riverboats, livery halls, museums, colleges, nightclubs, hotels ... London offers a more interesting selection of party venues than any other city on Earth.

This is the first comprehensive directory designed to help you find your way around the multitude of venues and identify the right one for your party – be it private or corporate, formal or casual.

We are very grateful to Champagne Mumm for their sponsorship. Their support has enabled us to spend time exploring many nooks and crannies of this most intriguing of cities and to find out about the enormous business of giving parties in London. Before we began our researches, we had little idea of the size of the iceberg whose tip we had occasionally glimpsed.

Our thanks must also go to the hundreds of people who have shown us around their venues and told us about their businesses. We hope that our impressions – for such they are – of the various venues and services have done them justice.

For his introduction to the world of party-giving we are particularly indebted to Andrew Clementson of The Richard Groves Catering Company.

On the venues themselves, the staff of the London Convention Bureau were good enough to allow us to tap their rich vein of knowledge.

At the beginning of our researches, William Bartholomew and Johnny Roxburgh very kindly gave us the benefit of their huge experience of organising parties great and small. To the latter, we are grateful for the valedictory thought that what parties are really all about, of course, is the people.

Richard Harden   **Peter Harden**

Costs

Introduction

Giving a party at the venues listed in this book can cost anything between £10 and £250 a head – more if you really try. If you are organising a major party for the first time, the following guidelines on expenditure may help to set you in the right direction.

Do ensure that you keep an eye on the "big picture" – it is very important not to compare specific costs in isolation. Look at the total costs involved in plan A and compare them with the total costs involved in plan B. For example, you may find that one venue is apparently, on the basis of its hire charge, cheaper than another but that, after taking the respective catering costs into account, the true picture is entirely different.

Where choice is possible, you should, of course, always get competing estimates for each of the different items.

Catering and drink will almost invariably consume the greater part of a party budget. The other main costs are usually venue hire and decoration. Sometimes, a marquee and/or entertainments can make up a significant part of the total cost.

Catering and drink

As a rule of thumb, expenditure on food and drink provided by an outside caterer will be roughly the same as eating in a restaurant providing comparable fare (although you still have to bear the additional cost of the venue). Like restaurants, caterers' charges vary widely.

The quite significant wine mark-ups and/or high corkage charges sometimes demanded can make quite a difference to total costs and you should make sure that you include them in your sums.

Entertainments

Examples: a discotheque can cost anything from £100 to £1000, although you should get something very respectable for £400 or so; a top after dinner-speaker, or a well-known dance band, might command £2-£3,000, or in some cases more, for an evening's work.

Costs

Venue hire

The costs of hiring the venues themselves usually fall within the following ranges:

£0-50 – most pubs and wine bars (and some nightclubs); you may have to guarantee a certain level of total "spend"

£50-£750 – most of the private venues in this book

£750 - £5,000 – grander galleries, museums, houses and livery halls and large nightclubs

£5,000 and up – about 15 of the largest and most prestigious venues listed in this book.

Hire charges can be affected by the day of the week, length of hire, purpose of hire and time of year (prices in the first quarter often being "softer"). Charges for some, but by no means all, venues are less if the venue is not being used to full capacity.

Decoration and theming

It is worth bearing in mind that apparently inexpensive venues may be less of a bargain when you factor in the expenditure on decoration which will be required to make them festive. Apparently expensive venues which are decorated to a high standard can be better value than they appear because they require much less work, and expense, to get them ready for the party.

To dress a medium size ballroom, you can spend several hundred pounds on balloons and other decoration. For floral decoration on any scale, it is not difficult to spend several thousand pounds.

The cost of fully theming a party can be very considerable, especially if a set is to be built. A more economical option is to find a venue that comes ready-themed, at least to an extent, and to build upon the base which it offers.

Marquee hire

As an example, the hire of a frame marquee large enough to hold a dinner dance for 100 people will generally cost upwards of £1000.

Private venues
•••••••••••••••••••••••••

*Venues available for exclusive hire and
venues with private rooms*

Private venues

Abbey Community Association SW1   £B, (300,200,200)
34 Great Smith St   222 0303   (233 3308)
No-frills Westminster hall and other rooms, with school-gym decor; suitable for a wide range of budget events.
/ 2 am; hirer's choice of caterer; smoking restricted;
Main Hall (300,200,200); Annex A & B & C (120,60); Bar (100,50).

Academy of Live & Recorded Arts SW18   £B-M, (300,250,200)
The Royal Victoria Patriotic Bldg,
Fitzhugh Gr, Trinity Rd   081-870 6475
This extraordinary, overblown Victorian building, in a Wandsworth park, houses a large, mirrored rehearsal room, with one of the largest sprung wooden floors in London – a characterful space opening off the very pretty cloister garden. / 1 am; vacations only; hirer's choice of caterer.

Accademia Italiana SW7   £M-E, (80,80)
24 Rutland Gt   225 3474   (589 5187)
This Knightsbridge Village townhouse hosts numerous and varied Italian art and cultural exhibitions; its airy, white-walled galleries and large outside terrace are ideal for receptions and there is quite a pleasant, first floor period room for dinners. / no weddings; 10.30 pm; eve only ex Mon all day; hirer's choice of caterer; no amplified music; no dancing; smoking restricted; Main Galleries (80,80); Spazio Club (80,40).

Africa Centre WC2   £B, (150,150)
38 King St   836 1973   (836 1975)
This is a quirky, atmospheric place, just off Covent Garden; the Victorian galleried hall, the main space, could with a little decoration be used for quite traditional events, but with food from the basement restaurant, and, by taking their advice on bands, this place has great theme party potential. / Mon-Thu midnight, Fri-Sat 3 am; in-house (Calabash African Restaurant); Main Hall (150,150); Rear Hall (80,80).

Ajimura WC2   £M, (–,20)
51-53 Shelton St   240 9424
The first Japanese restaurant in the UK (as they claim) is not as close to the cutting edge of London cooking as it was; much of the sterility and expense associated with later Nipponese arrivals is happily absent, however.
/ Private Rm (–,20).

Al Basha W8   £M, (–,60)
222 Kensington High St   938 1794
Good, if pricey, food comes graciously served at this Holland Parkside Lebanese; the glitzy basement private-room is an atmospheric spot for a celebration.
/ Private Rm (–,60).

Private venues

Al San Vincenzo W2 £M, (–,16)
30 Connaught St   262 9623
Belying its modest appearance, this family-run restaurant near Marble Arch offers some of London's best Italian food and friendly service; there is an intimate basement private room. / Private Rm (–,16).

**Alexandra
Palace & Park N22** £M, (6500,3000,2750)
Wood Gn   081-365 2121   (081-883 3999)
The heart of this complex, whose terraces benefit from panoramic views over London, is the enormous, strikingly decorated Victorian hall; there is scope, especially with the 196 acres of parkland, to organise the largest event, but smaller receptions and dinners fit quite comfortably in the Londesborough Room or Palace Restaurant. / 2 am; in-house caterers; Great Hall (6500,3000,2750); West Hall (2500,1500,1400); Palm Terrace (1500,–); Palace Restaurant (400,250,200); Londesborough Rm (200,130,100); Palm Court 1-5 (100,50); marquee site.

All Saints W10 £B-M, (–,20)
12 All Saints Rd   243 2808
Laid-back Notting Hill café/restaurant with a stylishly plain basement room. / 12.30 am; not Sun; Basement (–,20).

**All Saints -
The Crypt E14** £B-M, (180,140,140)
Newby Pl   538 9198   (987 1665)
Carefully renovated, large East End church crypt, with modern facilities for business and social events. / 2 am; not Sun morning; Main Hall (180,140,140).

Alma SW18 £B, (130,60)
499 Old York Rd   081-870 2537   (081-874 9055)
well-known Wandsworth pub whose upstairs parlour is available for dinners, drinks and "quiet discos". / midnight; not Sun; Private Rm (130,60).

Amadeus Centre W9 £M, (200,150,150)
50 Shirland Rd   286 1686   (266 1255)
Converted late Victorian Little Venice Chapel, dominated by a (non-functional) organ – quite character-ful and in good order, but you would need a lot of decoration to make it jolly; an ideal combination is a dinner in the Upper Hall and a disco below. / list of caterers; Upper Hall (200,150); Lower Hall (100,60).

L'Amico SW1 £M, (–,14)
44 Horseferry Rd   222 4680
Regularly packed with MPs, this nice but unremarkable basement Italian restaurant, a stone's throw from Westminster, has a couple of conspiratorial private rooms. / midnight; not Sat & Sun; Private Rm (–,14); Private Rm (–,8).

Private venues

Anchor SE1   £B-M, (120,70)
34 Park St   407 1577
Well-known riverside pub, down from London Bridge, which offers a complete range of options; for a party, you can hire the garden for a summer barbecue and outside disco; for a dinner, three upstairs rooms can be used, of which the best, the charming Shakespeare Room, boasts a great view and 200 year old panelling; for private beers and bar-billiards, Mrs Thrales Room is an intimate, characterful private bar. / midnight; Garden or adjoining Bar (80,–); Shakespeare Rm (–,25); Lower Chart Rm (–,30); Upper Chart Rm (–,70).

Annabel's W1   £E, (–,20)
44 Berkeley Sq   629 3558
London's top nightclub has facilities for small private parties; it is strictly members only.

Antelope SW1   £B-M, (70,48)
22 Eaton Ter   730 7781
Well-known Belgravia Pub, whose comfortable upstairs room is available for civilised lunches and dinners.
/ 11 pm; no amplified music; no dancing.

Apothecaries' Hall EC4   £M-E, (200,130)
Blackfriars Ln   236 1180   (329 3177)
The approach (through a small, cream courtyard, off a cobbled lane), an absolutely charming, pre-Fire hall, a sober Court Room and a Parlour decorated with apothecaries' jars through the centuries combine to make this one of the most delightful settings in London; they are reasonably flexible, but most of the bookings tend to be sit-downs. / 10.30 pm; not Sat eve & Sun; mid Aug - mid Sep hol; Party Ingredients; no dancing; Hall (200,130); Court Rm (–,22); Parlour (–,22).

Apsley House W1   £E, (200,110)
Hyde Pk Corner   938 8485   (938 8367)
Home to the Dukes of Wellington past and present, 'No 1 London' is arguably the grandest place for a medium size banquet available for hire (a dozen times annually) in London; 80 or fewer can recreate the Waterloo dinner, sitting at a single table; undergoing restoration by the V&A as we go to press. / companies only; eve only; list of caterers; no dancing; no smoking or candles.

The Argyll Arms W1   £B, (70,–)
18 Argyll St   734 6117
Very heavily decorated pub, just by Oxford Circus, with largish, pleasant private room. / 11 pm.

The Ark W11   £B-M, (–,28)
122 Palace Gdns Ter   229 4024
Old-established, pine-clad Notting Hill restaurant, well-known for its welcoming Alpine chalet atmosphere; the food is reasonably certain not to distract from the conversation. / Private Rm (–,28).

Private venues

Armourers' & Braisers' Hall EC2 £M-E, (125,81)
81 Coleman St   606 1199   (606 7481)
On the corner with London Wall, this fine, but not overbearingly grand, livery hall (1840s) is distinctively decorated; guests are generally received in the rich comfort of the gilt-walled Drawing Room and proceed to the armour-lined, vaulted hall, lit by the candles of the chandeliers. / no weddings or birthdays; 11.30 pm; not Sat & Sun; list of caterers; no amplified music; no dancing; Livery Hall (125,81); Drawing Rm (125,–); Court Rm (–,20).

L'Artiste Assoiffé W11 £M, (–,22)
122 Kensington Pk Rd   727 4714
Rambling, ' 60s Notting Hill restaurant, which some find very atmospheric; the private room is in the basement, but larger parties may take rooms in the main restaurant. / Private Rm (–,22).

Arts Club W1 £M-E, (200,160,120)
40 Dover St   499 8581   (409 0913)
Popular Mayfair address, whose manageable size and layout make for conviviality and where the mixed traditional and modern styles of the rooms produce an atmosphere of easy-going charm; a paved garden leads off the dining room. / 2 am; Dining & Drawing Rooms not Wed eve; 2 wks hol in Aug; list of caterers; Dining Rm (200,160,120); Drawing Rm (100,30); Bar & Conservatory (100,–).

Ascot Racecourse, Berks £M, (500,40)
Ascot   0344-20387   (0344-872208)
The Queen Anne Building (1990), overlooking the racecourse, has a number of small to medium size rooms available in different, traditional styles. / midnight; Letherby & Christopher; no music; no dancing; Buckhounds Bar (500,–); Norfolk Bar (100,–); King Edward VII (60,40); Abergavenny Bar (50,–); Brown Jack (50,26); Churchill (45,32); Hamilton (40,20); Crocker Bulteel (30,14); Gordon Carter (24,14).

Astoria WC2 £B, (1600,–)
157 Charing Cross Rd   434 9592   (437 1781)
Well-known, central, basic rock venue, used almost exclusively for concerts, but which has potential, especially with theming, for use by large, loud parties. / 3 am; usually not Fri, Sat; hirer's choice of caterer; alcohol in-house.

Athenaeum Hotel W1 £M, (60,40,40)
116 Piccadilly   499 3464   (493 1860)
On Green Park (no views sadly), this '70s hotel's Westminster Suite is a large, tastefully-decorated room which (especially in conjunction with the Richmond Suite) is versatile enough for most types of function. / midnight; Westminster Suite (60,40); Devonshire Suite & Terrace (50,–); Richmond Suite (20,10); Devonshire Suite (40,16).

Private venues

Au Jardin des Gourmets W1   £M, (–,55)
5 Greek St   437 1816   (437 0043)
Traditional, welcoming, slightly middle-aged Soho restaurant with accommodating service, above-average French cooking and a very strong wine list (it's owned by a wine-merchant); three comfortable upstairs private rooms are ideal for smartish, less formal occasions.
/ 1 am; Private Rm (–,55); Private Rm (–,25); Private Rm (–,14).

BAFTA Centre W1   £M, (300,200,200)
195 Piccadilly   465 0277   (734 1009)
While their decor is now modern, the club bars of the erstwhile 'Royal Institute of Painters in Watercolours' retain traces of c19 grandeur, adding to their attractiveness for receptions; this period character is absent from the function room, which nonetheless enjoys good views of St James's churchyard. / 1 am;
Roux Restaurants; Function Rm (200,200); Foyer Bar (120,–); Club Bars (200,–).

Bahn Thai W1   £M, (–,20)
21a Frith St   437 8504
This recently revamped Soho establishment is one of London's best-known Thai restaurants; the private room is on the second floor. / 1 am; Private Rm (–,20).

Bakers' Hall EC3   £B-M, (150,74)
9 Harp Ln   623 2223   (621 1924)
Located a short step from the Tower, at the foot of the company's own red-brick block; decoration throughout is in love-it-or-hate-it, modern style – the livery hall is a dark room, with deep-blue stained glass windows, while the basement Court Room is more conventional, with immaculate light wood panelling and furniture.
/ 11 pm; Aug hol; list of caterers; no amplified music; no dancing; smoking restricted; Livery Hall (108,74); Court Rm (60,26).

Balls Brothers   £B
2-3 Old Change Ct. EC4 248 8697	(150,–)
20 St James's St, SW1 321 0882	(300,94)
42 Threadneedle St, EC2 628 3850	(90,–)
6-8 Cheapside, EC2 248 2708	(80,–)
Bishopsgate, EC2 626 7919	(100,–)
Bucklersbury Hs, EC4 248 7557	(300,40)
Carey Ln, EC2 600 2720	(200,60)
Hays Galleria, Tooley St, SE1 407 4301	(150,100,100)
King Arms Yd, EC2 796 3049	(100,—)
London Wall, EC2 628 3944	(250,60)
St Mary at Hl, EC3 626 0321	(250,60)
Bishopsgate, EC2 626 7919	(100,—)

This well-known chain of wine-bars makes its branches available, given sufficient numbers, particularly at weekends (and see also the Hop Cellars); you can go direct to the individual wine bars or call their party service on 739 6466.

Private venues

Baltic Exchange EC3   £B-M, (300,130,130)
14-20 St Mary Axe   623 5501   (369 1623)
The trading floor was once one of London's more impressive, large evening venues; while restoration proceeds, the Queen's Room – a '50s basement banqueting suite – is available. / 11.30 pm; after 6 pm; in-house caterers; Queen's Rm (300,130); Directors' Dining Rm (–,24).

Balzac W12   £B, (–,45)
4 Wood Ln   081-743 6787
Cheerful Shepherd's Bush bistro, popular with the local BBC crowd, which serves man-sized portions of solid French fare; the large rear area is available privately.

Bank Of England Club SW15   £M, (260,220,180)
Priory Ln   081-876 8417   (081-878 7007)
Set in 42 acres of woodlands and every type of sports-field, this very well-maintained Roehampton club is tailor-made for grown-up sports days (including go-karting and the like); the Redgates Lodge or club restaurant are suitable for a wide variety of functions. / 11 pm; not Sun; in-house caterers; Redgates Lodge (150,80); marquee site.

Bank Of England Museum EC2   £M-E, (200,75)
Bartholomew St   601 5545   (601 5808)
Entered through the East Wall of the Bank, this museum does not conform to a dusty stereotype and is well suited to the restrained receptions for which it is made available; the lofty, reconstructed Bank Stock Office is more practical than the Rotunda, but is a less interesting space. / charities & companies only - no functions which might imply the Bank's approval of commercial ventures; 8.30 pm; after 5.30 pm, not Sat & Sun; in-house caterers; no amplified music; no dancing; no smoking; during temporary exhibitions (140,–).

The Bankers Club EC2   £M, (150,56)
7 Lothbury   606 5883   (600 3083)
Behind the Bank of England, what was formerly the Overseas Bankers Club has 1500 members (you need to be a banker to join); if you can find a member to host your function (or, indeed are eligible to join) it's worth considering for City entertaining, a clubby dinner or reception. / 11 pm; not Sat & Sun; in-house caterers; Cocktail Bar (150,–); Dining Rm (–,56); 9 smaller dining rooms.

Bankside Gallery SE1   £B-M, (180,60)
48 Hopton St   928 7521   (928 2820)
A pleasant, simple, red-walled gallery, this Southwark institution (home to the Royal Watercolour Society and Royal Society of Painter-Printmakers) is at the foot of a modern block, set back from the river. / 11 pm; Tue-Fri & Sun after 5 pm; hirer's choice of caterer; no amplified music; no smoking.

Private venues

Banqueting House SW1   £M-E, (500,375,375)
Whitehall   839 8918   (930 8268)
*The sole remaining fragment of the Palace of Whitehall;
Inigo Jones's stately c17 hall, with Rubens ceiling,
offers an impressive corporate venue; the undercroft
is an elegant space, available separately.* / *charities &
companies only; list of caterers; smoking restricted; Main Hall (500,375);
Undercroft (350,230).*

Bar Escoba SW7   £B-M, (70,40)
102 Old Brompton Rd   373 2403
*Well-known, young-scene South Kensington tapas bar,
there is an upstairs private room.* / *1 am; after 7 pm;
Private Rm (70,40).*

Bar Industria W1   £B, (200,–)
9 Hanover St   437 5534   (287 1747)
*Entry to this mid-sized Mayfair basement nightclub, done
out in minimalist, silver techno-decor, is down a steel-
panelled staircase through a small ante-room; there is
only one main space – half-bar, half dance-floor.* / *7 am;
not Fri & Sat; hirer's choice of caterer.*

Barbarella 1 SW6   £M, (–,–,150)
428 Fulham Rd   385 9434

Barbarella 2 SW7   £M, (–,–,140)
43 Thurloe St   584 2000   (584 2000)
See 'Paint the town rouge' – take over the whole place.
/ *3 am; not Sun, private hire Mon-Thu only.*

Barber-Surgeons' Hall EC2   £M, (250,120)
Monkwell Sq   600 1704
*This light, panelled livery hall, near the Barbican, is a
'60s remodelling in traditional style; it is available
primarily for business and livery functions.*
/ *no weddings; 10.30 pm; not Sat & Sun; Aug hol; Ring &
Brymer; no amplified music; no dancing; smoking restricted;
Livery Hall (250,120); Reception Rm (80,–).*

Barbican Centre EC2   £M-E, (550,240,240)
Barbican Centre   588 6971   (638 2061)
*The huge jungle-like Conservatory would not be out of
place in Kew Gardens and makes a dramatic setting
for a grand event; it can be used in combination with, or
independently, from the Barbican Art Gallery.* / *12.45 pm;
Searcy's; Conservatory (120,65); Conservatory
Terrace (250,150); Garden Rm (400,240,240); Art Gallery (450,–).*

El Barco Latino WC2   £B-M, (100,70)
Victoria Embankment   379 5496
*By Victoria Embankment, close to Temple tube, this
moored barge is potentially a fun venue for a party; the
food is Spanish and Latin American; they are geared to
dancing and have an outside deck for warm weather.*
3 am; in-house caterers.

Private venues

The Barley Mow W1 £B, (100,50)
8 Dorset St   935 7318
Weekend Trade in Marylebone is sufficiently quiet that this whole pub is available for parties on Saturday night – there is no hire charge, you just need to guarantee over 50 or so people. / midnight; avail Sat.

Basil Street Hotel SW3 £M, (300,170,120)
8 Basil St   581 3311   (581 3693)
This well-known Knightsbridge Edwardian establishment has a peaceful charm and lots of character; the dining room (available Saturdays) is the best room of all, while the large Parrot Club (downstairs) can be used for dancing. / midnight; Dining Room Sat only; Parrot Club eve & weekend only; Parrot Club (300,170,120); Dining Rm (220,154); Brompton Rm (120,67); Basil Rm (50,35); Mezzanine Rm (40,14); Room 246 (20,12).

Bath – Pump Room, Avon £M, (500,400,400)
Still St   0225-444477   (0225-447979)
If you are planning something special, Bath is very accessible by train, and the Georgian gentility and charm of the complex here is unmatched; a tour of the amazing Roman baths can be arranged. / 2 am; eve only; Milburns; Pump Rm (250,200,160); Concert Rm (200,150,110).

**The Battersea
Barge Bistro SW8** £B, (120,60,50)
Nine Elms Ln   498 0004
Not exactly easy to find, moored on the South Bank along from New Covent Garden market, this Dutch barge-restaurant makes an atmospheric place for a party, and is priced very affordably. / Upper deck (50,–); Captain's Rm (–,12).

Battersea Park SW8 £M, (10000,4000,4000)
Battersea Pk   081-871 8800   (081-871 7533)
By the riverside pagoda, you can have most kinds of marquee party (hire your own or Wandsworth Council can provide); for mega-marquee events (up to 10,000 people) there is the three acre British Genius Site.
/ midnight; hirer's choice of caterer; Riverside Terraces (500,300); British Genius Site (10000,4000,4000); marquee site.

Battersea Town Hall SW11 £B, (750,400,350)
Lavender Hl   081-871 7465
The Grand Hall – a pretty Victorian edifice, complete with organ – lives up to its name and offers a very characterful, economical venue for larger gatherings.
/ midnight; hirer's choice of caterer; Grand Hall (750,400,350); Lower Hall (200,150,110); Mezzanine Rm (40,–).

Beauchamp Place SW3 £M, (35,24)
15 Beauchamp Pl   589 4252
Trendily decorated Knightsbridge restaurant with a particularly fine, affordable wine list; its private room (rather more traditional in style than the restaurant) is quite stylish and not too expensive a spot for a reception or dinner. / not Sun; Private Rm (35,24).

Private venues

Beaulieu, Hants   £M-E, (2500,200,160)
John Montagu Bldg, Beaulieu
0590-612345   (0590-612624)
The National Motor Museum, the Domus (and ruined cloisters) of the c13 abbey, and the '70s Brabazon complex, provide a wealth of opportunity for most occasions – from wedding receptions to large corporate gatherings; for very grand affairs, the use of Palace House is also a possibility. / Ring & Brymer; smoking restricted; National Motor Museum (2500,–); Domus (180,120,80); Brabazon (300,200,160); marquee site.

HMS Belfast SE1   £M, (350,144,96)
Hay's Galleria   403 6246   (407 0708)
This WWII destroyer, permanently moored by Tower Bridge, offers a range of possibilities for medium sized events and the decks provide a central location for a summer drinks party. / 1 am; Ring & Brymer; Admiral's Quarters (35,20); Anteroom (75,–); Gun Rm (120,60,60); Wardroom (150,50,50); Ship Co's Dining Rm (240,144,96); Quarter Deck (350,–).

Belvedere W8   £M, (180,150)
Holland Ho, Holland Pk   602 1238
This restaurant – see 'Paint the town rouge' – does a roaring trade in sit-down receptions (occasionally with dancing), but to take the best, top, floor, you must hire the whole restaurant. / 3 am; Lower level (–,70); Middle level (–,20); Top level (–,60).

Benihana SW3   £M, (–,15)
77 King's Rd   No tel
See 'Paint the town rouge'. / Private Rm (–,15).

Bentleys W1   £M, (–,12)
11-15 Swallow St   734 4756
This very pretty, old-established English fish restaurant (now with a very contemporary menu) boasts a civilised, light first-floor private room. / not Sun; Private Rm (–,12).

Beotys WC2   £M, (–,60)
79 St Martin's Ln   836 8768
Solid, reliable, family-owned Theatreland restaurant with notably charming service and good food; for parties in the large private room, they are happy to add English staples to their unusual menu of French and Greek classics.
/ Private Rm (–,60).

The Berkeley SW1   £M-E, (450,180,180)
Wilton Pl   235 6000   (235 4330)
The wackily luxurious '70s decor of the ballroom and other banqueting rooms at this Knightsbridge Savoy Group hotel has recently been brought up to date (new carpets and murals); it maintains its high degree of individuality. / Ballroom (450,180,180); Waterloo Rm (70,30); Crystal Rm (120,50,50); Tattersall's Rm (50,25); Billet (15,12).

Private venues

The Berkshire W1   £M, (50,26)
350 Oxford St   629 7474   (629 8156)
The pretty, panelled top-floor Sonning Suite – suitable for dinners and smaller receptions – is the more richly furnished, better proportioned room available in this, modern wedge-shaped hotel. / 2 am; Sonning Suite (50,26); Sandhurst Suite (30,20).

Betjeman's EC1   £B, (75,35)
44 Cloth Fair   796 4981   (377 0806)
More than usually atmospheric wine bar in the ground floor of what was Sir John's Smithfield home; they will hire out at any time for private parties (weekends by special arrangement). / midnight.

Bill Bentley's EC2   £B, (60,40)
18 Old Broad St   588 2655
City wine bar with the unusual benefit of a paved garden; the garden cannot be reserved but, if you use the basement for an evening booking, it may be used (on a non-exclusive basis) for pre-dinner drinks. / not Sat & Sun.

Bishopsgate Institute EC2   £B-M, (360,180,130)
230 Bishopsgate   247 6844   (375 1794)
Victorian institute, to the North of the City, whose large main hall, with a little decoration and theming, has possibilities for big corporate parties. / companies only; midnight; hirer's choice of caterer; no smoking; Main Hall (360,180,130).

Blackheath
Concert Halls SE3   £B-M, (800,350,350)
23 Lee Rd   081-318 9758   (081-852 5154)
These characterful Victorian halls (claiming to be the first purpose-built concert halls in the country) are well-appointed and a local favourite for a whole range of events from wedding receptions to college balls. / 2 am; hirer's choice of caterer; Great Hall (500,350,250); Recital Rm (170,130,100); Webster Rm (75,60).

Bleeding Heart EC1   £M, (60,40)
Bleeding Heart Yd, Greville St   242 8238
Very good, characterful, cramped and difficult to find restaurant/wine bar, in the thin area north of Holborn, offering gutsy French cooking; the Champagne Room can be used privately in the evening and the whole place can be hired at weekends, when barbecues can also be arranged (in the yard); (see also St Etheldreda's Crypt).
/ Champagne Rm eve only; whole wb & BBQ Sat & Sun only; prefer live music; Champagne Rm (60,40).

Blenheim Palace, Oxon   £E, (500,300,300)
Woodstock   0993-811091   (0993-813107)
One of the finest English Baroque houses, set in 2,000 acres of Capability Brown gardens, offers unparalleled opportunities to impress; dinners are often followed by a military tattoo. / 11.30 pm; Jan-Feb hol; list of caterers; no amplified music; marquee site.

Private venues

Boardwalk W1   £B-M, (500,200,200)
18 Greek St   287 2051
See 'Paint the town rouge' – a fun place to take over for a large loud drinks party or disco. / 2 am; avail Sun-Thu; smoking restricted.

Bombay Brasserie SW7   £M, (–,150)
Courtfield Clo, Glouc. Rd   370 4040
Probably London's most famous Indian restaurant and on an imperial scale – if you guarantee 125 people, you can take the whole of the impressive conservatory. / no dancing.

Bonham's SW7   £M, (200,100)
Montpelier St   584 9161   (589 4072)
Knightsbridge auction rooms, available, subject to the constraints of the current hanging, for private hire; particularly suited to early evening receptions. / midnight; eve only; hirer's choice of caterer; no amplified music; no dancing.

Borscht & Tears SW3   £B-M, (–,70)
46 Beauchamp Pl   589 5003
Few private rooms in restaurants have as few frills as the 'hose-down' cellar at this notoriously rowdy Polish Knightsbridge restaurant, but few restaurants seem as tolerant of what happens in their private room; smaller parties can be accommodated in basement alcoves. / Private Rm (–,70).

Boyd's W8   £M, (–,40)
135 Kensington Church St   727 5452   (221 0615)
If you guarantee a minimum spend, you can take over this light and airy Kensington restaurant in its entirety; good English cooking.

Brahms & Liszt WC2   £B, (250,–)
19 Russell St   240 3661
The basement of this popular, quite atmospheric Covent Garden wine bar can be hired privately. / 1 am.

Bramah Tea & Coffee Museum SE1   £B-M, (250,–)
4 Maguire St   378 0222
The large mezzanine floor of the Butlers' Wharf Clove building – home to Mr Bramah's eccentric collection of over 1000 teapots and coffee-making machines – is a possibility for a reception; it would need some decoration to be festive. / 10.30 pm; eve only, post 6.30 pm; hirer's choice of caterer; no amplified music; no dancing; no smoking.

Brasserie Rocque EC2   £B-M, (500,120,90)
37 Broadgate Circle   638 7919   (628 5899)
Stylish, large, modern Brasserie which moonlights as a venue for all kinds of occasions; it's especially good in summer, when it is possible to spill onto the terrace by the Broadgate ice rink. / 1 am; Mon-Fri eve only, all day Sat & Sun; with Terrace (500,–); Inside (300,120,90).

Private venues

Bratts SW7   £B-M, (200,–)
3 Cromwell Rd   584 7258
Self-avowedly a haven for grown-up (just) public schoolboys, the Top Floor or Middle Bar of this South Kensington members' nightclub will consider private parties all night on less busy nights, and early evening at weekends (private hire ceases about 11 pm Fri, midnight Sat). / 3 am; Top Fl and Mid Bar, Tue & Wed – Top Fl or Mid Bar, Thur & Fri; Top Floor (100,–); Middle Bar (100,–).

Brewers' Hall EC2   £M, (170,80)
Aldermandbury Sq   606 1301   (796 3557)
The Brewers' Company is reasonably flexible about the use of its hall, whose quite simple but pleasant interconnecting rooms are available for a range of functions. / 11 pm; generally not Sat & Sun; Aug hol; list of caterers; no amplified music; no dancing; Livery Hall (130,80); Court Rm (40,20); Committee Rm (20,10).

The Brewery EC1   £M, (850,660,660)
Chiswell St   638 8811   (638 5713)
Just North of the Barbican, what started out as Whitbread's brewery is now their banqueting centre; the 250 year old Porter Tun room, with its huge unsupported wooden roof is very characterful and the converted vaults – Smeaton's and the City Cellars – are convivial; the remaining rooms are more conferency, if of high quality. / 1 am; not Sun; Porter Tun (850,350,350); King George III (700,300,300); Queen Charlotte (250,120,120); Smeaton's Vaults (250,100,100); Sugar Rms (150,100,100); The James Watt (120,66,66); City Cellars (100,50,40).

Brighton
Royal Pavilion, Sussex   £M-E, (150,90)
Brighton   0273-603005   (0273-779108)
George IV's splendid seaside palace offers the ideal setting for a Regency banquet. / companies only; 11 pm; eve only; in-house caterers; no amplified music; no dancing; smoking restricted; Banqueting Rm (–,90); William IV Rm (80,70); Queen Adelaide Suite (100,90); Great Kitchen (150,40).

Britannia W8   £B, (100,35)
1 Allen St   937 1864   (937 6905)
If you have over 40 guests, you can take the agreeable conservatory at the rear of this Kensington pub. / 11 pm.

Britannia
Intercontinental Hotel W1   £M, (120,80,80)
Grosvenor Sq   629 9400   (629 7736)
The large function-rooms which might be expected in a Mayfair hotel of this size are surprisingly lacking; the cosy Pine Bar is perhaps the best room, while the interconnecting Grosvenor rooms enjoy views of the square below. / Manhattan (120,80); Pine Bar (60,–); Grosvenor I (40,22); Grosvenor II (25,12).

Private venues

British Museum WC1   £E, (1000,450)
Great Russell St   323 8988   (323 8614)
Most events take place below the Nereid Monument (400BC), but the Duveen (Elgin Marbles) and Japanese Galleries may also be considered; the magnificent Joseph E Hotung Gallery of Oriental Antiquities is a relatively recent addition and suitable for large receptions; very high hire charges. / midnight; eve only; list of caterers; no music; no dancing; no smoking.

Broadgate Estates EC2   £B-E, (200,–)
Broadgate Centre   588 6565
Sites available for receptions include the Raised Garden Terraces around the Ice Rink, the Ice Rink and – hidden away north of Liverpool Street – Exchange Square (for which the centre has a special marquee); local wine bars and restaurants generally provide the catering (see Corney & Barrow and Brasserie Rocque). / avail Fri eve, Sat eve & Sun eve; Ice Rink not Apr-Oct; hirer's choice of caterer; Raised Garden Terrace (70,–); Ice Rink (200,–); Exchange Square Marquee (90,–).

Brocket Hall, Herts   £E, (180,150,150)
Welwyn   0707-335241   (0707-375166)
Superb c18 hall and estate, suited to the grandest of gatherings; "England's finest residential venue" they claim and with facilities including a Chippendale library, a private airstrip and an 18 hole golf course, they may well be right. / in-house caterers; marquee site.

Brown's Hotel W1   £M, (120,80,50)
Albemarle St   493 6020   (493 9381)
Mayfair stalwart epitomising a certain creaky, pleasantly worn, traditional English style; the ethos of the hotel and lack of sound-proofing preclude anything which might be called a bash, but it's well suited to genteel entertaining.
/ 11.30 pm; in-house caterers; no amplified music; Clarendon (120,80,50); Niagara & Roosevelt combined (100,70); Kipling (90,40); Roosevelt (60,45); Niagara (40,40); Hellenic (32,28); Lord Byron (12,12); Graham Bell (10,8); Albemarle (30,12).

Browns Club WC2   £B-M, (680,–)
4 Great Queen St   831 0802   (831 2228)
For a largish London nightclub, the decor of this place is uncharacteristically stylish. / 3 am; hirer's choice of caterer, alcohol in-house; Bar & dance-floor (300,–); VIP Rm (300,–); Small VIP Rm (100,–).

Bubb's EC1   £M, (–,10)
329 Cent Mkts, Farringdon Rd   236 2435
Old-fashioned Smithfield restaurant — a rambling arrangement of parlours, one of which may be used privately; the traditional cooking is heavy, quite good and pretty expensive. / Private Rm (–,10).

Private venues

Burgh House NW3   £B-M, (90,64)
New End Sq   431 0144
Charmingly located Queen Anne Hampstead house with a very pretty ground floor music room; especially suited to more sedate wedding receptions. / 10 pm; not Mon & Tue; in-house caterers; no amplified music; no dancing; no smoking.

Busabong Too SW10   £M, (–,25)
1a Langton St   352 7414
Cheerfully decorated Chelsea Thai restaurant, which provides tasty (though not particularly hot) food; if you supply enough people to more-or-less fill the mezzanine floor, where you sit bare-foot on floor cushions, you can have it to yourself. / Mezzanine (–,25).

Busby's W1   £B, (1000,1000)
165 Charing Cross Rd   434 9592
Large, subterranean dive, with a gallery surrounding its large dance-floor; "up for anything which is neither illegal nor destructive". / 3 am; avail Mon & Tue; in-house caterers.

Butchers' Hall EC1   £M, (250,164,164)
87 Bartholomew Cl   600 5777   (600 2777)
Smithfield livery hall in a traditional but fairly modest style; that said, this is a flexible venue, much used both for business and socially. / 1 am; 2 wks hol in Aug; Chester Boyd; live band only – no discos; Great Hall (250,164); Large Court Rm & Small Court Rm (150,80); Taurus Suite (120,80); Large Court Rm (–,45); Small Court Rm (50,24).

Cabinet War Rooms SW1   £M-E, (200,50,50)
King Charles St   930 6961   (839 5897)
Churchill's fascinating subterranean bunker, off Whitehall, offers interesting, snaking passageways for a reception; dining can take place in a no-frills, brick-walled room off the main museum; dancing is fine in principle, difficult to locate in practice; small day functions can be accommodated but without exclusive access to the galleries. / 11.30 pm; from 6.30 pm; dinner hirer's choice of caterer, lunch approved list of caterers; smoking restricted.

Cabot Hall E14   £M, (1000,400,350)
Canary Wharf   418 2536   (512 9117)
Like the rest of Canary Wharf, this hall at the foot of the tower (overlooking Cabot Square through a lofty bay window) is huge, finished to the highest standards and is vaguely American in feel; the smaller rooms are unimposing and quite jolly. / midnight; list of caterers; Hall (1000,400,350); Sebastian Rm (100,60); St Lawrence Rm (80,40); Cape Breton Rm (–,12); Nova Scotia Rm (–,8); Newfoundland Rm (–,8); marquee site.

Private venues

The Cadogan SW1   £M, (150,60)
75 Sloane St   235 7141   (245 0994)
Welcoming, fashionably-located, somewhat old-fahioned hotel which, for large parties, will consider allowing the use of its restaurant; there is also a nice private room.
/ midnight; Langtry Rm (100,32); Restaurant (150,60).

Café Club SE1   £B, (2000,400,400)
62 Union St   378 1988
Often likened to the Tardis – what is apparently a tiny, cramped jazz-café, near Blackfriars Bridge, leads onto very groovy vaults offering huge amounts of space for you to play around with; wild. / 3 am; not Fri & Sat; Café Club (100,40); The Vaults (2000,400,400).

Café de Paris W1   £B, (525,–)
3 Coventry St   437 5534   (287 1747)
Time brings its changes and what was one of the highest-society '30s rendez-vous is, having been rescued from its decayed state, now 'hot' on the club-circuit; much of the period elegance lingers and it's really quite a place.
/ 4 am, Thu 6am; avail Sun, Mon, Tue & Thu; hirer's choice of caterer.

Café Greenwich Park SE10   £B-M, (200,–)
Greenwich Pk   081-858 9695   (081-935 5894)
Although its private room is probably best suited to kids' parties, this park cafeteria has a wonderful location and – with its own private garden – would make a good spot for an outdoors evening party/BBQ for grown-ups (you can have a disco inside). / midnight; after 7.30 pm (winter 3 pm); hirer's choice of caterer; including Garden (200,–); Inside only (150,–); Upstairs Rm (80,–).

Café Lazeez SW7   £B-M, (100,50)
93-95 Old Brompton Rd   581 9993
Stylishly decorated, modern South Kensington Indian restaurant, with an upstairs room which can be taken in its entirety; the food is light, delicate and about as far from your average tandoori as is possible.

Private venues

Café Royal W1   £M, (3000,650,550)
68 Regent St   437 9090   (439 7672)
Eight remarkable floors of ballrooms, banqueting chambers, bars and restaurants; Forte-owned and conference-orientated, it offers size, flexibility and grandeur; the first three, Victorian, floors are more characterful than the 1920s extension upwards and the grandest option is probably to take over the Bar and wildly OTT rococo Grill Room; the cellar and Penthouse offer interesting options at the extremes – the one dimly-lit and atmospheric, the other with great views, if not the most stylish decor. / 2 am; in-house caterers;
4-Empire Napoleon (1000,650,550); 6-Dubarry (550,400,300); 2-Louis (350,270,200); 1-Elysee (300,220,160); 6-Dauphin (250,120); 5-Marquise or 2-Pompadour (200,120,80); 1-Derby & Queensbury (150,100,70); 5-George or 3-Nicols (150,70); 1-Domino (100,70,50); 3-Josephine (100,70);1-Cellars (80,50); 1-Lonsdale (50,40,40); 5-Tudor (60,18); 3-Club (40,30); 7-Trafalgar (30,18); 7-Hepplewhite (10,8); 8-Penthouse (40,24).

Café St Pierre EC1   £B-M, (150,45,45)
29 Clerkenwell Gn   251 6606   (490 1083)
Attractively done-out (if unscenically located) three-floor café/restaurant which moonlights at evenings and weekends for a variety of different functions – parties, weddings, dinners – not all with food; the middle and top floors can be hired individually. / 1 am; Ground Floor (60,35); Middle Floor (60,35); Top Floor (80,45).

The Caledonian Club SW1   £M-E, (250,120,120)
9 Halkin St   235 5162   (235 4635)
Belying the myth of Scottish dourness, this welcoming Belgravia Club lacks some of the stuffiness of its St James's cousins and is ideal for many kinds of receptions and dinners (with reeling possible in the Members Dining Room); the committee will consider events for non-members, primarily if someone has Scottish connections (though PR companies looking for Scottish theme evenings are discouraged). / 2 am; Members' Dining Room eve only; not Dec; no discos; jacket & tie; no children under 8; Selkirk (40,24); Stuart (65,52); Members Dining Rm (250,120,60); Smoking Rm (70,–); Oval (–,14).

Calthorpe Arms WC1   £B, (60,36)
257 Grays Inn Rd   278 4732
Friendly Bloomsbury pub with quite a smart, well-maintained private room. / Private Rm (60,36).

Canal Brasserie W10   £B-M, (200,70)
222 Kensal Rd   081-960 2732
Hiding in Canalot studios (on the banks of the Grand Union Canal), this lofty, stylish space is a weekday canteen, with food good enough to draw outsiders; a cool spot for weekend parties – there is an outside area for summer. / avail Sat, Sun & eve Mon, Tues.

Private venues

Canning House SW1 £B-M, (150,–)
2 Belgrave Sq   235 2303   (235 3587)
The first floor rooms of the Hispanic and Luso Brazilian Council, which overlook the square, are extremely popular for drinks parties – offering affordable grandeur at a very smart address, a stone's throw from Hyde Park Corner. / *10 pm; eve only, Sat all day, not Sun; hirer's choice of caterer.*

Cannizaro House SW19 £M-E, (100,80)
West Side, Wimbledon Common
081-879 1464   (081-879 7338)
Georgian mansion-hotel, prettily situated in Cannizaro Park on the edge of Wimbledon Common, with a good range of function rooms of various sizes; there are some period rooms, decorated in elegant traditional style.
/ *no amplified music; no dancing; Viscount Melville, Earl of Mexborough & Lady Jane (100,80); Viscount Melville (50,40); Oak Rm (35,24); Earl Of Mexborough & Lady Jane (45,35); Queen Elizabeth Rm (40,36); Boardroom (–,10).*

Canonbury Academy N1 £M, (120,80)
6 Canonbury Pl   359 6888   (704 1896)
Elizabethan house – Francis Bacon lived here – prettily situated in Canonbury, with a wide variety of attractive rooms (some with original ceilings) and two gardens; unfortunately, it's currently available for corporate functions only. / *companies only; 11.30 pm; hirer's choice of caterer; no smoking; no corkage; Long Gallery (120,80); 21 smaller rooms.*

La Capannina W1 £M, (–,25)
24 Romilly St   437 2473
Untouched by modern Italian fads, this Soho trattoria survivor from a different culinary age serves solid, decent fare and the private room downstairs is a cosy place for a dinner . / *not Sat L, Sun; Private Rm (–,25).*

The Capital SW3 £M-E, (35,22)
Basil St   589 5171   (225 0011)
Small, upmarket hotel, by Harrods, whose traditional decor is superimposed on a modern frame; the private dining suite is quite characterful and notably good cooking and wine are major attractions. / *Eaton (20,12); Cadogan (35,22).*

Captain Kidd E1 £B, (150,100,50)
108 Wapping High St   480 5759
One of the most popular places for food and drink in the Docklands, this riverside pub has an upstairs bar used regularly for celebrations. / *midnight; not Sun.*

Le Carapace NW3 £M, (–,12)
118 Heath St   435 8000
Pretty Hampstead restaurant with a very agreeable first floor private dining room and a pleasant sitting area; the food is quite good too. / *Private Rm (–,12).*

Private venues

Carpenters' Hall EC2   £M, (350,210)
Throgmorton Av   628 0833   (638 6286)
Forming the arch over the London Wall end of Throgmorton Avenue, this quite impressive Hall in distinctive '60s style is available once a week for business functions. / no weddings; Aug hol; list of caterers; no amplified music; no dancing; smoking restricted; Livery Hall (350,210); Reception Rm (230,–).

The Catherine Wheel W8   £B, (80,25)
23 Kensington Church St   937 3259
Kensington Pub whose private bar is like an intimate drawing room. / midnight.

Cavalry & Guards Club W1   £M, (300,130)
127 Piccadilly   499 1261   (495 5956)
This carefully maintained Edwardian club, overlooking Green Park, has a number of charming traditional rooms; for suitable functions, it may be worth trying to find a member to sponsor your event. / not Sun; in-house caterers; smoking restricted; Coffee Rm (300,130); Balaclava Rm (100,50); Peninsula Rm (180,90); Waterloo Rm (100,24); Double Bridal Rm (30,16).

Cecil Sharp House NW1   £B-M, (500,500,300)
2 Regent's Park Rd   485 2206   (284 0523)
The home of the English Folk Dance and Song Society has two fine, recently redecorated halls which are available for folk music and dancing with private receptions; there is a small garden. / 11 pm; in-house caterers; no amplified music; no discos; smoking restricted; Kennedy Hall (500,500,300); Trefusis Hall (140,140,100).

Central Club (YWCA) WC1   £B, (350,180,150)
16-22 Gt Russell St   636 7512   (636 5278)
What was the YWCA; the Queen Mary is a large, quite pleasantly worn hall, while the smaller rooms resemble class-rooms. / 2 am; in-house caterers; library - no smoking; Queen Mary Hall (350,180,150); Swiss Parlour (90,45); Hampstead Rm (70,35); Martin Rm (90,45); Martin Rm & Hampstead Rm (150,75); Library Rm (50,25).

Le Champenois EC2   £M, (250,120,110)
10 Devonshire Sq   283 7888
Large, stylish basement restaurant in the Cutlers' Gardens development; the modern French cooking is rather expensive. / 2 am.

Chapter 11 SW10   £M, (–,30)
47 Hollywood Rd   351 1683   (376 5083)
While the appeal of this airy, modish, modern British restaurant, off the Fulham Road, is wide-ranging, it must be the nicest restaurant in London to be notorious for stag and hen parties, the less sober of which are held in the not unpleasant "Brinkley bomb room". / 1 am; Private Rm (–,30).

Private venues

The Chariots SW3 £B, (600,60)
152 King's Rd   351 7141   (351 5270)
Even if this bar/restaurant/nightclub (formerly the Pheasantry) has never lived up to its great location (set back from the King's Road, in a private court-yard), the basement nightclub is not a bad venue; for large parties you might consider taking over the whole place. / 2 am;
Nightclub Tue & Wed; Basement Club (200,–); Bar (100,50);
First Floor Restaurant (–,60); Garden (100,50).

Chartered Accountants' Hall EC2 £M, (400,250,200)
Moorgate Pl   628 7060   (920 0547)
Elegant, attractive, extremely well-maintained City complex, including two interesting, traditional style rooms (Members' and Main Reception) and a tasteful modern hall. / 1 am; Leith's Good Food; Great Hall (400,250);
Members' Rm (100,30); Main Reception Rm (120,60);
Restaurant & Wine Bar (150,100).

Chartered Institute of Public Finance & Accountancy WC2 £M, (70,45)
3 Robert St   895 8823   (895 8825)
Though perhaps a little institutional, this Adam house offers a fine view over the Embankment from its fourth floor committee room, which is suitable for receptions or dinners; the lower floor rooms are more suited to business entertaining. / 10 pm; not Sat & Sun; Owen Bros;
no amplified music; no dancing; no smoking; Committee Rm 4 (60,40);
Council Chamber (70,45); Conference Rm (70,–).

The Chelsea SW1 £M-E, (200,120,120)
Sloane St   235 4377   (235 3705)
This modern Knightsbridge hotel has unusually crisp style; its modern banqueting rooms all open off the balcony of a small glazed atrium giving quite an intimate effect. / 2 am; Sloane Suite (200,120,120); Chelsea Rm (15,12).

Chelsea Football Club SW6 £B-M, (600,220,220)
Fulham Rd   610 2287   (610 3894)
No-frills, but big banqueting suites, available on non-match days. / London Catering Services;
Executive Club Rm (400,220); Trophy Rm (120,–);
Sponsors Lounge (100,60); Box (–,12).

The Chelsea Gardener SW3 £B-M, (500,150)
125 Sydney St   352 5656   (352 3301)
There are few acre-sized gardens in Chelsea; this one – the garden centre at Chelsea Gardeners' Market – is available for summer soirées. / midnight; after 6.30 pm – preferably not Sat & Sun; hirer's choice of caterer; no dancing;
smoking restricted; Shop (400,–); Conservatory (–,90).

Private venues

Chelsea
Harbour Rooms SW10   £M, (400,220,200)
Chelsea Harbour   351 4433   (352 7868)
This purpose-built suite of banqueting/conference rooms, on the edge of the 'village', best suits themed events; there is also a large hard-core site for marquees. / midnight; list of caterers; Turner & Carlyle Rms (300,220,200); Turner Rm (200,90); Carlyle Rm (180,70,60); Reception Rm (80,–); marquee site.

Chelsea
Old Town Hall SW3   £B-M, (480,400,250)
King's Rd   937 5464   (938 3468)
For a large event, this civic hall is grand, well-maintained, centrally-located and affordable; unfortunately, its listed building status forbids the soundproofing which would enable it to run after 11.30 pm, discouraging many events for which it would otherwise be suitable. / 11.30 pm; Crown Catering; Main Hall (480,400,250); Small Hall (150,100); Cadogan Suite (150,90).

Chelsea Physic Garden SW3   £M, (400,100)
66 Royal Hospital Rd   352 5646
A seventeenth century, 3 1/2 acre botanical garden, hidden away in Old Chelsea; the indoor accommodation is ordinary, but this is a fascinating spot for an outdoor summer drinks party (although deadly nightshade and ponds make it unsuitable for kids). / 10.30 pm; Apr-Sep, eve only; hirer's choice of caterer; no amplified music; no dancing; Private Rm (150,100); marquee site.

Chez Gerard W1   £B-M, (50,25)
31 Dover St   499 8171
Well-known for, some say, London's best steak-frites; for parties, this Mayfair establishment has an interesting stone-walled downstairs room; alternatively their mezzanine balcony can be used privately.
/ Private Rm (50,25); Mezzanine (–,25).

Chez Nico at Ninety
Grosvenor House Hotel W1   £E, (–,20)
90 Park Ln   409 1290   (355 4877)
Star chef Nico Ladenis's fairly recently established Mayfair base has an elegant, conventionally decorated private room. / closed Sat & Sun; Private Rm (–,20).

Chiang Mai W1   £B-M, (–,10)
48 Frith St   437 7444
The Thai cooking at this Soho restaurant is better than most, although service can be slow; there is a small, modern upstairs private room and a larger, less pleasant basement. / Private Rm (–,10).

Private venues

Chiswick House W4
Burlington Ln   081-570 7728   (081-862 5847)
While the House is run by English Heritage and hardly available at all for functions, the large gardens, run by Hounslow Council, have a number of sites suitable for marquee functions. / Sun-Thu 11pm, Fri & Sat midnight; hirer's choice of caterer; marquee site.

Christie's SW1   £M-E, (600,200)
8 King St   839 9060   (925 2751)
The grand galleries of this St James's auctioneer are, subject to other requirements, sometimes made available for functions. / 3 am; Mon-Fri after 6 pm, all day Sat, Sun not 2-5 pm; hirer's choice of caterer; no dancing; no smoking.

Chuen Cheng Ku W1   £B, (–,500)
17 Wardour St   437 1398   (434 0533)
Vast (400 seater), gaudy, Chinatown restaurant set in a building some of whose rooms retain quite a degree of period grandeur and all of which (capacity 30 and up) can be used privately with sufficient numbers; with their famous trolley dim-sum, it is particularly a place for a big lunch-party.

Church House SW1   £M, (250,200,160)
Dean's Yd   222 9011   (233 1439)
This recently refurbished '40s building is well appointed, but retains a rather arid feel; that said, it is an extremely central location, just by Parliament, and not too expensive; wedding receptions are a growing part of their business. / 1 am; not Sun; Crown Catering;
Harvey Goodwin Suite (250,200,160); Hoare Memorial Hall (250,150); Bishop Partridge Hall (180,120); Smaller rooms (–,25).

Church's W8   £B-M, (150,12)
20 Kensington Church St   938 2336
New owners are smartening things up at this simple but quite popular Kensington wine-bar, changing it into more of a club and extending possibilities for parties. / 2 am; whole place – all day Mon-Thu & until 11 pm Fri & Sat; Private Rm (–,12).

Churchill W1   £M, (300,240,180)
Portman Sq   486 5800   (486 1255)
This modern, marbled luxury hotel north of Oxford Street has a good range of banqueting facilities. / 1 am;
Chartwell Suite (300,240,180); Chartwell I (200,144,80); Library (80,60); Chartwell II (100,96,40); Edward Suite (80,40); Victoria Suite (80,40); Court Suite (–,14).

Cibo W14   £M, (–,55)
3 Russell Gdns   371 6271
Olympia Italian restaurant with rather unusual, bright decor and quite good food; it can be hired in its entirety for parties or alternatively it subdivides into areas of varying sizes and degrees of privacy.

Private venues

Circa W1   £B, (300,60,60)
59 Berkeley Sq   499 7850   (499 0051)
Very '80s, designer bar/café at the foot of Saatchi's Berkeley Square HQ; the basement bar moonlights as a club and is a good deal for a party, especially with dancing; after 11 pm, the ground-floor café becomes available for those tired by exertions below. / 3 am; upstairs not before 11 pm; hirer's choice of caterer, alcohol in-house; Downstairs (175,60,60); Upstairs (125,60).

Cittie of Yorke WC1   £B, (300,90,90)
22 High Holborn   242 7670
By the entrance to Gray's Inn, the main bar is one of the largest and most characterful of any pub in London, with brass pipes, wooden alcoves and a high wooded ceiling; you can also hire the Cellar Bar – a long, thin, white-walled vault, or the relatively ordinary Front Bar. / 1 am; in-house caterers; Main Bar (300,90,90); Front Bar (80,40); Cellar Bar (80,65,40).

City Livery Club EC4   £B-M, (400,160)
Victoria Embankment   936 2891   (936 2893)
On the Embankment, up from Blackfriars Bridge, the club has its accommodation in the Victorian building of Sion Theological college; with the sponsorship of a member (of which there are 1,200 amongst livery companies and City businesses), it is possible to hold a reception in the Library – a lofty room with a vaulted wood ceiling; otherwise there is the club's ground floor Dining Room and Bar. / 10.30 pm; Dining Room & Library eve only; Crown Catering; no amplified music; no dancing; Dining Rm (300,160); Stanley Bell Rm (100,50); Members Bar (70,–); Library (400,–).

City Miyama EC4   £M-E, (–,10)
17 Godliman St   489 1937
For a private Japanese dinner in the City this is one of the smartest places; the cooking is predictably pricey but of good quality. / Private Rm (–,10).

City Of London Club EC2   £M, (500,120,96)
19 Old Broad St   588 7991   (374 2020)
Charming, clubby early Victorian institution (the oldest club in the City) whose archetypal, first-floor smoking room is one of a number of fine period rooms available for entertaining; there are also agreeable modern rooms around an internal garden; the club has 1,200 members – mostly bankers and stockbrokers – who must hold or sponsor any event. / 1 am; in-house caterers; Upper Smoking Rms (200,–); Garden Rm (100,50); Visitors Rm (75,50); Main Dining Rm (300,120,96); Bar (50,–).

The Clachan W1   £B, (150,50)
34 Kingly St   734 2659
With its own street-entrance, this Soho pub, behind Liberty's, has an upstairs private bar which is comfortably furnished by pub standards. / 11.30 pm; not Sun; Highland Bar (150,50).

Private venues

Clandon, Surrey   £M, (280,200,160)
West Clandon, Guildford   0483-222482
The marble-floored, ground floor rooms of this c17 National Trust house can be used for receptions and grand dinners; for dancing or less formal functions the restaurant in the vaults can be used, or you can erect a marquee on the lawn. / midnight; Limited availability; in-house caterers; amplified music in restaurant only; dancing in restaurant only; no smoking; no red wine; no photography; Restaurant (280,200,160); Marble Hall (280,180); Saloon (180,100); marquee site.

Claridge's W1   £M-E, (800,210,180)
Brook St   629 8860   (872 8092)
Society's favourite hotel offers a suite of function rooms which, for simple elegance, have few peers; Royal Suites are sometimes made available for more intimate entertaining, for which the Orangery is also suitable; once or twice a year, for very special occasions, the beautiful foyer, reading room and restaurant may be used. / 2 am; Ballroom (400,210,180); Drawing Rm or French Salon or Mirror Rm (120,70); Private Suite (50,20); Orangery (-,14).

The Clink SE1   £B-M, (350,230,160)
1 Clink St   403 6515   (403 5813)
A stone's throw from London Bridge, this former prison (the granddaddy clink of them all) and erstwhile brothel (the Bishop of Winchester's) is now a tourist attraction, following prostitution through the ages; geared to parties – particularly the large medieval-style upstairs-room – it's a good place for an office bash or similar event. / 2 am; after 6 pm in museum; prefer Castle Catering - may negotiate hirer's choice of caterer; Museum (100,60); Winchester Hall (250,160,110).

Cliveden, Berks   £E, (250,160,160)
Taplow   0628-668561   (0628-661837)
The rococo French Dining Room at the Astors' Thames-side palazzo is one of England's finest dining rooms – or take the whole place to entertain 160 of your closest friends. / French Dining Rm (-,50); Churchill Boardroom (100,28); Mountbatten Rm (-,14); marquee site.

Clothworkers' Hall EC3   £M-E, (350,224)
Dunster Ct, Mincing Ln   623 7041   (283 1289)
One of the grandest, best maintained halls in the City – it is made available on a limited basis, primarily for business, livery and charity functions; guests proceed from a contemporary and quite unusual reception hall up to the elegant Drawing Room on the first floor, off which opens the Livery Hall – a '50s chamber built on traditional lines. / no weddings; 11 pm; not Fri-Sun; Aug & Sep hol; Graison; no amplified music; no dancing; smoking restricted; Livery Hall (350,224); Drawing Rm (224,-).

The Coal Hole WC2   £B, (100,-)
91 Strand   836 7503
Large, well-known West End pub, whose downstairs bar can be taken over exclusively. / 11 pm; not Fri night or Sun.

Private venues

**Coates Karaoke Bar &
Restaurant EC2** £B, (200,100,100)
45 London Wl   256 5148   (382 9373)
*Industrial chic City wine bar with good pizzas; guarantee
a good turn-out and you can hold a very inexpensive
knees-up here.* / midnight; Mon-Wed eve only, Sat by negotiation.

**Cobden's Working Men's
Club and Institute W10** £B-M, (400,200,150)
170-172 Kensal Rd
*Off the north end of Ladbroke Grove, this club (1880,
the oldest of its type in southern England) has
developed a certain recherché credibility in media circles;
its characterful hall is sometimes made available for
parties.*

The Coliseum WC2 £B-M, (120,80)
St Martin's Ln   836 0111   (836 8379)
*Europe's largest lyric theatre has a number of good-
looking rooms; the Royal Retiring, Stoll and Arlen rooms
would all make pleasant places in which to entertain
around a performance; the panelled Dutch bar is possibly
the most convivial and most suitable to be used for a
stand-alone reception.* / Gardner Merchant; Dutch Bar (100,–);
Royal Retiring Rm (25,12); Stoll Rm (20,12); Arlen Rm (12,8);
Terrace Bar (120,80).

**Commonwealth
Institute W8** £M, (1500,750,750)
Kensington High St   603 4535   (602 7374)
*This unusual Holland Park building is too little known; it
has a very nice 'feel' to it and offers interesting
possibilities for large garden parties, themed events or
more conventional celebrations; it's quite good value too
and, most unusually, has a lot of on-site parking.* / 1 am;
list of caterers; Comm Galleries (1500,750,750); Lawn (850,–);
Jehangir and Board Rms or Comm Brasserie (120,80);
Art Gallery (500,300,250); marquee site.

Congress Centre WC1 £B-M, (400,250,200)
23-28 Gt Russell St   580 5664   (580 8827)
*Not only champagne socialists can party at the TUC's
fine '50s memorial building, which is interested in
expanding its social business; the glass-walled Marble
Hall, overlooked by a huge Epstein statue, is an elegant
modern reception space, while the Congress Hall suits
dinners and dances.* / midnight; in-house caterers; no smoking;
Marble Hall (200,–); Congress Hall (400,250,200); Restaurant (–,150);
Board Rm (–,20).

Private venues

The Connaught W1   £M-E, (–,22)
Carlos Pl 499 7070 (495 3262)
London's most discreet hotel has nothing so brash as a ballroom; there are two sharply contrasting private dining rooms – the extraordinarily pretty Regency Carlos Suite, including a small glazed ante-room, and the smaller, rather sober Georgian room. / Regency Carlos Suite (–,22); Georgian Rm (–,12).

Conrad Hotel SW10   £M, (300,200,160)
Chelsea Harbour 823 3000 (352 8174)
This waterside hotel looks down on the marina; it is carefully fitted to a high standard and has a good range of accommodation, most of which is slightly corporate in feel. / Henley Suite (300,200,160); Compass Rose or Thames (200,100,80); Henley I (150,120); Harbour (75,50); Henley II or Henley III (70,40); Nelson (–,12); Wellington (–,8).

The Conservatory SW11   £B-M, (100,45)
Ransome's Dock, 35-37 Parkgate
081-874 8505 (071-924 2438)
Extraordinary modern rooftop conservatory (fully heated in winter), perched on top of a riverside building by Albert Bridge; it boasts plants, sculptures, fountains and terraces; access is via a spiral staircase. / midnight; hirer's choice of caterer; no amplified music; no dancing.

Conway Hall WC1   £B-M, (350,160,140)
25 Red Lion Sq 242 8032
On the corner of a Bloomsbury square, the South Place Ethical Society (the UK's largest humanist group) makes its converted music-hall accommodation available for summer weddings, Christmas parties, evening drinks, etc; the ground floor is well laid out to be taken over in its entirety – it's a little shabby at present, but refurbishment is promised. / midnight; large Hall not Sun pm Oct-Apr; hirer's choice of caterer; Large Hall (350,160,140); Small Hall (100,–); Lobby / Bar Area (100,–).

Coopers Arms SW3   £B-M, (60,30)
87 Flood St 376 3120
Much above-average Chelsea pub with a very good upstairs dining room; ship's dining table for up to 24. / midnight; in-house caterers; no amplified music; no dancing; Private Rm (60,30).

Coopers' Hall EC2   £M, (60,30)
13 Devonshire Sq 247 9577 (377 8061)
Livery hall – Georgian in origin – used for some business functions as well as livery dinners; it is available primarily to an established circle of former users but applications from newcomers will be considered. / 10.30 pm; not Sat & Sun; Aug hol; Jean Alexander Food Flair; no amplified music; no dancing.

Private venues

Corney & Barrow EC2 £B
19 Broadgate Circle, EC2 628 1251   (300,60)
5 Exchange Sq, EC2 628 4367   (80,30)
Lloyd's of London, EC3 621 9201   (150,50)
44 Cannon St, EC4 248 1700   (120,70,70)
3 Fleet Pl, EC4 329 3141   (100,30)
109 Old Broad St, EC2 638 9308   (50,28)
Well-known chain of superior City wine bars; Cannon St is best suited to discos, though their flagship is impressively situated above the Broadgate skating rink (where use of the terrace gardens is also possible, see Broadgate Estates); the Lloyd's Building wine bar (with the benefit of an outside terrace) is particularly stylish while Old Broad St is a single-roomed, old fashioned parlour. / sometimes available Mon-Fri, also Sat & Sun.

Costa's Grill W8 £B, (–,12)
12-14 Hillgate St 229 3794
This popular Notting Hill stalwart of a restaurant offers solid Greek food at knock-down prices; there is a basic basement room for cheap and cheerful celebrations.
/ not Sun; Private Rm (–,12).

Cottons Atrium SE1 £M, (200,–)
London Bridge 626 3411
With a view over the City, this large, lofty riverside office-block foyer is a mite businessy, but quite glossy; the waterfalls and palm trees add interest. / midnight; eve only, not Sun; hirer's choice of caterer.

Courtauld Institute WC2 £E, (350,–)
Strand 873 2677
This gem of a collection (now in its beautiful new Somerset House home) is sometimes made available for private views or evening receptions. / 9.30 pm; list of caterers; First Floor (150,–).

Crazy Larry's SW10 £B-M, (500,–)
533 King's Rd 376 5555 (352 1659)
This large nightclub, off the King's Road, is, for post-teeny-boppers, a good let-your-hair-down venue. / 2.30 am; eve only; hirer's choice of caterer, alcohol in-house.

The Criterion W1 £M-E, (400,200)
Piccadilly Circus 925 0909
Huge and striking, this gilded and mosaicked neo-Byzantine restaurant, off Piccadilly Circus, can be hired in its entirety, or the rear raised area can be used separately for drinks parties; to take the whole place, the required total spend level is high, making large drinks/buffet parties the most realistic proposition.
/ Terrace (100,60).

Private venues

Crown & Goose NW1 £B-M, (40,20)
100 Arlington Rd   485 2342
Trendily updated Camden Town pub – complete with candelabra and fake oils – with a pleasant private room in the same vaguely artsy style; it serves better than usual modern British pub-grub. / Private Rm (40,20).

Crown & Greyhound SE21 £B, (150,80,50)
73 Dulwich Village   081-693 2466
The only pub in Dulwich Village has a second floor room, with its own entrance, which is, of its kind, one of London's best; the decor is quite modern. / midnight.

The Crown and Two Chairmen W1 £B, (100,60)
31 Dean St   437 8192
Well-known Soho media watering-hole with characterful upstairs bar available for hire. / midnight; not Sun & Sat in winter.

The Crown Tavern EC1 £B, (200,30)
43 Clerkenwell Gn   250 0757
Peacefully situated, north of Smithfield – at weekends this pleasant pub can be taken over in its entirety if you have sufficient numbers; for the rest of the week there is an upstairs bar which can be used by parties of 40 and up. / whole pub Sat, possibly Sun – Private Room Mon-Fri; Upstairs Bar (60,30).

Cumberland Hotel W1 £M, (800,750,570)
Marble Arch   724 0087   (262 2248)
This hotel at the west end of Oxford Street has a number of useful and surprisingly pleasant function rooms; the highly unusual Production Box, with a ceiling of space-deck lighting frames, lends itself to events and theme parties; the ballroom-like Carlisle Suite (with the interesting adjacent Gloucester Room) is large, high-ceilinged and in a modern style; other rooms are more business-like. / 3 am; Production Box (800,750,570); Carlisle Suite (500,350,325); Gloucester (200,100).

Cutty Sark SE10 £M-E, (180,80)
King William Wk   081-858 2698   (081-858 6976)
In its riverside Greenwich dry-dock, the two decks of this most famous tea-clipper play host to many kinds of party and you can use the outside top deck in summer; the Captain's Room, open for viewing during functions, can be used for dinners only with special permission from the trust; a drawback is the pillars and permanent displays which reduce available space. / 11.30pm; eve only; hirer's choice of caterer; no dancing; no smoking (not even on outside decks); Tween Decks (180,80); Lower Hold (180,80); Captain's Rm (–,12).

Private venues

Czech Club NW6   £B, (300,200)
74 West End Ln   372 5251
This West Hampstead emigrés club offers worn grandeur, warm atmosphere, economy and interesting, if not sophisticated, food. / in-house caterers.

Dan's SW3   £M, (–,30)
119 Sydney St   352 2718   (352 3265)
Pretty or twee, to taste, this Chelsea house which is especially well-known for its conservatory (available for private hire) and garden dining also has a downstairs private room. / Conservatory (–,30); Private Room (-,20).

Dartmouth House W1   £M, (240,150,150)
37 Charles St   493 3328   (495 6108)
The imposing Mayfair HQ of the English Speaking Union offers some fine, well-maintained and characterful rooms, particularly suitable for weddings and other receptions. / midnight; Crown Catering; Long Drawing Rm (140,100); Ballroom (100,60); Small Drawing Rm (75,36); Terrace (100,–).

Davy's Wine Bars   £B, (300,250,200)
Bangers: 2-12 Wilson St, EC2   377 6326
Bangers Too: 1 St Mary at Hl, EC3   283 4443
Bishop of Norwich: 91-93 Moorgate, EC2   920 0857
Bishop's Parlour: 91-93 Moorgate, EC2   588 2581
Bottlescrue: 53/60 Holborn Viaduct, EC1   248 2157
Bung Hole: WC157 High Holborn, WC1   242 4318
Burgundys Ben's:102 Clerkenwell Rd, EC1   251 3783
Champagne Charlies: 17 The Arches, WC2   930 7737
The Chiv: 90-92 Wigmore St, W1   224 0170
Chopper Lump: 10c Hanover St, W1   499 7569
City Boot: 7 Moorfields High Wk, EC2   588 4766
City Flogger: 120 Fenchurch St, EC3   623 3251
City FOB: Lower Thames St, EC3   621 0619
City Pipe: Foster Ln, EC1   606 2110
City Vaults: 2 St Martin's-le-Grand, EC1   606 8721
Colonel Jaspers: 190 City Rd, EC1   608 0925
The Cooperage: 48-50 Tooley St, SE1   403 5775
Crown Passage Vaults: 20 King St, SW1   930 6157
Davy's of Creed Lane: 10 Creed Ln, EC4   236 5317
Dock Blida: 50-54 Blandford St, W1
Grapeshots: 2-3 Artillery Passage, E1   247 8215
Guinea Butt: Borough High St, SE1   403 5775
Gyngleboy: 27 Spring St, W2   723 3351
The Habit: 65 Crutched Friars, EC3   481 1131
Lees Bag: Gt Portland St, W14   636 5287
The Mug House: 1-3 Tooley St, SE1   403 8343
The Pulpit: 63 Worship St, EC2   377 1574
Shotberries: 167 Queen Victoria St, EC4   329 4759
Skinkers: 40-42 Tooley St, SE1   407 9189
The Spitoon: 15-17 Long Ln, EC1   726 8858
Tapster: 65 Buckingham Gt, SW1   222 0561
Truckles Of Pied Bull Yard: off Bury Pl, WC1   404 5338
Tumblers: 1 Kensington High St, W8   937 0393

Private venues

Davy's Wine Bars (contd)
Udder Place Wine Rooms: 1-6 Milk St, EC2   600 2165
The Vineyard: 1 St Katharine's Way, E1   480 6680
Branches of London's largest wine bar chain offer a re-assuringly samey olde-worldiness; sections are available privately prior to weekday closing times and thereafter (and at weekends) the whole place can be used for drinks parties, dinners or discos (just guarantee a certain number); Skinkers is arguably the best of the bunch; party enquiries may be made to the branch or to 171 Greenwich High Rd, SE10 - tel 081-858 6011.

Design Museum SE1   £M, (300,–)
Shad Thames   403 6933   (378 6540)
Next to Butler's Wharf, Sir Terence Conran's International-style museum has a large, white-walled foyer available for parties (and, for those who wish to view them, the collections above can be left open to view); summer receptions can spill through the large floor-to-ceiling windows onto the riverside area, which has a magnificent view of Tower Bridge. / 3 am; after 5.30 pm; list of caterers; Entrance Hall (300,–).

Dickens Inn E1   £B-M, (110,110,110)
St Katharine's Way   488 1226   (702 3610)
Prettily located, at the edge of St Katherine's Dock, this large inn has a large warehouse-conversion function room used for discos and, on occasion, wedding receptions. / midnight; Nickleby Suite (110,110,110).

The Dickens' House Museum WC1 £B-M, (50,12)
48 Doughty St   405 2127   (831 5175)
Oliver Twist's and Nicholas Nickleby's Bloomsbury birthplace is a four floor c19 house, for the most part filled with display cabinets detailing their and their creator's life; entertaining takes place in the pleasant, quite atmospheric basement Library. / 11 pm; eve only, possibly all day Sun; hirer's choice of caterer; no amplified music; no dancing; smoking in garden only.

Diorama NW1
14 Peto Pl
This intriguing early c19 hall of entertainment, next to Regent's Park, was one of London's best party spots; the Crown Estates are currently refurbishing but it seems likely that a new lessee, in due course, will make the place available for functions.

The Dog & Duck W1   £B, (35,–)
18 Bateman St   437 4447
Media-heartland pub with quite attractive upstairs bar available for hire. / 1 am; no music; no dancing.

Private venues

Doggetts Coat & Badge SE1 £B-M, (200,70)
1 Blackfriars Bridge Rd   633 9081   (928 7299)
Huge Thames-side, modern pub complex, including conference-orientated rooms, with excellent views of the City and St Paul's, especially from the large terraces; it can be taken over in its entirety at the weekends.
/ 12.30 am; only large parties Sat & Sun; Restaurant (120,70); Terrace Bar (80,24); Boardroom (30,18).

Dolphin Square SW1 £B-M, (240,200,125)
Dolphin Sq, Chichester St   834 3800   (798 8735)
The main interest at this huge, very '30s apartment block is its unique ground floor restaurant, which has an ocean-liner feel and view over the internal swimming-pool – ideal for nautical or '30s theme balls; the low-ceilinged Chichester Suite is one of the few central rooms in which you can cater for your own dinner party. / 12.30 am;
Restaurant (Gardner Merchant) (240,200,125); Chichester Suite (hirer's choice of caterer) (100,55).

Dora House SW7 £B-M, (120,70)
108 Old Brompton Rd   373 5554   (373 9202)
The Royal Society of British Sculptors is housed in an unusually elegant turn-of-the-century house – an agreeable and not too expensive South Kensington venue.
/ over 30s preferred; midnight; hirer's choice of caterer; no amplified music; The Studio (80,70); Salon (40,20).

The Dorchester W1 £M-E, (1000,550,450)
53 Park Ln   629 8888   (495 7351)
Glamorous opulence distinguishes the rooms at this recently revitalised Mayfair hotel; all of the rooms have real style, from the subtly-mirrored Ballroom, which is approached through a series of ante-rooms, down (or rather up) to the extraordinary fairy-tale setting of the 8th floor Penthouse with terrace, fountain and spectacular view. / Ballroom (1000,550,450); Orchid (250,160,120);
Park Suite (100,70,60); Holford (80,40); Pavilion (60,40);
Penthouse (30,18); Boardroom (20,12); Library (10,–).

La Dordogne W4 £M, (–,28)
5 Devonshire Rd   081-747 1836
Chiswick's No 1 restaurant is a cosy, very Gallic spot; they have a private room and, for large parties, one of the main restaurant rooms can be used. / only large parties Sat L & Sun L; Private Section (–,28); Private Rm (–,14).

Downstairs At 190 SW7 £M, (60,70)
190 Queensgate   581 5666   (581 8172)
This well-known South Kensington establishment serves a generally successful, eclectic fish menu; the private room – sumptuous, fun and overblown – comes complete with exotic tented ceiling; for bigger parties the whole restaurant can be hired. / not Sun; Private Rm (40,24);
Green Rm (60,–).

Private venues

Dr Johnsons' House EC4   £B-M, (80,–)
17 Gough Sq   0308-868118   (0308-868995)
Apart from its literary associations (and associated bric-à-brac), the charm of this five-storey house, hidden away off Fleet Street, is that it is, most unusually, a plain Georgian house in central London (and the decoration, in keeping with the period, is very neutral); available only for early evening receptions. / 9 pm - possibly later; not Sun; eve only; hirer's choice of caterer; no amplified music; no dancing; smoking restricted.

Drapers' Hall EC2
Throgmorton Av   588 5001
Behind the Bank of England, this livery hall is one of the City's finest; we include it primarily for completeness as its use by those outside the company is extremely restricted.

The Draycott SW3   £M, (40,–)
24 Cadogan Gdns   730 6466   (730 0236)
Small, plushly converted town-house club/hotel, behind Peter Jones, whose Drawing Room is available for moderately sized receptions; in summer, guests can spill through French windows onto the large, peaceful communal gardens. / no amplified music; no dancing; Drawing Rm (40,–).

Drones SW1   £M, (–,34)
1 Pont St   235 9638
See 'Paint the town rouge' – impressionist reproductions grace the walls of the downstairs private room.
/ Private Rm (–,34).

Duke of Albemarle W1   £B, (40,20)
6 Stafford St   493 9051
Comfortable, slightly old-fashioned, room over a Mayfair pub, for which there is no charge for parties.

Duke of Clarence W11   £B, (100,50)
203 Holland Pk Av   603 5431
Hospitable Notting Hill pub whose quite large rear conservatory can be used privately. / midnight; Conservatory (100,50).

Duke of York's HQ SW3   £B-M, (2000,500,500)
King's Rd   730 8131   (414 5560)
The fashionably located TA HQ is a stone's throw from Sloane Square; the gymnasium-style Cadogan Hall is very popular by virtue of its size plus the affordability and flexibility it offers (although some effort on decoration is a good investment) and marquees can be erected to add space; newly refurbished, the London Irish Mess is worth enquiring about for quite smart dinners and receptions, while for very large events the drill square can be used as a marquee site. / music ends 1 am; hirer's choice of caterer; Lawn (2000,–); Cadogan Hall with marquee (500,500,500); Cadogan Hall (500,200,250); London Irish Mess (60,30); marquee site.

Private venues

Dukes Hotel SW1   £M-E, (120,70,50)
35 St James's Pl   491 4840   (493 1264)
Traditional, late-Victorian St James's establishment where, surprisingly, the attractive roof-terrace is the star-attraction (but not for its view); winter entertaining can be accommodated in the more conventional private rooms – the suites here suit intimate dinners well. / 2am, roof terrace 11 pm; Roof Terrace (100,36); Marlborough Suite (120,70,50); Batchelor Suite (–,12); Single Suite (18,8); Double Suite (70,16).

Dulwich College SE21   £B-M, (800,400,300)
Dulwich Common   081-693 3737   (081-693 6319)
Impressively equipped Victorian school in its own extensive, leafy grounds, which offers a variety of possibilities for functions and entertainments (especially sports-related) of varying sizes; moderate prices and there is a no-corkage policy. / midnight; avail out of term only; in-house caterers; smoking restricted; Christenson Hall and Upper Dining Rms (800,400,300); Great Hall (500,250,200); Cricket Pavilion (250,–); Lower Hall or North and South Cloisters (120,–); Old Library (–,50); marquee site.

Dulwich Picture Gallery SE21   £M-E, (300,200)
College Rd   081-693 5254   (081-693 0923)
The UK's oldest picture gallery, designed by Soane and housing works by Rembrandt and Canaletto, offers an unusual, atmospheric and rather charming venue.
/ midnight; avail after 6 pm, and all day Mon; list of caterers; no dancing; no smoking; no flash photography; marquee site.

Durrants Hotel W1   £B-M, (80,55)
George St   935 8131   (487 3510)
One of London's few privately-owned, characterful hotels, this comfortable Marylebone spot boasts two nice, panelled, ground floor rooms; the more recent basement banqueting suite is more ordinary. / midnight; Edward VII Rm (80,55); Oak Rm (60,24); Armfield Rm (25,12).

Dyers' Hall EC4   £M-E, (–,57)
10 Dowgate Hl   236 7197
Small, early Victorian hall, available to suitable hirers for luncheons and dinners only. / 11 pm; not Aug & Sep; in-house caterers; no amplified music; no dancing.

East India Club SW1
16 St James's Sq   930 1000   (321 0217)
This St James's Club has enough members to be relatively indifferent about attracting functions from non-members; however, if you can find one of their number (6,000 or so) to act as host (and be present), the rooms are very good for clubby dinners and receptions.

Private venues

Eatons EC3   £B-M, (400,160,150)
1 Minster Pavt   283 2838   (283 7275)
In a new development off Mincing Lane, this is a pleasant modern City wine bar/restaurant with its own banqueting suite; the restaurant may be hired for evening and weekend drinks parties and dinners; the banqueting suite is sub-divisible and can accommodate sit downs from 10 upwards. / 1 am; Banqueting Suite (275,160,150).

Eatons SW1   £B-M, (–,12)
49 Elizabeth St   730 0074
Comfortably lived-in Belgravia townhouse restaurant suited to convivial, if not grand, gatherings. / not Sat & Sun; Private Rm (–,12).

El-Cid SW10   £B-M, (150,70,70)
333 Fulham Rd   352 9463
This small first-floor nightclub, dominated by its large bar, makes a cosy, fun spot for a party with its raised seating area and a tiny dance-floor; you can take it over all night, or, less expensively, have it privately until about 11.30 pm. / 2 am.

Electric Ballroom NW1   £B, (1100,400,400)
184 Camden High St   485 9006   (284 0745)
Rather nice, old-established, Camden Town dance hall, ideal for a large dance or major themed event. / 2 am; not Fri, Sat & Sun; hirer's choice of caterer, alcohol in-house.

11 Hobart Place SW1   £M-E, (30,20)
11 Hobart Pl   839 4071   (839 1702)
Narrow Edwardian house, behind Buckingham Palace, run by the Institute of Materials; for a formal meal, the two rooms – with Adam-style moulded ceilings and fire places – are worth considering and there is a small paved garden off one of the rooms for summer drinks.
/ 12.30 am; in-house caterers; smoking restricted; Edinburgh Rm (–,20); Garden Rm (30,20).

The Elizabeth Suite EC2   £M, (750,400,350)
59-67 Gresham St   606 7344   (606 2881)
Flexible accommodation in Mecca-Elizabethan style under a '50s office block, by the Guildhall, which is popular both for business-related and social events; the Spanish Room is ideal for dinner-dances (it gets booked solid in December) and a reasonable, all-in, Gala Package is offered. / 1 am; Graison; Spanish Rm (600,400,350); The Golden Hind (150,90,60); The Library (75,32); Willoughby Rm (–,12).

Empress Garden W1   £M, (–,36)
15-16 Berkeley St   493 1381   (491 2655)
This expensive, rather businessy, Mayfair Chinese restaurant has three basement private rooms.
/ Private Rm (–,36); Private Rm (–,12); Private Rm (–,10).

Private venues

English Garden SW3 £M-E, (–,50)
10 Lincoln St   584 7272   (581 2848)
Very similar to the English House (below); the decor of the upstairs private rooms is preferable to that of the rather overblown main restaurant (which may be taken in its entirety for larger parties). / Rm 1 (–,20); Rm 2 (–,10).

English House SW3 £M-E, (–,26)
3 Milner St   584 3002   (581 2848)
Chelsea townhouse restaurant decorated in a lavish Laura Ashleyesqe style which continues into the upstairs private rooms (the smaller opening onto a small outside terrace); the cooking is not inexpensive but consistent. / Front Rm (–,12); Blue Rm (–,6).

Equinox at the Empire WC2 £B-M, (1850,600,600)
Leicester Sq   437 1446   (287 2944)
Claiming the West End's largest dance-floor, this nightclub boasts all the high-tech gizmos you would expect and is used for a large range of day and evening functions; the Square Bar is effectively a mini-nightclub, available independently. / avail Sun & Mon eves and weekdays; Crown Catering; Club (1500,300); Square Bar (150,60,60).

L'Escargot W1 £M, (–,40)
48 Greek St   437 2679   (437 0790)
Recently relaunched Soho restaurant institution, with two good quality private rooms, of which the barrel-vaulted room with a single table is particularly distinctive. / not Sat L & Sun; Barrell Vaulted Rm (–,40); Private Rm (–,22).

L'Etoile W1 £M-E, (–,25)
30 Charlotte St   636 7189   (580 0109)
The heart of London's restaurant-land may have moved West, but the ancien régime food, service and atmosphere still draw many to this traditionalists' haven by the Tottenham Court Road. / not Sat L & Sun; Private Rm (–,25).

L'Express SW1 £B-M, (80,–)
16 Sloane St   235 9869
Immaculately styled, monochrome bar/café, underneath the Joseph shop, which, though rather long and thin (like many of its customers), offers affordable designer-style; they will consider evening receptions with light snacks. / no dancing.

La Famiglia SW10 £M, (–,40)
7 Langton St   351 0761   (351 2409)
This immensely popular, fashionable Chelsea Italian restaurant of long standing has a private room downstairs. / Private Rm (–,40).

Private venues

Fan Museum SE10   £M, (80,30)
12 Crooms Hl   081-853 3849   (081-293 1889)
Very pretty all around – both the fine collection of fans (housed in two recently-converted c18 Greenwich townhouses) and the mirrors and murals decor of the Orangery annex (opening onto the garden) where food is served; ideal for smaller weddings – comparatively inexpensive receptions can be organised. / 11 pm;
list of caterers; no amplified music; no dancing; no smoking; no drinks while viewing collection; Museum (80,–); Orangery (–,30).

Farmers' & Fletchers' Hall EC1   £M, (250,120)
3 Cloth St   600 5777   (600 2777)
Recently refurbished modern livery hall, decorated in a traditional style. / 1 am; Chester Boyd; no amplified music.

Feng Shang NW1   £M, (–,130)
Opp 15 Prince Albert Rd   485 8137   (267 2990)
Multi-floored Chinese theme-barge – floating on Regent's canal at the northern tip of the Park – which is, to some, quite a glam' venue for a large dinner or dinner-dance.
/ 1 am.

First Floor W11   £M, (100,35)
186 Portobello Rd   243 0072   (221 8387)
This New York style Notting Hill joint has one of the best-known and most distinctive restaurant private rooms in London; with its wonderful ambience and good and imaginative cooking, its appeal is to the younger at heart.
/ Private Rm (100,35).

Fishmongers' Hall EC4
London Bridge   626 3531
One of London's finest large halls, included for completeness only – it is generally unavailable to third parties, except sometimes to charities.

Footstool SW1   £B-M, (250,120,90)
St John's, Smith Sq   222 2779   (233 1618)
St John's light, flower-filled crypt is a lunch-spot popular with MPs (it has a division bell) and those attending on concert evenings; at other times it's available for most types of function. / 1 am.

Formula Veneta SW10   £M, (–,40)
14 Hollywood Rd   352 7612
Stylish, younger-scene Chelsea Italian restaurant, acclaimed by many for the quality of its food; the private area downstairs does not quite have the distinctive charm of the main restaurant. / Private Rm (–,40).

Private venues

Forte Crest
Regents Park W1 £M, (1200,550,500)
Carburton St   388 2300   (387 2806)
Quietly situated, rather Continental in feel, modernish Marylebone hotel (inevitably not adjacent to the Park); its particular attraction is the large, divisible Portland Suite which is well suited to dinner-dances. / 2 am;
in-house caterers; Portland Suite (1200,550,500); Albany (420,200); Clarence (250,150); Devonshire (250,130); Chester Suite (70,50); 1/2 Chester Suite (25,20).

Forte Crest St James's SW1 £M, (150,60)
Jermyn St   930 2111   (839 2125)
Perhaps still better known as the Cavendish, this St James's hotel boasts only one function room, traditional in style and mainly used for corporate events.
/ Private dining room (150,60).

41 Beak St W1 £M, (200,70,70)
41 Beak St   287 2057   (434 3085)
Soho media-scene members' club (serving good food) which, especially at Christmas, takes Saturday night parties from outsiders – often local companies. / 3.30 am;
Sat only; in-house caterers.

The Founders' Hall EC1 £M, (125,75,50)
1 Cloth Fair   600 5777   (600 2777)
Small, modern (1987) Smithfield hall, impressively designed; the intimate Livery Hall boasts striking contemporary decor; the Parlour is more conventional.
/ 1 am; Aug hol; Chester Boyd; no amplified music; Parlour (50,20); Livery Hall (125,75,50).

Four Seasons Hotel W1 £M-E, (750,400,325)
Hamilton Pl   499 0888   (499 5572)
Large, '70s hotel (formerly the Inn on the Park), overlooking Hyde Park, used for a fair number of grander events; the Pine Room is a grand setting for a small dinner and the plush Private Suites are worth considering for intimate occasions. / Park Rm (300,-);
Garden Rm (300,100,80); Pine Rm (60,40); Oak Rm (150,80,60); Ballroom (750,400,325); Sitting and Dining Rms (35,16).

Fox & Anchor EC1 £B-M, (-,24)
115 Charterhouse St   253 4838
Famous, atmospheric Smithfield pub – the best known of those serving early breakfast with Guinness; private breakfasts, grill lunches and dinners can be arranged in their agreeable upstairs parlour. / not Sun; Private Rm (-,24).

Foxtrot Oscar SW3 £B-M, (-,34)
79 Royal Hospital Rd   352 7179
This comfortably dated, Chelsea in-crowd hang-out is popular on account of its atmosphere, rather than its menu of erratically prepared staples; the basement is available for hire. /Basement (-,34).

Private venues

Frederick's N1   £M, (40,26)
Camden Pas   359 3902   (359 5173)
See 'Paint the town rouge' – the traditional Clarence Room is of a high standard – on Sundays, the whole restaurant is available for hire. / Clarence Rm (40,26).

The Freemason's Arms WC2   £B, (150,45)
81-82 Longacre   836 3115
Covent Garden pub with a large, pleasant upstairs bar, which is used for much more than typical pub functions. / 11 pm; no amplified music; no dancing.

French Institute SW7   £B-M, (120,40)
17 Queensbury Pl   589 6211   (581 5127)
The Salon de Réception of this South Kensington centre – a quite large, light, first floor room – suits smartish receptions and dinners; the Café Club, downstairs, is a modish, sandy-walled bar/café which can also cater for more informal private events. / midnight; hirer's choice of caterer; no amplified music; no dancing; Salon de Réception (80,30); Café Club (120,40).

Freud Museum NW3   £M, (120,50)
20 Maresfield Gdns   435 2002   (431 5452)
Spacious '20s Hampstead villa in which the great man lived his last days and where his daughter, Anna, lived until a decade ago; its domestic ambience makes it ideal for intimate gatherings, especially in summer when the charming, small garden can be used. / 11 pm; Wed-Sun after 5 pm, Mon & Tue all day; hirer's choice of caterer; no amplified music; no dancing; no smoking; House (80,20); House & Garden (120,50); marquee site.

The Fridge SW2   £B, (1100,–)
Town Hall Parade, Brixton Hl   326 5100   (274 2879)
Well-known, large Brixton nightclub. / 6 am; not Tue, Fri & Sat; hirer's choice of caterer, alcohol in-house.

Froebel Institute
College SW15   £B-M, (400,140,140)
Roehampton Ln   081-392 3305   (081-392 3331)
Grove House, in leafy Roehampton, is part of the Roehampton Institute; set in 25 acres, it is a little institutional but worth thinking of for weddings, cricket matches (especially as you can put a marquee up in the grounds) and similar events. / midnight; in-house caterers; smoking restricted; Terrace Rm (120,70); Main Common Rm (180,140); marquee site.

Front Page SW3   £B-M, (50,22)
35 Old Church St   352 2908
Prettily located Old Chelsea pub, with a reputation for food pretty good by pub standards; its panelled upstairs private room has a more ambitious menu than is offered below. / Private Rm (50,22).

Private venues

Fulham House SW6   £B-M, (200,150,150)
87 Fulham High St   384 2476
This plainly handsome Georgian house (with defensive cannon) houses a branch of the TA and is also a popular party venue; the main (drill) hall is a flexible gym-type space; the officers' mess offers traditional style. / 3 am; not Wed; hirer's choice of caterer; Main Hall (250,150,150); Officers' Mess (–,50).

Fulham Palace SW6   £M, (130,80,80)
Bishops Av   081-748 3020, x3528
Medieval palace, with courtyard, which was the home of the Bishops of London until the '70s; prettily situated in a park and potentially charming, but you should reckon to spend quite a lot on decoration. / 11 pm; hirer's choice of caterer; no smoking; Great Hall (100,80); Drawing Rm (100,80); Ante Rm (30,–); Drawing & Ante Rm (130,–); marquee site.

Fulham Town Hall SW6   £B-M, (500,300,230)
Fulham Broadway
081-748 3020   (081-741 5664)
Coming on-line in '94, Fulham Town Hall, on the Broadway, looks set to become a major venue; the heavily rusticated Edwardian building is extremely characterful inside and out and the large hall has just been tastefully renovated; next on the list is the Concert Hall due to re-open in '95. / 2 am; hirer's choice of caterer; Large Hall (500,300,230); Concert Hall (250,150,100).

Fung Shing WC2   £M, (–,28)
15 Lisle St   437 1539
Generally reckoned to be the best Cantonese restaurant in Chinatown, by whose standards, the restaurant, and the first-floor private room, are comfortably decorated. / Private Rm (–,28).

The Gaslight SW1   £B, (150,60)
4 Duke Of York St   930 1648
This St James's club leads a Jekyll and Hyde existence – during the week, a club for tired and lonely business executives, at weekends the red banquettes can come out and it's used as a nightclub or for private parties. / 2.30 am; avail Sat & Sun; in-house caterers.

Le Gavroche W1   £M-E, (40,20)
43 Upper Brook St   408 0881   (491 4387)
London's longest-established temple of Gallic gastronomy has an unusually grand, elegant, traditionally-styled private dining room, with its own small but comfortable sitting room. / not Sat & Sun.

Gay Hussar W1   £M, (–,12)
2 Greek St   437 0973
The atmosphere of this venerable, creaky Soho Hungarian restaurant permeates up to the cosy second-floor private room; surprisingly light, enjoyable dishes belie their heavy-sounding menu descriptions; service is extremely friendly. / not Sun; Private Rm (–,12).

Private venues

George Inn SE1   £B-M, (190,60)
77 Borough Hl St   407 2056
National Trust pub, just south of London Bridge – it is London's only remaining galleried coaching inn; set in its own (not very attractive) courtyard, it has a couple of quite pleasant private rooms, but the restaurant, some of which may be taken privately, is more characterful; best of all is the Old Bar which, with enough people, is available on an exclusive basis. / midnight; George (–,55); Talbot (–,25); Restaurant (–,60).

Glassblower W1   £B, (150,56)
42 Glasshouse St   734 8547
This pub on the fringe of Soho has a large, relaxed upstairs lounge bar with the odd bookshelf and lots of seating. / not Fri eve.

The Glasshouse Stores W1   £B, (150,50)
55 Brewer St   287 5278   (287 5278)
Cosy wine bar beneath a Soho pub; either or both arms of its U-configuration may be used privately. / midnight; One side (80,–).

Glaziers' Hall SE1   £M, (600,280,200)
9 Montague Cl   403 3300   (407 6036)
A '70s renovation left these early c19 rooms feeling slightly flat, though they are potentially very fine; the River Room's view more than compensates, however, and the hall and the other rooms offer flexible, not-too-expensive accommodation on a good scale. / 2 am; hirer's choice of caterer; smoking restricted; Hall (400,280,200); River Rm (200,120); Library / Court Rm (120,100).

Gloucester Hotel SW7   £M, (600,420,350)
4-18 Harrington Gdns   373 6030   (373 0409)
Modernish South Kensington hotel offering a range of quite agreeable and flexible banqueting facilities; refurbishment is promised as we go to press. / 2 am; Cotswold Suite (600,420,350); Cotswold - 1/2 (300,200,130); Harrington or Stanhope (50,45).

The Golden Lion SW1   £B, (120,20)
25 King St   930 7227
This St James's pub is usually closed at weekends, but for parties of over 100 they will open up for you; discos can be arranged in the nicer than usual upper room which is also available independently during the week for parties of 25 or more. / midnight; Mon-Fri eve only, Sat & Sun all day; in-house caterers; Theatre Bar (40,20).

Goldsmith's College SE14   £B-M, (500,250,200)
Lewisham Way   081-692 7171   (081-694 2234)
One of London's finest art schools, unglamorously located in New Cross; the lofty Great Hall opens straight off the entrance to the college and, though slightly worn, is in an interesting '30s style; (there are quite large student bars and rooms which are also available to boost space). / 2 am; Sutcliffes; Great Hall (500,250,200).

Private venues

Goldsmiths' Hall EC2   £M-E, (500,200)
Foster Ln   606 7010   (606 1511)
The epitome of majestic, classically styled grandeur, this early c19 livery hall, a stone's throw from St Paul's, is stately rather than stiff in atmosphere; the hall is available primarily to an established circle of former users for special events, but applications from newcomers will be considered. / midnight; not Sat & Sun; list of caterers; Livery Hall (500,200); Drawing Rm (200,–); Exhibition Rm (200,–).

Gopal's of Soho W1   £B-M, (–,20)
12 Bateman St   434 1621
For a comfortable Indian meal in a central location the private rooms of this low-key Soho restaurant are a good bet. / Private Rm (–,20).

Goring Hotel SW1   £M, (100,80)
Beeston Pl   396 9000   (834 4393)
Surprisingly tranquil given its Victoria location, one of London's few family-owned hotels affords some pretty rooms for entertaining – particularly the Small Garden and Large Lounges which offer views over, if not the use of, Mr Goring's large garden; the rather '70s, subterranean Ebury room is serviceable but less august. / Large Lounge Sat & Sun only; Small Garden Lounge (75,36); Drawing Rm (25,14); Large Lounge (weekends only) (100,80); Ebury Rm (100,50); Breakfast Rm (–,8).

Le Gothique SW18   £B-M, (400,250,200)
The Royal Victoria Patriotic Bldg, Fitzhugh Gr, Trinity Rd
081-870 6567   (081-870 1645)
Rather '70s restaurant whose particular appeal is its access to the very pretty cloister garden of its extraordinary OTT Victorian building, in a Wandsworth park; they may also be able to cater at the adjoining Academy of Live and Recorded Arts (see also). / 1 am; Restaurant (–,60); Patio (150,60); with Academy of Live & Recorded Arts (400,250,200).

Gray's Inn EC1   £M-E, (450,170,170)
High Holborn   405 8164   (831 8381)
The attractively cloistered surroundings of the inn make an excellent setting for social and business events of all types; the c17 hall is simply decorated but attractive. / midnight; not Sun; in-house caterers; Hall (300,170); Large Reception Rm (150,–); Landing (50,–); Reception area (30,–).

Green's SW1   £M-E, (50,34)
36 Duke St   930 4566
Club-like St James's restaurant and oyster bar offering simple, high-quality English food; an Establishment favourite, it is priced accordingly; the subterranean private rooms are not quite as character-ful as the main restaurant. / not Sun D; Private Rm (50,34); Private Rm (–,10).

Private venues

Grocers' Hall EC2   £M-E, (250,150)
Princes St   606 3113   (600 3082)
Rebuilt in 1970, the Grocers' accommodation, by the Bank of England, emerged relatively unscathed by the style-horrors of the period; the cream Piper room, named after the designer of its striking modern wall-hangings, may be used for receptions or dinners, while the Dining Room (complete with medieval gates) is an unusual modern re-creation of traditional style. / 11 pm; not Sun; Aug hol; in-house caterers; live music only; no discos; Dining Rm (250,150); Piper Rm (90,50).

Grosvenor Hotel SW1   £M, (150,120,100)
101 Buckingham Palace Rd   834 9494   (630 1978)
Despite its rather tired entrance (refurbishment promised), Victoria's railway hotel has some very attractive, atmospheric period rooms – especially the imposing, very bright Bessborough Room, a double-height treasure, complete with minstrel's gallery. / 1 am; Gallery Rm (150,120,100); Bessborough Rm (90,70,50); Warwick Rm (30,30); Belgrave or Wilton Rm (25,16).

Grosvenor House Hotel W1   £M-E, (1500,1500,1500)
86-90 Pk Ln   499 6363   (493 3341)
The Great Room – a two storey, unpillared space, originally built as an ice-rink – is the largest hotel room in Europe (they say) and hosts many major events; its fame tends to overshadow the other facilities here, which include a pretty ballroom in traditional style and 86 Park Lane – a complex of 18 recently refurbished dining and reception rooms all with natural light (catering for from 6 to 120) in a variety of styles, but principally clubby English. / 2 am; Great Rm (1500,1500,1500); Ballroom (750,550,500); Albemarle (150,120,80); Boardroom (-,22).

Grosvenor Rooms NW2   £B-M, (700,500,420)
92 Walm Ln, Willesden   081-451 0066   (081-459 7676)
Unpretentious, very '70s Willesden banqueting complex; it has the benefit of large kitchens available for use by external caterers, enabling, for example, ethnic requirements to be accommodated. / 2 am; hirer's choice of caterer; Grosvenor Suite (700,500,420); Executive Suite (300,180,180); Pearl Suite (200,120,120).

Guards Museum SW1   £M, (180,80,80)
Wellington Barracks, Birdcage Wk
414 3271   (414 3424)
Below the concrete of the Guards' regimental parade-ground, these modern galleries of regimental dress, weapons and regalia make a colourful backdrop especially for receptions or dinners; a free-standing marquee may be put up in the square, allowing greater numbers and dancing. / midnight; eve only; hirer's choice of caterer; no amplified music; no dancing; no smoking; marquee site.

Private venues

Guildhall EC2   £M-E, (1500,704)
Town Clerk, Corporation Of London, PO Box 270 / Aldermanbury 606 3030 (796 2621)
The City's c14 HQ is the venue for many state and civic occasions; City (and notable London) organisations can also apply, but use of the cathedral-like Great Hall is limited to special events such as mile-stone anniversaries; of the other rooms, the lofty Library is ecclesiastical in feel while the Crypts, with their stained glass and painted ceilings, are not at all gloomy; dancing is allowed but tends to be discouraged by the early closing time. / 11 pm; not Sun; list of caterers; no dancing in Great Hall; Great Hall (900,704); East Crypt (250,200); West Crypt (250,180); Livery Hall (250,200); Old Library (600,300).

The Guinea W1   £M, (30,20)
30 Bruton Pl 499 1210
Pleasantly old-fashioned Mayfair pub which is one of the few steakhouses in London, and one of the fewer tolerable ones; for a comfortable traditional meal they have a first-floor panelled boardroom. / Boardroom (30,20).

Gunnersbury Park W3   £B-M, (–,70)
Gunnersbury Pk 081-570 7728 (081-862 5847)
The Park is huge – just north of Kew Bridge; there are three simple park buildings available for weddings and similar events – the Small Mansion possibly enjoys the nicest position. / midnight; hirer's choice of caterer; Temple (–,50); Orangery (–,70); Small Mansion (–,70).

Guy's Hospital Tower SE1   £B-M, (150,120,100)
St Thomas St 955 4490 (955 4661)
On the 29th Floor of London's fourth highest block, the Robens Suite is the highest venue available for hire in London; the view is, predictably, magnificent, while the walk through the building to reach the suite is, predictably, not, though, once you are in, the decor is fine; weddings and so on are welcome. / midnight; in-house caterers.

Haandi NW1   £B, (–,50)
161 Drummond St 383 4557
The low-key basement room of this Little India establishment is undistinguished, but if surroundings are not important, professional service and some of London's best Indian cooking may more than compensate.

Haberdashers' Hall EC2   £M, (430,150)
Staining Ln 606 0967 (606 5738)
This Hall, near London Wall, is a quality '50s reconstruction in traditional style; the charming, pine-panelled Luncheon Room is the nicest room. / 11 pm; seldom Sat & Sun; Aug hol; list of caterers; no amplified music; no dancing; Main Hall (250,150); Court Rm (120,58); Luncheon Rm (–,20).

Private venues

Halcyon Hotel W11   £M-E, (100,80,70)
81 Holland Pk   727 7288   (229 8516)
Intimate, pretty and fashionable Holland Park townhouse hotel which offers attractive accommodation and good cooking. / *1 am; Restaurant (100,80,70); Suite 34 (40,20); Halcyon Suite (40,20).*

The Halkin SW1   £M-E, (150,75)
5 Halkin St   333 1000   (333 1100)
Slick, minimalist Italian style distinguishes this Belgravia hotel whose restaurant can be hired in its entirety; there is also a similar, smaller private room; the cooking is above average but not inexpensive. / *Private Rm (-,12).*

Ham House, Surrey   £M, (300,250)
Petersham   081-940 1950   (081-332 6903)
No functions are possible actually inside this National Trust c17 house, but you can use the Orangeryrestaurant or put a marquee up in the grounds, which overlook the river. / *midnight; eve only; not Jan & Feb; list of caterers; no amplified music; no dancing; no smoking; Orangery (100,60); marquee site.*

Hamilton House EC4   £M, (100,50)
1 Temple Av   353 4212   (353 3325)
This bright, lofty room, nicely decorated in traditional style, has windows on three sides and an excellent view of the Inner Temple Garden; the only disadvantage is that it is part of an office building and the entrance is rather business-like. / *11 pm; not Sat & Sun; Castle Catering; no amplified music; no dancing.*

Hamilton Suite W1   £M, (200,120,120)
5a Hamilton Pl   499 6555   (499 1230)
Formerly part of Les Ambassadeurs club upstairs; the vaguely exotic, lacquer-walled red room and relaxed Conservatory bar suit less formal functions, while the Marble Room and wood-panelled Hamilton Room are more traditionally clubby; its subterranean nature makes it more suitable for evening than lunch-time functions. / *3 am; in-house caterers; Conservatory Bar (80,40); Red Rm (150,100); Hamilton Rm (80,40); Marble Rm (25,14).*

Hamiltons Gallery W1   £M-E, (300,-)
13 Carlos Pl   499 9493   (629 9919)
London's leading photographic gallery, in Mayfair, offers an uncluttered, neutral but impressive central space for receptions. / *10.30 pm; not Sun; hirer's choice of caterer; no amplified music; no dancing; no smoking.*

Hammersmith Palais W6   £B, (2230,650,650)
242 Shepherd's Bush Rd   081-748 2812   (081-741 4994)
Well-known nightclub, just north of Hammersmith Broadway; the areas overlooking the large dance-floor may be taken privately. / *3 am; whole club Sun-Wed only; hirer's choice of caterer; alcohol in-house; Balcony Bar (400,-); VIP Bar (150,60).*

Private venues

Hammersmith Town Hall W6   £B, (850,450,300)
King St   081-748 3020
Huge, lofty, quite atmospheric '30s hall in good order.
/ *2 am; hirer's choice of caterer.*

Hampshire Hotel WC2   £M-E, (180,80,60)
Leicester Sq   839 9399   (930 8122)
With its view towards Trafalgar Square, the Penthouse is the best part of this Theatreland hotel; the basement banqueting rooms compare well with similar hotels, but style anglais is laid on with a trowel. / Romsey or Burley (45,30); Milton (40,25); Penthouse (180,80,60).

Hampton Court Palace, Surrey   £E, (1500,1000)
081-781 9508   (081-781 9509)
Wolsey's magnificent palace, adopted by Henry VIII, is occasionally used for major corporate and charity dinners; on a more intimate scale, the delightful, highly decorated Banqueting House in the grounds is used relatively frequently for medium size lunch and dinner parties. / *eve only; hirer's choice of caterer; no amplified music; no dancing; no smoking; no weddings; Great Hall (500,280); Banqueting House (–,60).*

Hampton Court Palace, Surrey, Tiltyard Restaurant   £M,(130,100,75)
East Molesey   081-943 3666   (081-943 5457)
Leith's prettily situated restaurant is the only part of the palace within most budgets. / *11 pm; no amplified music; marquee site.*

Hash Eleven W1   £B, (200,–)
11 Wardour St   287 3902   (713 0899)
Intimate, interesting and attractively decorated nightclub on the edge of Chinatown mostly dedicated to bar and seating space – there is a small upstairs dance-floor; those worried by associations with gay and fetish nights should look elsewhere. / *3 am; hirer's choice of caterer, alcohol in-house.*

Hayward Gallery SE1   £E, (250,–)
Belvedere Rd   921 0725   (928 0063)
The South Bank centre's art gallery has its fair share of prominent exhibitions, at which times it gets solidly booked for evening receptions; for such affairs, they have two two-hour slots per week. / *avail 6.30 to 8.30 Mon & Thu; list of caterers; no amplified music; no dancing; no smoking.*

Henry J Beans SW3   £B-M, (50,–)
195 King's Rd   352 9255
Chelsea burgeria, included solely for the rear section of its large garden which can be used privately for summer parties. / *no music; no dancing.*

Private venues

Hever Castle, Kent £M-E, (130,70)
Edenbridge   0732-865224   (0732-867860)
This intimate moated castle, substantially rebuilt by the Astors at the turn of the century, now benefits from an adjacent Tudor Village, making it especially suitable for residential events. / 12.30 am; in-house caterers; no amplified music; no dancing; Dining Hall (–,36); Tudor Suite (130,70).

Hilton on
Park Lane W1   £M-E, (1000,1000,1000)
22 Pk Ln   493 8000   (495 0716)
This landmark hotel has one of the capital's largest ballrooms (in a modern style) and also a full range of other accommodation for functions (especially dinner-dances); the fourth floor Serpentine Room, has one of the best views of any function room in London. / 3 am; Grand Ballroom (1000,1000,1000); Grand Ballroom - Section 1 (500,380); Grand Ballroom - Section 2 (450,350); Harvest Rm (200,150); Curzon Suite (300,200,150); Crystal Palace Rm (250,130,100); Coronation Rm (150,90,60); Pompei Rm (65,50); Serpentine Rm (30,16).

The Hippodrome WC2   £B-M, (1650,440,440)
Leicester Sq   437 4311   (434 4225)
London's best-known central nightclub is sufficiently well maintained that it would suit any crowd; it boasts an extremely impressive light system and is technically well equipped for major corporate events, in which they do big business. / Hirer's choice of caterer; Auditorium (1200,220,220); Balcony – Restaurant (450,175,175); Star Bar (120,30,30).

RS Hispaniola WC2   £M, (250,170,170)
Victoria Embankment   839 3011   (321 0547)
Moored permanently by Hungerford Bridge for the last 25 years, this erstwhile Clyde steamer is now quite a smart boat on which to entertain; both decks have outside outside areas front and rear. / 1 am; in-house caterers; Top Deck (120,80); Main Deck (250,170).

Hodgson's WC2   £M, (–,12)
115 Chancery Ln   242 2836
Unusually pretty restaurant, near the Public Record Office, which has quite good food and an attractive private room. / not Sat & Sun; Private Rm (–,12).

Holderness House EC2   £B, (300,150,150)
51-61 Clifton St   377 9237
No-one would call either the location or the common parts of this four-floor modern TA base north of the City glamorous; but it is fairly inexpensive and once you are in the drill hall it is, especially with decoration, quite agreeable. / 1 am; hirer's choice of caterer; Hall (300,150,150); Rifleman's Bar (–,20).

Private venues

Holiday Inn – Mayair W1   £M, (100,72)
Berkeley St   493 8282   (629 2827)
As befits the area, the banqueting rooms here are fitted out with a little more class than that for which the chain is renowned. / Stratton Suite (100,72); Presidential Suite (60,20); Buckingham (40,8); Berkeley (25,6); Burlington (25,8).

Hollands W11   £B, (100,60)
6 Portland Rd   229 3130
The airy conservatory at the rear of this Holland Park Filipino restaurant and wine bar makes an ideal spot for an informal party. / 3 am; Conservatory (–,40).

Hollyhedge House SE3   £B-M, (500,500,300)
Blackheath   694 0375
For an affordable big bash, the vast drill hall at this army centre on the edge of Blackheath is ideal (though it could use a little decoration); for club dinners and the like it may be worth enquiring about the Officers' Mess.
/ 2 am; hirer's choice of caterer; Hall (500,500,300); Officers Mess (–,40); marquee site.

Holy Trinity Brompton
Church Hall SW7   £B, (250,200)
Brompton Rd   581 8255
Behind the church, the hall is pretty basic, though with large windows opening onto a garden; fashionably located, but availability is pretty restricted. / HTB weddings, charities or parochial only; 10.30 pm; hirer's choice of caterer; no amplified music; no dancing.

Honourable
Artillery Co EC1   £B-M, (2500,1000,300)
Armoury Hs   606 4644   (628 0949)
Armoury House, the HAC's north City home, looks onto 7 acres of fields; options include the atmospheric, if basic, Queen's Room, the Albert Room (a large drill-hall used for parties, often with a marquee liner as decoration) and, for smarter events, the Long Room (using the fine Court Room for pre-dinner drinks); organisers of mega-functions (for up to 2,500) should consider using the huge amount of kit they assemble for their annual June ball while it is still up – a rig much cheaper than you could possibly DIY. / 11.45 pm; Albert not Tue & Wed eve; Long Room eve only except rare whole house bookings; Graison; Court Room — no smoking; Marquee (2500,1000); Albert Rm (500,350,300); Long Rm (250,180); Medal Rm (60,40); Court Rm (60,–); Queen's Rm (70,50); marquee site.

Hop Cellars SE1   £B, (330,90,90)
24 Southwark St   403 6851   (403 4237)
This large, pleasant wine bar can be used in conjunction with the overhead Hop Exchange (see below) to which there is a private staircase; there are also private function rooms, done out in off-the-peg traditional good taste. / after 8 pm and Sat & Sun all day; Malt Rm (150,90,70); Porter Rm (75,50).

Private venues

Hop Exchange SE1   £B, (350,250,220)
24 Southwark St   403 2573   (403 6848)
In the hinterland to London Bridge, this lofty, cream and green Victorian hall – with wrought iron galleries and a more modern, translucent roof – offers a large, atmospheric venue to those prepared to think a little about lighting and decoration; there is a private entrance from the Hop Cellars (see above). / *1 am; after 8 pm, all day Sat & Sun; hirer's choice of caterer.*

The Horniman At Hay's SE1   £B, (300,70)
Hays Galleria, Tooley St   407 3611   (357 6449)
High-ceilinged Hay's Galleria riverside pub which, despite being a recent conversion, is atmospheric and comfortable; on Saturday with enough people (100+ at night, more during the day) you can take the place over and just be charged at the bar; there are comfortable but less characterful banqueting rooms downstairs. / *midnight; whole pub avail all day Sat & Sun night; in-house caterers; Frederick John Horniman Rm (100,70).*

Howard Hotel WC2   £M-E, (200,70)
Temple Pl   836 3555   (379 4547)
This small, luxurious, modern, business-orientated hotel by the Temple offers fairly compact accommodation for functions; there are two first floor suites with river views, which are most suitable for sit-downs; the ground floor Fitzalan Suite has a view of the internal brick garden. / *1 am; in-house caterers; Arundel Suite (150,50); Fitzalan (200,70); Westminster (40,18); Surrey (20,12).*

HQ NW1   £B, (350,80)
Camden Lock   485 6044
Basic but atmospheric, first floor Camden Lock music club and restaurant – an ideal spot to dance the night away, especially for a younger crowd. / *2 am; Mon-Thu only; in-house caterers.*

Hubble & Co EC1   £B-M, (400,120,80)
55 Charterhouse St   253 1612
Agreeable wine bar/restaurant opposite Smithfield Market; a characterful warehouse conversion, there is a private area for dining, or you can hire one or both floors for a wide variety of events, including large dance parties. / *2.30 am; Wine Bar (200,120,80); Basement Restaurant (200,120,80); Private Rm (–,10).*

Hurlingham Club SW6   £M, (1000,650,650)
Ranelagh Gdns   731 0839   (736 7167)
Elegant, Georgian Fulham 'country club' in its own extensive grounds; it is one of the prettiest places near to central London and has an impressive suite of rooms well suited to wedding receptions, dances or summer barbecues, in all of which they do big business; a member's sponsorship is required. / *2 am; in-house caterers; Quadrangle Suite (500,250); Palm Court Suite (200,100).*

Private venues

Hyatt Carlton Tower SW1 £M-E, (650,320,300)
Cadogan Pl   235 5411   (235 9129)
Luxurious, traditionally-styled, modern Knightsbridge hotel whose ballroom has the benefit of a separate entrance (see also Rib Room). / Ballroom (650,320,300); Drawing Rm (–,48).

Hyde Park Hotel SW1 £M-E, (650,275,230)
66 Knightsbridge   235 2000   (235 4552)
Externally overbearing red brick Knightsbridge edifice; inside, there is much charming Edwardian detail and one of the most impressive suites of inter-connecting entertaining rooms available in London – in cream, blue and gold – with splendid views of the park; popular for grander weddings. / Ballroom (450,275,230); Ballroom & Knightsbridge Suite (650,–); Knightsbridge Suite (225,160); Park Suite (120,60,40); Loggia (60,36); King Gustav Adolf Suite (150,70); 19 Private Salons (–,12).

ICA SW1 £M, (300,200,100)
The Mall   930 0493   (873 0051)
Overlooking the Mall, the Nash room – a grand first floor room in Carlton House Terrace – is the high-point, with the adjacent Brandon Room available to add capacity; the institute's well-maintained, white-walled galleries can also be made available for receptions; recently-opened roof terraces provide a rather special open-air drinks party venue. / 1 am; in-house caterers; Nash (150,100); Brandon (150,100); Exhibition Galleries (300,–); Terraces (300,–).

Iceni W1 £B, (500,–)
11 White Horse St   495 5333   (409 2537)
With a great entrance just off Shepherd's Market, the best part of this budget temple to '70s kitsch is arguably the unadorned third floor terrace; this is not to do down the quite groovy, vaguely homespun charm of the rest of the club; the owners were not able to give us a precise capacity and we have made a conservative estimate. / 3.30 am; not Wed, Fri & Sat; in-house caterers; Ground Floor (175,–); First (dance) Floor (175,–); Second (bar) Floor (175,–); Terrace (100,–).

Ikkyu W1 £B-M, (–,12)
67 Tottenham Ct Rd   636 9280
This impossible-to-locate Japanese basement, near Goodge Street tube, serves excellent quality, unusually affordable Japanese food; they have a traditional rivate tatami room (shoes off). / 11 pm; not Sat; Tatami Rm (–,12).

The Imagination Gallery WC1 £M-E, (500,180,180)
South Crescent, 25 Store St   323 3300   (323 5810)
One of London's most impressive spaces; you cross a sci-fi-style, apparently fragile metal bridge (which spans the building's atrium – also available for hire) to reach this 5th floor gallery; it has a light and airy feel and a full length balcony with a very good view of Bedford Square. / midnight or by negotiation; sometimes Sat & Sun; in-house caterers; no children; Atrium and Mezzanine (500,–); Gallery (300,180).

Private venues

Imperial City EC3   £M, (–,12)
Cornhill   626 3437
In the vaults below the Royal Exchange, this extremely stylish Chinese restaurant brings an unusual degree of glamour (and culinary skill) to the City; behind a frosted glass wall, a side vault is available for private lunches and dinners. / not Sat & Sun; Private Vault (–,12).

Imperial College SW7   £B-M, (120,60)
170 Queensgate   225 6115   (589 9348)
Despite an uninspiring façade, the ground floor of the Rector's residence is very pleasant – offering possibilities for, amongst other occasions, business meals, small weddings, and summer receptions; the flexible council room is most used, though nicest is the lovely Music Room (aka the Solar) whose French windows lead into the garden; prices are very reasonable.
/ midnight; Sat & Sun by rector's permission, Mon-Fri eve only except Council Room all day; in-house caterers; no amplified music; no smoking; Council Rm (120,60); Solar (40,–); Dining Rm (–,40).

Imperial War Museum SE1   £M-E, (1000,300,300)
Lambeth Rd   416 5394   (416 5374)
This historic site (it includes part of the original Bedlam hospital) is also one of the most impressive venues and comes ready-themed with guns, planes and tanks; various galleries can be added to the lofty central atrium for extra reception space, while the trench and blitz experiences can also be open during events; the boardrooms are in the period part of the building.
/ 1 am; after 6 pm; hirer's choice of caterer; smoking restricted; Exhibition Hall (800,300); Festival Balconies (200,–); Boardroom 1 (75,50); Boardroom 2 (40,20).

L'Incontro SW1   £M-E, (–,30)
87 Pimlico Rd   730 6327   (730 5062)
Noisy, glamorous, opulent, stylish (and expensive), this monochrome Italian restaurant near Sloane Square has a smart private basement dining room and bar. / 1 am; Private Rm (–,30).

Inner Temple Hall EC4   £M-E, (450,250,250)
Temple   797 8181   (797 8178)
Inner's hall is a post-war reconstruction, but in a pleasant, panelled traditional style; the Parliament Chamber is very agreeable. / 2 am; eve only; Aug hol; in-house caterers; Hall (450,250); Luncheon Rm (100,–); Parliament Chamber (175,80); marquee site.

Private venues

Innholders' Hall EC4   £M-E, (150,91)
College St   236 6703
Sombre but striking, this c17 Hall, near Cannon Street, was substantially restored after the blitz; it is accessed via an intimate pretty hall and reception room, both of which have only recently been completed. / *charities & companies only; 11 pm; not Sat & Sun; Aug hol; Jean Alexander Food Flair; no amplified music; no dancing; Hall (150,91); Court Rm (30,25).*

Institute of Directors SW1   £M, (350,250,150)
116 Pall Mall   839 1233   (930 9060)
Built as a club, the full stateliness of this large, white Nash edifice is most apparent in the Waterloo and Nash rooms, both of which lead off the magnificent staircase; for business-related functions particularly, the institute offers affordable grandeur and there are 30,000+ members who can sponsor an event. / *11 pm; Letherby & Christopher; Nash (350,250,150); Burton (150,80); Waterloo (120,70); Trafalgar II / St James (50,35); Trafalgar / Spears (40,20).*

Institute of Materials SW1   £M-E, (250,100,100)
1 Carlton Ho Ter   839 4071   (839 1702)
At the end of this famous terrace overlooking the Mall, this recently refurbished institution offers a good sense of occasion but is not overbearingly grand; unfortunately, its regulations preclude it from hosting certain events. / *12.30 am; in-house caterers; no discos; smoking restricted; Bessemer Rm (30,18); Library (100,60); Council Rm (120,100).*

Institution of Civil Engineers SW1   £M, (400,300,250)
1 Gt George St   222 7722   (976 0697)
The high-ceilinged lobby, staircase, and, in particular, the huge marbled Great Hall of this impressive building, just off Parliament Square, all possess much neo-classical ('30s) grandeur; highly flexible, its rooms offer possibilities ranging from grand dinners and weddings to fashion shows and the whole would make a good setting for a ball. / *2 am; London Catering Services; Great Hall (400,300,250); Smeaton Rm (120,100); Brunel Rm or Council Rm (100,80); Old Members Rm (40,20); Restaurant (250,250).*

Institution of Mechanical Engineers SW1   £M, (200,150)
1 Birdcage Wk   222 7899   (222 4557)
Although the common parts and entrance of this prettily located St James's institute are rather, well, institutional, the panelled Council room, the Hinton room (park views) and the oddly striking Marble Hall are all well suited to quite grand entertaining – the last being the best for receptions. / *10 pm; London Catering Company; no amplified music; no dancing; no smoking; Marble Hall (200,150); Hinton (120,80); Council (70,45).*

Private venues

The Insurance Hall EC2 £M, (350,210)
20 Aldermanbury   606 3835   (726 0131)
A cosy institution, behind the Guildhall, which is flexible, by City standards; although the hall has quite a capacity, it is much less imposing than some of its local competition – which may be no bad thing – and the feel inside is of a small Edwardian town hall; the Council Chamber (with a small museum attached) is an atmospheric corner room. / midnight; Chester Boyd; smoking restricted; Great Hall (350,210); Ostler Hall (150,75); Pipkin Rm (40,30); Morgan Owen Rm (20,16); President's Rm (–,8); Committee Rm 1 (–,14); Committee Rm 2 (–,20).

Inter-Continental W1 £M-E, (1400,850,700)
1 Hamilton Pl, Hyde Pk Corner   409 3131   (409 7460)
As we go to press, the large ballroom suite of this luxurious hotel, currently in very dubious '70s taste, is being refurbished; what is currently the top-floor nightclub is being refitted as the Windsor Suite with stunning (we are told) views over Hyde Park. / 2 am; Grand Ballroom Suite (1400,850,700); Park Suite (600,144,120); Windsor Suite (180,100,100); Byron Rm (100,90,40).

Internat. Students Hse W1 £B, (800,200,200)
229 Portland St   631 3223   (636 5565)
This impressively housed student hostel is geared to student and club discos (as well as conference business); the cafeteria is a surprisingly stylish venue, with the gym-like theatre standing out among the other rooms; the hostel will consider arranging garden parties in Park Crescent gardens for charities or worthy organisations. / 2 am; Theatre (500,200); Restaurant (200,-); Marylebone Rm (200,130); Albany Rm (–,40).

Irish Club SW1 £B-M, (250,100,100)
82 Eaton Sq   235 4164   (235 4247)
Become a member here (if you are Irish by birth, marriage or descent) and this Eaton Square townhouse-club provides one of London's smartest, modestly-priced addresses; it may seem a little down at heel by day, but at night its faded grandeur comes into its own. / 12.30 am; hirer's choice of caterer; Munster Rm (150,100,100); Leinster Rm / Ulster Rm (70,40); Connaught Bar (150,–).

Ironmongers' Hall EC2 £M, (250,170)
Shaftesbury Pl, Barbican   606 2726   (600 3519)
Even though it is enveloped by the Barbican, from the inside this '20s faux-Medieval hall (complete with panelling, stone flags and stained glass) almost feels like the genuine article; the upstairs Drawing Room and Livery Hall are most impressive. / midnight; not Aug; list of caterers; no dancing; Banqueting Hall (250,170); Drawing Rm (100,–); Court Rm (–,80); Luncheon Rm (100,50).

Private venues

Ivy WC2 £M, (150,60)
1 West St   379 6077   (497 3644)
Revamped theatreland restaurant – popular with a glamorous (especially thespian) crowd – where the style is updated traditional and the international cooking excellent; up steep spiral stairs inside the entrance there is a panelled private room where up to 32 can sit at the same table. / 2 am; Private Rm (150,60).

Jakes SW10 £B-M, (–,60)
Hollywood Rd   352 6884
Recently resurrected '70s restaurant with a perfectly preserved menu of English staples of the period, served in comfortably modern surroundings; the basement private room is large and agreeable.

Jason's SW11 £B, (–,60)
50 Battersea Pk Rd   622 6998   (498 0091)
Behind sinister tinted windows, this cheap and cheerful Battersea Greek restaurant, is a south of the River favourite; private parties may take over its cellar. / not Sun.

Jazz Café NW1 £B-M, (350,300,270)
5 Parkway   916 6060   (916 6622)
See 'Paint the town rouge' – this stylish Camden Town venue would suit a wide variety of parties and functions; the balcony restaurant and bar can be hired separately.
/ Sun-Thu midnight, Fri & Sat 2 am; in-house caterers; Balcony (–,80).

Jongleurs at Camden Lock NW1 £M, (–,450,450)
Middle Yd, Camden Lock   924 2766   (924 5175)
Jongleurs at The Cornet SW11 £M, (–,300,300)
49 Lavender Gdns   924 2766   (924 5175)
See 'Paint the town rouge' – the party-planner owners can theme the show or the venue to the host's requirements and, at Camden, a firework display can be organised over the Lock. / 2 am; avail Mon-Thu; in-house caterers.

Julie's Restaurant & Wine Bar W11 £M, (–,45)
133-137 Portland Rd   229 8331   (229 4050)
This seductive, eclectically-decorated Holland Park labyrinth is one of London's best known restaurants for parties; the best rooms are the panelled Banqueting Room, which has a single oval table, and the Garden Room; the staff are generally given high marks for letting things run and run – the bill can too. / 1 am; Sat L, wb only; Banqueting Rm (–,24); Garden Rm (–,32); Conservatory (–,17); Gothic Rm (–,45); The Tomb (wb) (–,14); The Gallery (wb) (–,10).

K Warehouse E6 £B-M, (1000,1000,1000)
Royal Victoria Dock   512 0455   (512 0222)
Pending the recovery of the property market, the huge wooden shell of this grade II, c19 East End warehouse is available for theming; there are few facilities on site.
/ midnight; hirer's choice of caterer; smoking restricted;
Space 1 (1000,1000,1000); Cavern 1 (500,500,500);
Cavern 2 (500,500,500).

Private venues

Kaya Korean W1   £M, (–,22)
22-25 Dean St   437 6630
This Soho Korean restaurant serves very decent, quite pricey, food; the place is themed, but not to the point of tackiness, and there are a couple of private areas hiding behind bamboo walls. / not Sun D; Private Rm (–,22).

Kempton Park, Middx   £M, (1500,650,650)
Sunbury-on-Thames   0932-786199   (0932-761565)
Pleasant modern banqueting suite, adjacent to the racecourse. / 2 am; Ring & Brymer; Runnymede Suite (500,400,350); Hampton Suite (200,140); Thames Suite (170,120); Paddock Suite (160,120); Lanzarote (40,–); marquee site.

Ken Lo's Memories SW1   £M, (–,20)
67-69 Ebury St   730 7734   (730 2992)
One of the few places in the Victoria area which can accommodate a business celebration, say, in reasonable style; the food is satisfactory but do not mistake this Chinese restaurant for the landmark it once was.
/ midnight; not Sun; Private Rm (–,20).

Kensington Conservative Association W8   £B, (60,30)
23a Stratford Rd   937 0457   (937 8895)
Kensington Tories have the unusual benefit of owning their own premises, in a very pretty street; their main meeting room is available for drinks and dinner parties.
/ midnight; hirer's choice of caterer.

Kensington Palace Thistle W8   £M, (200,160,130)
De Vere Gdns   937 8121   (937 2816)
Facing Kensington Gardens, the rosily bland function rooms of this mid-range hotel are pleasant of their type.
/ Duchess (200,160,130); Marchioness (100,80,60); Park (–,30); Countess Princess (60,20); Baroness (25,16).

Kenwood House NW3   £E, (–,80)
Hampstead Ln   081-348 1286
English Heritage's policy on making this beautiful Hampstead Heath house available changes over the years; occasionally the lovely Dining Room or Orangery may be made available for special occasions. / 10.30 pm; Orangery (–,80); Dining Rm (–,35).

Kenwood House, Old Kitchen NW3 £M, (100,80)
Hampstead Ln   081-341 5384
The only part of the house regularly available is the Old Kitchen Restaurant – an airy, attractive, stone-flagged room, generally used for wedding receptions. / 10.30 pm; in-house caterers.

Kettners W1   £B, (–,60)
29 Romilly St   437 6437   (434 1214)
See 'Paint the town rouge' – the first and second floor dining rooms may be used for private functions. / midnight; Oak Rm (–,60); Blue Rm (–,30); Soho Rm (–,16).

Private venues

Kew Bridge Steam
Museum, Middx   £M, (300,270,170)
Green Dragon Ln, Brentford   081-568 4757
Producers of Dr Who and Frankenstein movies are just some of those who have used the dramatic potential offered by the Steam Hall; this venue is not too expensive as museums go and is much used for many kinds of functions from wedding receptions to themed company events. / no college events or under-30 birthdays; 1 am; generally eve only; hirer's choice of caterer; Steam Hall (150,100); Water Hall (200,170).

King David Suite W1   £M, (600,450,380)
32 Gt Cumberland Pl   387 4300
Gentiles take note: although this pleasant, subterranean, '60s, traditional-style dining suite is beneath a synagogue, goyim are most welcome; the well-maintained facilities, decorated in quite subdued taste, are one of the nicer legacies of the period and, though just by Marble Arch, are little known. / not Fri pm or Sat; Kosher catering only (including drinks); Main Rm (600,450,380).

King of Diamonds EC1   £B, (80,50)
Greville St   405 0999
This modern pub, off Holborn, is not beautifully situated, but its unusual, first-floor Garden Bar and terrace are ideal for summer parties; for winter there is a more ordinary downstairs bar available for private hire.
/ midnight; Garden Bar (80,50); Cellar Bar (80,50).

King's College WC2   £B-M, (450,220,160)
Strand   351 6011   (352 7376)
The college's main hall is well maintained, quite grand and suitable for a wide range of functions; the first floor council room is not a bad place for a reception. / 1 am; hirer's choice of caterer; Great Hall (450,220,160); Council Rm (80,–).

Knebworth House, Herts   £M-E, (600,240,350)
Knebworth   0438-812661   (0438-811908)
This c15 house has been much altered over the years and retains features of all periods; it is rather fairy-tale in appearance and not too enormous in scale – together with the more practical barns, there is scope for many entertainments and activities. / 2 am; in-house caterers; House (320,50); Manor Barn (300,140,190); Lodge Barn (250,100,100); Manor & Lodge Barns (550,240,350); Geodesic Dome (600,–); marquee site.

Knightsbridge Place SW1   £M, (100,50)
116 Knightsbridge   225 3512
Very central, but relatively unknown, this wittily decorated modern Italian restaurant (formerly called Dell'Arte) has an unusually spacious downstairs private room and is reasonably priced by the standards of the area. / Private Rm (100,50).

Private venues

The Kosher Luncheon Club E1   £B, (–,120)
13 Greatorex St   247 0039
The restaurant that time forgot, where lunch is served daily in an East End gym-style hall (attached to a synagogue); at night they will open for private dinners; the simple Kosher menu is strong on fish and sufficiently well done to appeal to all tastes. / 11 pm.

SB Lady Gwynfred E14   £M, (80,46,36)
Fishermans Wk   895 9779   (895 9779)
Permanently moored in the dock next to Canary Wharf; this floating restaurant, open to all for lunch, is otherwise available for private hire; the 90 year old barge is quite well decked out; (the aft section of roof can be lifted off on summer's days). / 3 am; Mon-Fri eve only, all day Sat & Sun.

The Lamb Tavern EC3   £B, (100,50)
Leadenhall Market   626 2454
One of the City's best pubs, in the centre of the atmospheric, covered market, has two bars for private early evening hire – the upstairs restaurant overlooking the market, or the downstairs Dive – an Edwardian tiled, vaulted cellar. / 9.30 pm; not Sat & Sun; no amplified music; no dancing; Dining Rm (100,50); The Dive (100,–).

The Lanesborough SW1   £M-E, (100,60,30)
Hyde Pk Corner   259 5599   (259 5606)
Neo-classical landmark, recently converted into a glossy hotel and furnished in rather overblown Empire/clubby style; a variety of lofty, medium-sized rooms and a romantically prettified wine cellar are available for functions. / 2 am; Wilkins Rm (50,30,30); St George's Rm (80,50); Wine Cellar (–,14); Westminster Rm (60,40); Wellington Rm (100,60).

Langham Hilton W1   £M, (500,300,220)
Portland Pl   636 1000   (323 2340)
London's first purpose-built grand hotel is slowly losing its post-refurbishment, new-out-of-the-wrapping look; rooms veer from charming to soulless, the former category including the extremely grand ballroom, the Ambassador's Room and the Memories of Empire restaurant (soon to be converted to a function room). / 3 am; Ballroom (500,300,220); Ambassadors' Rm (60,40); Memories of Empire (350,160); Portland Suite (190,110); Cumberland Rm (15,10); Regent Rm / Welbeck Rm / Wimpole Rm (60,40).

Lansdowne Club W1   £B-M, (200,90,120)
9 Fitzmaurice Pl   629 7200   (408 0246)
This large Mayfair club has a lot of slightly worn charm and, with a member's sponsorship, offers a very central, and quite economical, venue; highlights include the elegant ballroom and the striking art deco Thirties Room. / in-house caterers; Ballroom (200,90); Thirties Rm (70,48); Blue Rm (60,24).

Private venues

Larry's Wine Bar WC2 £B, (100,70,70)
Mercer St   836 0572
Below the Mountbatten Hotel, a pleasant, well-proportioned brick-walled space. / 2 am.

Lauderdale House N6 £B-M, (180,80)
Waterlow Pk, Highgate Hl   081-348 8716
Pretty c16 Highgate house, overlooking the park; much used for wedding receptions and other social events; Nell Gwyn was here. / no 21sts; 1 am; not mon; 3 wks hol in Jan; hirer's choice of caterer; smoking restricted; Lower Gallery (180,80); marquee site.

Launceston Place W8 £M, (–,30)
1A Launceston Pl   937 6912   (938 2412)
One of most discreet, comfortable and English of restaurants, hidden away in Kensington; it was recently extended to include a comfortable private room and there is also a larger semi-private area. / Private Area (–,30); Private Rm (–,14).

The Law Society WC2 £M, (350,220,150)
113 Chancery Ln   242 1222   (320 5955)
This fine, early c19 building has been sensitively developed over the years and recently comprehensively refurbished; the premises have a comfortable grandeur and surprising degrees of charm and flexibility; the Old Council Chamber, with its vast mirror-polished oval table, stands out, but there is a good range of rooms for most occasions. / 1 am; Charters (Sutcliffe Grp); Common Rm (350,220,150); Grill Rm (70,40); Old Council Chamber (–,30); Members Dining Rm (125,100,80).

Leadenhall Tapas Bar EC3 £B, (70,45)
27 Leadenhall Mkt   623 1818
Through the round window, the view from the top-floor private room is of the interesting Edwardian market below; the room itself is quite stylish, and, with the reasonably priced provisions, well worth considering for more than just after-work City drinks. / 11 pm; Sat & Sun larger parties only.

Leeds Castle, Kent £M-E, (2000,180,160)
Maidstone   0622-765400   (0622-735616)
"The loveliest castle in the whole world", Norman in origin, provides a great range of entertaining possibilities, both within the moated castle and in the surrounding park – from a c17 tithe barn to an underground grotto at the centre of the maze; for a real day-trip, you can travel on the Orient Express. / State Dining Room – companies only; in-house caterers; Henry VIII Banqueting Hall (250,100); State Dining Rm (150,60); Gate-tower (120,70); Fairfax Hall (250,180,160); Dog Collar Museum (120,–); Cedar Lawn (2000,–); Grotto (50,–); marquee site.

Private venues

Legends W1   £B-M, (350,–)
29 Old Burlington St   437 9933
Modern, quite '80s, two-level Mayfair nightclub, stylishly done out with sandy walls and lots of stainless steel. / 3 am; hirer's choice of caterer, alcohol in-house; Mezzanine (100,–); Downstairs (200,–).

Leighton House W14   £M-E, (150,92)
12 Holland Pk   602 3316   (371 2467)
Extraordinary Aesthetic Movement Victorian house and art gallery, with a Moorish hall and much charm; ideally suited to a special dinner or a music recital and reception. / 11 pm; eve only, not Sun; Leith's Good Food; no amplified music; no dancing; smoking restricted; Arab Hall (70,–); Dining Rm (–,30); Studio (–,92).

Leith's W11   £M-E, (–,40)
92 Kensington Pk Rd   229 4481
Comfortably time-warped Notting Hill restaurant providing modern British fare in well-preserved, '60s style surroundings; the private room, in the same style as the restaurant, is sub-divisible. / Private Rm (–,40).

Leoni's Quo Vadis W1   £B-M, (175,150)
26-29 Dean St   437 4809   (434 9972)
Comfortable, traditional style Soho Italian restaurant – an almost extinct breed – with grand premises, professional service and an unusually large private room, where stand-up receptions are among the possibilities; Marx lived here and guests may view his room. / Private Rm (175,150).

Leven is Strijd E14   £M, (50,20)
West India Docks   987 4002   (987 4002)
One of the few Docklands venues, this permanently-moored narrow barge caters for dinners for six and more people in cosy and unusually private surroundings. / midnight.

Ley-Ons W1   £B, (–,180)
56 Wardour St   437 6465
For a Chinese blow-out, the lofty-ceilinged basement of this large Soho establishment is the most stylish amongst its large Soho/Chinatown peers.

Limelight W1   £M, (600,200,200)
136 Shaftesbury Av   434 0572   (434 1761)
Converted West End church – one of London's more civilised nightclubs; the large domed hall retains many of its original fittings and is suitable for receptions and dinners; overlooking the main dance-floor, private dinner parties can be arranged in the Annex, and the comfortable, traditional Study Bar can also be used as a private area; in the crypt, the tented VIP club is a more louche affair. / 3 am; Truly Scrumptious; Gallery & Dome (400,200,200); Club VIP (250,80,80); Study Bar (70,30); Annex (–,20).

Private venues

Lincoln's Inn WC2   £M-E, (600,320,250)
Lincoln's Inn   405 1393   (831 1839)
For 'medieval' magnificence, the Great Hall (actually 1845), set in the quiet of the Inn's gardens, is difficult to better – ideal for a grand reception – while the drawing room is perfect for a stately dinner; the real c15 Old Hall across the lawn is smaller and, in its way, more atmospheric; you can use an outside caterer, but hire charges are much less if you don't. / 11.30 am;
hirer's choice of caterer; Great Hall (600,320,250); Drawing Rm (100,40); Old Hall (250,130,70).

Lindsay House W1   £M, (–,20)
21 Romilly St   439 0450
Discreet Soho townhouse restaurant, decorated in a rich, slightly Disneyesque antique style, but well done and with very charming private rooms, especially the larger; good food too. / Private Rm (–,20); Private Rm (–,12).

The Little Ship Club EC4   £B-M, (400,100,100)
Upper Thames St   236 7729   (236 9100)
Newly redeveloped (1991), comfortable and smart river-side yacht-club whose only real disadvantage is to share its entrance with a car park (though guests may be welcomed at the river entrance); it enjoys excellent views.
/ *1 am; Dining & Club rooms: Mon-Fri after 6pm (summer only) & all day Sat & Sun; Jean Alexander; Library (100,50); Chart Rm (–,10); Dining Rm (120,90); Club Rm & Bar (120,–).*

Lloyd's Of London EC3   £M, (800,350,250)
1 Lime St   623 7100, x 5434   (626 2389)
The large ground-floor Captain's Room restaurant in Richard Rogers' remarkable building is available at night for functions; for receptions another possibility is the Old Library – a panelled hall from the market's old building transplanted into the frame of the new. / Captain's Room after 5 pm; in-house caterers; Captain's Rm (800,350,250); Conference Rm (100,60); Old Library (120,–).

The London Dungeon SE1   £M-E, (400,300,150)
28 Tooley St   924 2444   (978 5178)
Boasting "a perfectly horrible experience", this highly successful London Bridge museum of the macabre (with its newly added Jack-the-Ripper experience) is great fun; the high-ceilinged vaults are at their best when full. / 3 am; after 7.30 pm; Moving Venue.

London Marriott W1   £M, (900,500,500)
Grosvenor Sq   493 1232   (491 3201)
A large, surprisingly characterful, subterranean '70s ballroom, with unusual barrel-vaulted ceiling, is this Mayfair hotel's most interesting feature.
/ *Westminster Suite (900,500,500); Hamilton Rm (65,45); John Adams Suite (50,25); Dukes Suite (30,15).*

Private venues

London Metropole W2   £M, (–,60)
Edgware Rd   402 4141   (724 8866)
Aspects the Rooftop Restaurant (24th Floor) of this Bayswater/Marylebone hotel is one of London's highest available for exclusive hire; views accordingly. / *1 am.*

London Palladium W1   £M, (300,–)
Argyll St   437 2274   (434 1217)
Atop the main staircase of this famous theatre, the large, light Cinderella bar attracts a fair number of daytime receptions; the atmosphere is of comfortably worn grandeur. / *day only; Gardner Merchant; Cinderella Bar (300,–).*

London Press Centre EC4   £B-M, (700,450,350)
New St Sq   353 6211   (583 3441)
Flexible and economical for a large central venue (just off Fleet Street) – and not just for business; the down-side is that (although some updating is planned) this modern complex largely remains a monument to the any-colour-as-long-as-it's-brown school of interior design (fluorescent strips too); it's cheap, and you can party all night, but allow a fair budget for decoration. / *Ring & Brymer; Caxton Suite (700,450,350); Pepys Suite (400,300,150); Boswell Rm / Johnson Rm (70,60); Milton Rm (–,12).*

London Rowing Club SW15   £B, (250,100)
Embankment   081-788 0666
The first of the line of boathouses on the Putney 'hard', London is a good and economical spot for informal receptions and discos – especially in summer on the terrace, which enjoys a great view of the Thames.
/ *midnight; hirer's choice of caterer.*

London Scottish SW1   £B-M, (300,160,120)
95 Horseferry Rd   630 0411   (414 3487)
Very unusual Pimlico TA hall, reconstructed from pieces transported from the regiment's old building; colourful Victorian vaulting and galleries rise from a modern, wood-floored base, which incorporates the old entrance and fireplace; with the messes also available it is suitable for many different types of event. / *1 am; not Tue & some Sat & Sun; hirer's choice of caterer; Hall (300,160,120); Officers' Mess (100,50); Queen Elizabeth Club (80,–).*

The London Television Centre SE1 £M, (100,60)
South Bank TV Centre, Upper Ground
261 3225   (261 3200)
Although the uses of the 18th floor conference rooms of this South Bank block, whose views are magnificent, include occasional parties and weddings, the suite is most suitable for corporate receptions and dinners.
/ *12 pm; hirer's choice of caterer; Westminster or St Pauls (50,20); Westminster & St Pauls (100,60).*

Private venues

London Transport Museum WC2 £M, (400,300)
Covent Gdn   379 6344   (836 4118)
Originally a Victorian flower market, this airy, iron and glass museum facing Covent Garden is home to a collection of old buses, tubes, trams and trains; as we go to press, it is again taking bookings for after its post-refurbishment reopening. / charities & companies only; midnight; from 6.30 pm; list of caterers; smoking restricted; no spirits or fortified drinks.

The London
Welsh Centre WC1 £B, (200,200,100)
157 Grays Inn Rd   837 3722
The light, gym-type hall here is largely used for rehearsals, but also for parties; the barn-like bar upstairs is suitable for informal drinks. / midnight; not Sun; hirer's choice of caterer, but all drinks through centre; dancing only in hall; Main Hall (200,200,100); Lower Hall (150,80); Bar (100,–).

London Zoo NW1 £M-E, (2000,800,240)
Regent's Pk   586 3339   (586 3910)
This really is one of the best venues – few are immune to the childish delight of partying among the animals; there are two banqueting suites but the real attraction is to be out barbecuing among the tigers or drinking among the reptiles – 'animal encounters' can be arranged; space and the variety of locations make for great flexibility – you can even arrive by canal boat. / 2 am; Animal houses, eve only; in-house caterers; Regency Suite (380,200,240); Marquee (2000,800); Reptile House (180,–); Insect House (60,–); Raffles Bar and Restaurant (150,100); marquee site.

Lord's NW8 £M, (600,260,260)
St John's Wood Rd   286 2909   (266 3170)
The home of cricket boasts a modern, purpose-built banqueting centre. / 1 am; not match days; National Leisure Catering; Ballroom (350,260,170); Toynbee (350,260,150).

Lou Pescadou SW5 £M, (–,30)
241 Old Brompton Rd   370 1057
Reliable, if not inexpensive, French Earl's Court fish restaurant, well-known for its authentic atmosphere and cooking; basement private room. / Private Rm (–,30).

Lundonia House WC1 £B, (400,80,60)
24 Old Gloucester St   242 7367   (405 1851)
AKA the October gallery, this former C of E girls' school is a good size to be taken over in its entirety and includes a small garden; the simple converted galleries have potential for numerous small to mid-sized functions, with the more richly decorated, upstairs club-room available for more restrained affairs; events with some kind of artistic tie-in are particularly encouraged. / 11 pm, Fri & Sat 1 pm; hirer's choice of caterer; smoking restricted; Ground Floor (200,80,60); Top Floor Theatre (60,–); Space Biospheres Club (40,10).

Private venues

Madame Tussaud's NW1   £M-E, (600,300,300)
Marylebone Rd   935 6861   (465 0862)
London's most-visited, longest-running tourist attraction (168 years), is also one of its top party venues; various sections may be hired – with the Garden Party a whisker ahead of the more traditional Grand Hall in popularity; the Chamber of Horrors is an optional extra (not a stand-alone venue), as is the new £10m 'Spirit of London Experience' – a cab-ride through the capital's history.
/ 2 am; after 6.30 pm; list of caterers; Garden Party (250,70); Grand Hall (450,300,250).

Mall Galleries SW1   £B-M, (600,300)
The Mall   930 6844
A short step from Admiralty Arch, the Main Gallery at the Federation of British Artists offers a cavernous space for a function; the East Gallery is smaller and more inviting.
/ 11 pm; from 5 pm; hirer's choice of caterer; no amplified music; no dancing; Main Gallery (500,300); East Gallery (100,80); North Gallery (80,50).

Mao Tai SW6   £M, (–,26)
58 New King's Rd   731 2520
Slightly high-tech, Parson's Green Chinese restaurant, well-known for its good food, efficient and friendly service and fairly high prices; the private room is upstairs. / Private Rm (–,26).

Marble Hill House TW1   £M-E, (60,50)
Richmond Rd   081-892 5115
Set in 66 acres bordering the Thames, this c18 English Heritage house is sometimes available for grand functions, the Great Hall being the main area used. / no weddings; no amplified music; no dancing; no smoking.

Maximus W1   £B, (600,–)
14 Leicester Sq   734 4111   (434 0993)
Medium-sized central venue, well-known on the dance-club circuit; the VIP suite can be hired separately from the club. / 3 am, Fri & Sat 6 pm; hirer's choice of caterer; VIP (100,–).

The Mayfair W1   £M, (500,300,240)
Stratton St   629 7777   (629 1459)
Large, quite grand '20s Mayfair hotel whose only really distinctive function room is the large, rose-hued Crystal Room – named for its three huge, modern, wedding cake chandeliers. / Crystal Rm (500,300,240); Devon Suite (60,–); Lansdowne Suite (120,80,60); Berkeley Suite (60,30); Curzon Suite (50,30); Stratton (30,12).

Mekong SW1   £B, (–,24)
46 Churton St   834 6896
Atmospheric Pimlico Vietnamese restaurant, whose characterful cellars are suited to a jolly (if not terribly inexpensive) get-together. / Private Rm (–,24).

Private venues

Mélange WC2   £B-M, (-,40)
59 Endell St   240 8077   (379 9129)
Self-consciously quirky Covent Garden restaurant with quite good modern British food and a nice atmosphere; the de-constructed-almost-to-the-point-of-destruction upper room is the one used privately. / not Mon L, Sat L & Sun; Private Rm (-,40).

Mercers' Hall EC2
Ironmonger Ln   726 4991
What is probably the richest of the livery companies tell us that their hall is never available to outsiders; we mention it only for completeness – unless you have a special 'in', you can save the cost of the call.

Merchant Taylors' Hall EC2   £M-E, (500,280)
30 Threadneedle St   588 7606   (528 8332)
In the heart of the City, this very grand, reconstructed (post War) medieval hall is the most imposing of the livery halls to be made available to outsiders with reasonable frequency; it comes complete with cloisters and a paved garden; the Parlour is heavily panelled and the Drawing Room is particularly pretty and convivial. / 2 am; not Sun; in-house caterers; Great Hall (500,280); Parlour (180,80); Cloisters (120,-); Library (40,-).

Le Meridien W1   £M-E, (400,250,210)
21 Piccadilly   734 8000   (437 3574)
The elegant and understated Georgian and Adam rooms are the highlights of this smart, central hotel, which has quite a range of facilities for business and social events.
/ Georgian (400,250,210); Edwardian (350,200,150); Adams / Regency (125,80); New Function Rms (160,100).

Mermaid Theatre EC4   £B-M, (150,70)
Puddle Dock, Blackfriars   410 0102   (410 0202)
The River Room, which is used for a wide range of social events from student parties to wedding receptions, lives up to its name, having a good view of the river and Blackfriars' Bridge; the Blackfriars Room (one floor up) is higher, lighter and has a more impressive view. / 1 am; Crown Catering; River Rm (150,70).

Le Mesurier EC1   £M, (-,24)
113 Old St   251 8117
With the decor of a café and the trappings of a restaurant, this place serves the only decent top-range food in a forsaken area of the City (and comes complete with monopoly prices); worth consideration by locals or those planning a relaxed, intimate evening or weekend function. / not Mon-Fri L.

Private venues

Middle Temple Hall EC4   £M-E, (500,300,300)
Temple   353 4355   (583 3220)
Middle's fine Tudor hall is an impressive, historic setting for dinners and receptions of all types; more comfortable are the Bench Apartments, available separately; the garden is intensively used for summer parties. / midnight; closed Aug and short vacations; in-house caterers; Hall (500,300,180); Parliament Chamber (130,56); Queen's Rm (80,20); Smoking Rm (100,–).

Le Midi SW6   £B-M, (–,14)
488 Fulham Rd   386 0657
This cheerful provençal restaurant, off Fulham Broadway, is a local favourite; the upstairs private room comes highly recommended. / not Sat L & Sun; no amplified music; no dancing; Private Rm (–,14).

Mimmo d'Ischia SW1   £M, (–,30)
61 Elizabeth St   730 5406
Sociable Belgravia Italian restaurant, run by the jovial Mimmo as a good but rather overpriced quasi-club; there is a private room downstairs. / not Sat & Sun; Private Rm (–,30).

Ming W1   £B-M, (–,20)
35-36 Greek St   734 2721
Soho Chinese where the smartness of the decor and quality of the cooking are both well above-average; the private basement, though not quite as nice as the main restaurant, is worth considering. / not Sun; Private Rm (–,20).

The Ministry of Sound SE1   £B, (1100,–)
103 Gaunt St   378 6528   (403 5348)
Boasting Europe's biggest and loudest sound system, this converted warehouse near Elephant and Castle is a key venue if you are serious about your clubbing; the VIP is easier to hire than the whole club. / 6 am; whole club not Sat & Sun; hirer's choice of caterer; VIP (300,–).

Minogue's Bar N1   £B, (80,30)
80 Liverpool Rd   354 4440
Atmospheric Islington Irish pub/restaurant with much above-average food; the upstairs private room is in the same, slightly old-fashioned style of down-below, with lofty ceilings. / 11 pm; not Mon-Wed eve; Private Rm (80,30).

Mirabelle W1   £M-E, (200,150,100)
56 Curzon St   499 4636
Classic French Mayfair restaurant, recently revived after a ten year hiatus; it never seems to hit the headlines but the food is not bad and the slightly tweely decorated rooms seem well suited to functions – this is probably one of the more reasonable and agreeable places to organise a small, comfortable, central dinner-dance and would make a good place for a wedding reception. / Pine Rm (–,30); Oak, Garden and Teppan-Yaki Rms (–,10).

Private venues

Mitsukoshi SW1 £M-E, (–,24)
14-16 Regent St   930 0317   (839 1167)
A little bright and efficient, but by Japanese standards this smart basement (below the department store) is welcoming and stylish; there are two private rooms, one Japanese (tatami), one western. / Western Rm (–,24); Tatami Rm (–,12).

Mon Plaisir WC2 £M, (–,30)
21 Monmouth St   836 7243   (379 0121)
Theatreland classic restaurant, half a century old; it has great character and good food and makes an ideal place for a West End celebration. / not Sun; Private Rm (–,30).

Monkey Island, Berks £M-E, (150,120,100)
Bray   0628-23400   (0628-784732)
Idyllic islet, accessible only by footbridge or boat; the hotel, early c18 in origin, has some charming rooms and a lovely garden. / River Rm (150,120,100); Boardroom (–,16).

Monkeys SW3 £M, (–,10)
1 Cale St   352 4711
Civilised Chelsea Green Anglo-French restaurant with one of London's nicest restaurant private rooms.
/ not Sat & Sun; (–,10).

Mortons Club W1 £M, (220,100,100)
28 Berkeley Sq   499 0363   (495 3160)
Fashionable yet unpretentious Mayfair townhouse club, whose attractive, updated traditional dining room overlooks the square; the downstairs bar is more racy and the basement room a comfortable place for a gathering; non-members events can sometimes be accommodated. / Sat ex D & Sun; in-house caterers; Restaurant & Bar (220,100,100); Downstairs Rm (80,42).

Mosimann's Belfry SW1 £M-E, (140,70)
11b West Halkin St   235 9625   (245 6354)
Celebrity chef, Anton Mosimann's converted Belgravia church/club; the comfortable dining room and gallery bar are very convivial and up in the Belfry, each private room is decorated to reflect its corporate sponsor (most gimmicky being the Baulthaup Room which overlooks the kitchen through a glass wall); non-members' events – weddings particularly – are occasionally accommodated.
/ members' club; Dining Rm (140,70); Harvey Nichols (80,50); Wedgewood (60,40); Alpha Romeo (25,10); Gucci (–,12); Baulthaup (–,6).

Motcomb's SW1 £M-E, (40,30)
23 Motcomb St   235 3092   (245 6351)
Belgravia restaurant, with its own townhouse for private dining; it has a nice pine-panelled dining room especially suited to parties of a dozen or more around a single table; separate reception room. / not Sun; no music; no dancing; McClue Suite (40,30).

Private venues

Mount Royal Hotel W1   £M, (400,300,250)
Bryanston St   629 8040   (499 7792)
Just refurbished, all the banqueting rooms at this hotel off Oxford St have been well done, if in rather corporate off-the-peg good taste. / 1 am; Edinburgh /
Hyde Park (400,300,250).

The Mountbatten WC2   £M, (120,80,50)
Seven Dials, 20 Monmouth St   836 4300   (240 3540)
Off the foyer, the comfortable, elegant Drawing Room (limited availability) is this centrally located hotel's best point; the basement function rooms are quite interesting of their type; (see also Larry's Wine Bar).
/ Drawing Rm (100,60); Earl (120,80,50); Viceroy (35,18).

Mr Kong WC2   £B-M, (–,40)
21 Lisle St   437 7341
This Chinatown basement looks nothing special, but it's pleasant enough and the outstanding, affordable food and easy-going service make it one of London's best places for a Chinese feast. / Private Basement (–,40).

Museum Of Childhood E2   £M, (125,60)
Cambridge Heath Rd   081-980 3204   (081-980 4759)
This Victorian construction in which the V&A originally grew up (nicknamed the 'Boilerhouse', it was taken down and re-constructed a stone's throw from Bethnal Green tube) now houses that museum's collection of toys and games; the lofty central area (the Marble Floor) can be used for receptions, and there is also a function room; plans for a café may restrict function space. / midnight; after 6.30 pm; hirer's choice of caterer; no amplified music; no dancing;
no smoking; Marble Floor (150,–); Summerly Rm (120,70).

Museum of Garden History SE1   £B-M, (300,70)
St Mary's Ch, Lambeth Palace Rd
401 8864   (401 8869)
St Mary-at-Lambeth church, in its new life, is a pleasant spot for receptions and has a manicured c17-style garden (which is a little noisy during the week); in keeping with the tranquil nature of the museum, only fairly sedate events are countenanced but they have recently acquired a nearby Victorian school building which may permit greater flexibility.
/ 1 am; not Sat; eve only; list of caterers; no discos;
no corkage; St Mary-at-Lambeth (100,70); School (300,–).

Private venues

Museum of London EC2   £M-E, (400,200,200)
London Wall   600 3699   (600 1058)
Bordering the Barbican, this Museum's internal high-ceilinged, concrete style is similar to that of the concert halls and houses an interesting collection, including the Lord Mayor's coach; the spaces seem better suited to receptions than dinners and the large, well laid-out central garden is available in summer. / 2 am; after 6 pm, all day Mon; hirer's choice of caterer; smoking restricted; Lord Mayor's Coach Gallery (250,150); Medieval Gallery (150,–); Eighteenth Century Gallery (100,60).

Museum of Mankind W1   £M-E, (200,100)
6 Burlington Gdns   437 2224   (323 8614)
This heavy Victorian building, originally London University's HQ, is now the Mayfair home of the BM's ethnic collections; the entrance hall is most suited to entertaining but all-in-all it seems quite expensive unless the venue is particularly appropriate. / midnight; after 6.30 pm; list of caterers; no amplified music; no dancing; no smoking.

Museum of the Moving Image SE1   £M-E, (250,100,100)
South Bank   815 1304   (815 1378)
This light-hearted South Bank museum (attached to the National Film Theatre) is a festive venue for most types of party; you too can be a TV star in the on-site studios, with actors substituting for the other glitterati; tours of the exhibits are available; (it may be worth enquiring after the Festival Pavilion – a rather remarkable clear tent-like structure right by the river; though prohibitively expensive to put up for a single event, if it is already up it is not too expensive). / midnight; from 6 pm; in-house caterers; smoking restricted; The Festival Pavilion (400,200).

National Army Museum SW3   £B-M, (450,90)
Royal Hospital Rd   730 0717   (823 6573)
If you are looking for a venue with martial associations in a smart area (next to the Royal Hospital), this rather unwelcoming building may be worth considering. / 11 pm; from 6 pm; list of caterers; Art & Uniform Galleries (450,90); Templer Galleries (100,50); Council Chamber (40,20).

National Liberal Club SW1   £M, (750,260,260)
Whitehall Pl   930 9871   (839 4768)
This large institution, just off Whitehall, is – with its impressive, high-ceilinged, tiled Edwardian rooms – one of the best, large, characterful venues in London for a large ball (weekends only); the accommodation is suitable for most big occasions and benefits from a large outside terrace; the two rooms permanently available for hire are less special. / 2 am; rooms marked * avail Sat & Sun only; in-house caterers; David Lloyd George (250,140); Lady Violet (70,50); Smoking Rm * (400,–); Dining Rm * (300,124); Terrace * (250,150).

Private venues

National Portrait Gallery WC2 £E, (300,70)
2 St Martin's Pl   306 0055   (306 0058)
Of London's major galleries, this is among the least institutional in feel; if you wish to dine, the second floor Stuarts galleries or the long, thin first-floor Victorian galleries are available, but the dimensions of the latter better suit standing receptions. / no weddings or birthday parties; midnight; after 6.30 pm; list of caterers; no amplified music; no dancing; no smoking.

National Westminster Hall EC2 (300,150)
Old Broad St
Nat West do not publicise this impressive hall under their tower, which is occasionally made available to suitable third parties; if you are organising an event for an established organisation it may be worth approaching them via one of the leading caterers.

Natural History Museum SW7 £M-E, (1400,600,450)
Cromwell Rd   938 9123   (938 9290)
The monumental Victorian Main Hall, complete with prehistoric monsters, particularly lends itself to parties (although good decoration and lighting are a must) and it is one of the top venues; other galleries (eg Mammals) add reception capacity with Lasting Impressions – a small, modern, quite cool gallery – an interesting option for small dinners. / 1 am; from 7 pm (day time functions in Spencer room); list of caterers; 85 dBA max; 78 dBA avg; Central Hall (1400,600,450); North Hall (250,180,150); Spencer Gallery (200,120); Mammal Gallery (200,–); Gem Stone Floor (400,150); Lasting Impressions (200,50).

Naval & Military Club W1 £B-M, (1200,200,200)
94 Piccadilly   499 5163   (499 2891)
The 'In & Out' is large, rambling and faded, but its crustiness is part of its charm and the place is not unduly imposing; with its secret-garden courtyard, summer receptions can be accommodated in particularly fine style, but the club is also a good choice for dinners; sponsorship of events by a member is essential.
/ 1.30 am; in-house caterers; Coffee Rm (400,200,130); Smoking Rm (300,–); Regimental Rm (100,70); Palmerston Rm (100,42); Egremont (100,42); Cambridge (–,10); Courtyard (80,–); Cowdray (30,20); Piccadilly (50,25); Octagon (30,16).

Neal St WC2 £M-E, (–,20)
26 Neal St   836 8368
Popular Covent Garden Italian restaurant, whose cleanly-styled downstairs room maintains the smooth styling of the main room; prices here tend infamously upwards.
/ not Sat & Sun; Private Rm (–,20).

Private venues

New Connaught Rms WC2   £B-M, (600,540,400)
Gt Queen St   405 7811   (831 1851)
One of London's oldest sets of banqueting suites (two centuries old) is predominantly used by business and the Masons (this was once an annex of the neighbouring Temple); the Grand Hall in particular, with its three huge chandeliers, offers size and lingering grandeur. / Sun only; am, L & pm only; brasserie eve & Sat & Sun only; in-house, but hirer's choice of caterer on Sunday; Balmoral & Grand Hall (600,540,400); Edinburgh & Drawing Rm / Cornwall & Crown (300,260,170); York & Warwick & Kent (200,140,120); Devon / Stafford (90,60); Oxford / Cambridge (50,25); Penthouse (50,32); Brasserie (300,200,180).

New Zealand House SW1   £B-M, (120,80,80)
80 Haymarket   930 8422   (839 4580)
The most exciting view in London – certainly from rooms available for hire – is to be had from the eighteenth floor of the New Zealand High Commission, an unusually fine (if intrusive) example of '60s high-rise architecture; the glass-walled Penthouse itself is well-appointed with a large terrace from which you can enjoy all 360° of landmarks and parks; short-notice cancellation is always a slight risk. / midnight; hirer's choice of caterer.

The Nosh Brothers SW6   £M, (–,45)
773 Fulham Rd   736 7311   (221 5031)
See 'Paint the town rouge' – the simply decorated basement may be taken by parties of 25 and up.

Nôtre Dame Hall WC2   £B, (300,200,160)
6 Leicester Pl   437 9363
Tatty but atmospheric, circular dance hall – in fact a church crypt; its main drawback is that its central location, just off Leicester Square, ensures that it is usually fully booked. / midnight; hirer's choice of caterer.

Now & Zen WC2   £B-M, (–,40)
4a Upper St Martin's Ln   497 0376   (437 0641)
Unusually stylish Theatreland Chinese, with a double-height, glazed frontage – the basement private room is one of the better places for a Chinese feast in comfortable, modern surroundings. / Private Rm (–,40).

Nº 1 Yacht Club WC2   £M, (250,75,75)
Victoria Embankment   379 9939   (379 9185)
New nightclub, housed on a moored steamer near the Temple; it aspires to exclusivity but, while it is becoming established, is available for hire for a range of events. / 3 am; in-house caterers; Dining Rm (150,75); Oak Rm (50,–); Cocktail Bar (70,–).

The O-Bar W1   £B, (150,–)
83-87 Wardour St   437 3490
Permanently packed with a youngish crowd, this newly-established, three-floor Soho bar will, for a sufficiently large party, give you a floor to use privately. / 3 am; Restaurant (150,–); Basement (120,–).

Private venues

Odette's NW1   £M, (–,30)
130 Regent St   586 5486
This multi-mirrored, Primrose Hill favourite – North London's smartest restaurant – has one of the sweetest private rooms in London, feeling rather like eating in a nice below-the-stairs cupboard; it overlooks the downstairs conservatory which can also be hired.
/ not Sat L & Sun; Private Rm (–,9); Conservatory (–,30).

The Old Operating Theatre Museum & Herb Garret SE1   £B-M, (150,–)
9a St Thomas St   955 4791
Bizarre and fascinating c19 operating-theatre, up tortuous spiral stairs in the belfry of a church near London Bridge; now housing a collection of surgical instruments and pickled internal organs – tough to beat for a drinks party with a touch of the macabre. / midnight; eve only, all day Mon; hirer's choice of caterer; no smoking.

Old Refectory W8   £B-M, (250,120,80)
Campden Hl Rd   351 6011   (352 7376)
Leafily located Kensington outpost of King's College, whose attractive, barrel-roofed hall is used for weddings and parties; french windows, which give onto a slightly unkempt garden, can be used as an entrance, which is otherwise through the college building. / midnight; hirer's choice of caterer.

Old Royal Observatory SE10   £E, (80,–)
Romney Rd   081-858 4422
Survey London from this lofty, 0° vantage-point in Greenwich Park; the charming, recently renovated top-floor Octagon is one of the few surviving Wren interiors, and its long narrow windows have one of the best views of the metropolis; available on a limited basis. / 11 pm; list of caterers; no amplified music; no dancing; no red wine; Octagon Rm (80,–).

The Old Thameside Inn SE1   £B, (150,–)
Clink St   403 4243
This riverside pub has a stone-floored, large cellar bar available for private parties where you can also have a disco; they can rope off a section of their terrace overlooking the river for 40 or so people. / midnight; Cellar Bar (150,–).

Opera Terazza! WC2   £B-M, (100,50)
45 East Ter, The Piazza   379 0666   (497 9060)
This Italian theme Forte establishment, over Covent Garden market, may seem a little dated and serve food which is OK only, but the balcony – which can be hired for large parties – is one of the best al fresco locations in London. / Terrace (100,50).

Private venues

Orangery (Holland Park) W8   £M, (300,70)
Holland Pk   602 7344   (371 2467)
This must be one of the prettiest spots in London, an enchanting c18 building, on an intimate scale and glazed on three sides. / 11.30 pm; contract caterer; no amplified music; With marquee (300,–); Orangery (150,70).

Orangery (Kensington Palace) W8   £M-E, (200,100)
Kensington Palace   937 9561   (376 0198)
Beautifully situated, at the back of the Palace, this lovely, long, white-painted Queen Anne summer house is made available ten or so times a year for prestigious celebrations. / charities & companies only; eve only; avail May - Sep only; Justin de Blanc; no amplified music; no dancing.

Oval SE11   £M, (350,240,180)
Kennington   735 6884   (582 8151)
Large, modernish banqueting suite adjacent to the cricket ground. / National Leisure Catering; Banqueting Suite (350,240,180).

Oxford & Cambridge Club SW1   £M, (120,60,60)
71 Pall Mall   930 5151   (930 9490)
Those who spent their salad days at the Varsity (or who have friends who did) should bear this St James's institution in mind; a member must be involved with any function. / in-house caterers; Marlborough (120,60); Edward VII (40,20); Princess Marie Louise (100,50).

Painters' Hall EC4   £M, (250,180)
9 Little Trinity Ln   236 6258
Near Mansion House, this hall is quite modest compared to some of its grand City brethren; decor is quite spare, with the hall (re-opened in the '60s) painted in cool shades; discos are not permitted but flexibility is otherwise the keynote; the small, yellow Painted Chamber is particularly charming. / 1 am; Aug; Ring & Brymer; no amplified music; Livery Hall (250,180); Court Rm (150,60); Painted Chamber (–,14).

Palace Theatre W1   £M, (250,100)
Cambridge Circus   434 0088
Mainly used privately for entertaining after shows, the beautiful Stalls Bar at this landmark on the edge of Soho can also be used for daytime receptions and lunches. / before 4.30 pm & after shows; hirer's choice of caterer; no amplified music; no dancing; Stalls Bar (250,100).

La Paquerette EC2   £B, (100,60)
Finsbury Sq   638 5134
By the green, at the centre of the square, this small bar/café has a garden and is available for barbecues, parties and bowling evenings; at the weekends you can take over the whole place. / 1 am; in-house caterers.

Private venues

Park Lane Hotel W1   £M-E, (1000,600,550)
Piccadilly   499 6321   (499 1965)
Rather charming, family-owned Mayfair hotel; the star is the large Ballroom, with its superb art deco entrance but some of the other rooms, for example the imposing Oak Room, also offer some unusually characterful possibilities. / Ballroom (1000,600,550);
Tudor Rose Rm (400,200,140); Oak Rm (140,80,50);
Garden Rm (150,120,100); Orchard Suite (80,40);
Mirror Rm (40,40); Drawing Rm (30,20);
Boardroom (20,16).

Paulo's W6   £B-M, (-,20)
30 Greyhound Rd   385 9264
The Torres family's home, off the Fulham Palace Road, is a welcoming, long-established, very inexpensive, Brazilian, eat-all-you-can buffet-restaurant; over 15 people may book their downstairs room. / not Sun.

Peacock House W14   £M, (200,40)
8 Addison Rd   603 6374   (602 8652)
Extraordinary late Victorian Holland Park house (by the same architect as the better known Leighton House) with a mosaicked entrance hall; it is used on several weekends a year for wedding receptions and, for bigger events, has a lawn suited to large marquees. / 10.30 pm
Sat, 4 pm Sun; Sat & Sun only; hirer's choice of caterer; amplified music must end by 9 pm; Main Hall & Lounge (200,40); marquee site.

Pentland House SE3   £B-M, (200,200,200)
Old Rd   081-692 7171   (081-694 2234)
The key attraction of this rather battered c17 house (one of Goldsmith College's lodging houses) is a fabulous, large and well maintained garden; the Refectory is also a possibility although some effort on decoration would be a good investment; there is no kitchen. / midnight;
hirer's choice of caterer; Marquee / Lawn (200,200); Hall (150,100);
marquee site.

Pewterers' Hall EC2   £M, (150,70)
Oat Ln   606 9363   (600 3896)
This livery company's mid-sized '60s hall is sometimes made available for dinners and receptions. / no weddings;
midnight; no amplified music; no dancing; Livery Rm (150,70);
Court Rm (150,-).

Phene Arms SW3   £B, (50,30)
9 Phene St   352 8391
Chelsea pub, known particularly for its pretty garden, with a reasonable party room above. / 11 pm; no amplified
music; no dancing; Upstairs Rm (50,30).

Phillips W1   £M-E, (250,100)
101 New Bond St   629 6602   (629 8876)
The larger sale-rooms of this Mayfair auction house are sometimes made available for receptions and dinners; there is also a dining room available for private hire. /
in-house caterers; no amplified music; no smoking;
Private Dining Rm (-,14).

Private venues

Photographers' Gallery WC2   £B-M, (150,80,80)
5 Great Newport St   831 1772   (836 9704)
On the fringe of Covent Garden, the nicest parts of this modern gallery are rather long and thin and the newly refurbished cafeteria tends to be the focus for functions.
/ midnight; not Tue – Sat pre 7 pm; Hungry for Business; no amplified music; no dancing; smoking restricted.

Pigeon SW6   £B, (–,26)
606 Fulham Rd   736 4618
This basic Fulham restaurant has been popular with successive waves of young professionals and locals for loud dinners in the downstairs dining room.
/ eves only; Private Rm (–,26).

Pimlico Wine Vaults SW1   £B, (50,38)
19-22 Upper Tachbrook St   834 7429
Rather superior wine bar, near Victoria, particularly popular with œnophiles; the setting of the main bar is quite atmospheric and there is also a panelled private room. / 11.30 pm; Private Rm (50,38).

Pinewood Studios, Bucks   £M, (600,150,150)
Pinewood Rd, Iver   0753-656953   (0753-656147)
The country house at the centre of this famous studio complex accommodates large parties in its Ballroom (off which there opens a theatre in which you can dance); smaller get-togethers happen in its Great Gatsby or Green Rooms; big productions might consider a marquee in the gardens. / 1 am; in-house caterers; Ballroom (200,150); Green Rm (150,80); Great Gatsby Rm (150,100); Gardens (marquee) (600,–); marquee site.

Pitcher & Piano SW10   £B, (60,28,28)
214 Fulham Rd   352 9234
On the divide between Chelsea and Fulham, the room over this well-known bar is very popular for drinks parties as, for the money (no room hire), it is one of the more civilised spots in town. / 11.15 pm.

Pizzeria Condotti W1   £B, (–,40)
4 Mill St   499 1308
This well-known, quite smart Mayfair spot offers possibilities for a stylish, quite inexpensive, central party in its downstairs room. / not Sun; Private Rm (–,40).

The Place Below EC2   £B-M, (150,70)
St Mary-le-Bow, Cheapside   329 0789
Cramped, cheery City crypt-restaurant, recently expanded, which is packed every lunchtime for its inexpensive, well cooked vegetarian dishes; at other times it may be used for private parties; unlicensed – reasonable corkage. / 11.30 pm; not Thu & Fri; no smoking.

Private venues

Plaisterers' Hall EC2
1 London Wall   606 7908
The Plaisterers' modern hall belies its relatively inconspicuous entry at the base of an office block – it is on an impressive scale and decorated in grand traditional style; available primarily for City-related functions.

The Plough WC2 £B, (45,30)
27 Museum St   626 7964
Friendly, creaky well worn pub across from the BM; if you are happy to do without a private bar, their room comes free. / 11 pm; no amplified music; no dancing.

Poissonnerie de l'Avenue SW3 £M, (–,25)
82 Sloane Av   589 2457
Upmarket, old-fashioned Chelsea fish parlour, popular with a mature crowd in spite of rather ordinary food; there is a well-appointed first-floor private room. / not Sun; Private Rm (–,25).

Polish Hearth Club SW7 £B-M, (200,130)
55 Exhibition Rd   589 4670   (435 8562)
For faded, old-fashioned charm, this South Kensington emigrés' club scores highly; a characterful, quite grand, mid-priced venue which will consider most kinds of event. / 1 am; in-house caterer; Restaurant (–,90); First Floor (200,130).

Polish Social &
Cultural Association W6 £B, (750,200,200)
238-246 King St   081-741 3225   (081-746 3798)
Like at many emigrés' clubs, it is the time-warp atmosphere which many find striking; the building is quite a basic '60s construction; most of their functions are weddings or conferences. / 1 am; Restaurant not Sat D & Sun L; in-house caterer; Lowiczanka Restaurant (200,150,110); Malinova Rm (200,200,200); Conference Theatre (300,200,160).

Pomegranates SW1 £M, (–,12)
94 Grosvenor Rd   826 6560
Characterful, dimly-lit, mirrored Pimlico basement restaurant, offering a long, eclectic menu. / not Sat L & Sun; Private Rm (–,12).

La Pomme d'Amour W11 £M, (–,35)
128 Holland Pk Av   229 8532
Middle-aged, but comfortable and quite pretty in a rather twee way, this Holland Park restaurant has a particularly nice room at the rear which is used for parties. / not Sat L & Sun; Private Rm (–,35).

Le Pont de la Tour SE1 £M, (–,20)
Butlers Wharf   403 8403   (403 0267)
The private room may lack the Tower Bridge view of the main restaurant – which is one of London's most glamorous and a business favourite – but it is a swish, popular setting nonetheless. / Private Rm (–,20).

Private venues

Porchester Centre W2 £B-M, (600,500,400)
Queensway 792 2919
Ornate, panelled art deco ballroom – a gem hidden away in a very municipal-looking Bayswater building – which is not very expensive and has lots of character; the marbled turkish baths are occasionally used by those in search of the off-beat. / 1 am; hirer's choice of caterer; Ballroom (600,500,400); Baths (200,100).

HMS President EC4 £B-M, (350,200,160)
Victoria Embankment 583 2652 (583 2840)
For a big, limited-budget bash, this WW 1, Q-class boat, moored just above Blackfriars Bridge, offers good value and the sense of occasion that being afloat brings; the rooms need decoration to be festive. / 2 am; in-house caterers; Drill Hall (250,200,160); Gun Rm (100,50); Quarter Deck (100,–); Wardroom (120,60); Captain's Quarters (–,30).

Punters EC4 £B, (80,40)
5 Abchurch Yd, Abchurch Ln 623 2355
Prettily located subterranean City wine bar whose restaurant is available in the evenings for drinks parties.

Quaglino's SW1 £M, (60,40)
16 Bury St 930 6767 (839 2866)
London's most striking restaurant has a salon privé with an (optional) ring-side view of the main floor below; the style is slickly modernistic, fireplace notwithstanding.
/ Private Rm (60,40).

Quayside E1 £M, (–,50)
World Trade Centre, 1 St Katherine's Way
481 0972 (488 3482)
Competent French cooking and a view of St Katherine's dock (in summer, from the terrace) are the attractions here; the slightly dated surroundings of the restaurant and private room appear to best advantage under a soft evening light (see also World Trade Centre). / not Sat L & Sun D; Private Rm (–,50).

TS Queen Mary WC2 £M, (300,110,110)
Victoria Embankment 240 9404 (497 8910)
Converted steamer moored by Temple tube and done out in best Bass banqueting style; most notable for its characterful wardroom bistro (which can be hired just for drinks) which has an outside deck in summer; private areas on another deck can be set aside for a BBQ. / 1 am; Queen Mary Suite (300,110,110); Captain's Suite (150,70); Carvery (200,100); Wardroom Bistro (100,50).

Queen's Eyot, Berks £M, (80,60)
Monkey Island Ln 0753-671219 (0753-671244)
Eton's island retreat has an impressive modern clubhouse reached by ferry; uses of the eyot stretch from corporate sports to wedding receptions. / midnight; in-house caterers; Permanent Marquee (250,150); marquee site.

Private venues

Queen's House SE10   £E, (200,150,150)
Romney Rd   081-858 4422   (081-312 6632)
Sandwiched picturesquely between the Royal Naval College and Greenwich Park, this highly unusual house (by Inigo Jones et al) has been restored to a spanking new state (displeasing purists); the grand, lofty, square Great Hall and pretty Orangery are the areas most used – for larger occasions additional spaces, inside and out, can be used in varying combinations.
/ after 7 pm; list of caterers; live bands only; no discos; Great Hall (150,100); Henrietta Maria Suite (200,150); Orangery Suite (150,30); Van De Velde Suite (150,135); Treasury (120,–); Loggia (30,–); marquee site.

Queens Ice Skating W2   £B, (1000,–)
Queensway   229 0172   (229 1818)
If your plans are not sufficiently ambitious to stage your own private ice spectacular at this large Bayswater rink you might consider jazzing up the basic private room which is regularly used for kids' parties. / 2 am; hirer's choice of caterer.

Raffles Dining Room SW3   £M-E, (150,50,50)
King's Rd   352 1091   (352 9293)
This intimate Chelsea nightclub, decorated in comfortable traditional style, is available to non-members before 11 pm and all day Sunday. / non-members before 11pm & Sun only; 3 am; before 11 pm & all day Sun; list of caterers; Dining Rm (50,30).

Ranger's House SE10   £M-E, (120,80)
Chesterfield Wlk   081-853 0035
On the border of Greenwich Park, overlooking Blackheath, the fine Gallery Room of this c18 English Heritage house – home to the Suffolk Paintings Collection – is available for dinners. / no weddings; midnight; list of caterers; no amplified music; no dancing; no red wine; marquee site.

The RAW Club WC1   £B, (450,–)
112a Gt Russell St   637 3375   (637 3965)
Underneath the Tottenham Court Road YMCA, this high-ceilinged basement nightclub comes heavily themed (currently aquatic) and has a large dance-floor; the Gardening Room (which is, well, like a garden) is available privately most nights. / 6 am; whole club Mon-Wed only; hirer's choice of caterer, alcohol in-house; The Gardening Rm (60,–).

Red Fort W1   £M, (–,200)
77 Dean St   437 2525
One of London's better-known Indian restaurants (if not a particular favourite of ours), has a large basement available privately. / Private Rm (–,200).

Private venues

Reform Club SW1 £M-E, (500,120,500)
104 Pall Mall   930 9374   (930 1857)
The beautiful, august lobby of this St James's club is quite superb and an ideal centrepiece for a ball; the Coffee room and the sombre Library are also very grand and there are smaller dining rooms for as few as 14; the club has recanted its more liberal '80s hiring policy and a member must now be actively involved in any function.
/ 2 am; in-house caterers; Library (300,150); Coffee Rm (300,150).

The Regent W1 £M-E, (500,360,310)
222 Marylebone Rd   631 8000   (631 8080)
Skillful updating of a Victorian building (it was the St Marylebone railway hotel) has provided London with some of its grandest public rooms; the marbled Ballroom and the oak Drawing Room are most impressive, without being overbearing; for smaller sit-downs, the Tower Suite (glass roofed and with a view of the atrium) and the Boardroom (once the BR boardroom) have individual attractions. / 1 am; in-house caterers; Ballroom (500,360,310); Champagne Rm (70,30); Drawing Rm (300,160,110); Music Rm (310,210,140); Empire Rm (360,160,110); Boardroom (–,20); Gazebo (40,–).

Regent's College NW1 £M, (400,200,200)
Inner Circle, Regent's Pk   487 7540   (487 7657)
A great position, in the heart of the Park, makes this a very attractive venue; the rooms available are light and airy, in good decorative order and only somewhat institutional; the Tuke Common Room benefits from a particularly leafy prospect. / 2 am; ARA; Herringham Hall (110,90); Knapp Gallery (80,50); Tuke Common Rm (80,–); Refectory (400,200,200); marquee site.

Rembrandt Hotel SW7 £M, (250,200,180)
11 Thurloe Pl   589 8100   (589 5223)
This agreeable South Kensington hotel, near the V&A, offers good, flexible banqueting accommodation. / 1 am; Edward (80,60); Charles (60,22); James (90,90); Princes (–,10); Elizabeth (80,40); Victoria (20,15); Elizabeth & Victoria (70,58,38).

Rib Room
Hyatt Carlton Tower Hotel SW1 £M-E, (–,16)
2 Cadogan Pl   235 5411
This luxurious Knightsbridge roasts, grill and seafood restaurant has a dark-panelled Boardroom for private dining. / Boardroom (–,16).

Private venues

The Ritz W1   £M-E, (250,120,120)
150 Piccadilly   493 8181   (493 2687)
The Ritz's strength is in stylish small to medium size rooms; in decor, the Marie Antoinette suite lives up to its name – it can be used for large functions in conjunction with the Palm Court; the Trafalgar Suite is also impressive; for very notable dinners, the Louis XVI main restaurant may be available; the Italian Garden is an interesting, if slightly noisy, summer drinks possibility.
/ live music only ;Palm Court & Marie Antoinette (250,120,120);
Marie Antoinette Suite (80,60); Palm Court (250,90); Trafalgar Suite (–,20);
Berkeley Suite Reception Rm & Dining Rm (80,30);
Berkeley Reception Rm (30,20); Berkeley Dining Rm (40,30);
Restaurant (–,120); Italian Garden (150,–).

Rochester Hotel SW1   £B-M, (90,50,50)
69 Vincent Sq   828 6611   (233 6724)
The impeccably maintained, very English decor can seem a shade overpowering; still, hire of the bar and restaurant of this Pimlico hotel could work well for a smartish, informal meal; (see also Rochesters wine bar, below). / 3 am; in-house caterers; Bar & Restaurant (–,35);
Victoria Suite (70,50); Rochester Suite (30,30); Wine Bar (90,–).

Rochesters SW1   £B, (70,–)
69 Vincent Sq   828 6611   (233 6724)
This high-ceilinged, light Pimlico wine bar lends itself well to casual drinks parties; dancing is possible at a push.
/ 3 am; eve only.

Rock Circus W1   £M-E, (250,60,60)
London Pavilion, Piccadilly Circus
734 7203   (734 8023)
It's difficult to get a clearer theme than this homage to rock-stars, complete with moving Animatronic figures; the show is the high-point of the venue; keeping in theme, the adjoining Rock Island Diner offers inexpensive catering possibilities. / 2 am; from 6.30 pm; list of caterers.

Rock Garden WC2   £B, (800,300)
4 The Piazza   497 3154
Best-known for its touristy upstairs burger-joint – the vaults downstairs are one of London's older rock venues cum nightclubs; its all very clean-cut and offers combinations for parties of many different sizes (especially, for bigger events, in conjunction with their Gardening dance-club in the vaults next-door). / 6 pm;
in-house caterers; Standalone (400,–); with Gardening Club (800,–).

Rodos WC2   £B, (–,40)
59 St Giles High St   836 3177
Stuck out on a limb, behind Centre Point, this long-established, family-run taverna offers good grub and an atmospheric upper room great for those feeling hungry and boisterous. / not Sat L & Sun; Private Rm (–,40).

Private venues

The Roof Gardens W8 £M-E, (420,230,180)
99 High St Kensington   937 7994   (938 2774)
Set amidst two extraordinary acres of mature gardens on the roof of the old Derry & Toms store, this well-known, highly popular venue is arguably London's best of the non-membership nightclub variety and is widely used for social and corporate events. / 3 am; not Thur eve &
Sat eve; in-house caterers.

Rose Garden Restaurant W1   £B-M, (500,50)
Inner Circle, Regent's Pk   935 5729
This park café opens onto a large garden; it's worth considering for events ranging from summer discos to kids' parties. / 2 am; hirer's choice of caterer;
Prince Regent Rm (75,50).

Royal Academy of Arts W1   £E, (1000,250)
Burlington Hs, Piccadilly   439 7438   (287 6312)
The c17/18 private rooms of the Royal Academy are among the most charmingly impressive of any in London; it may also be possible to organise functions around gallery exhibitions (and particularly the Summer Exhibition); dining is a privilege extended only to corporate members. / 9 pm (receptions); after 6.30 pm;
list of caterers; no smoking; Private Rms (350,100); Summer
Exhibition (1000,250); General Assembly Rm (-,40).

Royal Aeronautical Society W1   £M, (160,120)
4 Hamilton Pl   499 3515   (499 6230)
Although slightly institutional in feel, much of the original grandeur of this impressive c19 townhouse, just off Hyde Park Corner, remains; a terrace opens off the Argyll room.
/ midnight; London Catering Services; Council Rm & Bar (80,40);
Argyll Rm & Hawker Rm (160,120); Hawker Rm (25,12);
Sopwith Rm (60,30); Handley Page (60,40); Brabazon (25,12);
Terrace (120,-).

Royal Air
Force Museum NW9   £M-E, (1400,370,370)
Grahame Pk Way, Hendon
081-205 2266   (081-205 8044)
Although other galleries are available, the Battle of Britain Hall is the most used for functions – as well as the aircraft (from both sides) it has interesting displays on the blitz, making it a natural for themed events; the helipad can be used for marquees. / after 6 pm; list of caterers;
no smoking; Bomber Command Hall (700,-); Main Aircraft Hall (700,-);
Battle Of Britain Hall (400,370,370); marquee site.

Private venues

Royal Albert Hall SW7 £M-E, (3000,2000,1300)
Kensington Gore   589 3203   (823 7725)
You can entertain huge numbers in great style here, although, once more than just the Arena is used, the necessity of people eating in the stalls, circle and boxes is a slightly odd arrangement; smaller events may be arranged in private rooms – some of them lovely – either around a performance, or at other times on a stand-alone basis; the Prince of Wales, Henry Cole and Elgar Rooms are best. / 3 am; Ring & Brymer; smoking restricted; Arena (750,360,350); Elgar Rm (220,160); Prince Of Wales Rm (45,30); Henry Cole Rm (30,20); Victoria Rm (120,80); Picture Gallery (200,140); The Gods (500,300).

Royal Botanic Gardens, Surrey £M-E, (400,200)
Kew, Richmond   081-332 5616   (081-332 5610)
Of the famous glasshouses, the Temperate House may be used for grand entertaining; there is a gallery which is more generally available for dinners and receptions and also a new marquee site. / 11 pm; after 5.30 pm; list of caterers; no dancing; no smoking; Kew Gardens Gallery (150,80); Temperate House (400,200); marquee site.

Royal College of Art SW7   £B-M, (900,700,700)
Kensington Gore   584 5020   (225 1487)
Large, white-walled galleries looking onto Kensington Gardens; they offer large open spaces for inexpensive events – from a private view to a party – and are an ideal blank canvas on which to create more lavish themed parties; the upstairs Fellows Common Room (with outside terrace), hung with pictures by famous alumni, suits receptions and dinner can be served in the adjoining Fellows Dining Room. / 2 am; large functions eve & Sat & Sun only; hirer's choice of caterer; some areas - no red wine; Entrance Gallery (200,-); Henry Moore Gallery (900,700,700); Gulbenkian Upper Gallery (350,200); Gulbenkian Lower Gallery (150,80); Senior Common Rm Dining Rm (-,70); Sitting Rm and Bar (200,-).

Royal College of Music SW7   £M-E, (400,250,200)
Prince Consort Rd   589 3643   (589 7740)
Offering a fair degree of Victorian grandeur, the Concert Hall of this South Kensington institution opens directly off the college's marbled foyer; the cute Britten Theatre (seats 402) is available for those who want to kick off with a show or recital, and the council room is available for small dinners; the Donaldson Room (use by permission of the Director) is the most attractive. / 1.30 am; out of term best; hirer's choice of caterer; no smoking; red wine restricted; Concert Hall (400,250,200); Donaldson Rm (80,40); Council Rm (30,24).

Private venues

Royal Garden Hotel W8 £M, (1500,600,550)
High St Kensington   937 8000   (938 4532)
'Seventies hotel, prominently situated by Kensington Palace, with one of the larger ballrooms in London; during the winter the Royal Suite, which enjoys sixth floor views over Kensington Gardens, may be hired for lunch or dinner parties. / 1 am; *Palace Suite (1500,600,550); Kensington Suite (150,80,80); Balmoral Suite (150,120,90); Sandringham & Osborne Suite (100,70,50); Royal Suite (60,28).*

Royal Geographical Society SW7   591 3000   £B-M, (350,120,120)
1 Kensington Gore   589 5466   (584 4447)
Although it is a mite institutional, this Society just south of Hyde Park, is comparatively flexible about what it will entertain and offers a great address with very characterful surroundings at competitive rates. / midnight; *Lodge; Main Hall (120,100); New Map Rm (150,–); Tea Rm (60,40); Council Rm (–,24); Everest Rm (–,14); Reading Rm (–,10).*

Royal Green Jackets W1   £B-M, (450,180,120)
56 Davies St   629 3674   (414 3488)
This Mayfair TA outpost, just off Oxford Street, offers a basic, large gym-type hall for a bash, though with decoration it might be worth considering for weddings etc; its two mess bars are not particularly pretty, but broad-minded about bookings for stag and less sober lads' nights. / 2 am; not Wed; *Richmond Sundrey; Hall (450,180,120); St George's Club (200,–); Sergeants Mess (100,–).*

Royal Holloway College, Surrey   £B-M, (650,200,170)
Egham Hl, Egham   0784-443046   (0784-437520)
The impressive Picture Gallery of this extraordinary Victorian confection (with an impressive collection of art of the period) makes a great and unusual venue for a dinner; out of term you can use the adjoining Dining Hall which is larger and almost as impressive when dressed; with marquees, capacities up to 3,000 are realistic. / 1 am; *Dining Hall only in vacs; in-house caterers; no smoking; Picture Gallery (300,150); Founders Dining Hall (350,200,170); marquee site.*

Royal Horseguards Thistle Hotel SW1   £M, (100,100,60)
Whitehall Ct   839 3400   (925 2263)
With access to a terrace overlooking the river, the Thames Suite of this very central hotel, is quite pretty and the Boardroom a possibility for a business meal; other rooms are very conference-orientated. / 2 am; *Boardroom (–,12); Thames (100,100,60).*

Private venues

Royal Horticultural
Halls SW1   £B-M, (2000,1200,1000)
80 Vincent Sq   828 4125   (834 2072)
These large, flexible halls can transcend their flower-show function (although the cost of the decoration to do so is worth bearing in mind); the older hall, bordering the Square, is traditional in style, with a glazed, vaulted ceiling; over the road, the younger hall, a creation of the '30s, is a glass and concrete hangar which would not be wholly out of place in a sci-fi 'B' movie. / 1 am;
London Catering Services; Old Hall (1000,500,400);
New Hall (2000,1200,1000).

Royal Institute of
British Architects W1   £M, (400,210,150)
66 Portland Pl   580 5533   (255 1541)
The heart of this '30s institute is its lofty hall, reached by an extremely imposing staircase; with almost as much window as wall, it's an impressive space for any type of gathering; up more stairs, the South Room is pleasant if less notable. / midnight; not Sat & Sun; Sutcliffe; no amplified music; smoking restricted; Florence Hall (400,210,150); South Rm (70,40).

Royal Institution of
Great Britain W1   £B-M, (300,–)
21 Albemarle St   409 2992   (629 3569)
This large Mayfair institute, where Faraday 'discovered' electricity, unfortunately reserves the fine main entrance in its huge neo-classical façade for royalty; it has three pleasantly creaky rooms suitable for receptions. / 9.30 pm; not Sat & Sun; Crown Catering; no amplified music; no dancing; smoking restricted; Council Rm (50,–); Anteroom (150,–);
Long Library (150,–).

Royal Lancaster W2   £M, (2500,2000,1300)
Lancaster Ter   262 6737   (706 3571)
This blot on the Hyde Park landscape has one of the capital's largest ballrooms, recently refurbished to a high standard (gizmos include retractable chandeliers) and is very much nicer than the exterior might lead one to expect; for an hotel of such a size it is unusually thinly provided with smaller accommodation, but the two very large rooms do subdivide. / 2 am; Nine King's Suite (2500,2000,1300); Westbourne Suite (1300,1120,600);
Gloucester Suite (200,85,70).

Royal Majestic Suite NW6   £M, (300,220,200)
196 Willesden Ln   081-459 3276   (081-451 0920)
Pleasant, well-maintained Kosher banqueting hall in Willesden. / 12.30 am; not available Sat in Summer or Fri all year or Jewish festivals; in-house caterers; Ground Floor (300,220,200);
First Floor (120,70,70).

Private venues

Royal National Theatre SE1   £M, (1200,150)
South Bank   928 2033   (620 1197)
Most entertaining here happens around shows, but at other times the theatre's spaces are available for all events; Ovations restaurant and the Terrace Bar café suit functions best (used particularly for Christmas parties), while the Olivier Stalls (with outside terrace) is a pleasant, lofty foyer-space for a reception.
/ 2 am; only related events on performance-nights; in-house caterers; smoking restricted; Ovations (180,120); Terrace Café (220,150); Richardson Rm (25,14); Olivier Stalls Foyer (500,120); Olivier Circle Foyer (50,–); Lyttelton Exhibition Area (300,–); marquee site.

Royal Opera House WC2   £M-E, (300,100)
Bow St   240 1200, x214   (497 8030)
The splendid Crush Bar is sometimes used for entertaining during the day. / 3 am; in-house caterers; no amplified music; no dancing.

Royal Over-Seas League SW1   £B-M, (200,200,100)
Park Pl   408 0214   (499 6738)
The smaller rooms of these two imposing St James's houses are better suited to entertaining than the larger ones in the '30s annex (the nicest, the Park room, is smallest of all); once grand, the decor is now pleasantly worn in. / midnight; not Sun; in-house caterers;
Hall Of India & Pakistan (200,200,100); St Andrew's Hall (150,80,60); Wrench (50,32); Mountbatten Rutland (45,32); Bennet-Clark (30,16); Park (15,11).

Royal Parks Executive Agency SW1
298 2000
There is an ever more flexible policy on the use of these parks (including Hyde, Green, St James's and Greenwich Parks) for functions; if you have an idea for an event (or, say, want to erect a marquee on their 'patches' next to Spencer or The Queen's House), their attitude is "it can't hurt to ask".

Royal Society Of Arts WC2   £M, (250,170,150)
8 John Adam St   930 5115   (321 0271)
Composed of five converted c18 houses, off the Strand; the vaults below the society offer gallery-type space with brick ceilings and are the most versatile for parties, if rather bitty; the other rooms are a mixture of white-walled galleries and recently updated period rooms.
/ 1 am; Catering & Allied; All Vaults (250,170,150);
Benjamin Franklin Rm (150,95,60); Gallery (150,–); Tavern Rm (70,48); Folkestone Rm (30,20); Vault 1 (100,60); Vault 2 (50,36); Vault 3 (30,24); Vault 4 (75,50).

Private venues

Royal Veterinary College NW1   £B-M, (300,130,110)
Royal College St   387 2898   (388 2342)
'Thirties building with a comfortable ambience, a good variety of accommodation (much of it in period style) and offering a lot of flexibility; conveniently located and not too expensive, its institutionality is part of its charm.
/ hirer's choice of caterer; smoking restricted; Great Hall (250,130,110); Council Rm (55,35); Clarence Rm (80,70); Northumberland Rm (90,70); York Rm (50,–); Connaught Rm (60,20); Cambridge Rm (50,20); College Principal's Suite (–,12); Garden (300,–).

RSJ SE1   £M, (–,20)
13A Coin St   928 4554
This modern British South Bank restaurant-favourite offers good value for money (and for wine enthusiasts a collection of 200 Loire wines); its private room shares the restrained blue and yellow decor of the main restaurant.
/ Private Rm (–,20).

Rubens Hotel SW1   £M, (200,140)
Buckingham Palace Rd   834 6600   (828 5401)
Facing the Royal Mews, this Victoria hotel has quite agreeable banqueting facilities, fairly modern in style.
/ 1 am; kitchen; Rembrandt Rm (80,50); Old Masters Restaurant (200,140).

Ruby's W1   £B, (200,–)
49 Carnaby St   287 3957   (287 9468)
This small basement, by day a dance studio, has wood floors and mirrors on the walls; it is not nearly as tacky as the street outside and worth considering for a budget bash. / 2 am; hirer's choice of caterer.

Rules WC2   £M, (75,48)
35 Maiden Ln   379 0258   (497 1081)
Claiming to be London's oldest restaurant, this ultra-traditional, panelled English establishment, off Covent Garden, has some of the best private dining rooms in the capital. / Charles Dickens Rm (60,40); King Edward VII Rm (40,25); Greene Rm (75,48).

RUSI Building SW1   £M, (150,90)
Whitehall   930 5854   (321 0943)
Faded charm lingers at this Whitehall institute, making it a characterful, if not quite grand, venue; the Duke of Wellington hall is the most interesting room – its D-shape best suiting receptions – with the Council Chamber or reading room more appropriate for dinners; refurbishment is planned. / 2 am; hirer's choice of caterer; no amplified music; no dancing; Duke Of Wellington Hall (150,90); Council Chamber (50,20); Library & McGarel-Groves Reading Rm (100,50); McGarel-Groves Reading Rm (80,60).

Private venues

Russell WC1   £M, (650,350,300)
Russell Sq   837 6470   (837 2857)
How sad that the area surrounding this splendid Victorian hotel should have fallen from grace; despite the Forte treatment, most of the rooms, many of them marbled, retain their impressive period charm – the Warncliffe and Woburn (adjoining) offer size, the Library and King's bar clubbiness. / 2 am;
Warncliffe Suite (650,350,300); Bedford Suite (80,50);
Woburn Suite (600,350,300); Grafton Suite (80,50); Ormond Suite (60,48);
Guilford Suite (40,30); Library (40,15); Boardroom (–,8); Bar (60,–).

Saatchi Gallery NW8   £M-E, (1000,300)
98a Boundary Rd   624 8299   (624 3798)
An exceptional uncluttered white space, seeming all the more extraordinary for opening off an ordinary St John's Wood street; the gallery's avant-garde display changes periodically. / companies only; 11 pm; Mustard Catering;
no amplified music; no dancing; no smoking.

Saddlers' Hall EC2
40 Gutter Ln   726 8661   (600 0386)
This livery company hall is included for completeness only – use is generally restricted to organisations known to their court.

Saigon W1   £B-M, (–,50)
45 Frith St   437 7109
While the food at this Soho Vietnamese is only good in parts, it has a comfortably dated sultry atmosphere; you can take upstairs privately.

St Andrew Golf Club EC4   £B-M, (300,80,80)
Allhallows Ln   283 1335
In the arches of Cannon Street railway bridge – the lofty main vault bar and mezzanine restaurant are well suited to a party, reception or dinner. / 1 am; not Sun.

St Bartholomew's Hospital EC1   £M, (240,190)
West Smithfield   601 8019   (601 7899)
Ascend the Hogarth staircase to find one of the most atmospheric halls in London (c18), all cream, gold and dark wood – a little shabby perhaps, but only in the nicest way; it's part of the main quad at Bart's, so its use must not disturb the patients; that said, they seem pretty flexible. / 11.45 pm; list of caterers; no amplified music;
no dancing; Great Hall (240,190); Guild Rm (40,22);
Peggy Turner Rm (40,14); Treasurer's Rm (40,18);
Henry VIII Committee Rm (50,12).

St Botolph's Hall EC2   £B-M, (–,150)
Bishopsgate   588 3388
Undergoing major restoration work as we go to press (re-opening '94), this oak-panelled Victorian church hall, next to Liverpool Street, is used for receptions, dinners and Christmas parties for local City firms. / midnight;
hirer's choice of caterer; Upper Hall (–,150); Lower Hall (–,45).

Private venues

St Bride Foundation Institute EC4 £B, (175,90)
Bride Ln, Fleet St   353 3331   (353 1547)
Bright, characterful, Victorian institution, attractively situated near the 'wedding cake' church of the same name; star attraction is the Bridewell Hall, which, though well decorated, still occasionally doubles up as a Badminton court. / 10 pm; not Sat & Sun; hirer's choice of caterer; no music; no dancing; no smoking; Bridewell Hall (175,90); Farringdon Rm (75,40).

St Etheldreda's Crypt EC1   £B, (280,180,130)
14 Ely Pl   242 8238
London's oldest Catholic Church will allow wedding receptions and reasonably sedate parties in its undercroft; arrangements and catering are via the Bleeding Heart restaurant and wine bar (see listing). / no 21sts.

St John's Hill SW11   £B-M, (250,150,150)
St John's Hl   924 5264   (924 2626)
Housed in a large, red-brick Victorian building, opposite Clapham Junction, the Drill Hall of this branch of the TA is used for a variety of functions – 21sts, weddings, etc. / 2 am; hirer's choice of caterer; Drill Hall (250,150,150); Officers Mess (100,40); Sergeant's Mess (100,45).

St Martin
In The Fields WC2   £B-M, (350,200,150)
5 St Martin's Pl   839 4342   (839 5163)
This atmospheric church crypt on Trafalgar Square (which is a café by day) is a very good venue for a central party. / charities & companies preferred; 2.15 am; after 7pm, not Sun; in house caterers.

St Moritz W1   £B, (120,–)
159 Wardour St   437 0525
Despite its fame as a headbangers' music venue, this Soho basement of swiss grottos – dance-floor, bar, and seating areas – lends itself well to parties. / 3 am; avail Mon-Thu; hirer's choice of caterer, alcohol in-house.

St Peter's Hall W11   £B-M, (250,120)
59a Portobello Rd   792 8227
Extremely atmospheric, whitewashed Edwardian school-building with a tiny central courtyard and a variety of light lofty rooms, suitable for drinks parties for Portobello-bohemians or, with decoration, for weddings, etc. / midnight; Lower & North Halls eve only in school terms; hirer's choice of caterer; smoking restricted; North Hall (200,120); Lower Hall (100,50); Upper Hall (120,80).

St Quentin SW3   £M, (–,20)
243 Brompton Rd   581 5131   (584 6064)
Glittering Knightsbridge brasserie with good French atmosphere and food, and notably good service; the downstairs private room is pleasant, if not quite as grand as the restaurant. / Private Rm (–,20).

Private venues

St John's Gate EC1   £M, (290,120)
St John's Ln   253 6644   (490 8835)
North of Smithfield market, this romantic medieval gatehouse – home to the Order of St John – is a local landmark; the stately, mock-medieval Chapter Hall is a lofty, panelled room used for dinners and receptions; the Council Chamber actually in the gatehouse is similar and smaller; currently being refurbished, the Garden Cloisters of the order's church may be worth considering for marquee or garden parties. / midnight; hirer's choice of caterer; no discos; Chapter Hall (220,120); Council Chamber (–,25); Garden Cloisters (250,–); marquee site.

St Stephens Constitutional Club SW1   £M, (300,100,100)
34 Queen Anne's Gate   222 1382
Smart, yet unimposing, businessmen's club boasting a garden looking out onto St James's Park; a nice size to be taken over in its entirety, say for a wedding – it brings a good sense of occasion without stuffiness. / 3 am; eve only ex Sat & Sun; in-house caterers; Dining Rm (200,100); Bar (80,–); Garden Rm (60,28).

St Thomas's Hospital SE1   £M, (200,100)
St Thomas's Hospital, 2 Lambeth Palace Rd
922 8181   (261 9690)
Situated among the rather drab buildings of this hospital, opposite Parliament, the recently renovated hall and committee room are quite grand and can host many types of function. / midnight; hirer's choice of caterer; no amplified music; smoking restricted; Governors' Hall (200,100); Grand Committee Rm (50,18); marquee site.

Salters' Hall EC2
Gutter Ln   588 5216
Included for completeness only, the Salters are very restrictive with respect to the events which they will allow in their hall.

San Martino SW3   £M, (–,20)
103 Walton St   589 3833
Marty and his merry men provide a more than usually hospitable, old-style welcome at this still-fashionable, not inexpensive Chelsea Italian restaurant; the private room, upstairs, is white-tiled and unadorned. / Private Rm (–,20).

The Sanctuary WC2   £M-E, (250,80,80)
12 Floral St   240 9635   (497 0410)
This unique, luxury Covent Garden health spa is about as exotic a setting as central London affords – you can twist by the pool, complete with palms and the odd tropical fish; private parties are the only times that this tranquillity is invaded by men. / 12.30 am; Sat, Sun, Mon, Tues eve; hirer's choice of caterer.

Private venues

Sandown Park
Racecourse, Surrey   £M, (4000,2500,2000)
Sandown Pk, Esher   0372-462592   (0372-468762)
Modern racecourse-side facilities, available for all occasions. / Ring & Brymer; Tote Hall (4000,2500,2000); Lower Tote Hall (1000,800,600); Claremont (650,550,400); Wolsey (400,250,200); Cavalry Bar (150,120,80); Ardross (350,250,180); Tack and Saddle (250,200,150); Lawn Suite (100,80,40); Persimmon (75,60).

Les Saveurs W1   £M-E, (–,10)
37a Curzon St   491 8919
Luxurious Mayfair restaurant, fairly recently established and beginning to make quite a culinary name for itself; the impeccable blandness of the decor is less apparent in the small ground-floor function room than in the main restaurant; service is irreproachable. / not Sat & Sun.

The Savoy WC2   £M-E, (800,500,400)
Strand   836 4343   (240 6040)
This famous, central, luxurious, riverside hotel is the default choice for grander corporate and many social events – it has a range of characterful accommodation in differing period styles, some with a river view.
/ Lancaster Rm (800,500,400); Abraham Lincoln Rm & Manhattan Rm (400,240,180); River Rm (350,120,120); Beaufort (120,60); Pinafore (80,40); Gondoliers (50,28); Mikado (35,18); Patience (30,24); Iolanthe (25,12); Sorcerer (18,6).

Le Scandale W1   £B, (500,–)
53-54 Berwick St   437 6830
The '70s disco kitsch – glitter-painted walls and ceilings, glow-lights and mirrors – is laid on pretty thick at this large nightclub, just south of Oxford Street; its associations are touristic rather than trendy, but only the painfully hip would feel inhibited from using it for a big bop. / 3.30 am; avail Tue-Thu; hirer's choice of caterer, alcohol in-house; Front or Rear Bar (200,–).

School Of Pharmacy WC1   £B-M, (300,150)
29-39 Brunswick Sq   753 5800   (278 0622)
Slightly institutional by nature, but pleasant, pair of '30s halls, with large windows facing onto the square; this venue has potential for many kinds of function. / midnight; Aug hol; in-house caterers; Assembly Hall (–,150); Refectory (300,140).

Science Museum SW7   £M-E, (700,330,170)
Exhibition Rd   938 8190   (938 8112)
The fourth-floor Flight Gallery and ground floor Space Gallery are the most popular places to party in the museum; the lofty, East (entrance) hall can accommodate larger dinners while, amongst the galleries available for receptions, the medically-related Wellcome Galleries are most regularly used. / 1 am; from 6.30 pm; list of caterers; no smoking; Flight Gallery (400,200,170); Wellcome Gallery 1 (125,–); Wellcome Gallery 1 & 2 (250,–); Fellows' Rm (200,130); Launch Pad (350,–); East Hall (700,330); Space Gallery (200,–).

Private venues

Scone E14   £M, (40,28)
Millwall Dock   515 8826   (515 8826)
Clare Hunter and David Ireland's home is an old Thames sailing barge, permanently moored just by Cross Harbour DLR station; comfortably furnished, partially gas-lit and with the galley opening onto the dining room, it is a more than usually intimate, relaxed setting for a dinner or reception; much of their business is corporate. / midnight; in-house caterers; no music; no dancing.

Seafresh SW1   £B, (–,80)
80-81 Wilton Rd   828 0747
Large, well-known Pimlico fish and chip shop that is comfortable by chippie standards; they have access to a large private room for big bashes. / not Sun; Private Rm (–,80).

Searcy's SW1   £M-E, (300,200,180)
30 Pavilion Rd   823 9212   (823 8694)
A very well-known address and, for those without their own London townhouse in which to entertain, this discreet building makes an excellent substitute, being homely yet grand; many different sizes of party can be accommodated with different combinations of rooms.
/ 1 am; Searcy's.

Selfridge Hotel W1   £M, (300,282,228)
Orchard St   408 2080   (409 2295)
Woody, comfortable, modern hotel behind the department store; the Drawing Room (in fact a large, light, traditional dining room) is the nicest room; the long, divisible Selfridge Suite, decorated in yellow and red, offers flexible space. / 2 am; in-house caterers;
Selfridge Suite (300,282,228); Drawing Rm (30,25); marquee site.

Serpentine Gallery W2   £M-E, (350,240,170)
Kensington Gdns   402 6075   (402 4103)
Set back from the road dividing Kensington Gardens from Hyde Park, this c20 art gallery – converted from intriguing '30s tea-rooms – is an interesting reception or dinner venue, depending on the current installations; park-views and the garden come into their own in summer. / 11 pm (9 pm for receptions); from 6pm; list of caterers; smoking sometimes restricted.

Shampers W1   £B, (120,90,45)
4 Kingly St   437 1692   (437 1217)
During the week, private dinners and receptions take place in the basement of this bubbling Soho wine bar; at the weekends, for parties, you can have the whole place to yourselves. / 12.30 am; Upstairs or Downstairs (60,45).

Private venues

Sheekey's WC2 £M, (-,30)
28-32 St Martins Ct   240 2565
Old-established theatreland fish restaurant – the cooking is rather up and down – with a traditional, clubby feel and a loyal, older following; downstairs there is an attractive function room, while upstairs a very impressive section with heavy tiles and mirrors can be curtained off.
/ not Sat L & Sun; Private Rm (-,12); Section (-,30).

Shelleys W1 £B, (70,40)
10 Stafford St   493 0337
Un-pubby, pleasant, modernish top floor bar above this Mayfair inn. / 1 am.

Shepherd's SW1 £M, (-,30)
Marsham Ct, Marsham St   834 9552
Bright, art-filled, modern and clubby – this English restaurant in Westminster has a comfortable private roo which is a shade grander than the main restaurant; there is a charge for its use.

Sheraton Belgravia SW1 £M, (100,50)
20 Chesham Pl   235 6040   (259 6243)
For a mid-sized dinner or reception this Belgravia hotel has a couple of serviceable private rooms; a large nook in the alcoved restaurant would make quite a good place for a private dinner. / no dancing; Dining Rm (100,50); Study and Library (70,22); Alcove in Dining Rm (-,14).

Sheraton Park Tower SW1 £M-E, (250,130)
101 Knightsbridge   235 8050   (235 8231)
Prominent, cylindrical Knightsbridge luxury hotel with a range of four first floor function rooms in '70s/traditional style; the main room, the Trianon Room has the benefit of an Astroturfed terrace overlooking Lowndes Square, which may be used for barbecues. / Trianon Rm (250,150); Buckingham Rm (50,40).

Shuckburgh Arms SW3 £B, (100,-)
47 Denyer St   589 8382
You can take over the skylit side-room, and rather inaccessible yard of this Chelsea pub – summer barbecues a possibility. / 12.30 am; Garden (30,-).

Simpsons of Cornhill EC3 £B, (50,74)
38 1/2 Cornhill   626 9985
Well-known, popular Dickensian City institution with two smallish bars that may be used privately; (the very good value restaurant may also be used in the evenings, though its booth-seating cuts down suitability for large functions). / Amy's Bar or Wine Bar (50,-); Restaurant (-,74); Grill (-,50).

Private venues

Simpsons-in-the-Strand WC2   £M, (160,160,100)
100 Strand   836 9112   (836 1381)
Nowhere can compete with the solid Edwardian charm of this most English of restaurants; the Smoking Room downstairs (claiming to be the oldest bar in London) is perfect for a mid-sized dinner; it and the other fine period rooms and cocktail bar can be used for dinners and receptions and the South Room also has a dance-floor; (the restaurant rooms, capacity 150 and 130, are sometimes available for special occasions). / 1 am;
Smoking Rm (100,45); South Rm (145,145,100).

Sir John Soane's Museum WC2   £E, (–,30)
13 Lincoln's Inn Fields   405 2107   (831 3957)
One of the most remarkable, quirky houses in the world is (half a dozen times a year) made available, at huge expense, for parties of between 24 and 30 people; a pre-dinner tour of Soane's Egyptian treasures and his paintings (including the original Rake's Progress) can be arranged and dinner is served in the dark, and very antique dining room and library. / 2 am; Tue-Sat after 6 pm, Mon all day, not Sun; list of caterers; no amplified music; no dancing; no smoking.

606 Club SW10   £B-M, (150,150)
90 Lots Rd   352 5953
Trendy, late-night, cellar jazz club where the food is surprisingly good; for private hires there is no fee – just a minimum catering-spend; the place is impossible to find, down an anonymous staircase opposite the power station. / 1.30 am; not Fri & Sat; in-house caterers.

Ski Club of Great Britain SW1   £B-M, (180,100,100)
118 Eaton Sq   245 1033
Grand it ain't — location notwithstanding — but this informal, homely club is an extremely good, very affordable, central spot for parties, weddings and less formal dinners and get-togethers; a member's sponsorship for events is required, although it is not too difficult to obtain; the place is a nice size to take over in its entirety, but individual rooms can be hired. / 1 am; hirer's choice of caterer; Arnold Lunn Rm (80,40); Council Rm (40,20); Landing (40,20); D'Egyers Bar (60,–); Bistro (40,40).

Skinners' Hall EC4   £M-E, (300,170,170)
8 1/2 Dowgate Hl   236 5629   (236 6590)
Imposing, but charming, the Skinners' Company's accommodation near Cannon Street, entered via a courtyard, offers a number of possibilities; the restored c17 Hall (with Victorian murals) is rich and red; the other rooms are grand, in a relaxed country house style; there is a modern roof garden, with fountain, for fair-weather receptions. / 2 am; not Sun; 6 weeks hol around Aug; list of caterers; smoking restricted.

Private venues

Slug & Lettuce SW1 £B-M, (50,25)
11 Warwick Way   226 3864
Bright, well-maintained room over a comfortable, hospitable Pimlico pub.

Smith's Gallery WC2 £B-M, (800,300,250)
56 Earlham St   836 6252   (836 4769)
Ten years old, these Covent Garden galleries, housed in a stylishly converted warehouse, are a major party venue; flexibility exists for many different kinds of event.
/ hirer's choice of caterer; Maximum (800,300); Gallery 1 (250,120); Gallery 2 (150,80); Gallery 3 (80,40); Casbar (100,60); Wine Bar (100,50); Restaurant (350,250).

Soho Soho W1 £M, (80,60)
11-13 Frith St   494 3491
The stylish, modern 'salon privé' is one of London's better restaurant private rooms; cooking standards are high.
/ Salon Privé (80,60).

Solange's WC2 £B-M, (-,50)
11 St Martin's Ct   240 9936
A traditional French Theatreland spot which offers unexciting but decent classic dishes and friendly service; there is a cosy upstairs room available privately. / not Sat L & Sun D; Private Rm (-,50).

Sotherby's W1 £M-E, (400,300)
34 New Bond St   493 8080   (409 3100)
Unlike their rivals, Sotherby's are quite restrictive about the use of their galleries, making them available only a few times a year, usually for charity-related events.
/ midnight; not Sat & Sun; list of caterers; no amplified music; no dancing; no smoking.

The South Bank Centre SE1 £M-E, (500,250)
Belvedere Rd   921 0600   (928 0063)
The unadorned Chelsfield room is the centre's main function room, though during the day some of its other spaces can be used; when the sun shines, the views afforded by the huge glass walls are memorable; for big-budget productions you always have the option of having your own private concert. / no weddings; limited evening availability; National Leisure Caterers; no smoking;
Hong Kong & Chelsfield Rm (250,150); Sunley Pavilion (40,20); Queen Elizabeth Hall Foyer (500,250); Level 5 External Terrace (200,-).

Southwark Tavern SE1 £B, (200,-)
22 Southwark St   403 0257
For a weekend party you can hire the whole of this pub just South of London Bridge, which has an atmospheric, quite cramped cellar-bar. / 1.30 am; avail Sat.

Spaghetti House W1 £B, (-,50)
15 Goodge St   636 6582
This three-floor monument to '50s Italian restaurant kitsch offers an inexpensive spot for a jolly gathering.
/ 1 am; Private Section (-,50).

Private venues

Spanish Club W1   £M, (180,90)
5 Cavendish Sq   580 2750   (436 7188)
Overlooking the square, the pretty, quite grand first floor room of the Spanish Chamber of Commerce is available for receptions and dinners. / 2 am; hirer's choice of caterer; no amplified music; no dancing; Alfonso XIII Rm (180,90).

Spencer House SW1   £E, (600,120,120)
27 St James's Pl   409 0526   (493 5765)
One of London's most impressive venues and within the budget of very few; this c18 palace, bordering Green Park, was restored in the mid-'80s to its former glory (with paintings from the Royal collection and furniture on loan from the V&A); there are room combinations for all size of dinner or reception and dancing (subject to Royal Parks' permission) can be arranged in a marquee in the garden. / 1 am; not Sun in day; Aug & Jan hol; in-house caterers; dancing only in marquee; smoking restricted.

Spitting Image Museum WC2   £M, (100,–)
1 Cubits Yd   240 0393   (240 0719)
Just off Covent Garden, for a light-hearted reception this workshop-attraction offers an Animatronic puppet-show, the story behind how the puppets are made and the chance to rub shoulders with the stars themselves. / 1 am; after 6.30 pm; hirer's choice of caterer; no smoking.

The Stafford SW1   £M-E, (100,42)
16 St James's Pl   493 0111   (493 7121)
Dinner in its wonderful, musty, 350 year old wine-cellars (which are still very much in use) is this cosy St James's hotel's special attraction; the other entertaining rooms are pretty but less remarkable. / 12.30 am; The Cellar (75,42); Panel Rm (–,10); Sutherland Rm (40,24); Panel Rm & Sutherland Rm (100,40); Pink Rm (–,10); Argyll Rm (30,14); Pink Rm & Argyll Rm (50,14).

Stakis St Ermins SW1   £M, (250,200,200)
Caxton St   222 7888   (222 6914)
The very characterful, old-fashioned ballroom is the headline feature of this Victoria hotel, whose proximity to Westminster makes its smaller rooms favourites for political entertaining. / 1 am; hirer's choice of caterer; Ballroom (250,200,200); Balcony (100,100); York / Clarence (40,30); Cameo (35,20).

Stanley House SW10   £B-M, (175,100,80)
552 King's Rd   351 6011   (352 7376)
Flexibility, affordability and access to the garden combine to make this outpost of King's College a very popular venue; it is a pleasant suite of rooms in an attractive Georgian house just on the right side of the Chelsea/Fulham border. / music until 1 am; hirer's choice of caterer; marquee site.

Private venues

Staple Inn WC1   £M, (250,120)
High Holborn   600 5777   (600 2777)
Prettily situated off a cobbled courtyard, this panelled Victorian medieval-style hall (now the home of the Institute of Actuaries) is lofty, plain and handsome; the adjoining, panelled Council Chamber is also agreeable.
/ midnight; Chester Boyd; no amplified music; Hall (250,120); Council Chamber (70,40).

Star Tavern SW1   £B, (50,–)
6 Belgrave Mws   235 3019
A private bar is available at the 1992 Evening Standard pub of the year, which is hidden away off Belgrave Square. / 11 pm; Bar (50,–).

Stationers' Hall EC4   £M-E, (400,205,175)
Ave Maria Ln   248 2934   (489 1975)
One of the more accommodating of the livery halls – even dancing is permitted, if at an extra charge; the hall itself, c17 (restored), is dark-panelled and bannered; the gilded Court Room and the plainer Stock Room are also agreeable; sadly, the courtyard is entered through the arch of a '50s block. / 1 am; Aug hol; list of caterers; no smoking in Court Room; Livery Hall (400,205,175); Stock Rm (80,46); Ante Rm (–,20); Court Rm (150,80).

Stoke Newington Town Hall N16   £B-M, (700,500,450)
Stoke Newington Church St   081-986 3123
The large municipal suite here is regularly used for wedding receptions and similar large celebrations.
/ 2 am; hirer's choice of caterer.

Strand Palace Hotel WC2   £B-M, (300,225,180)
Strand   836 8080   (257 9503)
Despite some minor tacky additions over the years, the battered art deco Ballroom retains a fair amount of faded character, especially the still–impressive entrance; the other rooms are ordinary. / 2 am; Birley (300,225,180).

Streatham Megabowl   £M, (216,–)
142 Streatham Hill   081-678 6007   (081-674 3463)
Mega-bowling party? – You can hire one or both floors, and, though there is no drinking on the 36 lanes, there is a fair-sized bar area around which to stage festivities.
/ midnight, Fri & Sat 1 am; First floor (120,–).

Subterania W10   £B, (650,–)
12 Acklam Rd   916 6060   (916 6622)
Trendy Notting Hill nightclub, where, once inside, you forget that the club is set into the Westway fly-over; a smaller party would not feel lost here – on the most popular nights you can have a party privately only until normal club hours. / 2 am; until 11 pm Fri & Sat, all night Sun-Thu; hirer's choice of caterer.

Private venues

The Sun WC2   £B-M, (–,35)
Longacre   836 4520
Of its type, this finely decorated salon, over an old Covent Garden pub, is one of the most civilised in London; it is used for sit-downs only (there are many masonic functions here). / 1 am.

Suntory SW1   £E, (–,12)
72 St James's St   409 0201   (499 7993)
This St James's restaurant is top of the line for prestige Japanese corporate entertaining – the atmosphere is dry, the food good and the prices punishing. / 11 pm; not Sun; Tatami (–,12); Teppan-Yaki (–,7).

Le Suquet SW3   £M, (–,30)
104 Draycott Av   581 1785
West London's best and most authentic French fish restaurant transports you from Chelsea to Cannes – not least in the two upstairs private rooms; the service is no less Gallic than the atmosphere. / Private Rm (–,30); Private Rm (–,16).

SW1 Club SW1   £B, (860,400,330)
191 Victoria St   828 7455   (828 7753)
Atmospherically tatty, fashionable, centrally located dance hall. / 6 am; not Wed, Sat, Sun; hirer's choice of caterer, alcohol in-house.

Sweetings EC4   £M, (120,30)
39 Queen Victoria St   248 3062
This quirky City fish parlour is a famous lunch-spot; what's less well-known is that they will do private evening parties, at which optional extras include jazz and cod 'n' chips wrapped in the newspaper of your choice. / midnight; eve only, not Sat & Sun; no discos.

Syon Park (Banqueting), Middx   £B-M, (600,450,350)
London Rd, Brentford   081-568 0778   (081-568 4308)
Modern, purpose-built banqueting complex, benefiting from views of the garden of Syon House. / midnight; Payne & Gunter; Terrace Rm (120,80); Lakeside Rm (280,130); Camellia Rm (200,110); Conservatory Lounge (60,48); Garden Rm (300,146); marquee site.

Syon Park (Conservatory), Middx   £M, (500,250,200)
Brentford   081-560 0881   (081-568 0936)
Vast, imposing glasshouse, suitable for a whole range of events, and very popular; hire includes access to a large ornamental garden. / midnight; not day, Wed-Sun, Apr-Sep; hirer's choice of caterer; Great Conservatory (500,250,200).

Private venues

Syon Park (House), Middx   £E, (350,150)
Brentford   081-560 0881   (081-568 0936)
The Duke of Northumberland's superb palace (Robert Adam) may be hired for suitable events; this is the only great London house still privately owned. / midnight; hirer's choice of caterer; no amplified music; no dancing; smoking restricted; no red wine; House (350,150); marquee site.

Tall House SE1   £M, (200,70)
134 Southwark St   401 2929
A haven from desolate Southwark, this three floor house decorated in Charles Rennie Mackintosh-style is a local business favourite; the modern British dishes lack inspiration but the wine list is good and reasonably priced; the private room is available all day, while the whole building may be hired in the evening or at the weekend. / Private Rm (20,16).

Tallow Chandlers' Hall EC4   £M, (120,97)
4 Dowgate Hl   248 4726
Charming c17 livery hall, set back in its own courtyard; it's quite grand, but has a very agreeable, relaxed atmosphere. / no weddings; 11.15 pm; not Sat & Sun; not mid-July to end-Aug; Payne & Gunter; no amplified music; no dancing; Livery Hall (120,97); Parlour (60,30).

The Tank EC1   £B-M, (–,30)
57-59 Charterhouse St   251 4129
A converted Smithfield warehouse restaurant where the Chinese cooking is quite good, but where the feel is not even vaguely oriental; there is a private room in a part of the building away from the restaurant. / not Sat & Sun.

Tate Gallery SW1   £E, (500,200)
Millbank   821 1313   (630 8270)
If you wish to hold a function in the Tate's impressive galleries you will need to become a sponsor or corporate member – which might be worth considering for a sufficiently grand event. / sponsors only; list of caterers; no amplified music; no smoking; Clore Gallery Foyer (200,–); Clore Gallery Reading Rm (50,–); Sackler Octagon (400,120); Pre Raphaelite and 19th Century Gallery (500,200); Lodge (25,10); Rex Whistler Restaurant (–,90).

Tatsuso EC2   £M, (–,10)
32 Broadgate Circle   638 5863   (638 5864)
The basement of this modern City Japanese restaurant is much less slick than its ground floor and has two private rooms; one is a traditional tatami room (shoes off) and the other is in ordinary western style. / not Sat & Sun; Private Rm (–,10).

Private venues

The Tattershall Castle SW1   £B, (250,100,100)
Victoria Embankment   839 6548   (839 1139)
Permanently moored, along from Hungerford Bridge, this paddle-steamer Pub is something of a tourist paradise; they have a nightclub available privately early in the week, or the Bridge, which is an interesting but thin room with wonderful views; no outside decks can be taken privately. / 2 am; avail Sun, Mon & Wed; in-house caterers; Steamers Discotheque (250,100,100); Bridge (30,-).

Temple Island, Oxon   £M-E, (150,36)
c/o Henley Royal Regatta HQ
0491-572153   (0491-575509)
A fantasy location, this recently-restored Georgian island folly, picturesquely sited at the start of the Henley Regatta course, can be reached only by boat; difficult to beat for summer entertaining – if you want simple, picnic-type catering, you can arrange your own. / list of caterers; Inside (-,36); Marquee (150,-).

Theatre Museum WC2   £M-E, (250,70)
Russell St   836 7891
Housed in the old Covent Garden flower market, the V&A's collection of stage paraphernalia can be viewed prior to drinks or a meal in the pastiche Edwardian theatre-foyer in the basement; quite an interesting place for a theme event, but not, in itself, particularly festive.
/ midnight; hirer's choice of caterer; no amplified music; no disco; smoking restricted; Paintings Gallery (250,70).

Theatre Royal WC2   £M, (300,150)
Drury Ln, Catherine St   836 3687   (836 6465)
Archetypal, red walled and gilt decorated theatre, whose impressive Grand Salon is available daytimes and Sundays; the Stoll Moss VIP service (see 'Paint the town rouge') can organise functions (in, for example, the Royal Retiring Room) around the current show. / 1 am; avail Mon-Sat before 6 pm, all day Sun & if no current show; Gardner Merchant; Grand Salon (300,150); Royal Retiring Rm (40,20); Board Rm (40,20); Prince Of Wales Suite (16,-); Duke of Bedford (-,4).

Thierry's SW3   £M, (-,35)
342 King's Rd   352 3365
Very good, cosy, red-walled Chelsea bistro, offering assured cooking and good value; the basement is available privately.

Throgmorton's EC2   £B-M, (400,100,100)
27 Throgmorton St   588 5165
Amazing City labyrinth of underground restaurants and bars behind the Bank of England; the Oak Room, in the deepest bowels, is the most flexible room; the whole place is available for larger events (ie 150+) on a Saturday. / Short & Long Rm not Mon-Fri L, whole place Sat only, not Sun; in-house caterers; Oak Rm (200,100,100); Short Rm (100,-); Long Rm (80,-).

Private venues

Tower Bridge EC3 (300,–)
Tower Bridge   403 3761   (357 7935)
As we go to press, the major refurbishment of this miracle of c19 engineering makes its availability for functions unclear, but some resumption is likely; a return to previous arrangements would mean the long thin walkways between the towers could be used for receptions, while, with special permission, you could have drinks parties in the engine room. / Walkways (300,–); Engine Rm (50,–).

Tower Thistle E1 £M, (400,250,225)
St Katharine's Way   481 2575   (488 4106)
Views distinguish this fairly unremarkable, large '70s hotel; there is a magnificent close-up of Tower Bridge from the reception area to the Tower suite (which has its own entrance) and bird's-eye versions of the same vista (and of St Katherine's Dock) from the penthouse Raleigh and Spenser suites. / Tower Suite (York Rm & Lancaster Rm) (400,250,225); Raleigh or Spenser (100,24).

Trafalgar Tavern SE10 £B-M, (500,250,200)
Park Rw   081-858 2437   (081-858 2688)
Famous, riverside Greenwich institution (rather too large for a tavern) with magnificent views of the river through the high picture windows of the first-floor function rooms; the Nelson Room (site for the annual Ministerial Whitebait Dinner) is a large ballroom-type chamber; the Hawke & Howe Bar is themed like a galleon and a good place for a shindig. / 2 am; Nelson Suite (500,250,200); Hawke & Howe Bar (60,–).

Trinity House EC3 £M, (120,120,120)
Tower Hl   480 6601   (480 7662)
Fine, late-Georgian HQ of the UK's lighthouse authority; the Court Room is an elegant chamber, and the view of the Tower of London from the Library is magnificent.
/ 1 am; list of caterers; no smoking in Court Room; Court Rm (120,80); Library (102,120); Pepys Rm (–,28); Luncheon Rm (–,20).

La Truffe Noire SE1 £M, (55,40)
29 Tooley St   378 0621
This London Bridge French restaurant has high culinary aspirations, to which it generally lives up; while the upstairs dining room and bar are rather chi-chi, the downstairs bistro and bar are much more characterful and offer a small patio. / Upstairs Bar (–,16); Upstairs Dining Rm (–,40); Downstairs Bistro (55,35).

Turners SW3 £M, (–,55)
87-89 Walton St   584 6711
This recently refurbished, high quality Chelsea restaurant has a sensible arrangement whereby large parties can use a neighbouring art gallery for a pre-dinner reception.

Private venues

Turnmills EC1   £B, (500,150)
63b Clerkenwell Rd   250 3409
London's first nightclub with a 24-hour dance licence, this warehouse conversion in the middle of nowhere (north of Farringdon tube) is the ultimate stop for hardened all-night ravers; it's not at all seedy and its numerous areas offer flexibility for different sizes of party, either privately, or around other events.
/ hirer's choice of caterer, alcohol in-house.

Tuttons WC2   £B-M, (–,45)
11-12 Russell St   240 3228   (379 9979)
Below this large English brasserie overlooking Covent Garden, the white-painted brick cellars are very atmospheric; provisions are unadventurous staples.
/ Larger Cellar (–,45); Smaller Cellar (–,25).

22 Jermyn St SW1   £M, (–,12)
22 Jermyn St   734 2353
For an intimate setting for a lunch or dinner party the traditionally decorated sitting rooms of this small, soothing, understated, central suite-hotel are sometimes used by non-residents. / no amplified music; no dancing.

Twickenham Banqueting Centre TW1   £M, (400,200,200)
Rugby Rd, Twickenham   081-891 4565   (081-744 2104)
Pleasant, modern, purpose-built banqueting suite. / 2 am; Payne & Gunter; Rose Rm (400,200); West Pavilion Suite (350,175); Club Rm (150,75).

Two Chairmen SW1   £B, (50,22)
39 Dartmouth St   222 8694
Atmospheric, clubby top room in Westminster pub. / 11 pm; in-house caterers; no amplified music; no dancing.

University of London Boat Club SW15   £B, (100,70,70)
Putney Embankment   081-994 5928
The UL boathouse, just upstream from Chiswick Bridge, is large and rambling; it's not exactly a palace, but for a big knees-up it is affordable and in a good location; you can have summer barbecues. / midnight; Outdoors (250,–).

University of London Union WC1   £B, (400,–)
Malet St   580 9551   (436 4604)
Yoo-loo, as it's affectionately known, is not particularly beautiful (being tailor-made for big, studenty dance-parties) but does the job and is used, for instance, by local businesses at Christmas; the wine bar/restaurant (which also has a roof-terrace) is the area used most but there is also the larger Manning Hall. / 1 am; not Mon-Fri in term time; in-house caterers; Palms Wine Bar & Restaurant (250,–); Wine Bar (120,–); Manning Hall (400,–).

Private venues

University Women's Club W1 £M, (100,65)
2 Audley Sq   499 2268   (499 7046)
With a member's sponsorship, many kinds of events are possible amidst the faded gentility of this Mayfair establishment, which, especially at the weekend (when it can be hired in its entirety) would be ideal for smaller weddings; attractions include a pretty garden, a fine library and a secret room and terrace, entered through a fake set of library shelves. / 2 am; Dining Room Sat & Sun only; Eaton Management; Drawing Rm (60,50); Library (100,50); Red Rm (14,8); Dining Rm (–,65).

Upper Refectory Suite SW6 £B-M, (150,75)
King's College, Manresa Rd   351 6011   (352 7376)
On Carlyle Square, just off the King's Road, this suite of Old Common Room and Quiet Room is part of a King's College outpost built in the '60s; worth considering for more informal parties. / midnight; hirer's choice of caterer; no amplified music; no dancing.

Upstairs At 58 W11 £B, (120,–)
58 Ledbury Rd   229 4620
This comfortable, in-crowd Notting Hill club is in rooms over the Walmer Castle; on off-peak nights, they will consider making it available to non-members. / not Thu-Sat; no amplified music; no dancing.

Vanderbilt Hotel SW7 £M, (125,100,100)
68-86 Cromwell Rd   589 2424   (225 2293)
The listed Vanderbilt Suite of this South Kensington hotel is decorated in extraordinary French château style; there is other accommodation, but it is all much more business-like. / 2 am; Vanderbilt Suite(40,20).

Vat's WC1 £B, (130,60,40)
51 Lamb's Conduit St   242 8963
Convivial, street-level Bloomsbury wine bar, whose back-room restaurant is atmospheric, if slightly dated; at week-ends the whole place is up for hire. / Mon-Fri restaurant only; Restaurant (100,60,40).

The Vaults EC1 £B, (250,120,120)
Chiswell St   588 2642
Opposite The Brewery, this more-than-usually atmospheric vault wine bar occupies the other half of Whitbreads' old cellars; sections for up to 100 may be hired during the week and the whole place at the weekends. / midnight; whole place Sat & Sun only.

The Viceroy NW1 £B-M, (275,200,150)
3-5 Glentworth St   486 3515
The brick-and-plaster decor of this large, spacious Marylebone establishment is smart in a very un-European way; there is a private room, but the whole restaurant can be hired and claims a good trade in Indian celebrations – corporate and social. / 1.30 am; not Sat; Private Rm (35,20).

Private venues

Victoria & Albert Museum SW7   £E, (700,300)
Cromwell Rd   938 8366   (938 8367)
The high point here (until the Raphael Cartoon Court – one of London's most beautiful reception venues – re-opens at Christmas '94) is the wildly OTT Gamble and Morris suite, whose splendid, tiled Victorian interior housed the museum's original restaurant; larger dinners can be housed under the entrance Dome, usually used in conjunction with the Medieval Treasury, while for receptions there are various options amongst which the Toshiba Gallery and the Pirelli garden are most popular.
/ midnight; mostly eve only; list of caterers; no amplified music; no dancing; no smoking; some areas, no red wine; Gamble Rm (including Morris Rm) (400,190); Morris Rm (80,40); Raphael Cartoon Court (600,–); Dome, Medieval Treasury (& Pirelli Garden) (700,300); Other Galleries (250,–).

Victoria & Albert Museum Café SW7   £B-M, (300,150,120)
Exhibition Rd   581 2159
This café-with-a-museum-attached offers an atmospheric, lofty, brick-vaulted space in which many kinds of party are possible; its private room is suitable for smaller or daytime functions. / 1 am; whole place eve only; Milburns; Painted Rm (60,40).

Victoria Pump House SW8   £B, (100,–)
Battersea Pk   081-871 7530   (081-871 7533)
Prettily located by a lake in the South East corner of the park, this smallish square shaped tower (converted into four levels of pleasing small art galleries) is a good place for receptions; the upper two floors are often not available. / midnight; after 6 pm; hirer's choice of caterer; no smoking; Two Floors (60,–).

Villandry Dining Rooms W1   £M, (–,50)
89 Marylebone High St   487 3816   (486 1370)
This annex to a Marylebone foodie shop serves delicious, fairly simple dishes in plain, cramped but quite atmospheric surroundings; available for private hire at evenings and weekends.

Wag W1   £B, (600,–)
35 Wardour St   437 5534   (287 1747)
On the fringe of Chinatown, you can hire either floor of this well-known central nightclub; it's not scruffy but nor does it have the rather antiseptic feel of some of the major West End discos. / 7 am; hirer's choice of caterer, alcohol in-house; Bottom Floor (300,–); Top Floor (300,–).

Private venues

Waldorf Hotel WC2   £M, (800,420,420)
Aldwych   836 2400   (836 7244)
The most exciting possibility offered by this well-known, recently refurbished establishment is the use of its famous Palm Court (in conjunction with the Adelphi suite) for receptions and dinner-dances large enough to merit it; for smaller functions, Charter 1 is a pleasant room while the Aldwych is the private dining room with most character. / in-house caterers; Adelphi Suite &
Palm Court (800,420,360); Adelphi 1 (250,80); Adelphi 2 (150,60);
Adelphi 3 (350,150); Charter 1 (300,90); Charter 2 (400,280,230);
Somerset (60,50); Aldwych (60,45); Kingsway (48,20);
Westminster or Waterloo or Tavistock (20,12).

Walkers Of St James's SW1   £B, (200,150)
32a Duke St   930 0278
Modernised, but not too much, St James's cellar wine bar; the whole place can be used at weekends. / midnight; in-house caterers.

Wallace Collection W1   £E, (350,100)
Manchester Sq   935 0687
The Collection has recently begun to make rooms of its c18 palace available for stately receptions; most popular are the large Gallery 22 (key attraction – the Laughing Cavalier), the c18 French Painting, the Furniture and the Armour galleries; there is also a courtyard. / companies only;
11 pm; after 6.30 pm; list of caterers; no amplified music; no dancing;
no smoking; Great Gallery (350,100); Gallery 17 (50,24);
Arms and Armour (40,–).

Walton's SW3   £B, (–,24)
121 Walton St   584 0204
Romantic Chelsea English establishment whose consistently good cooking is reassuringly expensive; the distinctive decor of the upstairs private room is sumptuously vivid rather than overpowering.
/ Private Rm (–,24).

Wandsworth
Civic Suite SW18   £B, (800,800,550)
Wandsworth High St   081-871 6394   (081-871 7560)
Remodelled '30s suite of rooms, decorated quite comfortably in municipal style; ideal for a dinner-dance.
/ midnight; hirer's choice of caterer; Civic Suite (800,–); Civic Hall (475,–);
Banqueting Hall (400,–); Reception Rm (30,–); Vip Lounge (30,–).

Washington Hotel W1   £M, (110,100,80)
Curzon St   499 7000   (495 6172)
This modern, Mayfair establishment is less characterless than many of its type; the basement function room is only a little business-like and, for dinner-dances, use of the main restaurant is a possibility. / 1 am; in-house caterers;
Richmond Suite (110,60,45); Richmond 1 (40,25); Richmond 2 (60,30);
Restaurant (–,100,80).

Private venues

Watermen &
Lightermen's Hall EC3   £M, (110,72)
16-18 St Mary-at-Hill   283 2373   (283 0477)
An appealing mix of characterful charm, flexible attitude and a fair degree of stateliness (but not pomposity) makes this, the only Georgian livery hall, ideal for a wide variety of business and social events. / no 21sts;
in-house caterers; no amplified music; no dancing;
Freemen's Rm (110,72); Court Rm (70,37).

HQS Wellington WC2   £M-E, (200,125)
Victoria Embankment   600 5777   (600 2777)
The Master Mariners' hall, a Second World War naval sloop, boasts a fine location (opposite the Royal National Theatre); its hall, in the bowels of the ship, bears little sign of its floating location, but the other rooms are more nautical in flavour (with fine models of ships) and have an airy charm; the decks provide a fine location for a summer party. / 1 am; Chester Boyd; no amplified music;
Court Rm (200,125); Model Rm and Library (125,30);
Reception Area (50,-); Afterdeck (160,80).

Wessex House SW11   £B, (200,100)
1A St John's Hl   622 6818
Characterful, rather seedy dance hall at Clapham Junction, ideal for a real bop. / 3 am; in-house caterers.

West Wycombe Caves, Bucks   £M, (250,50,50)
West Wycombe Pk   0494-524411   (0494-471617)
A favourite out-of-town venue, these, the caves, which were the meeting place for the Hellfire Club, are available for many different kinds of function. / 2 am; after 6.30 pm;
hirer's choice of caterer; no smoking.

Westbury Hotel W1   £M, (150,100,80)
Bond St at Conduit St   629 7755   (495 1163)
This smartly located '50s hotel provides a series of unremarkable but pleasant function rooms. / 1 am;
Mount Vernon Rm (150,100,80); Pine Rm (120,80,60);
Brighton Rm (60,40); Regency Rm (40,20).

Westminster
Boating Base SW1   £B-M, (500,230,170)
136 Grosvenor Rd   821 7389
Located on the river by Dolphin Square, the base offers an unusually central location which can be turned to most types of function; it is not luxurious, but prices are reasonable and there are good facilities; they increase capacity in summer by tenting over the piers and for major events marquees may be erected in the adjoining park. / 1 am; hirer's choice of caterer; Total Facility
with Marquee (500,230); Total Facility (250,120);
Edgson Rm & Buttery (200,80); Edgson Rm (150,60); Crow's Nest (20,18);
marquee site.

Private venues

Westminster Cathedral Hall SW1   £B, (300,–)
42 Francis St   834 7452   (834 4257)
Refurbishing as we go to press, this currently dingy but potentially very fine Edwardian hall, behind the Cathedral, should re-emerge as a grand church hall, fit for most kinds of occasion; as it has interconnecting doors with the Archbishop's house, music cannot be particularly loud. / 10.30 pm; Wed & occasional Sat only; in-house caterers.

Westminster College SW1   £B, (200,150)
76 Vincent Sq   828 1222   (498 1097)
Bordering the square, this catering college's Escoffier room – a well-maintained period room – is fine for a small private dinner, or the faded-but-characterful, rather '50s restaurant can be used; obviously, the college prefer their students to cater but negotiation is sometimes possible.
/ 11.30 pm; not during college hrs; hirer's choice of caterer, though prefer students; Restaurant (200,150); Escoffier (50,32).

Westminster Conference Centre SW1   £M, (150,70)
12 Gt George St   222 7000   (222 9430)
Just off Parliament square, the Royal Institution of Chartered Surveyors offers traditional rooms and easy-going atmosphere rather than grandeur; most of the rooms would be fine for a dinner, with the small York room apparently particularly popular; most convivial is the Members' Club Room which is sometimes made available for receptions. / midnight; Crown Catering; no amplified music; no dancing; smoking restricted; Edinburgh Rm (60,–); York Rm (–,8); Cambridge Rm (80,22); Lancaster / Warwick (25,14); Gloucester (40,24); Members Club Rm (150,–); Restaurant (120,70).

Westway Studios W11   £M-E, (1200,500,500)
8 Olaf St   243 8410
Notting Hill film studios whose large, empty spaces are ideal for theme evenings; these are usually organised by on-site Buzz Productions (see entry in Party Planners).
/ hirer's choice of caterer; Studio 1 (750,500); Studio 2 (590,390); Studio 3 (300,200); Studio 4 (150,100).

The White Horse SW6   £B, (100,65)
Parsons Gn   736 2115
Well-known, atmospheric Parson's Green pub, overlooking the green; there is a large upstairs private room. / midnight.

White House Hotel NW1   £M, (175,100,90)
Albany St, Regent's Pk   387 1200   (388 0091)
Rather anonymous Marylebone hotel whose kitsch, subterranean Albany Room has most to recommend it. / in-house caterers; Albany (175,100,90).

Private venues

White Tower W1 £M, (–,16)
1 Percy St   636 8141
Wonderful creaky Greek restaurant, with solid cooking and ancient waiters, which is a great favourite for long liquid business lunches; there is a second floor private room in similar style to the restaurant proper.
/ Private Rm (–,16).

Whitechapel Art Gallery E1   £B-M, (500,60,60)
80-82 Whitechapel High St   377 5015   (377 1685)
This agreeable, spacious gallery on the fringes of the City is particularly suitable for early evening receptions.
/ eve only, not Wed; hirer's choice of caterer; alcohol in café area only; Meeting Rm (–,35); Café (–,60).

Whittington's EC4 £M, (80,40)
21 College Hl, Cannon St   248 5855
Cooking among the City's best (in an updated Anglo-French style) distinguishes this characterful cellar restaurant and wine bar, which is sited in Dick's old home. / 1 am; eve only, not Sat & Sun; Restaurant (–,40); Wine Bar (80,–).

Wilson's W14 £B
236 Blythe Rd   603 7267
This rather sparsely furnished Brook Green restaurant serves good British food, quite inexpensively; a downstairs private room is scheduled to open in late '93. / not Sat L & Sun D.

Wiltons SW1 £M-E, (–,16)
55 Jermyn St   629 9955
Clubby, old-established, expensive St James's English restaurant with a ground floor private room. / not Sun; Private Rm (–,16).

Winchester House Club SW15 £M, (180,130,180)
Lower Richmond Rd   622 6229
The first floor Victorian River Room extension of this Queen Anne house is an agreeable, light, airy room, perhaps particularly suited to wedding receptions; the club is a summer favourite on account of its pretty walled garden which borders the Thames. / 1 am; AM & PM Catering; River Rm (180,110,70); Turner Rm (–,16); River Lawn (–,–,180); Front Lawn (–,130); marquee site.

Private venues

WKD NW1   £B, (300,120,60)
18 Kentish Town Rd   267 1869
What was part of the Camden Town Sainsbury's car-park has been reclaimed with a mixture of breeze-blocks, corrugated metal and halogen lamps, with surprisingly stylish results; by day a veggie café, by night it is an up-and-coming blues/jazz venue; the mezzanine has a view of the stage and is worth considering for a private bash; for raves, you can hire a section of the car-park which they have yet to attend to. / 2 am; whole club, Mon & Tue only (poss Wed & Thur) – mezzanine, all week; in-house caterers; Ground Floor (150,–); Mezzanine (150,60,60); Car park (120,–).

World Trade Centre E1   £B-M, (500,350,280)
St Katherine's Way   488 2400   (265 0459)
Large glass walls give a fine view of St Katherine's marina from this hall – actually the Centre's foyer; the decor is rather dated. / 3 am; from 4 pm; in-house caterer.

Wynkyn de Worde EC4   £B, (–,10)
1 St Brides Pas, Bridge Ln   936 2554
Hidden off Fleet Street, this agreeable wine bar/restaurant has large windows overlooking a small terrace; available for parties at weekends. / Private Rm (–,10).

Xenon W1   £M-E, (700,–)
196 Piccadilly   734 9344   (734 3416)
Central discotheque, used for media-related parties (sometimes together with BAFTA), cabarets and product launches. / 3.30 am; not Tue, Fri, Sat nights; hirer's choice of caterer, alcohol in-house; Main Rm (600,–); Piano Bar (Gr Floor) (120,–).

Ye Olde Cheshire Cheese EC4   £B, (150,60)
145 Fleet St   353 6170   (353 0845)
Rambling, aged, atmospheric pub whose food is not at all bad and where many of the nooks and crannies can be used for lunch, dinners or drinks. / midnight; not Sun eve; Cellar Bar (150,60); Johnson's or Williams Rm (80,55); Johnson's Bar (70,–); Snug Bar (40,–); Director's Rm (25,10).

Zen SW3   £M, (–,20)
Chelsea Cloisters, Sloane Av   589 1781
This Chelsea Chinese restaurant is comfortably worn and produces enjoyable food; the ground-floor private room is similar to the main dining room. / Private Rm (–,20).

Zen Central W1   £M-E, (–,22)
20-22 Queen St   629 8089
London's smartest Chinese restaurant, in the centre of Mayfair, is also one of its best and the leading example of the slick style of the rest of its group; there is a private room behind the frosted glass at the rear. / Private Rm (–,22).

ZeNW3 NW3   £M, (–,25)
83 Hampstead High St   794 7863
Extremely stylish, minimalist Hampstead Chinese restaurant which has a top floor private room.
/ Private Rm (–,25).

Moving venues
....

Trains and boats and 'planes

Moving venues

TRAIN

Orient Express SW1   £E, (–,200)
Victoria Station   620 0003   (620 1210)
These nine famous carriages can take you anywhere in the UK – popular destinations being Bath, Leeds Castle and York; non-exclusive hirers are directed to Goodwood Travel who arrange trips on the 'three legends' – the Orient Express, Concorde and QEII (Goodwood Travel Ltd, Concorde Hs, Stour St, Canterbury, Kent CT1; tel 0227-763336, fax 0227-762417). / not Wed, Thur, Fri & Sun in summer.

BOATS

Parties on boats have a number of attractions. The sense of occasion which being afloat brings is certainly one of them, although, where parties on the Thames are concerned, the key factor, for many, is the absence of licensing restrictions.

Bateaux London WC2   £M-E, (–,160)
Victoria Embankment   925 2215   (839 7793)
One of the top two boats on the river, if a little touristy – see 'Paint the Town Rouge'.

Beric Sailing Barge E1   £B-M, (60,22)
St Katherine's Dock   220 7218
Aged Thames sailing barge, with a largely unmodernised hold, available either for static St Katherine's Dock parties, or functions on the move (but the boat must be back in dock by dusk). / Stationary (60,22); Afloat (40,22).

Catamaran Cruisers WC2   £B-M, (300,240,240)
Victoria Embankment   987 1185   (839 1034)
Largest operator on the river, in terms of numbers of boats; only their flagship, the Naticia, is actually a catamaran; (boats marked * have relatively limited galleys and are better suited to trips than full-blown entertaining). / hirer's choice of caterer, except Naticia; Naticia (300,240,240); Pridla (270,108); Chevening * (195,–); Abercorn (160,54); Valulla * (160,–); Viceroy * (100,–).

Chas Newen Marine Co SW15   £B-M, (12,12)
The Embankment   081-788 4587   (081-780 2339)
Some of the pencil-thin launches which follow the Boat Race are available for river trips; one has a covered section. / hirer's choice of caterer; no high heels; Panache, Majesty or Pomery (12,12).

Chelsea Luxury Charters SW10   £M-E, (12,12)
Chelsea Harbour   351 9680   (352 4534)
Agency which can provide small yachts, motor yachts or launches for luxury trips; happy to act as your agent for larger parties too.

Moving venues

City Cruises E14   £B-M, (250,110,110)
PO Box 67   515 4948   (538 8445)
The two larger boats (Mayflower Garden and Eltham) are suited to large floating hoe-downs, the smaller ones (Westminster and Halary) to more formal entertaining.
/ hirer's choice of caterer; Mayflower Garden (250,110,110); Eltham (175,90,90); Westminster (100,70,70); Halary (30,24).

Crown River Cruises EC4   £B-M, (120,60,60)
HMS President, Blackfriars Bridge   936 2033   (583 2840)
Family-run cruise company, which does slightly more corporate than social business. / hirer's choice of caterer; Suerita (120,60,60); Spirit of London (80,36,36).

Floating Boater W2   £B-M, (100,50,40)
Little Venice,1 Bishops Bridge Rd   724 8740
Trips from Little Venice to Camden; built in 1990, the Prince Regent is an Edwardian-style canal-boat, with all mod cons, and can cope with year-round entertaining; the 80 year old Lapwing narrow-boat is less weather-proofed and best suits summer receptions. / midnight; hirer's choice of caterer; Prince Regent (100,50,40); Lapwing (50,22).

Interceptor Launch, Essex   £M-E, (26,21)
46 Fairfield Ave, Upminster   0708-225570
This 57', twin-engined launch is about the only luxury cruiser of this capacity available for hire on the river.

Jason's Trip W9   £B-M, (75,120,24)
Blomfield Rd, Little Venice   286 3428   (266 4332)
For trips on Regent's Canal, the smaller Lace Plate accommodates more formal sit-down functions while the Jason or Holland narrow boats are more for trips and 'stand-ups'; their Courtyard base has an awning, and can also act as a venue in itself; standard time for a cruise is three hours. / midnight; hirer's choice of caterer; Lace Plate (30,24,24); Jason Holland (75,-); Holland (75,-); Courtyard (-,120).

The Lady Daphne SE1   £B-M, (60,26)
St Katherine's Dock   702 2457   (702 2252)
Seventy year old Thames sailing barge, whose interior has been quite comfortably modernised with sofas and a bar; parties may be held in dock or on the move (though the moving part must be over by dusk). / dusk; hirer's choice of caterer; Stationary (60,26); Afloat (40,26).

Maidenhead Steam Navn., Berks   £B-M, (110,50)
Taplow   0628-21770   (0628-773802)
Cruise the upper reaches of the Thames (Windsor to Marlow) on this company's two boats of very different ages – the SL Belle, a 99 year old cruiser restored along Edwardian lines or the 6 year old purpose-built Edwardian, which is less characterful but better kitted out for entertaining. / midnight; Edwardian (110,50); Belle (80,30).

Moving venues

Mainstream Leisure SW15   £B-M, (180,148,148)
32 Chartfield Ave   081-788 2669   (081-785 3406)
This established party-giving company run two boats; the well-known Elizabethan paddle-steamer is one of the top boats on the Thames; the Lady Rose barge plies the canals from Little Venice on the Regent's Canal; they are also happy to act as agents to organise a party on one of the other Thames boats. / midnight; Elizabethan (180,148,148); Lady Rose of Regents (50,36,36).

Thames Leisure, Kent   £B-M, (250,120,120)
Chislehurst   081-467 6314   (081-467 2060)
'Mom and pop' operation which does a wide range of events from corporate cruises to college parties. / hirer's choice of caterer; The Miyuki (250,120,120); The Tideway (100,40,40).

Thames Pleasure Craft EC3   £B-M, (150,75,50)
Tower Pier   709 9697   (481 3226)
The Golden Salamander is their boat more suited to formal entertaining, while, with its open top-deck, the Captain James Cook is better suited to summer cruising. / Golden Salamander (150,50,50); Captain James Cook (75,75).

Tidal Cruises SE1   £B-M, (250,220,220)
Lambeth Pier   928 9009   (401 2894)
Mid-ranking company offering four boats suitable for parties and cruises. / hirer's choice of caterer; Royal Princess (250,220,220); PV Viscountess (210,150,150); Hurlingham (180,132,132); Old London (130,106,106).

Turk Launches, Surrey   £B-M, (150,100,60)
Thames Side, Kingston   081-546 2434   (081-546 5775)
For trips above Richmond Lock (eg to Hampton Court); the Yarmouth Bell (complete with paddle-wheels) and Empress of India are c19 cruisers; the Kingston and Richmond Royale are tripping boats while the New Southern Belle is a Mississippi-style paddle-steamer. / 1 am; Empress Of India (75,40); Richmond Royale (50,-); Kingston Royale (90,-); New Southern Belle (150,100,60); Yarmouth Belle (125,40).

Woods River Services SE3   £M-E, (230,168,168)
PO Box 177, Blackheath   481 2711   (481 8300)
Few would dispute that the two-deck Silver Barracuda is the Queen of the River though her cost of hire largely limits use to corporate entertaining; the smaller Silver Dolphin is a slightly more affordable option. / Silver Barracuda (230,168,168); Silver Dolphin (90,68,68).

PLANE

Concorde   £E, (-,100)
British Airways, Gatwick Airport, Gatwick
0293 668213   (0293-668331)
As well as for destinations throughout the world, you can charter the big C for hops over the Bay of Biscay or the Channel and be home in time for tea; for non-exclusive hires enquire to Goodwood Travel (see Orient Express).

Action venues

Venues for competitive parties

Action venues

GO-KARTING

Pro-karting, as insiders like to call it, revolves (for amateurs anyway) around racing smallish single-engine Karts capable of about 40 mph.

Many of the tracks are indoors, and offer a variety of different race formats (lasting several hours), including heats (several short races) and endurance (one long race, sometimes with pit stops).

Prices for most sessions are something over £25.

Buckmore Park, Kent
Chatham   0634 201562   (0634 686104)
Off Junction 3 of the M2, this 700m track is set in 250 acres of Parkland; they have a host of equipment in addition to pro-karts.

Formula Fun W3
2606 Western Ave   081-752 0554
This old 40,000 sq ft (ex Littlewoods) warehouse has a 300m track; parties of up to 80 can be accommodated.

Formula 1 Chelsea SW6
191 Townmead Rd   371 0202   (371 7333)
New 300m circuit, in a converted warehouse by Chelsea Harbour, complete with tunnels, bank curves and a sophisticated electronic scoreboard; it is unusually smartly fitted out

Playscape Pro Racing SW4
Triangle Pl   498 0916   (498 6467)
The first indoor kart-racing company, they have two converted bus garage race-ways for battling it out at Clapham ('Silverstone') and Battersea ('Brandshatch').

Team Daytona W12
54 Wood Ln   081-749 2277   (081-749 7831)
There are two tracks in the same building (in what was an M&S warehouse) opposite the BBC; Daytona, a 400m circuit, is used for pro-karting; Indianapolis, an oval track, has more powerful cars decked out like Formula 1 races, and is for endurance-style races only; maximum numbers on both tracks – 66; they will go as late as 2am.

Action venues

PAINTBALL

A great stag night and corporate entertaining favourite; most days cost something round £40 for which you will generally be provided with goggles (which must be worn at all times), a gun, pellets and lunch.

Some people take this 'sport' very seriously and, if you are a smaller group, it is worth some caution as to who you are to be combined with to make up numbers. To make up a complete group of your own, you generally need twenty to thirty people.

Increasingly under 18s are being allowed to join in the fun. Some site-owners warn, though, that below 16 children generally take the whole thing rather too seriously.

Electrowerkz Two EC1
7 Torrens St   837 6419
For urban London Paintball, this 30,000 sq ft converted warehouse right next to Angel tube takes some beating; they have two packages - one for three, one for five hours; minimum age 16.

The Paintball Company NW7
40 Barnet Way   081-959 4440
Just outside the M25 (near junction 22) this site boasts six combat areas, with possibilities for jungle, village and bridge attacks; you need at least 30 to play alone; 14 is the absolute minimum age, 16 preferred.

Skirmish, Hants
Alton   0256-381628   (0256-381356)
About an hour outside London, David Shaylor's woodland paintball site has an excellent array of old WWII bunkers, trenches, etc; stag parties and the like might like to enquire after his barn, which he will sometimes make available for over-night stays – it's staggering distance from the local pub.

Skirmish, Bucks
14 Bourdon St W1   493 0270
Toby Halls is a well-reputed Paintball organiser who runs a 20 acre High Wycombe site.

Skirmish, Surrey
Dormansland   0342 870870
One of the first UK paintball companies (they claim) their site is close to junction 6 of the M25; they have 17 acres with a three story fort, jungle bridges and assorted other areas; kids' days are possible.

Action venues

Survival Game, Hants
Basingstoke   081-780 0480
Near Junction 5 of the M3, a 40 acre site; 16-18 year olds can sometimes be accommodated.

Survival Game, Kent
Dartford   0634 864173
They have two sites; urban takes place in the passages and grounds of a disused hospital on the outskirts; woodland is an area of gulleys, clearings and forts near Sidcup.

QUASAR
The latest, and most modernistic version of adult cowboys and Indians. Opposing teams are equipped with laser guns, the object being to zap the opposing team's chest-packs. The computer keeps score. Some of their branches run 'happy hours' with cut price rates at quiet times.

Quasar branches
Frobisher Rd, N8   081-348 9798
13 Coventry St, W1   734 8151
2 Hardwicks Way, SW18   081-871 9817
124 Ladbroke Gr, W10   243 8088
Edgware Rd, NW2   081-208 4141

Paint the town rouge

Festive spots around the capital

Paint the town rouge

TOP SPOTS

American Bar at the Savoy WC2
Strand   836 4343
Still, after half a century, the best cocktail bar in London and the best way of easing into a night on the town; jacket & tie.

Bateaux London WC2
Victoria Embankment   925 2215
London now has an answer to Paris's bateaux mouche – this hyper-modern flat deck cruiser plies the river for two hour lunch and dinner trips; it's not a cheap experience and a slightly touristy one, but it is all pretty well done.

Bibendum SW3
81 Fulham Rd   581 5817
If money presents no object, this would be many people's choice for a celebration dinner – the food and the ambience created by the glamorous modern setting are reckoned by many to be London's best.

Blakes SW7
33 Roland Gdns   370 6701
If you are intent on blowing as much money as possible on a single meal, this still fashionable, seductively decorated South Kensington basement restaurant has its attractions and its reputation as a romantic setting is unmatched

Blue Elephant SW6
4 Fulham Broadway   385 6595
London's best-known Thai restaurant is a large, dramatic, extremely romantic setting for a night out; the food sometimes reaches the heights – the bill never fails.

Bombay Brasserie SW7
Courtfield Clo, Glouc. Rd   370 4040
London's best-known Indian restaurant seems to be re-establishing a reputation for decent cooking, as well as the undoubtedly impressive scale of its setting; as long as you banish any thoughts that "Indian = cheap", this is quite a good place to party.

Le Caprice SW1
Arlington Hs, Arlington St   629 2239
See-and-be-seen, Manhattan-style St James's brasserie with an enormous reputation for glamour and consistency; its proportions cut it out more for smaller celebrations and even for these you should book well ahead.

China Jazz NW1
29-31 Parkway   482 3940
This stylish, modern Camden Town Chinese restaurant is a great party destination if cost is not a particular issue; the food is good, the service friendly and there is jazz nightly.

The Connaught W1
Carlos Pl   491 0668
For traditional celebration this gleaming panelled Edwardian dining room at this most discreet of Mayfair hotels is unsurpassed; the food, the ambience and, perhaps most of all, the service preserve the best of another age.

Paint the town rouge

Ivy WC2
1 West St   836 4751
Revamped in traditional style, this glamorous and comfortable Theatreland English restaurant has an ever-strengthening all-round reputation; popularity with theatre-goers (and those from the other side of the footlights) keeps it going till late and it's a good place for parties containing mixed age-groups.

L'Incontro SW1
87 Pimlico Rd   730 6327
Glamorous, opulent, noisy Pimlico Italian restaurant; its buzzing metropolitan style is its main strength.

Julie's W11
135 Portland Rd   229 8331
The eclectic decoration, seductive ambience and friendly service of this Holland Park restaurant labyrinth make it – despite food which is rather ordinary and expensive – one of London's most consistent party favourites.

Langan's Brasserie W1
Stratton St   493 6437
The magical atmosphere lingers at this Mayfair legend; some find that this compensates for high prices, average food and service which is sometimes rather star-struck.

Launceston Place W8
1A Launceston Pl   937 6912
Charm and discretion (not to mention pretty good food) are the keynote attractions of this particularly nicely located Kensington restaurant, which is one of the very nicest places for a civilised (but not stuffy) celebration.

Maroush W2
21 Edgware Rd   723 0773
It's not the greatest address, but this glitzy, Lebanese restaurant has established itself as one of the best of its type; there is a prix-fixe dinner with music, dancing and belly-dancing nightly.

Odette's NW1
130 Regent's Park Rd   586 5486
North London's only really glamorous, quality restaurant (and priced accordingly) is romantically decorated (mainly with a huge collection of mirrors) and a comfortable place for a civilised celebration.

Le Pont de la Tour SE1
Butlers Wharf   403 8403
The stunning view from this stylish Tower Bridge-side restaurant (especially from the window seats) combined with reliable Anglo-French food makes this, for many people, one of the best spots for a celebration.

Roof Gardens W8
99 High Street Kensington   937 7994
On Thursdays and Saturdays, with advance booking, groups of up to 25 can dine and dance at this intriguing nightclub venue – set among two acres of mature gardens eight floors above Kensington High Street.

Paint the town rouge

San Lorenzo SW3
22 Beauchamp Pl   584 1074
If you want a party illuminated by diamonds and stars, then this is still the restaurant for you; the cooking and – for mortals – the service can lack sparkle, and come at a glittering price.

Savoy Grill WC2
Strand   836 4343
This wonderful dining room exudes an unequalled sense of understated power and glamour; its reputation as a power-lunch spot risks overshadowing its night-time existence as one of the very best places for a celebration.

Savoy River Room WC2
Strand   836 4343
The most elegant dinner-dance in town tips off nightly at this extremely romantic dining room, whose best tables overlook the river; a great favourite for birthdays and anniversary celebrations.

Stoll-Moss Theatres VIP Service W1
21 Soho Sq   494 5222
London's largest theatre group offers packages for celebrating around a show, which have the major advantage of being bookable the day before; the evening includes being greeted and looked after throughout – champagne, nibbles and, if desired, meals in private rooms (sometimes the royal retiring rooms); they stress their flexibility to accommodate larger groups.

The Ritz W1
150 Piccadilly   493 8181
One of London's few pleasant grown-up dinner-dance spots; to dine in the magnificent Louis XVI restaurant is one of London's most magical experiences and you can trip the night away in the famous Palm Court.

The River Café W6
Thames Wf, Rainville Rd   385 3344 am; 381 8824 pm
Some find the atmosphere at this trendy Hammersmith restaurant a little spare for a celebration, especially at the price; however, the trek to its obscure location and its glamorous reputation give a sense of occasion and the modern Italian cooking is, at its best, extraordinary.

Windows on the World Hilton Hotel W1
22 Park Ln   493 8000
For an expensive dinner-dance evening in glitzy surroundings, the Hilton's rooftop restaurant is uniquely well equipped, and the view is magnificent; alternatively, a drink in the cocktail bar is a good prelude to dinner elsewhere.

Zen Central W1
20-22 Queen St   629 8089
Modern Mayfair surroundings and some of London's best oriental cooking made this stylish, airy restaurant a natural (but, some can find, rather sterile) place for a celebration.

Paint the town rouge

MID-PRICE PLACES

Albero & Grana SW3
89 Sloane Ave   225 1048
Fashionable, stylish, buzzing Chelsea Spanish restaurant – ideal for a big dinner party (as long as you don't want to talk to each other); tapas parties in the trendily decorated bar are an informal, less expensive option.

Anna's Place N1
90 Mildmay Park   249 9379
One of North London's most notable long-running restaurants, Anna Hegarty's individualistic spot offers unusually good food of an unusual type – Scandinavian – and not too expensively; an airy place with a very cosy atmosphere.

Barbarella 1 & 2
1) 428 Fulham Rd, SW6   385 9434
2) 43 Thurloe St, SW7   584 2000
For an evening combining dining and disco, these South Kensington and Fulham cellars (done out in what might have been good taste 20 years ago) are some of the better non-membership places in town; and considering it is not the main point, the food is really quite good.

Beach Blanket Babylon W11
45 Ledbury Rd   229 2907
For trendily stylish decor, this lively bar/restaurant is one of London's top places; on the culinary front, the basement dining-room fails to live up to the rest of the experience, but for a fun meal you could do worse than taking over their 'gothic' section.

Belgo NW1
72 Chalk Farm Rd   267 0718
Extraordinary decor, waiters dressed as monks, a large collection of enjoyable Belgian Beers and a decent moules-based menu make a meal at this much talked about Camden Town restaurant something of an occasion; it's noisy, though.

Belvedere W8
Holland Hs, off Abbotsbury Rd   602 1238
A magical setting, overlooking Holland Park (floodlit by night) is the great strength of this airy, stylishly decorated restaurant which does a lot of party business; the modern style cooking can tend to unexciting.

Benihana
100 Avenue Rd, SW3   586 9508
77 King's Rd, SW3
A Swiss Cottage spectacle, this huge modern teppan-yaki (each table has a grill with its own chef) offers a flash but fun night out and for a snip (currently £12.95) the entire staff will join you in celebration with a rendition of the Benihana Happy Song; a new Chelsea basement sprouting of the chain is scheduled for after we go to press, promising a slightly younger atmosphere than at Swiss Cottage.

Paint the town rouge

Blue Print Café SE1
Design Mus, Butler's Whf   378 7031
Arguably London's best view from a restaurant makes a table at Terence Conran's striking Design Museum café (especially on the outside terrace) a memorable place to toast a special event.

Boardwalk W1
18 Greek St   287 2051
Young, fun Soho bar/restaurant (a few still remember it as Bill Stickers) serving a menu of mostly American staples.

Le Bouchon Lyonnais SW8
38 Queenstown Rd   622 2618
This consistent Battersea bistro is usually packed, often with parties of up to a dozen or so, which it absorbs quite efficiently.

Brixtonian SW9
11 Dorrell Pl   978 8870
For a party away from the West End beaten track, try this stylish late night Rhum bar off Brixton High Street; it has quite a lot of street-cred and not the least of its attractions is a range of over 100 rums; jazz nightly.

Brixtonian Backyard WC2
Neal's Yd   240 2769
An offshoot of the Brixton original, this Covent Garden spot brings a little bit of Caribbean colour to grey old London; the colourful modern bar is overlooked by a romantic, colonial-style dining room.

Buzkash SW15
4 Chelverton Rd   081-788 0599
With its walls crammed with ethnic clobber, this Putney Afghan restaurant is an atmospheric place; the unusual food is actually very good and a visit here is a good bet for a fun group experiment.

Café du Marché EC1
22 Charterhouse Sq   608 1609
Oddly located in a designer-rustic warehouse conversion, between Smithfield and the Barbican, this French restaurant is often praised for its combination of good food, buzzing atmosphere and jazz most nights – what more could you want for a party?

Café Lazeez SW7
93-95 Old Brompton Road   581 9993
Fashionable, but not too expensive, this South Kensington café/restaurant offers unusual, subtle dishes of Indian inspiration; they sometimes have live music and this is a very good place for a stylish but informal party.

Café Pacifico WC2
5 Langley St   379 7728
This noisy, genuine-American Tex-Mex Covent Garden restaurant has seen many competitors come and go – it remains a classic party destination; as it usually takes 45 minutes to get a table (no booking after early evening), and as there is nothing to do but drink Margueritas, many find themselves in the party mood long before they sit down.

Paint the town rouge

The Canteen SW10
Chelsea Harbour   351 7330
If you like a walk on the wild side, a trip to Chelsea Harbour provides not only a sense of occasion but also the opportunity to sample cooking inspired by star chef Marco Pierre White at quite reasonable cost and in elegantly glamorous surroundings.

Caravan Serai W1
50 Paddington St   935 1208
This cosy, richly rug-decorated Marylebone Afghani restaurant offers a good spot for a party, unusual both for its cuisine and its decor.

Caspers W1
6 Tenterden St   493 7923
The darling of stag and hen nights – if you fancy someone on the next table just pick up the 'phone (every table has one) and tell them so; yep, supremely tacky but extremely popular; as you would expect in so upmarket an establishment, no jeans.

Comedy Store W1
28a Leicester Sq   0426-914433
Well-known Leicester Square dive; food and surroundings are basic, but on the humorous side it's a reliable evening; there is no booking and you can only buy one ticket per person; there are late shows (around midnight) on Fridays and Saturdays.

The Criterion W1
Piccadilly Circus   925 0909
This striking, recently-reopened, marbled restaurant, on Piccadilly Circus, offers great bang-for-the-buck in the Sense of Occasion department and the Californian/ Italian cooking is pretty good; avoid early in the week though – on a quiet night the place can seem a bit sepulchral; the rear terrace bar is an excellent spot to start the evening off.

Cuba W8
11 Kensington High St   938 4137
Kensington Bar/restaurant – the restaurant upstairs is no great shakes but the party atmosphere in the basement continues until quite late.

Cuba Libre N1
72 Upper St   354 9998
This quite lavishly decorated, swinging Islington restaurant consistently attracts a fun, lively crowd, making it a good place for louder celebrations.

Daphne's SW3
110-112 Draycott Ave   589 4257
Chelsea restaurant with a modern Italianate menu and impressive decor; its real strength however is that it offers a level of glamour quite unusual in London and is not tremendously expensive; a particularly good place for smaller parties.

Paint the town rouge

Dell'Ugo W1
56 Frith St   734 8300
This buzzing, modish Soho restaurant has a name for innovative and not too expensive cooking; there are three floors – it gets quieter (and more expensive) as you go up.

Dog House W1
187 Wardour St   434 2116
Soho cellar which is a hip mix of day-glo café and cramped funky cocktail bar; fun, and, if you stick around for dinner, the food is surprisingly good.

Dover Street Wine Bar W1
8-9 Dover St   629 9813
Of its type, this very atmospheric Mayfair dine and dance cellar is the best in London, with office parties and courting couples somehow co-existing quite happily; live music and disco nightly; no jeans.

Drones SW1
1 Pont St   235 9638
Glamorous, extremely pretty Belgravia bistro in a conservatory; as a culinary experience, it's on the expensive side, but it does have a lot of charm, and there is sometimes a cabaret.

Fakhreldine W1
85 Piccadilly   493 2424
Glitzy, rather dated, Mayfair Lebanese restaurant notable for its day-time view of Green Park; if you want a late party its particular attraction is that it keeps serving well after midnight.

La Famiglia SW10
7 Langton St   351 0761
This World's End Italian restaurant has been packing in the in-crowd for over two decades and remains one of the most consistent spots for parties of all sizes; the down-side is that it's pricey and that you may not be encouraged to linger.

First Floor W11
186 Portobello Rd   243 0072
While the downstairs bar is hip, almost to the point of intimidating, the upstairs New York-style café is a cool, comfortable setting – this combines with the good cooking to make it a very good party spot.

Florians N8
4 Topsfield Parade   081-348 8348
This extremely popular, informal Crouch End Italian is notable for the quality of its food and its buzzing atmosphere – a really good place for a decent party meal which should not break the bank.

Formula Veneta SW10
14 Hollywood Rd   352 7612
This Chelsea/Fulham border Italian restaurant is, on a good night, one of the best places for a stylish, young-at-heart night out.

Paint the town rouge

Frederick's N1
106 Camden Pas   359 3902
The scale of this attractive Islington restaurant-institution marks it out as a rather special place – especially for a place serving "real" food – and the place can absorb several parties at once without really noticing.

Gasworks SW6
87 Waterford Rd   736 3830
Despite its calculatedly disinterested service and drab food, this antique-filled Fulham spot has quite a following on account of its extraordinary, decadent atmosphere; not recommended for small groups – the enormous central table in the main room, for around a dozen or more, is the only table to have.

Glaisters SW10
4 Hollywood Rd   351 1011
The cooking at this Fulham/Chelsea bistro is nothing special but the place is very cosy and benefits from a large walled garden; it shouldn't break the bank either.

Jazz Café NW1
5 Parkway   916 6060
Styled with panache, the modern decor of this Camden Town spot could not be further from the dark and smokey cliché image of a jazz joint; there is a large balcony bar/restaurant, serving good and not expensive fare, which overlooks the stage.

Joe Allen WC2
13 Exeter St   836 0651
Theatreland American cellar-restaurant, famous for its good atmosphere and full till late (last orders, 1 am) – early booking is advised; not inexpensive and they don't take credit cards.

Jongleurs at the Cornet SW11
49 Lavender Gdns, SW11   924 2766
Jongleurs at Camden Lock NW1
Middle Yd   924 2766
On Thursday, Friday and Saturday nights, you can take in a comedy show, dine and disco all in one place at these very popular comedy-cabaret places; Battersea is more characterful, Camden more comfortable.

Kennys
2a Pond Pl, SW3   225 2916
70 Heath St, NW3   435 6972
Comfortable, Chelsea and Hampstead Cajun joints, with a lively, successfully transplanted American atmosphere; they carry on till fairly late.

Kensington Place W8
201-205 Kensington Ch St   727 3184
Not a place for a soothing gathering, but this huge, modern, glass-fronted restaurant near Notting Hill Gate is one of London's best, and not particularly expensive; be prepared for a high noise level though and, if you want to linger, it is probably better to book a late table.

Paint the town rouge

Madame Jo Jos W1
8 Brewer St   734 2473
Transvestite Soho cabaret so unthreatening you could take your grandmother; a giggle for office parties and the like – there is a disco at the end of the evening.

Mainstream Leisure SW15
32 Chartfield Ave   081-788 2669
If you are stuck for inspiration, consider this 25 year old party-planning company; some of their group evenings sound a mite tacky, but they offer a very wide range of ideas.

Le Midi SW6
488 Fulham Rd   386 0657
This fairly new Fulham Provençal restaurant – modern and relaxed in style – is good all round and an excellent place for a party.

Motcomb's SW1
26 Motcomb St   235 9170
Very welcoming, picture-hung, quite tightly-packed Belgravia basement; the attraction and the crowd are fairly traditional English but, for a fairly mature party, this place has a very good atmosphere.

Mr Wing SW5
242-244 Old Brompton Rd   370 4450
The best known "party-Chinese" restaurant in London – famous for its jolly atmosphere and the decor of its delightfully tacky jungle-basement.

Nam Long SW5
159 Old Brompton Rd   373 1926
The favourite of a fashionable, younger crowd, this stylish, low-lit South Kensington cocktail bar and restaurant is a great place for parties of up to a dozen or so.

Nikita's SW10
65 Ifield Rd   352 6326
The alcoves, or small main restaurant, of this richly decorated basement Russian restaurant on the Chelsea/Fulham border provide a perfect, very unusual, spot for an intimate party; people always seem to talk about the vodka when they mention this place.

The Nosh Brothers SW6
773 Fulham Rd   736 7311
Fairly recent, sparely decorated restaurant with unusually good, simple food, attracting a pretty trendy crowd – though physically situated in Fulham, the place's spiritual home is Notting Hill.

Orso WC2
27 Wellington St   240 5269
Central London's best-known modern Italian restaurant – in a Covent Garden basement – bubbles on till late and there is the odd famous face about; pressure on tables means it's best to book late if you don't want the party to be moved on; they don't take cards.

Paint the town rouge

Palio W11
175 Westbourne Grove   221 6624
This lofty, modern multi-level Notting Hill restaurant (under the same management as Soho's Dell'Ugo) offers good food, quite a lot of style and a good atmosphere.

Palookaville WC2
13A James St   240 5857
Covent Garden jazz venue whose brick-lined cellar offers a reasonably priced night out, or is quite a good post-dinner spot.

PJ's SW3
52 Fulham Rd   581 0025
Always packed, this buzzing Chelsea Euro-Sloane home-from-home offers upbeat atmosphere and good American-inspired food; perfect for young-at-heart parties of any age.

Planet Hollywood W1
13 Coventry St   287 1000
For a giggle, it might be worth the queue (bookings for 50 and up only) to munch quite expensive burgers in this well-executed, Tinseltown-setting, star-backed burgeria.

Players Theatre WC2
14 Villiers St   839 1134
Authentically Victorian (in concept) music hall near Charing Cross; after the show, you can dine on the premises simply but quite inexpensively.

Quaglino's W1
16 Bury St   930 6767
Monumental, instantly famous St James's restaurant whose sheer scale makes it a special place; there is music and dancing till 3 am on Fridays and Saturdays.

Rebato's SW8
169 South Lambeth Rd   735 6388
This out-of-the-way Vauxhall Spanish establishment is a fun spot worth the hike; the food is actually better in the Tapas bar, but the restaurant (go for the Paella) is lively, genuinely continental in feel and good for a relaxed celebration.

Ronnie Scotts W1
47 Frith St   439 0747
Soho's international-standard jazz venue offers an excellent place to cap an evening's celebration; admission also includes a disco and the place goes on till 3 am.

La Rueda SW4
68 Clapham High St   627 2173
Popular, big, boisterous Spanish restaurant – a good place for groups to let their hair down.

Sandrini SW3
260 Brompton Rd   584 1724
Glamorous Brompton Cross Italian restaurant, comfortable, well spaced, with good food and somehow not quite as expensive as you might expect – a good place for a more civilised sort of gathering.

Paint the town rouge

School Dinners Restaurant W1
1 Robert Adam St   486 2724
Would-be fantasy restaurant, where schoolgirls in gym-slips and suspenders serve lads' nights-out with spotted dick, verbal abuse and six-of-the-best; only the very mature find no enjoyment but most find it expensive and some complain of being pestered for tips.

Smollensky's Balloon W1
1 Dover St   491 1199
This younger scene, Mayfair restaurant has a regularly packed, characterful, cocktail bar; the American-style restaurant is a good place for a reasonably priced, central get-together.

Smollensky's on the Strand WC2
105 Strand   497 2101
Luxuriously fitted, large American formula bar/restaurant, on the fringe of Covent Garden, with a good atmosphere; it carries on until quite late and you can dance at the weekends.

Snows on the Green W6
166 Shepherd's Bush Rd   603 2142
Up and coming Brook Green restaurant, whose modern Italian cooking is generating a more-than-local reputation; perhaps not the most buzzing restaurant but a good party choice for people who care for their stomachs.

Sofra W1
18 Shepherd's Mkt   493 3320
Very good all-round, this Turkish restaurant in Shepherd's Market has bright decor, pleasant service and good food – a good place for parties of all sizes.

Tiroler Hut W2
27 Westbourne Gr   727 3981
If you are looking for a laugh, you can yodel the night away to the strains of the accordion at this Bayswater chalet restaurant.

Wembley, Greyhound Racing NW10
Wembley Stadium   081-902 8833
Wimbledon Greyhound Stadium SW17
Plough Ln   081-946 5361
A great venue for the armchair (well, dining chair) sportsman – you can watch the racing while you eat and you don't even need to move to bet (they come to you); this combination of excitement and inaction makes this a popular spot for celebrations and entertainment generally.

Wódka W8
12 St Alban's Grove   937 6513
Success has brought recent expansion at this welcoming, modish Kensington restaurant popular for smaller parties; the Polish food is surprisingly sophisticated and there is a large selection of flavoured vodkas to fuel the festivities.

Paint the town rouge

CHEAP AND CHEERFUL

Andrew Edmunds W1
46 Lexington St   437 5708
Welcoming, laid-back cramped wine bar/restaurant, in a characterful Soho townhouse which serves top-notch inexpensive modern British fare – gastronomically, its basement is one of best spots for a cheap and cheerful party.

Anemos W1
32 Charlotte St   636 2289
In spite of Greek fare which is not exactly what you would call special this beery place remains a favourite for stag and hen nights – learn the song before you go: A-ne-mos, A-ne-mos, A-ne-mos – A-ne-mos, A-ne-mos, A-ne-mo-o-os

Bar Madrid (incorporating Viva Brazil) W1
4 Winsley St   436 4649
A cross between a nightclub and bar, this large, swinging Spanish scene, just off Oxford Street, has quite good dancing but is a fun place just to hang around drinking.

Ben's Thai W9
93 Warrington Crescent   266 3134
For an inexpensive dinner, with a sense of occasion, this good Maida Vale Thai restaurant – in a charming, big Victorian room over a pub – is an excellent deal.

Big Easy SW3
334 King's Rd   352 4071
Good value, fun and boisterous, this Chelsea crab-shack is usually packed; they have special group menus - huge portions served on overturned dustbin lids - and the seafood can be quite good; beware the expensive cocktails which are not quite as wicked as they sound.

Bon Ton Roulet SW2
43 Tulse Hill   678 0880
This popular, inexpensive South London restaurant has recently moved and its new basement premises have alcoves ideal for parties of up to 16; no-corkage BYO and real food are not the least of the attractions.

Café Météor W6
158 Fulham Palace Rd   081-741 5037
Good French food, reasonable prices (and, usually, jazz) combine to make this Hammersmith brasserie a great budget party buy.

Le Casino SW1
77 Lower Sloane St   730 3313
Luxurious it ain't and the food's nothing to write home about, but this basic-but-fun cellar, off Sloane Square, is a huge favourite for groups;

Da Mario SW7
15 Gloucester Rd   584 9078
The reliability of the Pizza Express chain and the attraction of a cavernous basement disco combine to make this as cheap a (reasonably pleasant) spot as you will find for a big dine and dance party.

Paint the town rouge

Down Mexico Way W1
25 Swallow St   437 9895
An extraordinary place, a stone's throw from Piccadilly Circus; now an inexpensive Mexican restaurant, it was London's first Spanish restaurant and has an amazing tiled '20s interior; the food is no great shakes but the bar goes on till late and there are Latin disco nights Monday, Friday and Saturday.

Efes Kebab Houses 1 & 2 W1
80 Great Titchfield St   636 1953
175-177 Great Portland St   436 0600
The appeal of these Turkish Marylebone institutions is surprisingly wide-ranging; Efes I is darker, quieter and more relaxing – Efes II is the place for music and belly dancing; either way the party feast of meze and kebabs is very well prepared and good value.

Gourmet Diner W1
27 Wardour St   287 6578
A nice mixture of local atmosphere with smarter than usual decor make this one of the best places for a night on the Chinatown.

Hard Rock Café W1
150 Old Park Lane   629 0382
For a loud burger party, with a sense of occasion, this remains, after two decades, London's No 1 spot; if you want to spoil the fun, you can call ahead to avoid the queue.

Harvey's Café SW10
358 Fulham Rd   352 0625
This Chelsea/Fulham borders restaurant (converted from a pub) serves uncommonly good (modern British) food, for its type; the room is fashionably spartan.

House on Rosslyn Hill NW3
34a Rosslyn Hill   435 8037
Hampstead young crowd's characterful hang-out, well known for its bustling atmosphere.

Joe's Brasserie SW6
130 Wandsworth Bridge Rd   731 7835
Raucous young scene Fulham brasserie, wittily decorated; a good place for a "can't hear myself think" sort of party.

Kalamaras Micro W2
66 Inverness Mews   727 5082
Slightly tatty, charming Bayswater taverna always packed with locals; inexpensive and BYO (but not beer) – ideal for a cosy, cramped feast.

Kettners W1
29 Romilly St   437 6437
Still unrivalled, this huge, rambling Soho Edwardian restaurant – now with an inexpensive pizza and grills menu – brings an unequalled sense of occasion to budget meals and is particularly useful as an inexpensive kicking-off point for grander occasions (eg pre-ball dinners); the champagne bar provides the opportunity to blow the economies made in the restaurant.

Paint the town rouge

Khan's W2
13-15 Westbourne Gr   727 5420
This huge notorious Bayswater experience – a cross between an Indian Railway station and McDonalds – is good for a cheap, chaotic group meal; not a place for a whole evening though – they don't exactly encourage you to sit around.

Lemonia NW1
89 Regent's Park Rd   586 7454
One on its own – good, affordable Greek food and friendly service are the hallmarks of this large fashionable, Primrose Hill super-taverna.

Marine Ices NW3
8 Haverstock Hl   485 8898
This Camden Town Italian restaurant is always packed with representatives of all generations; there is a pizza and pasta menu, but the real point is the ices and sorbets, which are the best in London.

Nacho's
147-149 Notting Hill Gate W11   221 5250
79 Heath St NW3   431 0866
212 Fulham Rd SW10   351 7531
8 Battersea Sq SW11   924 6450
Tex-Mex restaurants that are the best of their type in London (frankly, something of an indictment of the capital); they are tailor-made for large, affordable gatherings.

New World W1
1 Gerrard Pl   434 2508
Once inside this enormous Chinatown restaurant, you could be in Hong Kong; it's all pretty unsophisticated but the novelty and festive atmosphere of trolley dim-sum particularly make a lunch party worth considering.

Osteria Basilico W11
29 Kensington Park Rd   727 9957
Trendy Notting Hill restaurant which attracts a good young following with its fashionably rustic decor and reasonable prices; the food in not really the attraction.

Palms–on–the–Hill W8
3 Campden Hill Rd   938 1830
This Kensington salad, burgers and pasta café is a swinging place of its type and is tough to better for a cheapo dinner.

Pizza on the Park W1
11 Knightsbridge   235 5550
By Hyde Park Corner, this high-ceilinged Pizza Express showpiece has a very enjoyable, atmosphere; a natural choice for an economical party at a smart address and the basement is quite a well-known jazz venue.

Pizza Pomodoro SW3
51 Beauchamp Pl   589 1278
This must be one of the most famous places in London to be almost completely invisible; a seedy, cramped Knightsbridge basement, where good pizza and live music are served up till late and there is an almost Latin buzz; larger parties will probably not be able to sit together.

Paint the town rouge

Ruby in the Dust
70 Upper St, N1   359 1710
102 Camden High St, NW1   485 2744
Young and fun bar/restaurants with a friendly atmosphere buoyed by cocktails and beers; the menu is a hotch-potch based around Tex-Mex and burgers.

Rumours WC2
33 Wellington St   836 0038
This throbbing Covent Garden cocktail bar is the closest London comes to a singles bar; if that does not sound too appealing, the more restrained basement is still not a bad place to start an evening's revels.

Star of India SW5
154 Old Brompton Rd   373 2901
London's most fashionable, but certainly not best, Indian restaurant's main strengths are its extraordinary Roman-style decor and the fact that it is always full – making it a reliable, characterful spot for a party.

Texas Lone Star SW7
154 Gloucester Rd   370 5625
This cavernous, noisy South Ken Tex-Mex saloon is wearing its years well; cheap, atmospheric and with both kinds of music – country and western – its main drawback is that it is almost invariably full.

Wine Gallery SW10
49 Hollywood Rd   352 7572
This cosy, unchanging Chelsea/Fulham fringe wine bar/ restaurant is particularly popular with a younger crowd; the downstairs divides into a number of semi-private areas ideal for informal dinners.

Services

All the services you need to add sparkle to your party

Services – Food & wine

CATERERS

Most of the caterers listed here hold themselves out to do most types of catering. We have tried to suggest why each of them may be more or less suitable for any particular event although caterers are generally only too pleased to have the opportunity to quote and will indicate if, for any reason, an occasion is not one for them.

The following list is necessarily selective and omits many excellent local firms who do not generally take on anything but small dinner or drinks parties. For such events, the best recommendation is to ask around. For larger events too, don't hesitate to speak to friends or others who have organised functions recently.

Different caterers charge for food, wine, service and crockery hire in different ways. When comparing companies, it is important to ensure that you are comparing like with like – make sure, for example, that both estimates include VAT.

Almost all caterers offer some degree of party planning service and can, to differing extents, co-ordinate a marquee, flowers and even entertainments in addition to the catering. If you want help with these, you should sound the caterers out on their approach at an early stage.

Above the Salt
93 Calbourne Rd SW12   081-673 5279   (081-944 7006)
Smaller events are the forte of this caterer particularly known for its canapés.

The Admirable Crichton
6 Camberwell Trading Est, Denmark Rd SE5
733 8113   (733 7289)
Acknowledged by its peers as one of the leading firms in the outside catering business; grand and extraordinary events are a forte.

Jean Alexander Food Flair
Riverway, Guildford, Surrey GU3
0483-571326   (0483-302496)
Medium-sized but diverse operation which combines some City work with a good measure of private business of all sizes.

AM & PM Catering
15-17 Ingate Pl SW8   622 6229   (720 8157)
Small but professional catering outfit which puts particular emphasis on service and visual presentation.

Beeton Rumford
The Richmond Suite, Earl's Ct Ex Hall SW5
370 8164   (370 8192)
Part of the P&O Group, this young company specialises in banqueting and the majority of its work is large scale City and corporate.

Blue Ribbon Catering Services
205 Camberwell Rd SE5   703 3517   (701 5103)
Traditional, small-scale family catering operation; not too expensive.

Food & wine – Services

Brazilian Party Co
27 High St W5   081-840 5522   (081-840 5522)
Just the catering, or, if you choose, music and dancing too, for parties of 30 to 250.

Butlers Catering
6 Holland Pk Mansions, Holland Pk Gdns W14
602 0390
Celia Butler has been in the business for over 20 years; she does all the cooking herself, but can arrange to cater for several hundred guests.

By Word of Mouth
22 Glenville Mews, Kimber Rd SW18
081-871 9566   (081-871 3691)
Top caterers; they stress their flexibility and their willingness to take on all types of work.

Café Suze
1 Glentworth St NW1   486 8216   (935 3827)
Kiwi caterer for small to medium size functions; antipodean ingredients are used when possible.

Canapé Direct
Unit 7, 81 Southern Rd W10   081-964 0240
An interesting selection of hot and cold canapés, delivered to your door.

Caroline's Kitchen
13 Cornwall Cr W11   229 4114
Everything is catered for, but small to medium sized buffets are the speciality.

Castle Catering Services
57-66 King James St SE1   928 3242   (821 1703)
Large, traditional, mainly corporate caterer, tending to do bigger-scale events.

Chariots of Fire
Unit 50, Metrostore Centre, Townmead Rd SW6
731 6802
Barbecue specialists.

Chelsea Catering Company
305 Fulham Rd SW10   351 0538   (376 5637)
Chelsea traiteur, in business for half a century, offering a fairly traditional range of dishes, with or without staff and equipment.

Classical Cuisine
23 Lavender Hill SW11   738 1688   (924 7510)
Simple dishes and good presentation are the twin aims of this recently established caterer for small to medium size events.

The Tessa Corr Catering Co
30 Beckwith Rd SE24   274 6196   (274 9514)
Larger-scale work is the speciality of this well-established company, quite a lot of whose work is arts-related.

Crown Catering
236 London Rd, Romford, Essex RM7
0708-744101   (0708-742480)
Mainly corporate and institutional caterers, often on a fairly large scale; they also do a lot of corporate hospitality work.

Services – Food & wine

Culinary Arts
67 Muswell Hill N10   081-883 3799
Not only vegetarians avail themselves of Nadine Abensur's non-meat catering; weddings and media-related work are specialities.

Danish Catering
25 Red Lion St WC1   430 1557   (430 1557)
Danish Catering, probably the oldest name in Scandinavian catering, recently merged with up-and-coming caterer Rosa de Souza; smörgaasbord, canapés and confectionery.

Dinner Jackets Catering
Unit 11, Gun Wharf Business Centre, Old Ford Rd E3   081-980 6814
Middle market caterer doing a mix of corporate work and weddings.

Eatons
7 Willow St EC2   729 5447   (729 7199)
One of the larger companies – boardroom, banqueting and outside caterers.

Feathers
108 New Bond St W1   499 9192   (499 7517)
Many large corporate clients go to this Liverpool-based company, which provides a national banqueting and events service.

Annie Fryer Catering
134 Lots Rd SW10   351 4333   (351 5044)
Well-established company, which does a wide range of events; a quality company where many leading caterers served an apprenticeship.

Gorgeous Gourmets
Gresham Way SW19   081-944 7771   (081-946 1639)
Flexible caterer providing diverse types of cooking for small to medium-sized events.

The Richard Groves Catering Co
Unit 4, The Swan Centre, Riverside Rd SW17
081-947 1213   (081-944 1895)
Up and coming general quality caterer with particular strength in larger, corporate and themed events.

Hamlin's of Kensington
3 Abingdon Rd W8   376 2191
Delicatessen-based firm which caters for small to medium sized parties on a fully-serviced or take-away basis.

Michael Jay The Freelance Chef
13 Tottenham St W1   580 5090
Mr Jay, who has been in the business for over 15 years, caters for a wide range of small to medium sized business and social events.

K & M Caterers
110 Forest Hill Rd SE22
081-299 1057   (081-693 9086)
"Catering to the City" is the motto here – livery halls are a speciality.

Food & wine – Services

Leith's Good Food
86 Bondway SW8   735 6303   (735 1170)
Pru Leith's reputation attracts a wide following to her eponymous catering firm, now under French ownership.

Letherby & Christopher
Cheney Ho, Oaklands Pk, Wokingham RG11
0734-773000   (0734-772111)
Known as a sporting event caterer (Ascot, for example), L&C generally concentrate their efforts on venues where they are the resident caterer, but they also do general outside catering.

The Lumsden Twins
Unit 24, Sleaford St SW8   622 0087   (498 1975)
Emma and Kate's quality catering operation has outgrown its dinner party origins and can now take on almost anything.

MacQuisten Mitchell
12 Palace St SW1   834 4627   (821 5819)
Small caterer with big aspirations and, unusually, very central kitchens.

Mange Tout
38 Melgund Rd N5   609 0640   (609 0640)
Audrey Knight caters for small to medium sized parties, often with an ethnic/vegetarian twist.

Philip Moore
Unit 7, Malham Rd Ind Est, Malham Rd SE23
081-699 7318   (081-291 6552)
Mid-range outfit, catering for a wide range of predominantly social gatherings.

Mosimann's
Unit 2, Morie St, Old York Rd SW18
081-875 9900   (081-870 8319)
The smart black outside catering vans of this celebrity chef grace many top-notch events.

Moveable Feasts
83/85 Holloway Rd N7   607 2202   (607 1555)
Well-established, medium-size caterer which prides itself on offering quality traditional food at reasonable prices.

Moving Venue
14 Calico Ho, Plantation Whf SW11
924 2444   (978 5178)
Medium-sized, fast-growing caterer, working mainly in the corporate market.

Mustard Caterers
1-3 Brixton Rd SW9   582 8511   (793 1024)
Mustard's reputation for being at the very top end of the more traditional caterers attracts a blue-chip business and social following.

New Quebec Quisine
13 New Quebec St W1   402 0476   (724 6581)
Mainly corporate caterer, offering Mediterranean cuisine and healthy eating; theatrical parties are a speciality.

Services – Food & wine

Occasions
21 Hotham Rd SW15   081-789 6307   (081-789 6307)
Young company establishing itself in the corporate market particularly.

Owen Brothers Catering
Units C3 & C4, Jaggard Way SW12
081-675 2905   (081-675 9175)
Flexible organisation, capable of dealing with functions large and small; package deal buffets delivered to your door.

Owens & Monteith
3 Phillips Hs 52 Goodge St W1   497 8014   (437 4541)
"Specialist caterers to the media industry" – themed catering for launches and other events.

Party Ingredients
Kirtling St SW8   627 3800   (720 6249)
Well-known operator which does significant amounts of corporate and social business.

Payne & Gunter
Mayfair Hs, Belvue Rd, Northolt UB5
081-842 2224   (081-845 2319)
Probably the largest of the independent caterers, well known for sporting event catering but big in banqueting too; they also take on smaller, mainly corporate work.

Platters
4 Berry St EC1   490 4949   (253 3788)
Everything from boardroom lunches to large weddings.

Alison Price
Unit 5, The Talina Centre, Bagleys Ln SW6
371 5133   (371 5671)
Top of the range general operator whose catering can come in a variety of national flavours.

Princes
Suite 505 Linen Hall, 156/170 Regent St W1
287 6444   (287 5230)
Traditional, mainly corporate caterer.

Richmond Caterers
17 Studley Grange Rd W7
081-567 9090   (081-566 3698)
Wide-ranging caterer, whose work comprises livery hall banquets, corporate work and larger-scale social entertaining.

Ring & Brymer
Manor Hs, Manor Farm Rd, Alperton, Middx HA0
081-998 8880   (081-991 9636)
Major banqueting specialists (now twinned with Town & County); their historical credits include Victoria's Coronation.

Searcy's
124 Bolingbroke Grove SW11   585 0505   (350 1748)
Long-established caterers particularly well known for their own premises at 30 Pavilion Road SW1, but also big in outside catering.

Food & wine – Services

Simply Delicious
Unit 5a, 15 Micawber St N1   490 4548   (490 4547)
Fairly new, upmarket outfit, catering for small to medium sized events; their standard menus look very appealing.

Tastefully Yours
13/15 Pensbury St SW8   978 1080   (978 1092)
"Japanese and European caterers" whose services, apart from sushi and oriental catering, include Japanese tea ceremonies and flower arrangements.

Top Nosh
24 Vincent Sq SW1   834 5109
Five year old firm offering reasonably priced classic catering dishes for cocktail and dinner parties.

Top Tier Catering
Unit 24, Rosemary Rd, The Swan Centre SW17
081-944 0490   (081-944 7467)
Smaller scale general caterer, mainly for corporate customers, but also some government departments.

Town & County
Manor Hs, Manor Farm Rd, Alperton, Middx HA0
081-998 8880   (081-991 9636)
Successors to J Lyons; Royal garden parties are the highest profile part of the activities of this wide-ranging outside caterer.

Uncommon Cooks
Bell Ho, 49 Greenwich High Rd SE10
081-469 0651   (081-692 3555)
Well-established, up-market firm, catering particularly for larger corporate events.

Lorna Wing
Studio 21, The Talina Centre SW6
731 5105   (731 7957)
Lorna Wing is (wrongly) assumed by many to be oriental – a perception enhanced by the exquisite design of many of her dishes, which is the trademark of her company.

KOSHER CATERERS

Toni & Herman Heller
Unit 9, GEC Industrial Est, Wembley HA9
081-904 1222   (081-385 0700)
Mid-price Kosher caterer, for all but the largest events.

Oberlander
1A Cecil Rd NW9   081-205 5994   (081-200 8253)
One of the top Kosher caterers, established in Berlin in 1895.

Tony Page
Unit 10, The Harp Business Centre, Apsley Way NW2   081-208 4321   (081-208 0700)
The most recently established of the leading Kosher caterers.

Schaverien
Unit 9, Trojan Ind Est, Cobbold Rd NW10
723 7933   (402 0399)
One of the leading Kosher caterers, in business for over half a century; large social and charitable events are the mainstay.

Services – Food & wine

CAKES

The following firms are specialists, generally capable of taking on almost any design. Harrods and Selfridges also have speciality cake departments and a number of the supermarket chains – Waitrose and Safeway for example – have sample books from which you can order a surprisingly wide range of special cakes.

Anne Fayrer Cakes & Flowers
66 Lower Sloane St SW1   730 6277
Novelty and traditional cakes; (the floral side of the business is almost exclusively bridal).

Jane Asher
4 Cale St SW3   584 6177
All kinds of celebration cakes with a tendency to the unusual; a lot of corporate and logo work.

Final Touch
Studios E & P, Canada Ho, Blackburn Rd NW6
625 9617   (372 0729)
Wedding cakes to traditional or modern designs, or something extraordinary

Margaret's Cakes of Distinction
224 Camberwell Rd SE5   701 1940
Specialists in classic ("with a twist") and West Indian cakes; "uptown cakes at downtown prices", they claim.

CATERING EQUIPMENT

If you want to organise catering yourself, but do not have enough china, glasses or chairs, the following companies will be able to help. Practice differs as regards charges for delivery, extra charges for returning items dirty and whether VAT is included in quoted prices. As always, ensure that prices you are comparing are quoted on a similar basis.

Brandon Hire
Unit 12, School Rd NW10   081-965 5357
Wide range of tableware, furniture and catering equipment hire; also marquees and lighting and heating equipment; very helpful colour catalogue.

DCS Fairs
105 Constantine Rd NW3   485 5313
Not strictly catering equipment suppliers, they do mainly exhibition props, some of which are just what you need for a big party – ashtrays, coat rails etc; also some theme items.

Gorgeous Gourmets
Gresham Way SW19   081-944 7771   (081-946 1639)
Good basic range of equipment available for hire from this outside catering company.

Jones
Kenbury St SE5   735 5577   (737 4374)
China, cutlery, glasses etc; detailed price list.

Just Hire
Unit 5, Davenport Centre, Renwick Rd, Barking IG11   081-595 8855   (081-984 1363)
Full range of catering equipment; illustrated brochure.

Food & wine – Services

Mitchell Linen Hire
26A Devonshire Cr NW7
081-346 0330   (081-346 0546)
Specialists in tablecloths and napkins – available in a wide range of colours.

Party Ingredients
Kirtling St SW8   627 3800   (720 6249)
Being part of a leading caterer enables this firm to offer a good selection of tasteful equipment.

Planner Catering (Equipment Hire)
Unit 9, Barratt Ind Pk, Gillender St E3   987 2102
China, cutlery, glasses etc; detailed price list.

Rayner's Catering & Equipment Hire
Banquet Hs, Hereward Rd SW17
081-767 8331   (081-682 2484)
Seventy year old family company offering a wide range of equipment; helpful brochure.

Taylor's Hire
389 Northolt Rd, Sth Harrow HA2   081-422 1627
Catering equipment and furniture hire.

STAFF

If you do not need caterers, but would like some staff to help out, the following will assist.

The Admirable Crichton
6 Camberwell Trading Est, Denmark Rd SE5
733 8113   (733 7289)
Leading caterer which can also provide staff only.

At Your Service
27 Effie Rd SW6   371 0912   (731 6592)
Only a year old, this upmarket staff agency already provides young, personable staff to many of the top caterers and to private individuals.

Elite Staff Services
10 Oxford Circus Ave, 231 Oxford St W1
494 3402   (287 4254)
Butlers and other staff from this agency which provides directors' dining room staff.

John (Personal Services)
99d Talbot Rd W11   792 1162
Traditional caterer and staff agency; sadly, since last year, liveried footmen are no longer available.

Massey's Agency
Premier Ho, 10 Greycoat Pl SW1   799 1417   (799 1069)
Staff agency (a century and a half old) mainly involved in permanent placements but also maintaining a register of occasional staff.

Universal Aunts
PO Box 304 SW4   738 8937
"Britain's original personal service bureau", established in 1921, offers all types of temporary help, including butlers, waitresses and washers-up.

Services – Food & wine

WINE

Almost all of the following will offer delivery (often free of charge), glass hire and sale-or-return (check the proportion you can return). Many of them also supply ice. If you are buying in quantity you should certainly shop around – you may find that even the big chains will offer special terms for larger orders.

John Armit
5 Royalty Studios, 105 Lancaster Rd W11
727 6846   (727 7133)
Upmarket merchant which has no shop but an enclopaedic (and beautifully produced) list.

Bentalls
Wood St, Kingston KT1   081-546 1001
Department store with above-average wine selection.

Berry Bros & Rudd
3 St James's St SW1   396 9666   (396 9611)
St James's merchant with wonderfully Dickensian premises; long, helpfully discursive list.

Caves de la Madeleine
82 Wandsworth Br Rd SW6   736 6145   (371 8324)
Parson's Green shop whose services include timed deliveries and, if desired, providing bottles semi-uncorked – don't forget you may want to return some, though.

Corney & Barrow
12 Helmet Rw EC1   251 4051   (608 1373)
Well-known City wine merchant; most of their sales are from their list, but they have a retail shop at 194 Kensington Park Road W11 (tel 221 5122).

Fortnum & Mason
181 Piccadilly W1   734 8040   (437 3278)
F&M's wide-ranging wine department specialises in the rare, the unusual and the unashamedly expensive.

Harrods
Knightsbridge SW1   730 1234
Harrods offers a good, if not inexpensive, selection of champagnes, wines and spirits and a high level of service.

Justerini & Brooks
61 St James's St SW1   493 8721   (499 4653)
Well-known St James's merchant; although they have a retail shop, they mainly deliver from their long list.

Lay & Wheeler
6 Colver St West, Colchester CO1
0206-577272   (0206-564488)
Well respected out-of-town merchants who emphasise the breadth of their "value for money" selections.

Lea & Sandeman
301 Fulham Rd SW10   376 4767   (351 0275)
Wines are carefully chosen by an enthusiastic team at this chain of two shops – the other is at 211 Kensington Church Street W8.

Party planners – Services

Oddbins
Head office 081-944 4400
Probably the leading off-licence chain in London, particularly well known for their Australian selections and their champagne offers.

Robersons
348 Kensington High St W14   371 2121   (371 4010)
High quality, recently established merchant, with a particularly wide range of stock.

Selfridges
Oxford St W1   629 1234
Department store with an impressive wine selection.

Soho Wine Supply Ltd
18 Percy St W1   636 8490
Old-established Soho suppliers, specialising in champagnes and whiskies.

Thresher
Regional office   0707-328244
Threshers are the UK's biggest retailers of wine – their more upmarket shops are called Wine Racks.

The Vintage House
42 Old Compton St W1   437 2592
Champagnes, malt whiskies, liqueurs and claret are the specialities of this Soho shop of long standing.

ICE

In case your needs are greater than your local off-licence can provide...

Ace Speedy Ice
13 Claylands Rd SW8   735 4966
The proprietor, Mr Marenghi, is a third-generation ice-monger; dry ice also available, with notice.

PARTY PLANNERS

If you are organising a big party there is a lot to be said for bringing in the professionals. With an event of any scale, it is a full time job to ensure that everything comes together on the night – a party planner will do the worrying for you. In addition, assuming you choose the right planner, you may get a better party for your money, with greater flair and professionalism.

The term "party planner" covers a multitude of sins. Many party planners have grown out of caterers or entertainers and their party planning business often emphasises their original speciality. Others are independent specialists who have no formal links with any particular caterers or other suppliers and are completely free to help you choose the right contractors for your event.

Services – Party planners

Some planners will get right down to the detail, for example ensuring that invitations are correctly addressed and organising the "placement" (table seating). Others will regard their job as done if they organise a good dinner and the band plays.

Some planners work on commission, others will charge a fee. Don't be afraid to ask the planners about their experience of events similar in type to that which you are contemplating – there should be no objection if you ask to speak to the people who gave them.

In the corporate area, "event managers" (or sometimes "event designers") compete with the party planners as organisers of parties. For a corporate client, there may be little practical difference between going to a party planner and an event manager.

The current party trend is away from "ordinary" parties to themed events and this development has led to the evolution of a new sort of expert. The "themers" concentrate on designing and realising either bespoke or standard themes for parties. Often they provide their services through party planners or event organisers. In other cases, however, they offer a complete party planning service.

The Admirable Crichton
6 Camberwell Trading Est, Denmark Rd SE5
733 8113 (733 7289)
Leading caterer, which also has a name for organising some of the most spectacular parties.

Alternative Corporate Entertainments
39 Guildford Rd, Lightwater GU18
0276-452131 (0276-452150)
Themed parties are the speciality here, with particular emphasis on finding unusual venues; in spite of their name, they do some private work.

Bailey Carr
13 Cinnamon Rw, Plantation Whf SW11
924 6400 (924 6366)
Event designer, serving the corporate market, especially the City.

Banana Split
11 Carlisle Rd NW9 081-200 1234 (081-200 1121)
Professional planner which puts a lot of emphasis on its design work; its discos are also well known.

William Bartholomew
18 The Talina Centre, Bagleys Ln SW6
731 8328 (384 1807)
One of the top all-round party planners – often cited by competitors as the man to beat.

Bentley's
26a Winders Rd SW11 223 7900 (978 4062)
Well-known firm which has organised some very prestigious parties.

Party planners – Services

Bojolly's & BJ Hire
Unit 4, Brentford Business Centre, Commerce Rd, Brentford TW8   081-568 6447   (081-569 9355)
Well-known firm whose particular strength is its access to its own wide range of lighting, audio visual equipment and banqueting furniture.

Mark Butler Associates
28 St Ann's Villas W11   603 8963   (603 2070)
"Creative event management" in the UK and abroad for the corporate market; music often plays a part.

Buzz Productions
Westway Studios, 8 Olaf St W11   243 8410   (221 9399)
Theming specialists; their Westway Studios base is a good site for themed events, but they also work elsewhere.

Chance
321 Fulham Rd SW10   376 5995   (376 3598)
Andrew Chance is one of the biggest names in party planning, particularly for events with a strong entertainments content.

Nicki Colwyn
29 Oakley Gdns SW3   351 2875   (376 8187)
Lady Colwyn's independent planning company does a wide range of corporate and private work; they emphasise their interest in organising anything from a dinner party to a ball.

Fait Accompli
32b Queensgate Mews SW7   581 0384   (581 3216)
Independent party planner, undertaking a wide range of assignments.

Fêtes
Charlton Ho, Searle Rd, Farnham GU9
0252-724888   (0252-724849)
Fairly newly-established planner able to take on parties large and small.

The Finishing Touch Entertainments Co
19 Warren Ave, Richmond TW10
081-878 7555   (081-878 8444)
Organisation of corporate and themed events.

Juliana's
Unit 7, Farm Ln Trading Centre SW6
937 1555   (381 3872)
Well-established firm, offering a full party-planning service.

Magnum Marketing
19 Churton St SW1   932 0006   (932 0676)
Specialists in discreet management of social and business functions for, among others, rock and screen stars.

Party Planners
56 Ladbroke Gr W11   229 9666   (727 6001)
Lady Elizabeth Anson, doyenne of the London party scene, is going strong into her fourth decade of party planning; she is not tied to any particular suppliers and emphasises her willingness to accommodate smaller budgets.

Services – Entertainments

Party Professionals
33 Kensington Pk Rd W11   221 3438   (243 2985)
Discreet, independent party planners who emphasise their detailed approach.

The Jonathan Seaward Organisation
2 Heliport Estate, Lombard Rd SW11
350 0033   (228 6213)
Well-reputed, wide-ranging party planner which takes on a good mix of work; also very strong on the technical side.

The Theme Makers
The Folly, Pinner Hill Rd, Pinner HA5
081-429 3000   (081-868 6497)
"Balloon displays, colour co-ordination and theme packages" – they have their own kit with which to provide themed environments.

Theme Traders
The Studio, 16 North Sq NW11
081-458 3253   (081-458 2462)
Bespoke or package themed party organisers; they can provide just the theming or organise the whole thing.

Ubique
2 Drayson Mews W8   937 6446   (938 3728)
Corporate event managers specialising in organising hospitality in innovative locations worldwide.

Ultimate Experience
209 St John's Hill SW11   738 2544   (738 2556)
Employee entertainments are the specialities of this corporate events manager.

ENTERTAINMENTS

If you have the budget, do consider whether a few hundred pounds spent on performers, perhaps some musicians, a magician or a caricaturist, might not help turn your party into a truly memorable event.

Music is, of course, the most common type of entertainment. The best way of finding the right musicians for your event is to go to an agency – they should be able to find not only a good band, but also one which is right for the party concerned.

Many of the agencies and consultancies below deal with entertainers of all types. Most of the general agencies can provide a disco and many of them can provide casinos and other themed events.

If you wish to seek out your own entertainers, refer to the "White Book", the "bible" of the entertainment business (in major reference libraries).

Acker's International Jazz Agency
PO Box 2328, London W8   937 1333   (937 1335)
Many top names on the books, not least Mr Acker Bilk and his Paramount Jazz Band.

Entertainments – Services

Alternative Arts
49/51 Carnaby St W1   375 0441   (437 9828)
Arts organisation concentrating on new artists and new ideas; worth getting in touch if you are looking for inspiration or introductions to up-and-coming performers.

John Austin Organisation
25 Delamere Gdns NW7   081-959 1501
John Austin's specialities are theme nights, discos, casinos and corporate events.

Paul Bailey Agency
22 Wolsey Rd, East Molesey, KT8
081-941 2034   (081-941 6304)
Entertainments and more; Mr Bailey also offers a comprehensive events management service, mainly to corporate clients.

Barn Dance Agency
62 Beechwood Rd, Croydon CR2
081-657 2813   (081-651 6080)
Any sort of folk music – pipers, Morris Men, Irish Ceilidh – as well as barn dancing and Wild West parties; very popular for weddings, apparently.

Cahill Entertainment
8 Brookside Close, Barnet EN5   081-449 6589
Mr Cahill does a lot of work for hotels and banqueting departments but emphasises that he can provide anything from a harpist to a band for any function.

Caledonian Enterprises
97 Erskine Rd, Sutton SM1
081-644 4744   (081-641 4135)
Any type of Scottish entertainment can be provided – pipes, drums, dancing.

Crowd Pullers
158 Old Woolwich Rd SE10
081-305 0074   (081-858 9045)
Street performers booking agency – clowns, jugglers, fire eaters, street bands, etc.

Crown Entertainments
103 Bromley Common, Bromley BR2
081-464 0454   (081-290 4038)
Entertainment agency which can provide a wide range of bands, cabaret acts and speakers.

Dark Blues Management
30 Stamford Brook Rd W6
081-743 3292   (081-740 5520)
"The live entertainment specialists" – a quality outfit with a quarter of a century's experience behind them.

Fox
101 Shepherd's Bush Rd W6   602 8822   (603 2352)
Radio DJs, TV presenters and personalities; also after-dinner speakers.

Gemini Entertainments
2 Adelaide Tavern, 15 Regents Pk Rd NW1
586 7422   (722 5220)
General entertainment agency.

Services – Entertainments

Grosvenor Productions
12 Sherwood St W1   734 6755
The entertainments, theming and production arm of Forte; their operations base is very broad, enabling them to offer an unusually wide range of services to outsiders – "budgets from £125 to £125,000".

The Highland Gathering
135 Colchester Rd E10   081-556 8914
Everything Hibernian, from "Highland Games" to a piper.

Lawson Ross Management
116 Finchley Ln NW4   081-203 0626   (081-203 8996)
Entertainment consultancy which now specialises in themed events.

Le Cap Entertainment
25 Dighton Court, John Ruskin St SE5   701 1205
Smaller scale entertainments, mainly personal; stag/hen night packages.

Jeremy Lee Associates
14A Goodwin's Ct WC2   240 0413   (240 0371)
Top after-dinner speakers and comedians; also cabarets.

Lively Sounds
149 Englefield Rd N1   354 7370   (359 7855)
Agent for a large number of freelance orchestral musicians and bands.

London Music Agency
Wayside, Epping Gn CM16   0992-578617   (0992-578618)
All types of music, but specialising in the unusual.

More Balls Than Most
323 Upper St N1   354 5660
Juggling supplies, jugglers and juggling workshops.

Norman Murray & Anne Chudleigh
235-241 Regent St W1   629 4817   (629 5668)
Comedians, singers and after-dinner speakers; manage some established names.

Music Management
PO Box 1105 SW1   976 6262   (584 7944)
Live music consultants – everything from a flautist to an opera.

National Association of Toastmasters
Albany Hs, Albany Cr, Claygate, Esher KT10
0372-468022   (0372-470057)
One of the two big toastmasters' associations (see also the Society of London Toastmasters) – they are happy to send out lists of members.

Party Jazz
26 Harold Rd E11   081-539 5229   (081-556 9545)
Small jazz agency providing bands of all sizes.

Penguins Entertainment
Hattons Lodge, Snow's Ride, Windlesham GU20
0753-833811   (0753-833754)
All sorts of party entertainments, from bucking broncos to a 20 piece steel band; also well known for their discos.

Entertainments – Services

Jo Peters
53 North End Hs, Fitzjames Ave W14
603 8930 (603 1839)
Jo concentrates on finding entertainers of all types, mainly for corporate clients; she does not represent any individual performers.

Nic Picot
79 Anglesmede Cr, Pinner HA5
081-863 2522 (081-427 5253)
General entertainment agency specialising in magic; helpful, priced brochure.

Prelude
36 Searchwood Rd, Warlingham CR3
0883-623118 (0883-623492)
General agency, offering a wide range of music and live entertainments and specialising in corporate work.

Prime Performers
The Studio, 5 Kidderpore Ave NW3
431 0211 (431 3813)
Consultants for all types of entertainments – "the largest consultancy in the UK", they claim.

The Puppet Centre Trust
BAC, 176 Lavender Hill SW11 228 5335 (978 5207)
Information and advice centre for all forms of puppetry; they can provide an information pack, and publish a directory of professional puppeteers.

Society of London Toastmasters
77 Kingsway, Betts Wood BR5 0689-830065
One of the two major groupings of toastmasters (see also National Association of Toastmasters).

Splitting Images Lookalike Agency
62 Ormonde Ter NW8 286 8300 (286 8300)
A famous fact to grace your party.

Sproule Entertainments
141 Praed St W2 706 1550
Mr Sproule's speciality is hotel work, which gives him contact with a wide range of entertainers.

Sternberg-Clarke
London Ho, 68 Upper Richmond Rd SW15
081-877 1102
Fairly new outfit which specialises in the unusual – didgeridoo players and Chinese acrobats, for example – as well as representing a number of jazz and dance bands and other entertainers.

The Talent Corporation UK
6 Star St WC2 724 4343
Star after-dinner speakers are the speciality of this agency.

Your Entertainment Services
26 Princes Pk Ave, Hayes UB3
081-561 5944 (081-561 4092)
Services include organising corporate dinner dances, family fun days and providing artists bands and discos.

Services – Entertainments

MILITARY BANDS

Blues & Royals
Combermere Barracks, Windsor, Berks SL4
0753-868222

Grenadier Guards
Wellington Barracks SW1   414 3267   (414 3443)

Irish Guards
Chelsea Barracks SW1   414 4519   (414 4530)

Life Guards
Hyde Park Barracks SW7   414 2531   (414 2525)

Welsh Guards
Chelsea Barracks SW1   930 4466

MURDER ENTERTAINMENTS

Accidental Productions (Murder by Accident)
76 Enfield Cloisters, Fanshaw St N1
613 0822   (739 3582)
Murder evenings or, for a change, a movie weekend, where the guests get involved in producing a film at short notice.

Initiative Unlimited
Merlin Hs, Unit 8, Mill Hill Industrial Est, Flower Ln NW7
081-959 6579   (081-959 4246)
Murder mystery company, claiming to offer a quality service at reasonable prices.

Murder my Lord?
Britannia Hs, 1-11 Glenthorne Rd W6
081-846 9491   (081-748 4250)
"We'll murder your managing director for cash; anytime, anywhere"; the script for the murder evening is written after research into the group concerned.

CHILDREN'S ENTERTAINMENT

There are many children's entertainers who help amuse the kids at parties – some of them are happy to take over the whole event. Local recommendations are probably the best way to find a clown or puppeteer brighten up your child's party – an alternative is to approach one of the general agencies listed under entertainments. The following are specialists in the area of looking after kids.

Crêchendo
St Luke's Hall, Adrian Mews, Ifield Rd SW10   259 2727
Crêchendo can organise an "action-packed" party (for kids aged 1 to 12) – your place or theirs; they also hire out bouncy castles and other equipment.

Event Playcare Management
Unit F16, Lea Valley Commercial Centre, Lee Valley Trading Est N18   081-345 6706   (081-345 6095)
Specialists in temporary crèche care.

Puddleduck
77 Inglethorpe St SW6   386 9693   (385 2829)
All-in themed kids' party organising service for those with a fair budget to spend; they can also do miniaturised real food (pizzas etc) which is apparently catching on for adult parties too.

Entertainments – Services

CASINOS AND INDOOR AMUSEMENTS

Casinos are a very popular after-dinner diversion, even if, thanks to the gaming laws, you can only win confetti money.

Blue Moon Casino
6E Atlas Village, Oxgate Ln NW2   081-200 8229
Casinos with croupiers.

Cabaret Casino Associates
3 Willow Ct, 98 Sidney Rd, Walton-on-Thames KT12   0932-252282   (0932-252283)
Casinos, race nights, Scalextric, bingo.

Carnival Promotions
1 Hartmoor Cl, Stokenchurch HP14   0494-483645
Casinos and indoor "games night" equipment – basketball machines, indoor clay pigeon shooting, etc.

Casino Entertainment Services
1 Kingsbridge, 172 Lordship Rd N16   081-809 1439
Gaming tables with or without croupiers; also racing evenings with radio-controlled racing cars.

Zona Virtual Reality
The Piazza WC2   240 3948
By putting on the headset, you enter a virtual world and fight either the computer or a human opponent, similarly equipped.

DISCOS

Banana Split
11 Carlisle Rd NW9   081-200 1234   (081-200 1121)
Discos from a well-known party planner.

William Bartholomew
18 The Talina Centre, Bagleys Ln SW6
731 8328   (384 1807)
Top-notch discos from one of the top party planners.

Chance
321 Fulham Rd SW10   376 5995   (376 3598)
One of the biggest names in quality discos.

Exclusive Discotheques
94 Warwick Ave, Thorpe Lea, Egham TW20
0784-471716   (0784-437199)
Reasonably priced discos.

Joffins
2 Heliport Estate, Lombard Rd SW11
350 0033   (228 6213)
The disco arm of the Jonathan Seaward organisation, one of the leading party planners.

Juliana's
Unit 7, Farm Ln Trading Centre SW6
937 1555   (381 3872)
One of the best-known names in quality discos.

Services – Entertainments

Mobi-Deque
14 The Village, Charlton SE7
081-319 3222   (081-319 3037)
Professional disco operators, established for over a quarter of a century, who can also provide internal lighting and PA systems; they also have a shop selling disco equipment and some party novelties.

Muzic Non Stop Soundz
Norland Hs, Queensdale Cr W11   371 4493
Discos and lasers.

Penguins Entertainment
Hattons Lodge, Snow's Ride, Windlesham GU20
0753-833811   (0753-833754)
Entertainment agency particularly known for its discos.

Sounds Good to Me
84 Rayleigh Rd N8   081-292 9124
A range of disco systems, with or without DJs; also stage lighting, club effects and smoke.

TKO Mobile Nightclub
35 Sorrells Cl, Chineham, Basingstoke RG24
0256-470041
Rather more than a disco – performs at some top venues.

Zinos
101 Farm Ln SW6   385 3439
Twinned with Juliana's and doing broadly the same sort of business, but with a more international slant; have their own marquees.

DISCO EQUIPMENT

Abbey Acoustics
775 Harrow Rd NW10   081-960 7212
Disco equipment hire.

Disco-Tech
775 Harrow Rd, College Pk NW10
081-960 7212   (081-968 0797)
Disco equipment hire.

PA Music
172 High Rd N2   081-883 4350
Sound, lighting and special effects hire.

Young's
20 Malden Rd NW5   485 1115
Wide range of disco equipment for hire; open 7 days.

FIREWORKS

End the party with a bang! The professionals emphasise that, unless you have an enormous budget, it is much better to have a short, impressive display than a longer, less intensive one.

Entertainments – Services

Anglia Fireworks
Tall Trees, The Causeway, Gt Horkesley, Colchester CO6
0206-272515   (0206-272985)
Specialising in imported fireworks, this family-owned company covers the whole range, including some quite large DIY packages, complete with video instructions.

Fantastic Fireworks
Rocket Hs, Redbourn, Herts
0582-485555   (0582-485545)
A speciality of this company is large scale productions combining fireworks with music and lasers; they also do packs for more modest events.

The Firework Company
Shine Hs, High St, Uffculme EX15
0884-840504   (0884-841142)
This fairly young firm has a helpful brochure setting out their various all-in packages catering for most price levels; they also do special displays and their literature is a helpful introduction to organising such an event.

Fox Fireworks
26 Queens Mews W2   243 0981   (791 1938)
London-based operator who has recently launched in France – useful if you want to arrange the inauguration of your château.

Le Maitre Fireworks
312 Purley Way, Croydon CR0
081-686 9258   (081-680 3743)
High-tech fireworks and effects company whose work has stretched from Rolling Stones concerts to the G7 Summit display at Buck House.

Pains Fireworks
The Old Chalkpit, Romsey Rd, Whiteparish SP5
0794-884040   (0794-884015)
A firm responsible for some of the biggest displays; they also offer "dancing waters" – fountains synchronised with music; very helpful brochure for their DIY packs.

Shell Shock
South Manor Farm, Bramfield, Nr Halesworth IP19
098684-469   (098684-582)
A relative newcomer, with some very impressive big display credits.

Standard Fireworks
Crosland Hill, Huddersfield HD4
0484-640640   (0484-658039)
As you would expect, the best-known name has a good DIY range; they also do displays.

LASERS

The following are the specialists. For smaller shows, consult the disco operators.

Laser Creations International
55 Merthyr Ter SW13   081-741 5747   (081-748 9879)
One of the top laser companies – they do the Royal Tournament each year.

Services – Marquees

Laser Dynamics
Giles Hs, Clunbury, Craven Arms SY7
05887-443   (05887-453)
Shropshire based company – laser shows throughout Europe.

Laser Grafix
Unit 15, Orchard Rd, Royston SG8
0763-248846   (0763-246306)
"The creative force in lasers" – like most of the big firms, they do a lot of corporate and large-scale work.

MARQUEES

The most traditional type is the canvas tent supported by poles with external guy-ropes, but on constricted London sites, a clear-span, or frame tent, which is free-standing, will probably be more suitable. The structure is only the beginning and you should explore the types of linings on offer and the availability of furniture and, if appropriate, dance floors and heating. All but linings can, of course, be organised separately, but one-stop shopping will be much simpler.

Barkers Marquees
47 Osborne Rd, Thornton Heath CR7
081-653 1988   (081-653 2932)
Full range supplier, a century old, also offering event organisation and allied services.

Basildon Marquee Hire
4 Little Spenders, Fryerns, Basildon SS14
0268-526674
Family-run frame tent business.

Black & Edgington
30 Marshgate Ln E15   081-534 8085   (081-534 4143)
One of the leading suppliers of marquees and other temporary structures.

Alfred Bull & Co
Woolbridge Meadows, Bypass Rd, Guildford GU1   0483-575492
Long established Surrey company, offering traditional and frame tents.

John M Carter
Industrial Est, Winchester Rd, Basingstoke RG22 4AB
0256-24434   (0256-816209)
Old-established family firm whose work stretches from relatively small private parties to agricultural shows.

Charles Dean
41 Baring St N1   226 2237   (226 4560)
Steel framed clearspan marquees.

Dyas Marquees
Portswood Hs, Third Ave, Millbrook, Southampton SO9
0703-788878   (0703-788224)
A division of Yeo Paull, one of the market leaders, offering a wide range of structures for private and corporate functions.

Decoration – Services

The London Marquee Co
5 Beechmore Rd, London SW11   610 1770
Recently established firm, closely integrated into a party organising company.

M&B Marquees
Premier Hs, Tennyson Dr, Pitsea, Basildon SS13 3BT   0268-558002   (0268-552783)
National network supplier of frame marquees of all sizes.

Marquees over London
319 New King's Rd SW6   731 6660   (736 9078)
Frame tents, suited to London's many constrained spaces.

Neptunus
5 Vigo St W1   734 2578   (434 3465)
One of the world's largest tent companies, specialising in major temporary structures for corporate and sporting occasions; they also do some private work.

Owen Brown
Station Rd, Castle Donnington DE7
0332-850000   (0332-850005)
The UK's largest supplier of marquees and temporary structures; they do a lot of upmarket corporate work.

Stitches
7a Highshore Rd SE15   732 4976   (277 8271)
Traditional and frame marquees.

FLORISTS

The following operators are the specialists, often involved in lavish arrangements and theming. In some cases the firms are effectively designers of whole sets in which flowers may be the leading, but not the solo, performer, sharing the limelight with herbs, fruits, shells and other props.

If you have a good local florist, they should be able to help with smaller occasions – the venue itself being another possible source of inspiration.

Blooming Marvellous
40 Battersea Rise SW11   223 9099
Well-established florist, specialising in the "wild and unusual".

Pattie de Clifford
65 Cowley Rd SW14   081-876 4265
Well recommended, smaller scale florist.

Caroline Dickenson
5 William St SW1   245 9599   (259 5014)
Society florist with Knightsbridge shop; a lot of top corporate and party planners' work; offers monthly courses.

Edward Goodyear
45 Brook St W1   629 1508
"Court florist", with four warrants to prove it.

Services – Decoration

Sophie Hanna Flowers
Arch 48, New Covent Gdn Mkt, Nine Elms Ln SW8
720 0841   (720 1756)
Upmarket firm which also offers a discreet party planning service.

David Jones and Noel Minett
108A Bishops Rd SW6   081-870 4394
Well-reputed florists, tending to a more traditional style.

Moyses Stevens
157 Sloane St SW1   259 9303   (259 9279)
The oldest-established florist is happy to provide anything, but their natural style is fairly traditional and informal.

Jane Packer
56 James St W1   935 2673   (486 5097)
In a dozen years, Jane Packer has built up a firm which, apart from a large party-related business, includes schools in London and Tokyo.

Palm Brokers
Cenacle Nursery, Taplow Common Rd, Burnham SL1
0628-333734   (0628-661047)
Short-term hire of trees, shrubs and tropical plants, for internal or external decoration.

Detta Phillips
274/276 Queenstown Rd SW8   498 2728
Well-reputed Battersea florist who does a good range of work, including some top venues.

Michael Pickworth
99 Notting Hill Gt W11   727 3222
Mr Pickworth has been in the business nearly a quarter of a century and does party business internationally.

Pulbrook & Gould
127 Sloane St SW1   730 0030   (730 0722)
The best of the big-name, shop-based florists – the training ground for many of the leading names who now have their own businesses.

Town & Country Flowers
131 Wandsworth Bridge Rd, SW6   736 4683
Well recommended firm whose business includes a lot of work with leading party planners.

Kenneth Turner
19 South Audley St W1   355 3880   (495 1607)
The top individual name in the business, with an international following; Mr Turner is widely credited with having initiated a complete change in the approach to flowers – regarding them as part of the overall decorative scheme rather than as a rather formalised addition to it.

ICE SCULPTOR

Duncan Hamilton
5 Lampton Hs Cl SW19   081-879 0693   (081-780 0291)
The UK's only full-time ice-sculptor; the clarity of Mr Hamilton's blocks of ice is such that they are in demand on the continent.

Decoration – Services

BALLOONS

With a little imagination, balloons can make even the barest space festive at relatively modest expense. The following firms provide either a full decoration service or the ingredients for DIY decorations. See also Party Shops.

The Balloon and Kite Emporium
613 Garratt Ln SW18   081-946 5962   (081-944 0027)
The name say it all: everything from a 5 inch latex balloon to a 30 foot blimp.

Balloon Factory
53e Clifton Gdns W9   289 7455   (266 3166)
Size is no object to the Jago family balloon firm – they used to do the Berkeley Square Ball - and they subcontract for some of the top party planners.

The Balloon Printery
27A Buckingham Rd E15   081-536 0686   (081-536 0686)
Small personalised orders – they say they will do singles, but 25 is probably more realistic.

The Balloon Works
233 Sandycombe Rd, Kew TW9
081-948 8157   (081-332 6077)
Commissions here extend from children's parties to corporate launches; balloon printing also available.

Balloonland
44 Warwick Lodge, Shoot Up Hill NW2
081-452 1587   (081-450 6357)
All types of balloon decoration; printing available.

Balloons and Parties Today
Unit A, 9 Park Rd, Hayes UB4
081-573 2077   (081-573 2077)
Balloon designers, tending to do larger, corporate business.

Balloons Inc
106 Windmill Rd, Brentford TW8
081-560 9520   (081 560 9147)
Large balloon cash and carry; they also organise basic and advanced balloon-art courses and workshops.

Balloons World Wide
23 Richmond Rd, Kingston KT2
081-547 2737   (081-974 5393)
Full-range supplier; also organise "balloon colleges".

BOC Gases
10 Priestley Rd, The Surrey Research Pk, Guildford GU2
0483-579857   (0483-505211)
"Balloon gas" (98% helium), floating balloon packs and dry ice; ring the head office number given for details of your nearest branch.

Busy Lizzie
49 Copenhagen St N1   833 0279
Floristry and balloons for a wide range of clients in Islington, the City and parts of the West End; balloons sculptures; happy to take on smaller jobs.

Services – Equipment

Just Balloons
127 Wilton Rd SW1   434 3039   (233 8224)
*Just about anything balloon-related you could think of –
from wedding decorations via product launches to blimps.*

Kite & Balloon Co
The Old Church, 160 Eardley Rd SW16
081-679 8844   (081-679 7792)
*"Adding knowhow to blowhow" – they should know how as
they are part of a group which does everything from making
balloon-making machinery to organising major inflatable
happenings; also balloon printing.*

West Side Balloons
43 Ormiston Gr W12   081-749 7931
*Balloon sculptures, mainly for weddings; also
small retail outlet.*

FLAGS AND BUNTING

Black & Edgington Flags
Orpington Tr Est, Sevenoaks Way, Orpington BR5
0689-839389   (0689-870236)
*The flags of the world and red, white and blue bunting for
hire; can also provide indoor flag-poles.*

Turtle & Pearce
31 Tanner St SE1   407 1301   (378 0267)
*Old established flag maker, which can also provide banners
(printed to order) and bunting.*

EQUIPMENT

It is relatively unlikely that you will want to deal with most
of the following firms! If you are having a party of sufficient
scale to justify their involvement, it is probable that you will
have a professional organiser doing it for you. However, if
you have decided to do it yourself, or just need, for example,
some lighting, the following firms can help.

Audio & Acoustics
United Hs, North Rd N7   200 2900   (700 6900)
Sound systems, lighting and staging.

The AV Company
278 Forest Rd E17   081-520 4321   (081-520 9484)
*Stage and interior lighting, sound systems of all sizes and
video screens.*

AVE
16 South Sea Rd, Kingston, Surrey KT1
081-549 7521   (081-549 6876)
Amplifying the spoken word is the speciality here.

Martin Bradley Lighting and Sound
69A Broad Ln, Hampton TW12   081-979 0672
*Practical, disco and effect lighting as well as sound systems
and smoke machines.*

Classic Lighting
9 Westglade, Farnborough GU15   0252-860330
Full range of indoor and external lighting.

Equipment – Services

Ecando Systems
Earl's Ct Exhib Centre, Warwick Rd SW5
244 6233   (370 8084)
Servicing Earl's Court for the last century gives this company unrivalled experience of support for mega-events.

Fisher Lighting
Unit 1, Heliport Ind Est, Lombard Rd SW11
228 6979   (924 2328)
One of the top firms, supplying a full range of internal and external lighting; son-et-lumières.

Gemini Productions
14 Morris Pl, Finsbury Pk Trading Est N4
263 6336   (263 8995)
Set builders, especially for corporate events; also hire dance-floors.

Glenby's
The Wooden Hs, Manton, Oakham LE15   081-673 2035
The Rolls-Royces of the travelling loo world, complete with attendants.

HSS Hire Shops
Have 22 London shops –
Call 0800 282828 for the nearest.
Bouncy castles, barbecues, heaters, crockery, festoon lights, balloon gas and more – a useful source for the more DIY sorts of parties.

RG Jones (Morden)
Beulah Rd SW19   081-540 9881   (081-542 4368)
PA systems for all types of events.

Jukebox Junction
12 Toneborough Abbey Rd NW8   328 6206
Modern jukeboxes for hire.

Midnight Design
Unit 1, Chelsea Bus Centre, 326 Queenstown Rd SW8
498 7272   (498 8845)
Full range decorative lighting specialists; although they aim mainly at the top end of the market, they also have a service for smaller themed parties.

Nostalgia Amusements
22 Greenwood Cl, Thames Ditton KT7   081-398 2141
Automata, slot machines and juke boxes, including a fully operational Edwardian amusement parlour; available, with suitably attired attendants, for theme evenings.

Rent-a-Loo
Building 5, Smallford Ln, St Albans AL4
0727-822120   (0727-822886)
Individual or multiple – chemical or plumbed in.

Spaceworks Furniture Hire
Unit W4, Lambs Business Pk, Tilberstow Hill, Sth Godstone RH9   0342-892333   (0342-893082)
Wide range of indoor and outdoor furniture; helpful colour catalogue.

Services – Transport

Starlight
5 Gateway Tr Est, Hythe Rd NW10
081-960 6078   (081-960 7991)
Leading, creative lighting and effects company which does many of the largest events nationally and on the continent.

Water Sculpture
St George's Studios, St George's Quay, Lancaster LA1
0524-64430   (0524-60454)
Byll Elliot has been orchestrating dancing fountains, indoor cascades and water installations of all types for more than two decades.

CARS

Eccentric, classic, impressive or merely practical...

Altarmobiles (MJ Ellard)
120 Holland Pk Ave W11   221 8244
Family firm, whose stable includes Alvis, Packard and Rolls-Royce.

American Classic Hire Co
63 Hewens Rd, Hillingdon UB10   081-561 2728
Peppermint green dream machines, etc.

Bond Enterprises
Gate Cottage, Campden Hill W8   229 6895
'30s American classics are the speciality.

Camelot Barthropp
Headfort Pl SW1   235 0234   (823 1278)
The Savoy Group's chauffeur-driven service, offering the range of top cars you would expect.

Dennis Carter
96a Clifton Hill NW8   723 9244   (372 1855)
Stretch Jaguars, Daimlers and Mercedes, with uniformed chauffeurs.

Fleetwood Classic Limousines
63 Carlton Hill NW8   624 0869   (372 2397)
Classic '50s American limos and English classics; also specialise in odd-ball requirements – ambulances, American police outriders, etc.

Huxley Car Hire Co
1 Donnington Rd, Kenton HA3
081-909 2251   (081-907 7994)
Wide range, mainly of modern limousines, but also including a 1932 white Rolls-Royce.

London Limousine Co
Carriage Hs, 6 Burrell St SE1   928 9280
Chauffeur-driven Jaguars and Mercedes.

Maxwell Car Services
138 Hammersmith Rd W6
081-748 3000   (081-748 7075)
Chauffeur-driven cars – Jaguars a speciality.

Star Express Limousines
12 Calthorpe St WC1   837 0793
All makes of American limos, including Cadillac and Lincoln.

Dress – Services

OTHER VEHICLES

CB Helicopters
Battersea Heliport, Lombard Rd SW11
228 3232   (738 0100)
The quickest way of leaving the party.

CBM Services
Redhill Rd, Cobham KT11   0932-864078   (0932-857660)
"Period and modern vehicle properties hire", including the oldest bus (1925) still in regular use.

Greenhill
152 Windmill Ln, Southall UB2
081-574 6915   (081-571 5916)
"Double-decker hospitality units" – ie big red buses with a bar downstairs.

London Carriage Company
The Coach Ho, 100 Gifford St N1   609 9462
Coaches and fours for hire.

London Coaches
Jews Rw SW18   081-877 1722   (081-877 1968)
Open-topped, and other, red buses and coaches.

COSTUME AND FANCY DRESS

The shops below stock everything from jokey animal outfits to authentic (and sometimes original) period clothing. Always ring to discuss whether the shop has roughly what you might want before making the journey – also a good precaution as they do not all keep very regular hours.

Aardvark
4 Ravey St EC2   739 3026
A wide range from budget fancy dress items to historical costumes, with a very large selection of ladies' original 20th century items; helpful leaflet.

Academy Costumes
50 Rushworth St SE1   620 0771   (928 6287)
Small range of high quality 20th century originals.

Angels & Bermans
119 Shaftesbury Ave WC2   836 5678   (240 9527)
"The world's largest costumier" offers, as a spokesman put it, "to fulfil any costume fantasy" from its vast range of ex-film/TV/theatre stock.

The Cavern
154 Commercial St E1   247 1889
Treasure trove of '60s and '70s clobber for hire; also some virgin items for sale.

City Dress Arcade
437 Bethnal Gn Rd E2   739 2645   (613 1917)
Fifth generation family enterprise, offering nearly a thousand costumes, relatively inexpensively – send for the unusually full brochure; also party novelties.

Services – Dress

Contemporary Wardrobe
The Horse Hospital, Colonnade WC1
713 7370 (713 7269)
Original '50s, '60s, '70s kit for hire; visits by appointment.

Laurence Corner
62-64 Hampstead Rd NW1   813 1010
Military outfits old and new for hire.

Costume Call
158 Munster Rd SW6   371 7211
Century-old theatrical costumiers, now mainly into parties, with an enormous selection; particular strength is '30s and earlier; also some fancy dress; by appointment only.

The Costume Studio
6 Panton Gr, Off White Lion St N1   388 4481 (837 5326)
Large range of period and theatrical costumes in good condition; from personal experience, we can recommend this place.

Culture Vultures
200 High Rd, East Finchley N2   081-883 5525
Fancy dress and costume; not too expensive; murder parties, '60s parties and militaria are strong points.

Escapade
150 Camden High St NW1   485 7384 (485 0950)
Well-stocked, mid-price fancy dress hire shop.

Royal National Theatre Costume Hire Department
Unit 15, 1/3 Brixton Rd SW9   587 0404 (820 9324)
Top quality and not especially expensive.

The Theatre Zoo
21 Earlham St WC2   836 3150
Mice to gorillas and everything in-between; also carnival make-up, wigs, masks and hats.

DRESS HIRE (MEN)

Dinner jackets, white tie and tails, kilts.

Austin Reed
103-113 Regent St W1   437 2140
Relative newcomer to the hire game; Austin Reed's operations are based in Regent Street, but you can be measured up in their other shops.

Lipman & Sons
22 Charing Cross Rd WC2   240 2310
"Never knowingly undersold", this formal wear emporium both sells and hires out; they offer group and student discounts.

Moss Bros
88 Regent St W1   494 0666
The name still practically synonymous with gents' dress hire.

Young's
19-20 Hanover St W1   437 4422
Hire chain with several London branches.

Party shops – Services

DRESS HIRE (WOMEN)

20th Century Frox
614 Fulham Rd SW6   731 3242
Evening and (more unusually) day wear for hire; hats and shoes for sale.

A Chance to Dance
57a Latchmere Rd SW11   350 1579
Evening wear and accessories for hire.

Frock Around the Clock
42 Vardens Rd SW11   924 1669
Evening wear and accessories for hire.

One Night Stand
44 Pimlico Rd SW1   730 8708
Evening wear and accessories for hire.

Puttin' on the Glitz
Pied Bull Ct WC1   404 5067
Ballgowns, cocktail and party dresses with matching gloves, bags and jewellery; also at Hays Galleria SE1 (tel 403 8107).

PARTY SHOPS

For one-stop shopping for smaller events, the following can be recommended as suppliers of balloons, novelties, decorations, masks, disposable plates and so on. Harrods Hospitality Shop also has a good range, including paper disposables in a big range of colours.

Barnum's
67 Hammersmith Rd W14   602 1211   (603 9945)
Very large, well-stocked party shop.

Circus Circus
176 Wandsworth Br Rd SW6   731 4128   (371 5949)
All round party shop; kids' party items a speciality; they also offer a children's party organising service.

Davenports
7 Charing X Underground Shopping Arcade, Strand WC2   836 0408
Third generation supplier of magic tricks ranging from simple to professional; also juggling balls and long, thin balloons to sculpture with.

Frog Frolics
15 Victoria Gr W8   581 5439   (584 2712)
Party shop specialising in kids' parties – they can also provide cakes; useful "parties by post" brochure.

Non-stop Party Shop
214/216 Kensington High St W8   937 7200
Well stocked all-round novelty shops offering a delivery service and a balloon decoration service; also at 694 Fulham Rd SW6 (tel 384 1491) and Chelsea Farmers' Market SW3 (tel 351 5771).

Oscar's Den
127/129 Abbey Rd NW6   328 6683   (625 4130)
Full-range party, balloon and equipment hire shop; children's entertainers also arranged.

Services – Photography etc

PHOTOGRAPHERS ETC
Belgrave & Portman Press Bureau
7 West Halkin St SW1   235 3227
Old-established wedding and social photographers – they claim 60 years and 100,000 weddings behind them.

Andrea Cunningham
19 Onslow Gdns SW7   581 3433
Photography is not the only way of capturing people – why not consider the services of an on-the-spot caricaturist?

BIPP PHOTOGRAPHERS

We are grateful to the British Institute of Professional Photography for the following list of social photographers within the M25. Their address is Fox Talbot House, Amwell End, Ware, Herts SG12 9HN (tel 0920-464011).

The letters LBIPP, ABIPP and FBIPP indicate respectively Licentiates, Associates and Fellows of the Institute – Fellowship is, of course, the highest level.

E & EC POSTCODES
Anthony Bartram LBIPP
Robert Anthony Studios, 160 Roman Rd E2   081-981 7971
Ken Bray ABIPP
223 High Rd, London E18   081-504 8463
Sidney Chevin LBIPP
24 High Rd, London E18   081-989 3801
Michael Ley LBIPP
238B Chingford Mount Rd, London E4   081-524 2825
Bruno Medici LBIPP
The Medici Studio, 5 Backhill EC1   278 6722

N & NW POSTCODES
Adam Adamou ABIPP
87 Green Lns N13   081-888 3275
Don Bartram LBIPP
10 Hawthorn Rd N18   081-807 1376
Stephen Christmas LBIPP
52 Berkeley Gdns N21   081-360 9894
Chris Chrysanthou LBIPP
27 Kingwell Rd, Hadley Wd, Barnet EN4   081-440 7073
Natwarlal Chudasama LBIPP
57 High Rd NW10   081-451 5697
Mrs Lupe Cunha LBIPP
843/845 Green Lns N21   081-360 0144
Fuat Erman ABIPP
28 Pk Ave N13   081-882 5793
Mark Gerson FBIPP
3 Regal Ln, Regents Pk Rd NW1   286 5894
Miss Nicola Hollins LBIPP
67 Redston Rd N8   081-341 2080
Paul Kaye FBIPP
Paul Kaye Studio Ltd, 20 Park Rd NW1   723 2444
Mrs Susannah Olins ABIPP
11 Fairfax Pl NW6   328 1623

Photography etc – Services

Kevin Parker LBIPP
Photo Assignments, 189 Edgware Rd, The Hyde NW9
081-205 9852
Miss Rena Pearl ABIPP
8A The Drive NW11   081-455 7661
Peter Phillips LBIPP
11 Grove End Gdns, Grove End Rd NW8   286 9129
Paul Wilmhurst ABIPP
Flambards Photography, 6 Chaseville Parade,
Chaseville Pk Rd N21   081-360 7187

S & SW POSTCODES
Alan Brown LBIPP
30 Sudbrooke Rd SW12   081-673 6070
Mrs Tessa Codrington LBIPP
73 The Chase SW4   622 3895
Mike Curry LBIPP
Ann Charles Photography, 61 Valleyfield Rd SW16
081-769 2950
Len Dance FBIPP
218 Fulham Palace Rd W6   381 0150
Ms Desi Fontaine LBIPP
62 Archway St SW13   081-878 4348
Ron Howard FBIPP
20 Aldbourne Rd W12   081-743 8194
Julian Kaye ABIPP
Simon Kaye ABIPP
Paul Kaye Studio Ltd, 74 New Bond St W1   491 4123
Miss Barbara Kleiner LBIPP
76 York Mansions, Prince of Wales Dr SW11   720 5061
James Norcott LBIPP
4 St Marks Pl SW19   081-946 0439
Alan Shawcross ABIPP
Grant White ABIPP
Anthony Buckley & Constantine Ltd, 109 Mount St W1
629 5235

ESSEX
Peter Cavalier ABIPP
7 Manford Way, Grange Hill, Chigwell IG7   081-501 2430
Stanley Hecquer LBIPP
1 Queens Mews, Queens Rd, Buckhurst Hill IG9   081-505 6226
Barry Johnston LBIPP
9 The Windsors, Lower Queens Rd, Buckhurst Hill IG9
081-505 3425
Ron Prince LBIPP
1st Floor, Romford Shopping Hall, Romford RM1   0708-724561
Mrs Roberta Ross LBIPP
1104 High Rd, Chadwell Heath, Romford RM6   081-597 8988

HERTS
Marisa D'Allesandro ABIPP
16 Ashdown Dr, Borehamwood WD6   081-207 1924
Brian Harris ABIPP
Studio B, 345 Watling St, Radlett WD7   0923-856545

Services – Photography etc

KENT

Miss Celine Barsley LBIPP
8 Oaklands Rd, Bexleyheath DA6   081-301 6563

Michael Bolt LBIPP
Kimberley Colour, 6 Norman Rd DA14   081-308 0060

Margaret Carvalho LBIPP
Hamilton-Jack Portrait Photography, 173 Croydon Rd, Beckenham BR3   081-658 7588

Robin Dawe LBIPP
35 Saxville Rd, Orpington BR5   0689-38435

Henry Gee LBIPP
246 High St, Bromley BR1   081-460 8444

John Lawrence ABIPP
14 Warwick Cl, Orpington BR6   0689-826587

Leslie Lockwood LBIPP
4 Crayford High St, Crayford DA1   0322-529950

MIDDX

Kaushik (Ken) Bathia ABIPP
24 Sudbury Ave, Wembley HA0   081-903 3294

David Brown LBIPP
92c Whitton Rd, Hounslow TW3   081-572 2030

Mrs Glenda Colquhoun ABIPP
21 Northcote Rd, St Margarets, Twickenham TW1
081-891 1704

David Cox LBIPP
Town Studio, 80 Lancaster Rd, Enfield EN2   081-367 7683

Peter Dyer FBIPP
Peter Dyer Photographs Ltd, 86 London Rd, Enfield EN2
081-363 2456

Charles Green FBIPP
309 Hale Ln, Station Rd, Edgware HA8   081-958 3183

Chris Hands ABIPP
Peter Dyer Photographs Ltd, 86 London Rd, Enfield EN2
081-363 2456

Leonard Hooper LBIPP
Gem Photographics, 26 Feltham Hill Rd, Ashford TW15
0784-255613

Malcolm Lunn LBIPP
62 First Ave, Bush Hill Pk, Enfield EN1   081-363 3300

Mrs Eileen Michel LBIPP
31 South Parade, Mollison Way, Edgware HA8
081-952 4711

Maurice Rubeck ABIPP
42 Church Rd, Stanmore HA7   081-954 8047

George Wells FBIPP
325 Kenton Rd, Harrow HA3   081-907 7741

SURREY

Pierre Marcar LBIPP
44A Bensham Grove, Thornton Heath CR7   081-771 1233

Mahmad Peerbacus LBIPP
Flat 2, 27 St Paul's Rd, Thornton Heath CR4   081-771 7088

Edward Phillips ABIPP
108 Stafford Rd, Wallington SM6   081-669 9444

Miscellaneous – Services

Eric Strange FBIPP
Dawson Strange Photography Ltd, Between Streets, Cobham KT11
0932-867161

Mrs Alison Trapmore ABIPP
Oatlands Studio, 7 Oatlands Dr, Weybridge KT13   0932-227935

SECURITY

Corps of Commissionaires
85 Cowcross St EC1   490 1125   (250 1287)
For more than a century, the corps has been providing smart, ex-servicemen commissionaires; they are all security-trained.

Group 4
10 Wapping Ln E1   488 3111   (480 7689)
The country's biggest security firm can provide professional event security; minimum hire charge is for ten hours.

STATIONERS

Aquila Press
The Maltings, 6 Palmers Hill, Epping CM16
0992-573131   (0992-561516)
Copperplate invitations; formerly of St James's, they do a lot of diplomatic work and have a keen eye for protocol.

Invitation 2000
80 Church St NW8   224 8820
Invitations in all languages and styles are the speciality; also bridal accessories and the "UK's largest range of bonbonierie (sugared almond favours)".

Smythsons
44 New Bond St W1   629 8558   (495 6111)
The grandest name in stationery.

The Wren Press
26 Chelsea Whf, 15 Lots Rd SW10
351 5887   (352 7063)
Suppliers of engraved stationery; their business incorporates that of Truslove & Hanson, formerly of Sloane Street.

INSURANCE

It's certainly worth talking to your broker, but surprisingly few people seem to be involved with event insurance. The following are among the specialists.

Insurex
The Pantiles Hs, 2 Nevill St, Tunbridge Wells TN2   0892-511500   (0892-510016)
Specialists in event insurance of various types.

Leslie & Godwin
6 Braham St E1   480 7200   (480 7450)
Specialists in theatrical/musical event insurance who will also quote for more general event cover.

Wedding Plan
Grand UK Insurance Services Ltd, 82 Upper St Giles St, Norwich NR2   0603-767699
Wedding, reception and honeymoon insurance packages.

Indexes

Private venues by type

Halls

Central
Abbey Community Centre *(SW1)*
Africa Centre *(WC2)*
Banqueting House *(SW1)*
Central Club (YWCA) *(WC1)*
Cobden's Working Men's Club *(W10)*
Conway Hall *(WC1)*
King's College *(WC2)*
Lincoln's Inn *(WC2)*
London Scottish *(SW1)*
The London Welsh Centre *(WC1)*
Nôtre Dame Hall *(WC2)*
Royal Green Jackets *(W1)*
Royal Horticultural Halls *(SW1)*
Staple Inn *(WC1)*
Westminster Cathedral Hall *(SW1)*

West
Amadeus Centre *(W9)*
Chelsea Old Town Hall *(SW3)*
Duke of York's HQ *(SW3)*
Fulham Town Hall *(SW6)*
Hammersmith Town Hall *(W6)*
Holy Trinity Brompton Church Hall *(SW7)*
Kensington Conservative Association *(W8)*
Old Refectory *(W8)*
Porchester Centre *(W2)*
St Peter's Hall *(W11)*

North
Alexandra Palace & Park *(N22)*
Cecil Sharp House *(NW1)*
Stoke Newington Town Hall *(N16)*

South
Academy of Live & Recorded Arts *(SW18)*
Battersea Town Hall *(SW11)*
Blackheath Concert Halls *(SE3)*
Hop Exchange *(SE1)*
St John's Hill *(SW11)*
St Thomas's Hospital *(SE1)*
Wandsworth Civic Suite *(SW18)*

East
Bishopsgate Institute *(EC2)*
Cabot Hall *(E14)*
Gray's Inn *(EC1)*
Holderness House *(EC2)*
Honourable Artillery Co *(EC1)*
Inner Temple Hall *(EC4)*
Middle Temple Hall *(EC4)*
National Westminster Hall *(EC2)*
St Bartholomew's Hospital *(EC1)*
St Botolph's Hall *(EC2)*
St Bride Foundation Institute *(EC4)*
St John's Gate *(EC1)*
World Trade Centre *(E1)*

Banqueting halls

Central
Café Royal *(W1)*
King David Suite *(W1)*
New Connaught Rooms *(WC2)*
Westminster Conference Centre *(SW1)*

West
Chelsea Football Club *(SW6)*
Chelsea Harbour Rooms *(SW10)*

North
Grosvenor Rooms *(NW2)*
Lord's *(NW8)*
Royal Majestic Suite *(NW6)*

South
The Conservatory *(SW11)*
Oval *(SE11)*
Twickenham Banqueting Centre *(TW1)*

East
Baltic Exchange *(EC3)*
The Brewery *(EC1)*
The Elizabeth Suite *(EC2)*

Outside London
Ascot Racecourse - Berks *(Berks)*
Kempton Park *(Middx)*
Sandown Park Racecourse *(Surrey)*
Syon Park (Banqueting) *(Middx)*

Livery halls

East
Apothecaries' Hall *(EC4)*
Armourers' & Braisers' Hall *(EC2)*
Bakers' Hall *(EC3)*
Barber-Surgeons' Hall *(EC2)*
Brewers' Hall *(EC2)*
Butchers' Hall *(EC1)*

Private venues by type

Carpenters' Hall *(EC2)*
Chartered Accountants' Hall *(EC2)*
Clothworkers' Hall *(EC3)*
Coopers' Hall *(EC2)*
Drapers' Hall *(EC2)*
Dyers' Hall *(EC4)*
Farmers' & Fletchers' Hall *(EC1)*
Fishmongers' Hall *(EC4)*
The Founders' Hall *(EC1)*
Goldsmiths' Hall *(EC2)*
Grocers' Hall *(EC2)*
Guildhall *(EC2)*
Haberdashers' Hall *(EC2)*
Innholders' Hall *(EC4)*
The Insurance Hall *(EC2)*
Ironmongers' Hall *(EC2)*
Mercers' Hall *(EC2)*
Merchant Taylors' Hall *(EC2)*
Painters' Hall *(EC4)*
Pewterers' Hall *(EC2)*
Plaisterers' Hall *(EC2)*
Saddlers' Hall *(EC2)*
Salters' Hall *(EC2)*
Skinners' Hall *(EC4)*
Stationers' Hall *(EC4)*
Tallow Chandlers' Hall *(EC4)*
Watermen & Lightermen's Hall *(EC3)*

South
Glaziers' Hall *(SE1)*

Houses

Central
Apsley House *(W1)*
Canning House *(SW1)*
Dartmouth House *(W1)*
11 Hobart Place *(SW1)*
Searcy's *(SW1)*
Sir John Soane's Museum *(WC2)*
Spencer House *(SW1)*

West
Chiswick House *(W4)*
Dora House *(SW7)*
Fulham House *(SW6)*
Fulham Palace *(SW6)*
Leighton House *(W14)*
Peacock House *(W14)*
Stanley House *(SW10)*

North
Burgh House *(NW3)*
Canonbury Academy *(N1)*
Freud Museum *(NW3)*
Kenwood House *(NW3)*
Lauderdale House *(N6)*

South
Hollyhedge House *(SE3)*
Marble Hill House *(TW1)*
Pentland House *(SE3)*
Queen's House *(SE10)*
Ranger's House *(SE10)*

East
Dr Johnsons' House *(EC4)*

Outside London
Beaulieu *(Hants)*
Blenheim Palace *(Oxon)*
Brighton Royal Pavilion *(Sussex)*
Brocket Hall *(Herts)*
Clandon *(Surrey)*
Ham House *(Surrey)*
Hampton Court Palace *(Surrey)*
Hever Castle *(Kent)*
Knebworth House *(Herts)*
Leeds Castle *(Kent)*
Syon Park (House) *(Middx)*
Syon Park (Conservatory) *(Middx)*

Museums

Central
British Museum *(WC1)*
Cabinet War Rooms *(SW1)*
The Dickens' House Museum *(WC1)*
Guards Museum *(SW1)*
London Transport Museum *(WC2)*
Museum of Mankind *(W1)*
Theatre Museum *(WC2)*

West
National Army Museum *(SW3)*
Natural History Museum *(SW7)*
Science Museum *(SW7)*
Victoria & Albert Museum *(SW7)*

North
Royal Air Force Museum *(NW9)*

South
Bramah Tea & Coffee Museum *(SE1)*
The Clink *(SE1)*
Cutty Sark *(SE10)*
Design Museum *(SE1)*
Fan Museum *(SE10)*
Imperial War Museum *(SE21)*
Museum of Garden History *(SE1)*

Private venues by type

Museum of the Moving Image *(SE1)*
The Old Operating Theatre Museum & Herb Garret *(SE1)*
Old Royal Observatory *(SE10)*

East
Bank Of England Museum *(EC2)*
Museum Of Childhood *(E2)*
Museum of London *(EC2)*

Outside London
Kew Bridge Steam Museum *(Middx)*

Galleries
Central
Courtauld Institute *(WC2)*
Hamiltons Gallery *(W1)*
ICA *(SW1)*
The Imagination Gallery *(WC1)*
Lundonia House *(WC1)*
Mall Galleries *(SW1)*
National Portrait Gallery *(WC2)*
Photographers' Gallery *(WC2)*
Royal Academy of Arts *(W1)*
Smith's Gallery *(WC2)*
Tate Gallery *(SW1)*
Wallace Collection *(W1)*

West
Accademia Italiana *(SW7)*
Royal College of Art *(SW7)*
Serpentine Gallery *(W2)*

North
Saatchi Gallery *(NW8)*

South
Bankside Gallery *(SE1)*
Dulwich Picture Gallery *(SE21)*
Hayward Gallery *(SE1)*
Victoria Pump House *(SW8)*

East
Whitechapel Art Gallery *(E1)*

Tourist attactions
Central
Rock Circus *(W1)*
Spitting Image Museum *(WC2)*

North
London Zoo *(NW1)*
Madame Tussaud's *(NW1)*

South
The London Dungeon *(SE1)*

Outside London
Royal Botanic Gardens *(Surrey)*
West Wycombe Caves *(Bucks)*

Colleges & Universities
Central
International Students *(W1)*
London School Of Economics *(WC2)*
University of London Union *(WC1)*
Westminster College *(SW1)*

West
Imperial College *(SW7)*
Royal College of Music *(SW7)*
Upper Refectory Suite *(SW6)*

North
Regent's College *(NW1)*
Royal Veterinary College *(NW1)*

South
Dulwich College *(SE21)*
Froebel Institute College *(SW15)*
Goldsmith's College *(SE14)*

Outside London
Royal Holloway College *(Surrey)*

Institutions
Central
BAFTA Centre *(W1)*
Chartered Institute of Public Finance & Accountancy *(WC2)*
Church House *(SW1)*
Institute of Directors *(SW1)*
Institute of Materials *(SW1)*
Institution of Civil Engineers *(SW1)*
Institution of Mechanical Engineers *(SW1)*
The Law Society *(WC2)*
Royal Aeronautical Society *(W1)*
Royal Institute of British Architects *(W1)*
Royal Institution of Great Britain *(W1)*
Royal Society Of Arts *(WC2)*
RUSI Building *(SW1)*

Private venues by type

School Of Pharmacy *(WC1)*

West
Commonwealth Institute *(W8)*
French Institute *(SW7)*
Royal Geographical Society *(SW7)*

East
Lloyd's Of London *(EC3)*
London Press Centre *(EC4)*
Trinity House *(EC3)*

Moored boats

Central
RS Hispaniola *(WC2)*
Thames Sailing Barge Wilfred *(WC2)*
HQS Wellington *(WC2)*
N° 1 Yacht Club *(WC2)*
TS Queen Mary *(WC2)*

South
HMS Belfast *(SE1)*

East
Leven is Strijd *(E14)*
HMS President *(EC4)*
Scone *(E14)*

Theatres

Central
The Coliseum *(WC2)*
London Palladium *(W1)*
Palace Theatre *(W1)*
Royal Opera House *(WC2)*
Theatre Royal *(WC2)*

West
Royal Albert Hall *(SW7)*

South
Royal National Theatre *(SE1)*
The South Bank Centre *(SE1)*

East
Mermaid Theatre *(EC4)*

Miscellaneous

Central
Astoria *(WC2)*
Christie's *(SW1)*
Congress Centre *(WC1)*
Dolphin Square *(SW1)*
Hamilton Suite *(W1)*
New Zealand House *(SW1)*
Phillips *(W1)*
St Martin In The Fields *(WC2)*
The Sanctuary *(WC2)*
Sotherby's *(W1)*

Westminster Boating Base *(SW1)*

West
Bonham's *(SW7)*
The Chelsea Gardener *(SW3)*
Chelsea Physic Garden *(SW3)*
Gunnersbury Park *(W3)*
Orangery (Holland Park) *(W8)*
Orangery (Kensington Palace) *(W8)*
Queen's Ice Skating Club *(W2)*
Westway Studios *(W11)*

North
Diorama *(NW1)*

South
Battersea Park *(SW8)*
Cottons Atrium *(SE1)*
Guy's Hospital Tower *(SE1)*
The London Television Centre *(SE1)*
Streatham Mega Bowl *(SW2)*

East
All Saints - The Crypt *(E14)*
Barbican Centre *(EC2)*
Broadgate Estates *(EC2)*
Hamilton House *(EC4)*
K Warehouse *(E6)*
St Etheldreda's Crypt *(EC1)*
Tower Bridge *(EC3)*

Outside London
Bath – Pump Room *(Avon)*
Pinewood Studios *(Bucks)*
Queen's Eyot *(Berks)*
Temple Island *(Oxon)*

Clubs

Central
Annabel's *(W1)*
Arts Club *(W1)*
The Caledonian Club *(SW1)*
Cavalry & Guards Club *(W1)*
East India Club *(SW1)*
41 Beak St *(W1)*
Irish Club *(SW1)*
Lansdowne Club *(W1)*
Mortons Club *(W1)*
Mosimann's Belfry *(SW1)*
National Liberal Club *(SW1)*
Naval & Military Club *(W1)*
Oxford & Cambridge Club *(SW1)*
Reform Club *(SW1)*
Royal Over-Seas League *(SW1)*

Private venues by type

Ski Club of Great Britain (SW1)
Spanish Club (W1)
St Stephens Constitutional Club (SW1)
University Women's Club (W1)

West
The Draycott (SW3)
Hurlingham Club (SW6)
Polish Hearth Club (SW7)
Polish Social & Cultural Association (W6)
Raffles Dining Room (SW3)

North
Czech Club (NW6)

South
Bank Of England Club (SW15)
London Rowing Club (SW15)
University of London Boat Club (SW15)
Winchester House Club (SW15)

East
The Bankers Club (EC2)
City Livery Club (EC4)
City Of London Club (EC2)
The Little Ship Club (EC4)
St Andrew Golf Club (EC4)

Nightclubs

Central
Bar Industria (W1)
Browns Club (WC2)
Busby's (W1)
Café de Paris (W1)
Circa (W1)
Equinox at the Empire (WC2)
The Gaslight (SW1)
Hash Eleven (W1)
The Hippodrome (WC2)
Iceni (W1)
Legends (W1)
Limelight (W1)
Maximus (W1)
The RAW Club (WC1)
Rock Garden (WC2)
Ruby's (W1)
St Moritz (W1)
Le Scandale (W1)
SW1 Club (SW1)
Wag (W1)
Xenon (W1)

West
Bratts (SW7)
The Chariots (SW3)
Crazy Larry's (SW10)
El-Cid (SW10)
Le Hammersmith Palais (W6)
The Roof Gardens (W8)
606 Club (SW10)
Subterania (W10)
Upstairs At 58 (W11)

North
Electric Ballroom (NW1)
HQ (NW1)
Jazz Café (NW1)
Jongleurs at Camden Lock (NW1)
WKD (NW1)

South
Café Club (SE1)
The Fridge (SW2)
Jongleurs at The Cornet (SW11)
The Ministry of Sound (SE1)
Wessex House (SW11)

East
Turnmills (EC1)

Wine & Cocktail bars

Central
Balls Brothers (SW1)
Brahms & Liszt (WC2)
Davy's Wine Bars
Larry's Wine Bar (WC2)
The O-Bar (W1)
Pimlico Wine Vaults (SW1)
Rochesters (SW1)
Shampers (W1)
Vat's (WC1)

West
Church's (W8)
Davy's Wine Bars
Hollands (W11)
Pitcher & Piano (SW10)

South
Balls Brothers (SE1)
Davy's Wine Bars
Hop Cellars (SE1)

East
Balls Brothers
Betjeman's (EC1)
Bill Bentley's (EC2)
Bleeding Heart (EC1)
Corney & Barrow
Davy's Wine Bars (EC2)
Eatons (EC3)
Leadenhall Tapas Bar (EC3)
Punters (EC4)
The Vaults (EC1)

Private venues by type

Pubs

Central
Antelope *(SW1)*
The Argyll Arms *(W1)*
The Barley Mow *(W1)*
Calthorpe Arms *(WC1)*
Cittie of Yorke *(WC1)*
The Clachan *(W1)*
The Coal Hole *(WC2)*
The Crown and Two Chairmen *(W1)*
The Dog & Duck *(W1)*
Duke of Albemarle *(W1)*
The Freemason's Arms *(WC2)*
Glassblower *(W1)*
The Glasshouse Stores *(W1)*
The Golden Lion *(SW1)*
The Plough *(WC2)*
Shelleys *(W1)*
Slug & Lettuce *(SW1)*
Star Tavern *(SW1)*
The Sun *(WC2)*
The Tattershall Castle *(SW1)*
Two Chairmen *(SW1)*
Walkers Of St James's *(SW1)*

West
Britannia *(W8)*
The Catherine Wheel *(W8)*
Coopers Arms *(SW3)*
Duke of Clarence *(W11)*
Phene Arms *(SW3)*
Shuckburgh Arms *(SW3)*
The White Horse *(SW6)*

South
Anchor *(SE1)*
Crown & Greyhound *(SE21)*
Doggetts Coat & Badge *(SE1)*
George Inn *(SE1)*
The Horniman At Hay's *(SE1)*
The Old Thameside Inn *(SE1)*
Southwark Tavern *(SE1)*
Trafalgar Tavern *(SE10)*

East
Captain Kidd *(E1)*
The Crown Tavern *(EC1)*
Bishop's Parlour *(EC2)*
Bishop of Norwich *(EC2)*
Dickens Inn *(E1)*
King of Diamonds *(EC1)*
The Lamb Tavern *(EC3)*
Simpsons of Cornhill *(EC3)*
Ye Olde Cheshire Cheese *(EC4)*

Restaurants

Central
Ajimura *(WC2)*
L'Amico *(SW1)*
Au Jardin des Gourmets *(W1)*
Bahn Thai *(W1)*
Bentleys *(W1)*
Beotys *(WC2)*
Boardwalk *(W1)*
La Capannina *(W1)*
Chez Gerard *(W1)*
Chez Nico *(W1)*
Chiang Mai *(W1)*
Chuen Cheng Ku *(W1)*
The Criterion *(W1)*
Drones *(SW1)*
Eatons *(SW1)*
Empress Garden *(W1)*
L'Escargot *(W1)*
L'Etoile *(W1)*
Footstool *(SW1)*
Fung Shing *(WC2)*
Le Gavroche *(W1)*
Gay Hussar *(W1)*
Gopal's of Soho *(W1)*
Green's *(SW1)*
The Guinea *(W1)*
Hodgson's *(WC2)*
Ikkyu *(W1)*
L'Incontro *(SW1)*
Ivy *(WC2)*
Kaya Korean *(W1)*
Ken Lo's Memories *(SW1)*
Kettners *(W1)*
Knightsbridge Place *(SW1)*
Leoni's Quo Vadis *(W1)*
Ley-Ons *(W1)*
Lindsay House *(W1)*
Mekong *(SW1)*
Mélange *(WC2)*
Mimmo d'Ischia *(SW1)*
Ming *(W1)*
Mirabelle *(W1)*
Mitsukoshi *(SW1)*
Mon Plaisir *(WC2)*
Motcomb's *(SW1)*
Mr Kong *(WC2)*
Neal St *(WC2)*
Now & Zen *(WC2)*
Opera Terazza! *(WC2)*
Pizzeria Condotti *(W1)*
Pomegranates *(SW1)*
Quaglino's *(SW1)*
Red Fort *(W1)*
Rib Room *(SW1)*
Rodos *(WC2)*
Rose Garden Restaurant *(W1)*
Rules *(WC2)*

Private venues by type

Saigon *(W1)*
Les Saveurs *(W1)*
Seafresh *(SW1)*
Sheekey's *(WC2)*
Shepherd's *(SW1)*
Simpsons-in-the-Strand *(WC2)*
Soho Soho *(W1)*
Solange's *(WC2)*
Spaghetti House *(W1)*
Suntory *(SW1)*
Tuttons *(WC2)*
Villandry Dining Rooms *(W1)*
White Tower *(W1)*
Wiltons *(SW1)*
Zen Central *(W1)*

West
Al Basha *(W8)*
Al San Vincenzo *(W2)*
All Saints *(W10)*
The Ark *(W11)*
L'Artiste Assoiffé *(W11)*
Balzac *(W12)*
Bar Escoba *(SW7)*
Barbarella 1 *(SW6)*
Barbarella 2 *(SW7)*
Beauchamp Place *(SW3)*
Belvedere *(W8)*
Benihana *(SW3)*
Bombay Brasserie *(SW7)*
Borscht & Tears *(SW3)*
Boyd's *(W8)*
Busabong Too *(SW10)*
Café Lazeez *(SW7)*
Canal Brasserie *(W10)*
Chapter 11 *(SW10)*
Cibo *(W14)*
Costa's Grill *(W8)*
Dan's *(SW3)*
La Dordogne *(W4)*
Downstairs At 190 *(SW7)*
English Garden *(SW3)*
English House *(SW3)*
L'Express *(SW1)*
La Famiglia *(SW10)*
First Floor *(W11)*
Formula Veneta *(SW10)*
Foxtrot Oscar *(SW3)*
Front Page *(SW3)*
Henry J Beans *(SW3)*
Jakes *(SW10)*
Julie's *(W11)*
Launceston Place *(W8)*
Leith's *(W11)*
Lou Pescadou *(SW5)*
Mao Tai *(SW6)*
Le Midi *(SW6)*
Monkeys *(SW3)*
The Nosh Brothers *(SW6)*

Paulo's *(W6)*
Pigeon *(SW6)*
Poissonnerie de l'Avenue *(SW3)*
La Pomme d'Amour *(W11)*
St Quentin *(SW3)*
San Martino *(SW3)*
Le Suquet *(SW3)*
Thierry's *(SW3)*
Turners *(SW3)*
V&A Museum Café *(SW7)*
Walton's *(SW3)*
Wilson's *(W14)*
Zen *(SW3)*

North
Le Carapace *(NW3)*
Crown & Goose *(NW1)*
Feng Shang *(NW1)*
Frederick's *(N1)*
Haandi *(NW1)*
Minogue's Bar *(N1)*
Odette's *(NW1)*
The Viceroy *(NW1)*
ZeNW3 *(NW3)*

South
Alma *(SW18)*
The Battersea Barge Bistro *(SW8)*
Café Greenwich Park *(SE10)*
Le Gothique *(SW18)*
Jason's *(SW11)*
Le Pont de la Tour *(SE1)*
RSJ *(SE1)*
Tall House *(SE1)*
La Truffe Noir *(SE1)*

East
Brasserie Rocque *(EC2)*
Bubb's *(EC1)*
Café St Pierre *(EC1)*
Champenois *(EC2)*
City Miyama *(EC4)*
Coates Karaoke Bar & Restaurant *(EC2)*
Fox & Anchor *(EC1)*
Hubble & Co *(EC1)*
Imperial City *(EC3)*
The Kosher Luncheon Club *(E1)*
SB Lady Gwynfred *(E14)*
Le Mesurier *(EC1)*
La Paquerette *(EC2)*
The Place Below *(EC2)*
Quayside *(E1)*
Sweetings *(EC4)*
The Tank *(EC1)*
Tatsuso *(EC2)*
Throgmorton's *(EC2)*
Whittington's *(EC4)*
Wynkyn de Worde *(EC4)*

Private venues by type

Hotels

Central
Athenaeum Hotel *(W1)*
The Berkeley *(SW1)*
The Berkshire *(W1)*
Britannia Intercontinental Hotel *(W1)*
Brown's Hotel *(W1)*
The Cadogan *(SW1)*
The Chelsea *(SW1)*
Churchill *(W1)*
Claridge's *(W1)*
The Connaught *(W1)*
Cumberland Hotel *(W1)*
The Dorchester *(W1)*
Dukes Hotel *(SW1)*
Durrants Hotel *(W1)*
Forte Crest St James's *(SW1)*
Forte Crest Regents Park *(W1)*
Four Seasons Hotel *(W1)*
Goring Hotel *(SW1)*
Grosvenor Hotel *(SW1)*
Grosvenor House Hotel *(W1)*
The Halkin *(SW1)*
Hampshire Hotel *(WC2)*
Hilton on Park Lane *(W1)*
Holiday Inn – Mayair *(W1)*
Howard Hotel *(WC2)*
Hyatt Carlton Tower *(SW1)*
Hyde Park Hotel *(SW1)*
Inter-Continental *(W1)*
The Lanesborough *(SW1)*
Langham Hilton *(W1)*
London Marriott *(W1)*
The Mayfair *(W1)*
Le Meridien *(W1)*
Mount Royal Hotel *(W1)*
The Mountbatten *(WC2)*
Park Lane Hotel *(W1)*
The Regent *(W1)*
The Ritz *(W1)*
Rochester Hotel *(SW1)*
Royal Horseguards Thistle Hotel *(SW1)*
Rubens Hotel *(SW1)*
Russell *(WC1)*
The Savoy *(WC2)*
Selfridge Hotel *(W1)*
Sheraton Belgravia *(SW1)*
Sheraton Park Tower *(SW1)*
The Stafford *(SW1)*
Stakis St Ermins *(SW1)*
Strand Palace Hotel *(WC2)*
22 Jermyn St *(SW1)*
Waldorf Hotel *(WC2)*
Washington Hotel *(W1)*
Westbury Hotel *(W1)*

West
Basil Street Hotel *(SW3)*
The Capital *(SW3)*
Conrad Hotel *(SW10)*
Gloucester Hotel *(SW7)*
Halcyon Hotel *(W11)*
Kensington Palace Thistle *(W8)*
London Metropole *(W2)*
The Rembrandt Hotel *(SW7)*
Royal Garden Hotel *(W8)*
Royal Lancaster *(W2)*
Vanderbilt Hotel *(SW7)*

North
White House Hotel *(NW1)*

South
Cannizaro House *(SW19)*

East
Tower Thistle *(E1)*

Outside London
Cliveden *(Berks)*
Monkey Island *(Berks)*

Private venues with outside areas

Venues with outside areas
(see also: Moving Venues – Boats)

Central
Arts Club *(W1)*
Dartmouth House *(W1)*
The Dorchester *(W1)*
Dukes Hotel *(SW1)*
11 Hobart Place *(SW1)*
El Barco Latino *(WC2)*
Guards Museum *(SW1)*
RS Hispaniola *(WC2)*
ICA *(SW1)*
Iceni *(W1)*
The Imagination Gallery *(WC1)*
International Students House *(W1)*
Lansdowne Club *(W1)*
Lincoln's Inn *(WC2)*
Mosimann's Belfry *(SW1)*
National Liberal Club *(SW1)*
Naval & Military Club *(W1)*
New Zealand House *(SW1)*
Opera Terazza! *(WC2)*
TS Queen Mary *(WC2)*
The Ritz *(W1)*
Rose Garden Restaurant *(W1)*
Royal Aeronautical Society *(W1)*
Royal Horseguards Thistle Hotel *(SW1)*
Royal Parks Executive Agency
Sheraton Park Tower *(SW1)*
Spencer House *(SW1)*
St Stephens Constitutional Club *(SW1)*
University of London Union *(WC1)*
University Women's Club *(W1)*
HQS Wellington *(WC2)*
Westminster Boating Base *(SW1)*

West
Accademia Italiana *(SW7)*
Belvedere *(W8)*
Canal Brasserie *(W10)*
The Chelsea Gardener *(SW3)*
Chelsea Physic Garden *(SW3)*
Chiswick House *(W4)*
Commonwealth Institute *(W8)*
Dan's *(SW3)*
The Draycott *(SW3)*
Duke of York's HQ *(SW3)*
Fulham Palace *(SW6)*
Gunnersbury Park *(W3)*
Henry J Beans *(SW3)*
Hurlingham Club *(SW6)*
Imperial College *(SW7)*
Orangery (Holland Park) *(W8)*
Orangery (Kensington Palace) *(W8)*
Paulo's *(W6)*
Peacock House *(W14)*
Polish Hearth Club *(SW7)*
The Roof Gardens *(W8)*
Serpentine Gallery *(W2)*
Shuckburgh Arms *(SW3)*
Stanley House *(SW10)*
V&A Museum *(SW7)*

North
Alexandra Palace & Park *(N22)*
Canonbury Academy *(N1)*
Cecil Sharp House *(NW1)*
Freud Museum *(NW3)*
Lauderdale House *(N6)*
London Zoo *(NW1)*
Regent's College *(NW1)*
Royal Air Force Museum *(NW9)*
Royal Veterinary College *(NW1)*

South
Academy of Live & Recorded Arts *(SW18)*
Anchor *(SE1)*
Bank Of England Club *(SW15)*
Battersea Park *(SW8)*
HMS Belfast *(SE1)*
Café Greenwich Park *(SE10)*
Cannizaro House *(SW19)*
The Conservatory *(SW11)*
Cutty Sark *(SE10)*
Design Museum *(SE1)*
Doggetts Coat & Badge *(SE1)*
Dulwich College *(SE21)*
Dulwich Picture Gallery *(SE21)*
Froebel Institute College *(SW15)*
Le Gothique *(SW18)*
London Rowing Club *(SW15)*
Marble Hill House *(TW1)*
Museum of Garden History *(SE1)*
Pentland House *(SE3)*
Queen's House *(SE10)*
Ranger's House *(SE10)*

Private venues for marquees

The South Bank Centre *(SE1)*
University of London Boat Club *(SW15)*
Victoria Pump House *(SW8)*
Winchester House Club *(SW15)*

East
Bleeding Heart *(EC1)*
Brasserie Rocque *(EC2)*
Broadgate Estates *(EC2)*
Gray's Inn *(EC1)*
Honourable Artillery Co *(EC1)*
Inner Temple Hall *(EC4)*
King of Diamonds *(EC1)*
Merchant Taylors' Hall *(EC2)*
Middle Temple Hall *(EC4)*
Museum of London *(EC2)*
La Paquerette *(EC2)*
HMS President *(EC4)*
Quayside *(E1)*
St John's Gate *(EC1)*
Skinners' Hall *(EC4)*

Outside London
Beaulieu *(Hants)*
Blenheim Palace *(Oxon)*
Brocket Hall *(Herts)*
Clandon *(Surrey)*
Cliveden *(Berks)*
Ham House *(Surrey)*
Hampton Court *(Surrey)*
Hever Castle *(Kent)*
Knebworth House *(Herts)*
Leeds Castle *(Kent)*
Monkey Island *(Berks)*
Pinewood Studios *(Bucks)*
Queen's Eyot *(Berks)*
Royal Botanic Gardens *(Surrey)*
Royal Holloway College *(Surrey)*
Syon Park *(Middx)*
Temple Island *(Oxon)*

Marquee Sites

Central
Guards Museum *(SW1)*
Spencer House *(W1)*
Westminster Boating Base *(SW1)*

West
Chelsea Physic Garden *(SW3)*
Chelsea Harbour Rooms *(SW10)*
Chiswick House *(W4)*
Commonwealth Institute *(W8)*
Duke of York's HQ *(SW3)*
Fulham Palace *(SW6)*
Orangery (Holland Park) *(W8)*
Peacock House *(W14)*
Stanley House *(SW10)*

North
Alexandra Palace & Park *(N22)*
London Zoo *(NW1)*
Regent's College *(NW1)*
Royal Air Force Museum *(NW9)*

South
Bank Of England Club *(SW15)*
Battersea Park *(SW8)*
Dulwich College *(SE21)*
Dulwich Picture Gallery *(SE21)*
Froebel Institute College *(SW15)*
Hollyhedge House *(SE3)*
Pentland House *(SE3)*
Queen's House *(SE10)*
Ranger's House *(SE10)*
Winchester House Club *(SW15)*

East
Hon. Artillery Co *(EC1)*
Inner Temple Hall *(EC4)*
St John's Gate *(EC1)*

Outside London
Beaulieu *(Hants)*
Blenheim Palace *(Oxon)*
Brocket Hall *(Herts)*
Clandon *(Surrey)*
Cliveden *(Berks)*
Ham House *(Surrey)*
Hampton Court, Tiltyard *(Surrey)*
Kempton Park *(Middx)*
Knebworth House *(Herts)*
Leeds Castle *(Kent)*
Pinewood Studios *(Bucks)*
Queen's Eyot *(Berks)*
Royal Botanic Gardens *(Surrey)*
Royal Holloway College *(Surrey)*
Syon Park *(Middx)*
Temple Island *(Oxon)*

Private venues – standing

CAPACITY LISTS

(Note: particularly with hotels, it may be possible to divide rooms to provide smaller accommodation.)

Venues listed by standing capacity

* **largest entry for venue**
† **dancing is possible at the venue (not necessarily in the room named)**

£E

1500	Hampton Ct Pal., Surrey *(Max*)*
1000	Brit. Mus. WC1 *(Max*)*
	Royal Acad. of Arts W1 *(Summer Exhib.*)*
700	V&A Mus. SW7 *(Dome, Medieval Treasury (& Pirelli Gdn)*)*
600	Spencer Hs† SW1 *(Max*)*
	V&A Mus. SW7 *(Raphael Cartoon Ct)*
500	Blenheim Pal.†, Oxon *(Max*)*
	Hampton Ct Pal., Surrey *(Gt Hall)*
	Tate Gall. SW1 *(Pre Raphaelite & c18 Gall.*)*
400	Tate Gall. SW1 *(Sackler Octagon)*
	V&A Mus. SW7 *(Gamble Rm (inc Morris Rm))*
350	Courtauld Inst. WC2 *(Max*)*
	Royal Acad. of Arts W1 *(Private Rms)*
	Syon Pk (Hs)†, Middx *(Max*)*
	Wallace Collection W1 *(Gt Gall.*)*
300	Nat. Portrait Gall. WC2 *(Max*)*
250	Cliveden†, Berks *(Max*)*
	Hayward Gall. SE1 *(Max*)*
	V&A Mus. SW7 *(Other Galls.)*
200	Apsley Hs W1 *(Max*)*
	Queen's Hs† SE10 *(Henrietta Maria Suite*)*
	Tate Gall. SW1 *(Clore Gall. Foyer)*
180	Brocket Hall†, Herts *(Max*)*
150	Courtauld Inst. WC2 *(First Fl)*
	Queen's Hs† SE10 *(Orangery or Van De Velde Suite)*
120	Queen's Hs SE10 *(Treasury)*
100	Cliveden†, Berks *(Churchill Boardroom)*
80	Old Royal Observatory SE10 *(Octagon Rm*)*
	V&A Mus. SW7 *(Morris Rm)*
50	Tate Gall. SW1 *(Clore Gall. Reading Rm)*
	Wallace Collection W1 *(Gall. 17)*
40	Wallace Collection W1 *(Arms & Armoury)*
30	Queen's Hs† SE10 *(Loggia)*
25	Tate Gall. SW1 *(Lodge)*

£M-E

2500	Beaulieu†, Hants *(Nat. Motor Mus.*)*
2000	Leeds Castle†, Kent *(Cedar Lawn*)*
	London Zoo† NW1 *(Marquee*)*
1500	Grosvenor Hs Htl† W1 *(Gt Rm*)*
	Guildhall EC2 *(Max*)*
1400	Inter-Continental† W1 *(Grand Ballroom Suite*)*
	Natural History Mus† SW7 *(Central Hall*)*
	RAF Mus.† NW9 *(Max*)*
1200	Westway Studios† W11 *(Max*)*
1000	Hilton on Pk Ln† W1 *(Grand Ballroom*)*
	Imp. War Mus.† SE1 *(Max*)*
	Park Ln Htl† W1 *(Ballroom*)*
	Saatchi Gall. NW8 *(Max*)*
	Dorchester† W1 *(Ballroom*)*
900	Guildhall EC2 *(Gt Hall)*
800	Claridge's† W1 *(Max*)*
	Imp. War Mus.† SE1 *(Exhib. Hall)*
	Savoy† WC2 *(Lancaster Rm*)*
750	Four Seasons Htl W1 *(Ballroom*)*
	Grosvenor Hs Htl† W1 *(Ballroom)*
	Royal Albert Hall† SW7 *(Arena*)*
	Westway Studios† W11 *(Studio 1)*
700	RAF Mus.† NW9 *(Bomber Command Hall or Main Aircraft Hall)*
	Science Mus.† SW7 *(East Hall*)*
	Xenon† W1 *(Max*)*
650	Hyatt Carlton Tower† SW1 *(Ballroom*)*
	Hyde Pk Htl† SW1 *(Ballroom & Knightsbridge Suite*)*
600	Christie's† SW1 *(Max*)*
	Guildhall EC2 *(Old Library)*
	Inter-Continental† W1 *(Park Suite)*
	Knebworth Hs, Herts *(Geodesic Dome*)*
	Lincoln's Inn† WC2 *(Gt Hall*)*
	Mme Tussaud's† NW1 *(Max*)*
	Xenon† W1 *(Main Rm)*
590	Westway Studios† W11 *(Studio 2)*
550	Barbican Ctr† EC2 *(Max*)*
	Knebworth Hs†, Herts *(Manor & Lodge Barns)*
500	Banqueting Hs† SW1 *(Main Hall*)*
	Goldsmiths' Hall EC2 *(Livery Hall*)*
	Hilton on Pk Ln† W1 *(Grand Ballroom - Section 1)*
	Imagination Gall.† WC1 *(Atrium & Mezz.*)*
	Merchant Taylors' Hall EC2 *(Gt Hall*)*
	Middle Temple Hall† EC4 *(Hall*)*
	Reform Club† SW1 *(Max*)*
	Royal Albert Hall† SW7 *(Gods)*
	Regent† W1 *(Ballroom*)*
	South Bank Ctr SE1 *(Queen Elizabeth Hall Foyer*)*
450	Barbican Ctr† EC2 *(Art Gall.)*
	Berkeley† SW1 *(Ballroom*)*
	Gray's Inn† EC1 *(Max*)*
	Hilton on Pk Ln† W1 *(Grand Ballroom - Section 2)*
	Hyde Pk Htl† SW1 *(Ballroom)*
	Inner Temple Hall† EC4 *(Hall*)*
	Mme Tussaud's† NW1 *(Grand Hall)*
420	Roof Gdns† W8 *(Max*)*
400	Barbican Ctr† EC2 *(Gdn Rm)*
	Claridge's† W1 *(Ballroom)*
	Criterion W1 *(Max*)*
	Le Meridien† W1 *(Georgian*)*
	London Dungeon† SE1
	Mus. of London† EC2 *(Max*)*
	Mus. of the Moving Image† SE1 *(Festival Pavilion*)*

Private venues – standing

Natural History Mus. SW7
(Gem Stone Fl)
Park Ln Htl† W1 *(Tudor Rose Rm)*
RAF Mus.† NW9
(Battle of Britain Hall)
Royal Botanic Gdns, Surrey
(Temperate Hs)*
Royal Coll. of Music† SW7
(Concert Hall)*
Science Mus.† SW7
(Flight Gall.)
Sotherby's W1 *(Max*)*
Stationers' Hall† EC4
(Livery Hall)*
Savoy† WC2
(Abraham Lincoln Rm & Manhattan Rm)

380 London Zoo† NW1 *(Regency Suite)*
360 Regent W1† *(Empire Rm)*
350 Banqueting Hs† SW1 *(Undercroft)*
Clothworkers' Hall EC3
(Livery Hall)
Inst. of Directors† SW1 *(Nash*)*
Le Meridien† W1 *(Edwardian)*
Savoy† WC2 *(River Rm)*
Science Mus. SW7 *(Launch Pad)*
Serpentine Gall.† W2 *(Max*)*
320 Knebworth Hs†, Herts *(House)*
310 Regent† W1 *(Music Rm)*
300 Beaulieu†, Hants *(Brabazon)*
Dulwich Picture Gall. SE21
(Max)*
Four Seasons Htl† W1
(Pk Rm or Gdn Rm)
Gray's Inn† EC1 *(Hall)*
Hamiltons Gall. W1 *(Max*)*
Hilton on Pk Ln W1 *(Curzon Suite)*
Imagination Gall.† WC1 *(Gall.)*
Knebworth Hs†, Herts
(Manor Barn)
Reform Club† SW1
(Library or Coffee Rm)
Regent† W1 *(Drawing Rm)*
Royal Opera Hs WC2 *(Max*)*
Searcy's† SW1 *(Max*)*
Skinners' Hall† EC4 *(Max*)*
Westway Studios† W11
(Studio 3)
250 Barbican Ctr† EC2 *(Conserv. Ter.)*
Caledonian Club† SW1
(Members Dining Rm)*
Dorchester† W1 *(Orchid)*
Grocers' Hall EC2 *(Dining Rm*)*
Guildhall EC2
(East Crypt, West Crypt or Livery Hall)
Hilton on Pk Ln† W1
(Crystal Pal. Rm)
Inst. of Materials† SW1 *(Max*)*
Knebworth Hs†, Herts
(Lodge Barn)
Leeds Castle†, Kent
(Henry VIII Banqueting Hall or Fairfax Hall)
Lincoln's Inn† WC2 *(Old Hall)*
Mme Tussaud's† NW1 *(Gdn Party)*
Mus. of London† EC2
(Lord Mayor's Coach Gall.)
Mus. of the Moving
Image† SE1 *(Max)*
Natural History Mus† SW7
(North Hall)
Phillips W1 *(Max*)*
Rock Circus† W1 *(Max*)*
Science Mus.† SW7
(Wellcome Gall. 1 & 2)
Sheraton Pk Tower† SW1
(Trianon Rm)
Ritz† W1 *(Palm Ct & Marie Antoinette*)*
Sanctuary† WC2 *(Max*)*
South Bank Ctr SE1
(Hong Kong & Chelsfield Rm)

Theatre Mus. WC2
(Paintings Gall.)*
230 Boat: Woods River Svcs† SE3
(Silver Barracuda)*
225 Hyde Pk Htl† SW1
(Knightsbridge Rm)
224 Clothworkers' Hall EC3
(Drawing Rm)
220 Royal Albert Hall† SW7
(Elgar Rm)
200 Apothecaries' Hall EC4 *(Hall*)*
Arts Club† W1 *(Dining Rm*)*
Bank of Eng. Mus EC2 *(Max*)*
Cabinet War Rms† SW1 *(Max*)*
Chelsea† SW1 *(Sloane Suite*)*
Goldsmiths' Hall EC2
(Drawing Rm or Exhib. Rm)
Hilton on Pk Ln† W1 *(Harvest Rm)*
Howard Htl WC2 *(Fitzalan)*
HQS Wellington WC2 *(Ct Rm*)*
Mirabelle† W1 *(Max*)*
Mus. of Mankind W1 *(Max*)*
Natural History Mus† SW7
(Spencer Gall, Mammal Gall. or Lasting Impressions)
Orangery (Kensington
Pal.) W8 *(Max*)*
Royal Albert Hall† SW7
(Picture Gall.)
Science Mus.† SW7
(Fellows' Rm or Space Gall.)
South Bank Ctr SE1
(Level 5 External Ter.)
180 Beaulieu†, Hants *(Domus)*
Cutty Sark SE10
('Tween Decks or Lower Hold)*
Hampshire Htl† WC2 *(Penthouse*)*
Inter-Continental† W1
(Windsor Suite)
London Zoo† NW1 *(Reptile Hs)*
Merchant Taylors' Hall EC2
(Parlour)
175 Inner Temple Hall† EC4
(Parliament Chamber)
160 HQS Wellington WC2 *(Afterdeck)*
150 Brighton Royal
Pavilion, Sussex *(Gt Kitchen*)*
Four Seasons Htl† W1 *(Oak Rm)*
Gray's Inn† EC1
(Large Reception Rm)
Grosvenor Hs Htl† W1 *(Albemarle)*
Halkin SW1 *(Max*)*
Hilton on Pk Ln† W1
(Coronation Rm)
Howard Htl WC2 *(Arundel Suite)*
Hyde Pk Htl† SW1
(King Gustav Adolf Suite)
Innholders' Hall EC4 *(Hall*)*
Inst. of Directors† SW1 *(Burton)*
Leeds Castle†, Kent
(State Dining Rm)
Leighton Hs W14 *(Max*)*
London Zoo† NW1
(Raffles Bar & Rest.)
Monkey Island†, Berks
(River Rm)*
Mus. of London† EC2
(Medieval Gall.)
Park Ln Htl† W1 *(Gdn Rm)*
Raffles Dining Rm† SW3 *(Max*)*
Ritz† W1 *(Italian Gdn)*
Royal Botanic Gdns, Surrey
(Kew Gdns Gall.)
Stationers' Hall† EC4 *(Ct Rm)*
Temple Island, Oxon *(Marquee*)*
Westway Studios† W11
(Studio 4)
140 Bank of Eng. Mus EC2
(during temporary exhib.s)

195

Private venues – standing

	Mosimann's Belfry† SW1 *(Dining Rm*)*
	Park Ln Htl† W1 *(Oak Rm)*
130	Hever Castle, Kent *(Tudor Suite*)*
	Middle Temple Hall† EC4 *(Parliament Chamber)*
125	Armourers' & Braisers' Hall EC2 *(Livery Hall or Drawing Rm*)*
	HQS Wellington† WC2 *(Model Rm & Library)*
	Le Meridien† W1 *(Adams / Regency)*
	Science Mus.† SW7 *(Wellcome Gall. 1)*
120	Barbican Ctr† EC2 *(Conserv.)*
	Berkeley† SW1 *(Crystal Rm)*
	Claridge's† W1 *(Drawing Rm or French Salon or Mirror Rm)*
	Dukes Htl† SW1 *(Marlborough Suite*)*
	Hyde Pk Htl† SW1 *(Pk Suite)*
	Inst. of Directors† SW1 *(Waterloo)*
	Inst. of Materials† SW1 *(Council Rm)*
	Leeds Castle†, Kent *(Gate-tower or Dog Collar Mus.)*
	Merchant Taylors' Hall EC2 *(Cloisters)*
	Ranger's Hs SE10 *(Max*)*
	Royal Albert Hall† SW7 *(Victoria Rm)*
	Savoy† WC2 *(Beaufort)*
	Xenon† W1 *(Piano Bar (Gr Fl))*
100	Arts Club† W1 *(Drawing Rm, Bar & Conserv.)*
	Brighton Royal Pavilion, Sussex *(Queen Adelaide Suite)*
	Cannizaro Hs SW19 *(Viscount Melville, Earl of Mexborough & Lady Jane*)*
	Criterion W1 *(Ter.)*
	Dorchester† W1 *(Pk Suite)*
	Dukes Htl† SW1 *(Roof Ter.)*
	Halcyon Htl† W11 *(Rest.*)*
	Inner Temple Hall† EC4 *(Luncheon Rm)*
	Inst. of Materials† SW1 *(Library)*
	Inter-Continental† W1 *(Byron Rm)*
	Lanesborough† SW1 *(Wellington Rm*)*
	Lincoln's Inn† WC2 *(Drawing Rm)*
	Middle Temple Hall† EC4 *(Smoking Rm)*
	Mus. of London† EC2 *(Eighteenth Century Gall.)*
	Stafford SW1 *(Panel Rm & Sutherland Rm*)*
90	Boat: Woods River Svcs† SE3 *(Silver Dolphin)*
	Grocers' Hall EC2 *(Piper Rm)*
80	Accademia Italiana SW7 *(Main Galls. or Spazio Club*)*
	Brighton Royal Pavilion, Sussex *(William IV Rm)*
	Dorchester† W1 *(Holford)*
	Lanesborough† SW1 *(St George's Rm)*
	Middle Temple Hall† EC4 *(Queen's Rm)*
	Mosimann's Belfry† SW1 *(Harvey Nichols)*
	Park Ln Htl† W1 *(Orchard Suite)*
	Royal Coll. of Music† SW7 *(Donaldson Rm)*
	Stationers' Hall† EC4 *(Stock Rm)*
	Ritz† W1 *(Berkeley Suite Reception Rm & Dining Rm or Marie Antoinette Suite)*
	Savoy WC2 *(Pinafore)*
75	Imp. War Mus.† SE1 *(Boardroom 1)*
	Stafford SW1 *(Cellar)*
70	Berkeley† SW1 *(Waterloo Rm)*
	Caledonian Club† SW1 *(Smoking Rm)*
	Dukes Htl SW1 *(Double Suite)*
	Leighton Hs W14 *(Arab Hall)*
	Regent† W1 *(Champagne Rm)*
65	Caledonian Club† SW1 *(Stuart)*
	Hilton on Pk Ln† W1 *(Pompeii Rm)*
60	Dorchester† W1 *(Pavilion)*
	Four Seasons Htl† W1 *(Pine Rm)*
	Hyde Pk Htl† SW1 *(Loggia)*
	London Zoo† NW1 *(Insect Hs)*
	Marble Hill Hs TW1 *(Max*)*
	Mosimann's Belfry† SW1 *(Wedgewood)*
	Lanesborough† SW1 *(Westminster Rm)*
50	Berkeley† SW1 *(Tattersall's Rm)*
	Cannizaro Hs SW19 *(Viscount Melville)*
	Claridge's† W1 *(Private Suite)*
	Gray's Inn† EC1 *(Landing)*
	Green's SW1 *(Private Rm*)*
	HQS Wellington WC2 *(Reception Area)*
	Inst. of Directors† SW1 *(Trafalgar II / St James)*
	Lanesborough† SW1 *(Wilkins Rm)*
	Leeds Castle†, Kent *(Grotto)*
	Raffles Dining Rm† SW3 *(DiningRm)*
	Savoy† WC2 *(Gondoliers)*
	Sheraton Pk Tower *(Buckingham Rm)*
	Stafford SW1 *(Pink Rm & Argyll Rm)*
45	Cannizaro Hs SW19 *(Earl of Mexborough & Lady Jane)*
	Hampshire Htl† WC2 *(Romsey or Burley)*
	Royal Albert Hall† SW7 *(Prince of Wales)*
40	Caledonian Club† SW1 *(Selkirk)*
	Cannizaro Hs SW19 *(Queen Elizabeth Rm)*
	Le Gavroche W1 *(Private Rm*)*
	Halcyon Htl† W11 *(Suite 34 or Halcyon Suite)*
	Hampshire Htl† WC2 *(Milton)*
	Howard Htl WC2 *(Westminster)*
	Imp. War Mus.† SE1 *(Boardroom 2)*
	Inst. of Directors† SW1 *(Trafalgar / Spears)*
	Merchant Taylors' Hall EC2 *(Library)*
	Motcomb's SW1 *(McClue Suite*)*
	Park Ln Htl† W1 *(Mirror Rm)*
	Regent† W1 *(Gazebo)*
	Ritz† W1 *(Berkeley Dining Rm)*
	South Bank Ctr SE1 *(Sunley Pavilion)*
	Stafford SW1 *(Sutherland Rm)*
35	Cannizaro Hs SW19 *(Oak Rm)*
	Capital SW3 *(Cadogan*)*
	Four Seasons Htl† W1 *(Sitting & Dining Rms)*
	Savoy† WC2 *(Mikado)*
30	Dorchester† W1 *(Penths)*
	11 Hobart Place SW1 *(Gdn Rm*)*
	Gray's Inn† EC1 *(Reception area)*
	Hilton on Pk Ln† W1 *(Serpentine Rm)*
	Innholders' Hall EC4 *(Ct Rm)*
	Inst. of Materials† SW1 *(Bessemer Rm)*
	Park Ln Htl† W1 *(Drawing Rm)*
	Ritz† W1 *(Berkeley Reception Rm)*

Private venues – standing

	Royal Albert Hall SW7 *(Henry Cole Rm)*
	Royal Coll. of Music† SW7 *(Council Rm)*
	Savoy† WC2 *(Patience)*
	Stafford SW1 *(Argyll Rm)*
26	Boat: Interceptor Launch, Essex *(Max*)*
25	Mosimann's Belfry† SW1 *(Alpha Romeo)*
	Savoy† WC2 *(Iolanthe)*
20	Capital SW3 *(Eaton)*
	Dorchester† W1 *(Boardroom)*
	Howard Htl WC2 *(Surrey)*
	Park Ln Htl† W1 *(Boardroom)*
18	Dukes Htl† SW1 *(Single Suite)*
	Savoy† WC2 *(Sorcerer)*
15	Berkeley† SW1 *(Billet)*
12	Boat: Chelsea Luxury Charters† SW10 *(Max*)*
10	Dorchester† W1 *(Library)*

£M

6500	Alexandra Pal. & Pk† N22 *(Gt Hall*)*
4000	Sandown Pk Racecourse†, Surrey *(Tote Hall*)*
3000	Café Royal† W1 *(Max*)*
2500	Alexandra Pal. & Pk† N22 *(West Hall)*
	Royal Lancaster† W2 *(Nine King's Suite*)*
1500	Alexandra Pal. & Pk† N22 *(Palm Ter.)*
	Commonwealth Inst.† W8 *(Comm Galls.*)*
	Kempton Pk†, Middx *(Max*)*
	Royal Gdn Htl† W8 *(Pal. Suite*)*
1300	Royal Lancaster† W2 *(Westbourne Suite)*
1200	Forte Crest Regents Pk† W1 *(Portland Suite*)*
	Royal Nat. Theatre† SE1 *(Max*)*
1000	Cabot Hall† E14 *(Hall*)*
	Café Royal† W1 *(4-Empire Napoleon)*
	Hurlingham Club† SW6 *(Max*)*
	Sandown Pk Racecourse†, Surrey *(Lower Tote Hall)*
900	London Marriott† W1 *(Westminster Suite*)*
850	Commonwealth Inst.† W8 *(Lawn)*
	Brewery† EC1 *(Porter Tun*)*
800	Cumberland Htl† W1 *(Production Box*)*
	Lloyd's of London† EC3 *(Captains' Rm*)*
	Waldorf Htl† WC2 *(Adelphi Suite & Palm Ct*)*
750	Nat. Liberal Club† SW1 *(Max*)*
	Elizabeth Suite† EC2 *(Max*)*
700	Brewery† EC1 *(King George III)*
650	Russell† WC1 *(Warncliffe Suite*)*
	Sandown Pk Racecourse†, Surrey *(Claremont)*
600	Elizabeth Suite† EC2 *(Spanish Rm)*
	Glaziers' Hall† SE1 *(Max*)*
	Gloucester Htl† SW7 *(Cotswold Suite*)*
	King David Suite† W1 *(Main Rm*)*
	Limelight† W1 *(Max*)*
	Lord's† NW8 *(Max*)*
	Pinewood Studios†, Bucks *(Gdns (marquee)*)*
	Russell† WC1 *(Woburn Suite)*
550	Café Royal† W1 *(6 Dubarry)*
500	Ascot Racecourse†, Berks *(Buckhounds Bar*)*
	Bath – Pump Rm†, Avon *(Max*)*
	Battersea Pk† SW8 *(Riverside Rm.s*)*
	City of London Club† EC2 *(Max*)*
	Commonwealth Inst.† W8 *(Art Gall.)*
	Cumberland Htl† W1 *(Carlisle Suite)*
	Hurlingham Club† SW6 *(Quadrangle Suite)*
	Kempton Pk†, Middx *(Runnymede Suite)*
	Langham Hilton† W1 *(Ballroom)*
	Mayfair† W1 *(Crystal Rm*)*
	Royal Nat. Theatre† SE1 *(Olivier Stalls Foyer)*
	Syon Pk (Conserv.)†, Middx *(Max*)*
430	Haberdashers' Hall EC2 *(Max*)*
420	Forte Crest Regents Pk† W1 *(Albany)*
400	Alexandra Pal. & Pk† N22 *(Pal. Rest.)*
	Chartered Accountants' Hall† EC2 *(Gt Hall*)*
	Chelsea Harbour Rms† SW10 *(Max*)*
	Chelsea Physic Gdn SW3 *(Max*)*
	Glaziers' Hall† SE1 *(Hall)*
	Inst. of Civil Engs† SW1 *(Gt Hall*)*
	Limelight† W1 *(Gall. & Dome)*
	London Transport Mus† WC2 *(Max*)*
	Mount Royal Htl† W1 *(Edinburgh / Hyde Pk*)*
	Nat. Liberal Club† SW1 *(Smoking Rm*)*
	Regent's Coll.† NW1 *(Refectory*)*
	Royal Inst. of Brit. Architects† W1 *(Florence Hall*)*
	Sandown Pk Racecourse†, Surrey *(Wolsey)*
	Tower Thistle† E1 *(Tower Suite (York Rm & Lancaster Rm)*)*
	Twickenham Banqueting Ctr† TW1 *(Rose Rm*)*
	Waldorf Htl† WC2 *(Charter 2)*
350	Café Royal† W1 *(2 Louis)*
	Carpenters' Hall EC2 *(Livery Hall*)*
	HMS Belfast† SE1 *(Quarter Deck*)*
	Insurance Hall† EC2 *(Gt Hall*)*
	Langham Hilton† W1 *(Memories of Empire)*
	Law Soc.† WC2 *(Common Rm*)*
	Lord's† NW8 *(Ballroom or Toynbee)*
	Oval† SE11 *(Banqueting Suite*)*
	Sandown Pk †, Surrey *(Ardross)*
	Twickenham Banqueting Ctr† TW1 *(West Pavilion Suite)*
	Waldorf Htl† WC2 *(Adelphi 3)*
300	BAFTA Ctr† W1 *(Max*)*
	Basil Street Htl† SW3 *(Parrot Club*)*
	Café Royal† W1 *(1 Elysee)*
	Cavalry & Guards Club W1 *(Coffee Rm*)*
	Chelsea Harbour Rms† SW10 *(Turner & Carlyle Rms)*
	Churchill† W1 *(Chartwell Suite*)*
	City of London Club† EC2 *(Main Dining Rm)*
	Conrad Htl† SW10 *(Henley Suite*)*
	Design Mus.† SE1 *(Entrance Hall*)*

Private venues – standing

Gloucester Htl† SW7 *(Cotswold - 1/2)*
Ham Hs, Surrey *(Max*)*
ICA† SW1 *(Exhib. Galls. or Ter.s*)*
Kew Bridge Steam Mus.†, Middx *(Max*)*
London Palladium W1 *(Cinderella Bar*)*
Nat. Liberal Club† SW1 *(Dining Rm *)*
Orangery (Holland Pk)† W8 *(With marquee*)*
Royal Majestic Suite† NW6 *(Ground Fl*)*
Royal Nat. Theatre† SE1 *(Lyttelton Exhib. Area)*
Selfridge Htl† W1 *(Selfridge Suite*)*
St Stephens Constitutional Club† SW1 *(Max*)*
Theatre Royal WC2 *(Grand Salon*)*
TS Queen Mary† WC2 *(Queen Mary Suite*)*
Waldorf Htl WC2 *(Charter 1)*

290 St John's Gate† EC1 *(Max*)*
280 Clandon†, Surrey *(Marble Hall or Rest.*)*
260 Bank of Eng. Club† SW15 *(Max*)*
250 Barber-Surgeons' Hall EC2 *(Livery Hall*)*
Bath – Pump Rm†, Avon *(Pump Rm)*
Brewery† EC1 *(Queen Charlotte or Smeaton's Vaults)*
Butchers' Hall† EC1 *(Gt Hall*)*
Café Royal† W1 *(6Dauphin)*
Champenois† EC2 *(Max*)*
Church Hs† SW1 *(Harvey Goodwin Suite or Hoare Memorial Hall*)*
East India Club SW1 *(Max*)*
Farmers' & Fletchers' Hall EC1 *(Max*)*
Forte Crest Regents Pk† W1 *(Clarence or Devonshire)*
Haberdashers' Hall EC2 *(Main Hall)*
Inst. of Civil Engs† SW1 *(Rest.)*
Ironmongers' Hall EC2 *(Banqueting Hall*)*
Limelight† W1 *(Club VIP)*
Nat. Liberal Club† SW1 *(David Lloyd George or Ter.*)*
Nº 1 Yacht Club† WC2 *(Max*)*
Painters' Hall EC4 *(Livery Hall*)*
Pal. Theatre W1 *(Stalls Bar*)*
Queen's Eyot†, Berks *(Permanent Marquee*)*
Royal Soc. of Arts† WC2 *(All Vaults*)*
RS Hispaniola† WC2 *(Main Deck*)*
Sandown Pk†, Surrey *(Tack & Saddle)*
St John's Gate† EC1 *(Gdn Cloisters)*
Stakis St Ermins† SW1 *(Ballroom*)*
Staple Inn WC1 *(Hall*)*
Rembrandt Htl† SW7 *(Edward & Charles & James & Princes (King Suite)*)*
Waldorf Htl† WC2 *(Adelphi 1)*
West Wycombe Caves†, Bucks *(Max*)*

240 Dartmouth Hs† W1 *(Max*)*
HMS Belfast† SE1 *(Ship Co's Dining Rm)*
St Bartholomew's Hosp. EC1 *(Gt Hall*)*
230 Carpenters' Hall EC2 *(Reception Rm)*
220 Basil Street Htl† SW3 *(Dining Rm)*

Mortons Club† W1 *(Rest. & Bar*)*
Royal Nat. Theatre† SE1 *(Ter. Café)*
St John's Gate† EC1 *(Chapter Hall)*

216 Streatham Mega Bowl SW2 *(Max*)*
200 41 Beak St† W1 *(Max*)*
Alexandra Pal. & Pk† N22 *(Loneborough Rm)*
Amadeus Ctr† W9 *(Upper Hall*)*
BAFTA Ctr† W1 *(Function Rm or Club Bars)*
Bath – Pump Rm†, Avon *(Concert Rm)*
Bonham's SW7 *(Max*)*
Café Royal† W1 *(5-Marquise or 2Pompadour)*
Chelsea Harbour Rms† SW10 *(Turner Rm)*
Churchill† W1 *(Chartwell I)*
City of London Club† EC2 *(Upper Smoking Rms)*
Conrad Htl† SW10 *(Compass Rose or Thames)*
Cottons Atrium† SE1 *(Max*)*
Cumberland Htl† W1 *(Gloucester)*
Glaziers' Hall† SE1 *(River Rm)*
Hamilton Suite† W1 *(Max*)*
Hurlingham Club† SW6 *(Palm Ct Suite)*
Inst. of Mechanical Engs SW1 *(Marble Hall*)*
Kempton Pk†, Middx *(Hampton Suite)*
Kensington Pal. Thistle† W8 *(Duchess*)*
Kew Bridge Steam Mus†, Middx *(Water Hall)*
Peacock Hs† W14 *(Main Hall & Lounge*)*
Pinewood Studios†, Bucks *(Ballroom)*
Royal Lancaster† W2 *(Gloucester Suite)*
Rubens Htl† SW1 *(Old Masters Rest.*)*
St Stephens Constitutional Club† SW1 *(Dining Rm)*
St Thomas's Hosp.† SE1 *(Governors' Hall*)*
Tall Hs† SE1 *(Max*)*
TS Queen Mary† WC2 *(Carvery)*

190 Langham Hilton† W1 *(Portland Suite)*
180 Belvedere† W8 *(Max*)*
Cavalry & Guards Club W1 *(Peninsula Rm)*
Chelsea Harbour Rms† SW10 *(Carlyle Rm)*
Church Hs† SW1 *(Bishop Partridge Hall)*
Clandon†, Surrey *(Salloon)*
Guards Mus.† SW1 *(Max*)*
Royal Nat. Theatre† SE1 *(Ovations)*
Spanish Club W1 *(Alfonso XIII Rm*)*
Winchester Hs Club† SW15 *(River Rm*)*

175 White Hs Htl† NW1 *(Albany*)*
170 Brewers' Hall EC2 *(Max*)*
Kempton Pk†, Middx *(Thames Suite)*
160 Kempton Pk†, Middx *(Paddock Suite)*
Royal Aeronautical Soc.† W1 *(Argyll Rm & Hawker Rm*)*
Simpsons- in-the- Strand† WC2 *(Max*)*

Private venues – standing

150	Bank of Eng. Club† SW15 *(Redgates Lodge)*
	Bankers Club EC2 *(Cocktail Bar*)*
	Brewery† EC1 *(Sugar Rms)*
	Butchers' Hall† EC1 *(Large Ct Rm & Small Ct Rm)*
	Cadogan SW1 *(Rest.*)*
	Café Royal† W1 *(5-George, 3-Nicols, or 1-Derby & Queensbury)*
	Chartered Accountants' Hall† EC2 *(Rest. & Wine Bar)*
	Chelsea Physic Gdn SW3 *(Private Rm)*
	Conrad Htl† SW10 *(Henley I)*
	Elizabeth Suite† EC2 *(Golden Hind)*
	Forte Crest St James's SW1 *(Private dining Rm*)*
	Grosvenor Htl† SW1 *(Gall. Rm*)*
	Hamilton Suite† W1 *(Red Rm)*
	HMS Belfast† SE1 *(Wardroom)*
	ICA† SW1 *(Nash or Brandon)*
	Insurance Hall† EC2 *(Ostler Hall)*
	Ivy WC2 *(Private Rm*)*
	Kew Bridge Steam Mus†, Middx *(Steam Hall)*
	Mus. of Childhood E2 *(Marble Fl*)*
	Nº 1 Yacht Club† WC2 *(Dining Rm)*
	Orangery (Holland Pk)† W8 *(Orangery)*
	Painters' Hall EC4 *(Ct Rm)*
	Pewterers' Hall EC2 *(Livery Rm or Ct Rm*)*
	Pinewood Studios†, Bucks *(Green Rm or Gt Gatsby Rm)*
	Royal Gdn Htl† W8 *(Kensington or Balmoral Suite)*
	Royal Soc. of Arts† WC2 *(Benjamin Franklin Rm or Gall.)*
	RUSI Building SW1 *(Duke of Wellington Hall*)*
	Sandown Pk, Surrey *(Cavalry Bar)*
	TS Queen Mary† WC2 *(Captain's Suite)*
	Twickenham Banqueting Ctr† TW1 *(Club Rm)*
	Waldorf Htl† WC2 *(Adelphi 2)*
	Westbury Htl† W1 *(Mount Vernon Rm*)*
	Westminster Conf. Ctr SW1 *(Members Club Rm*)*
145	Simpsons- in-the-Strand† WC2 *(South Rm)*
140	Dartmouth Hs† W1 *(Long Drawing Rm)*
130	Brewers' Hall EC2 *(Livery Hall)*
	Fulham Pal.† SW6 *(Drawing & Ante Rm*)*
	Hampton Ct, Tiltyard†, Surrey *(Max*)*
125	Mus. of Childhood E2 *(Max)*
	Founders' Hall† EC1 *(Livery Hall*)*
	Law Soc.† WC2 *(Members Dining Rm)*
	Vanderbilt Htl† SW7 *(Max*)*
120	BAFTA Ctr† W1 *(Foyer Bar)*
	Basil Street Htl† SW3 *(Brompton Rm)*
	Britannia Intercontinental† W1 *(Manhattan*)*
	Brewery† EC1 *(James Watt)*
	Brown's Htl† W1 *(Clarendon)*
	Butchers' Hall† EC1 *(Taurus Suite)*
	Canonbury Acad. N1 *(Long Gall. – there are 21 smaller Rms*)*
	Chartered Accountants' Hall† EC2 *(Main Reception Rm)*
	Commonwealth Inst.† W8 *(Jehangir & Board Rms or Comm Brass.)*
	Freud Mus. NW3 *(Hs & Gdn*)*
	Glaziers' Hall† SE1 *(Library / Ct Rm)*
	Haberdashers' Hall EC2 *(Ct Rm)*
	HMS Belfast† SE1 *(Gun Rm)*
	Inst. of Civil Engs† SW1 *(Smeaton Rm)*
	Inst. of Mechanical Engs SW1 *(Hinton)*
	Lloyd's of London† EC3 *(Old Library)*
	Mayfair† W1 *(Lansdowne Suite)*
	Mountbatten† WC2 *(Earl*)*
	Mus. of Childhood E2 *(Summerly Rm)*
	Oxford & Cambridge Club† SW1 *(Marlborough*)*
	Royal Aeronautical Soc.† W1 *(Ter.*)*
	Royal Majestic Suite† NW6 *(First Fl)*
	RS Hispaniola† WC2 *(Top Deck)*
	Streatham Mega Bowl SW2 *(Single Fl)*
	Sweetings EC4 *(Max*)*
	Tallow Chandlers' Hall EC4 *(Livery Hall*)*
	Trinity Hs† EC3 *(Ct Rm*)*
	Westbury Htl† W1 *(Pine Rm)*
	Westminster Conf. Ctr SW1 *(Rest.)*
110	Regent's Coll.† NW1 *(Herringham Hall)*
	Washington Htl† W1 *(Richmond Suite*)*
	Watermen & Lightermen's Hall EC3 *(Freemen's Rm*)*
102	Trinity Hs† EC3 *(Library)*
100	Alexandra Pal. & Pk† N22 *(Palm Ct 1-5)*
	Amadeus Ctr† W9 *(Lower Hall)*
	Ascot Racecourse†, Berks *(Norfolk Bar)*
	Brewery† EC1 *(City Cellars)*
	Mountbatten† WC2 *(Drawing Rm)*
	Brown's Htl† W1 *(Niagra & Roosevelt combined)*
	Cabot Hall† E14 *(Sebastian Rm)*
	Cadogan SW1 *(Langtry Rm)*
	Café Royal† W1 *(1Domino or 3-Josephine)*
	Cavalry & Guards Club W1 *(Balaclava Rm or Waterloo Rm)*
	Chartered Accountants' Hall† EC2 *(Members' Rm)*
	Churchill† W1 *(Chartwell II)*
	City of London Club† EC2 *(Gdn Rm)*
	Dartmouth Hs† W1 *(Ballroom or Ter.)*
	First Fl W11 *(Private Rm*)*
	Fulham Pal.† SW6 *(Gt Hall or Drawing Rm)*
	Goring Htl SW1 *(Ebury Rm or Large Lounge (weekends only)*)*
	Ham Hs, Surrey *(Orangery)*
	Hamilton Hs EC4 *(Max*)*
	Holiday Inn – Mayair W1 *(Stratton Suite*)*
	Inst. of Civil Engs† SW1 *(Brunel Rm or Council Rm)*
	Ironmongers' Hall EC2 *(Drawing Rm or Luncheon Rm)*
	Kensington Pal. Thistle† W8 *(Marchioness)*
	Kenwood Hs, Old Kitchen† NW3 *(Max*)*
	Knightsbridge Place SW1 *(Private Rm*)*

Private venues – standing

Lloyd's of London† EC3 *(Conf. Rm)*
London Television Ctr SE1 *(Westminster & St Pauls*)*
Oxford & Cambridge Club† SW1 *(Princess Marie Louise)*
Royal Gdn Htl† W8 *(Sandringham & Osborne Suite)*
Royal Horseguards Thistle Htl† SW1 *(Thames*)*
Royal Soc. of Arts† WC2 *(Vault 1)*
RUSI Building SW1 *(Library & McGarel-Groves Reading Rm)*
Sandown Pk†, Surrey *(Lawn Suite)*
Sheraton Belgravia SW1 *(Dining Rm*)*
Simpsons-in-the-Strand† WC2 *(Smoking Rm)*
Spitting Image Mus. WC2 *(Max*)*
Stakis St Ermins† SW1 *(Balcony)*
Tower Thistle† E1 *(Raleigh or Spenser)*
TS Queen Mary† WC2 *(Wardroom Bistro*)*
Univ. Women's Club W1 *(Library*)*

90 Brown's Htl† W1 *(Kipling)*
Grosvenor Htl† SW1 *(Bessborough Rm)*
Rembrandt Htl† SW7 *(James)*

80 Barber-Surgeons' Hall EC2 *(Reception Rm)*
Cabot Hall† E14 *(St Lawrence Rm)*
Chelsea Harbour Rms† SW10 *(Reception Rm)*
Churchill† W1 *(Library, Edward or Victoria Suite)*
Fan Mus. SE10 *(Mus.*)*
Freud Mus. NW3 *(Hs)*
Hamilton Suite† W1 *(Conserv. Bar or Hamilton Rm)*
Mortons Club† W1 *(Downstairs Rm)*
Queen's Eyot†, Berks *(Max)*
Regent's Coll.† NW1 *(Knapp Gall. or Tuke Common Rm)*
Rembrandt Htl† SW7 *(Edward or Elizabeth)*
Royal Aeronautical Soc.† W1 *(Council Rm & Bar)*
Rubens† Htl SW1 *(Rembrandt Rm)*
RUSI Building SW1 *(McGarel-Groves Reading Rm)*
Russell† WC1 *(Bedford Suite or Grafton Suite)*
SB Lady Gwynfred† E14 *(Max*)*
Soho Soho W1 *(Salon Privée)*
St Stephens Constitutional Club† SW1 *(Bar)*
Westminster Conf. Ctr SW1 *(Cambridge Rm)*
Whittington's EC4 *(Wine Bar*)*

75 City of London Club† EC2 *(Visitors Rm)*
Conrad Htl† SW10 *(Harbour)*
Dartmouth Hs† W1 *(Small Drawing Rm)*
Elizabeth Suite† EC2 *(Library)*
Goring Htl SW1 *(Small Gdn Lounge)*
HMS Belfast† SE1 *(Anteroom)*
Royal Soc. of Arts† WC2 *(Vault 4)*
Rules WC2 *(Greene Rm*)*
Sandown Pk†, Surrey *(Persimmon)*

70 Chartered Inst. of Public Finance & Accountancy WC2 *(Conf. Rm or Council Chamber*)*
Conrad Htl SW10 *(Henley II or Henley III)*
Forte Crest Regents Pk† W1 *(Chester Suite)*
Inst. of Mechanical Engs SW1 *(Council)*
Law Soc.† WC2 *(Grill Rm)*
Limelight† W1 *(Study Bar)*
Nat. Liberal Club† SW1 *(Lady Violet)*
Nº 1 Yacht Club† WC2 *(Cocktail Bar)*
Rembrandt Htl† SW7 *(Elizabeth & Victoria (Queen Suite))*
Royal Inst. of Brit. Architects† W1 *(South Rm)*
Royal Soc. of Arts† WC2 *(Tav. Rm)*
Sheraton Belgravia SW1 *(Study & Library)*
Staple Inn WC1 *(Council Chamber)*
Watermen & Lightermen's Hall EC3 *(Ct Rm)*

65 London Marriott† W1 *(Hamilton Rm)*

60 Ascot Racecourse†, Berks *(King Edward VII)*
Athenaeum Htl† W1 *(Westminster Suite*)*
Bleeding Heart EC1 *(Champagne Rm*)*
Britannia Intercontinental† W1 *(Pine Bar)*
Brown's Htl† W1 *(Roosevelt)*
Chartered Inst. of Public Finance & Accountancy WC2 *(Committee Rm 4)*
Coopers' Hall EC2 *(Max*)*
Downstairs At 190 SW7 *(Green Rm*)*
Holiday Inn – Mayair W1 *(Presidential Suite &)*
Kensington Pal. Thistle† W8 *(Countess Princess)*
Langham Hilton† W1 *(Ambassadors' Rm, Regent Rm , Welbeck Rm or Wimpole Rm)*
Mayfair† W1 *(Devon or Berkeley Suite)*
Quaglino's SW1 *(Private Rm*)*
Rembrandt Htl† SW7 *(Charles)*
Royal Aeronautical Soc.† W1 *(Handley Page or Sopwith Rm)*
Royal Gdn Htl W8 *(Royal Suite)*
Rules WC2 *(Charles Dickens Rm)*
Russell WC1 *(Ormond Suite or Bar)*
St Stephens Constitutional Club† SW1 *(Gdn Rm)*
Tallow Chandlers' Hall EC4 *(Parlour)*
Univ. Women's Club W1 *(Drawing Rm)*
Waldorf Htl† WC2 *(Somerset or Aldwych)*
Washington Htl† W1 *(Richmond 2)*
Westbury Htl† W1 *(Brighton Rm)*
Westminster Conf. Ctr SW1 *(Edinburgh Rm)*

55 La Truffe Noir SE1 *(Downstairs Bistro*)*

50 Ascot Racecourse†, Berks *(Brown Jack or Abergavenny Bar)*
Athenaeum Htl† W1 *(Devonshire Suite & Ter.)*
Basil Street Htl† SW3 *(Basil Rm)*
Berkshire W1 *(Sonning Suite*)*
Butchers' Hall† EC1 *(Small Ct Rm)*
City of London Club EC2 *(Bar)*
Founders' Hall† EC1 *(Parlour)*
Gloucester Htl† SW7 *(Harrington / Stanhope)*
Leven is Strijd E14 *(Max*)*

Private venues – standing

London Marriott† W1
(John Adams Suite)
London Television Ctr SE1
(Westminster / St Pauls)
Mayfair† W1 *(Curzon Suite)*
Nº 1 Yacht Club† WC2 *(Oak Rm)*
Royal Nat. Theatre SE1
(Olivier Circle Foyer)
Royal Soc. of Arts† WC2 *(Vault 2)*
RUSI Building SW1
(Council Chamber)
St Bartholomew's Hosp EC1
(Henry VIII Committee Rm)
St Thomas's Hosp.† SE1
(Grand Committee Rm)

48 Waldorf Htl† WC2 *(Kingsway)*
45 Ascot Racecourse†, Berks
(Churchill)
40 Ascot Racecourse†, Berks
(Hamilton)
Athenaeum Htl† W1
(Devonshire Suite)
Basil Street Htl† SW3 *(Mezz. Rm)*
Brewers' Hall EC2 *(Ct Rm)*
Britannia Inter-
continental† W1 *(Grosvenor I)*
Brown's Htl W1 *(Niagara)*
Downstairs At 190 SW7
(Private Rm)
Draycott SW3 *(Drawing Rm*)*
Frederick's N1 *(Clarence Rm*)*
Holiday Inn – Mayair W1
(Buckingham)
Inst. of Civil Engs† SW1
(Old Members Rm)
Insurance Hall† EC2
(Pipkin Rm)
Kempton Pk, Middx *(Lanzarote)*
Oxford & Cambridge
Club† SW1 *(Edward VII)*
Rules WC2 *(King Edward VII Rm)*
Russell† WC1
(Guilford Suite or Library)
Scone E14 *(Max*)*
St Bartholomew's Hosp EC1
(Guild, Peggy Turner or Treasurer's Rm)
Stakis St Ermins† SW1
(York / Clarence)
Theatre Royal WC2
(Royal Retiring Rm or Board Rm)
Vanderbilt Htl† SW7 *(Vanderbilt)*
Washington Htl† W1 *(Richmond 1)*
Westbury Htl† W1 *(Regency Rm)*
Westminster Conf. Ctr SW1
(Gloucester)

35 Beauchamp Place SW3
(Private Rm*)
HMS Belfast† SE1
(Admiral's Quarters)
Stakis St Ermins† SW1 *(Cameo)*
Mountbatten† WC2 *(Viceroy)*

32 Brown's Htl† W1 *(Hellenic)*
30 Ascot Racecourse†, Berks
(Crocker Bulteel)
Berkshire W1 *(Sandhurst Suite)*
Brown's Htl† W1 *(Albemarle)*
Cavalry & Guards Club W1
(Double Bridal Rm)
Fulham Pal.† SW6 *(Ante Rm)*
Grosvenor Htl† SW1
(Warwick Rm)
Guinea W1 *(Boardroom*)*
London Marriott† W1
(Dukes Suite)
Mayfair† W1 *(Stratton)*
Royal Soc. of Arts WC2
(Folkestone Rm or Vault 3)
Selfridge Htl† W1 *(Drawing Rm)*

25 Britannia Inter-
continental† W1 *(Grosvenor II)*

Forte Crest Regents Pk† W1
(1 / 2 Chester Suite)
Goring Htl SW1 *(Drawing Rm)*
Grosvenor Htl† SW1
(Belgrave or Wilton Rm)
Hamilton Suite† W1 *(Marble Rm)*
Holiday Inn – Mayair W1
(Berkeley or Burlington)
Kensington Pal. Thistle W8
(Baroness)
Royal Aeronautical Soc.† W1
(Hawker Rm or Brabazon)
Royal Nat. Theatre† SE1
(Richardson Rm)
Westminster Conf. Ctr SW1
(Lancaster / Warwick)

24 Ascot Racecourse†, Berks
(Gordon Carter)
20 Athenaeum Htl† W1
(Richmond Suite)
Basil Street Htl† SW3 *(Room 246)*
Brewers' Hall EC2 *(Committee Rm)*
Insurance Hall† EC2
(Morgan Owen Rm)
Rembrandt Htl† SW7 *(Victoria)*
Tall Hs† SE1 *(Private Rm)*
Waldorf Htl† WC2
(Westminster or Waterloo or Tavistock)

16 Theatre Royal WC2
(Prince of Wales Suite)
15 Langham Hilton† W1
(Cumberland Rm)
14 Univ. Women's Club W1
(Red Rm)
12 Brown's Htl† W1 *(Lord Byron)*
10 Brown's Htl† W1 *(Graham Bell)*

£B-M

2500 Hon. Artillery Co† EC1 *(Marquee*)*
2000 Duke of York's HQ† SW3 *(Lawn*)*
Royal Horticultural
Halls† SW1 *(New Hall)*
1850 Equinox at the Empire† WC2
(Max*)
1650 Hippodrome† WC2 *(Max*)*
1500 Equinox at the Empire† WC2
(Club)
1200 Hippodrome† WC2 *(Auditorium)*
Naval & Military Club† W1
(Max*)
1000 K Warehouse† E6 *(Space 1*)*
Royal Horticultural
Halls† SW1 *(Old Hall)*
900 Royal Coll. of Art† SW7
(Henry Moore Gall.*)
800 Blackheath Concert
Halls† SE3 *(Max*)*
Dulwich Coll.† SE21
(Christenson Hall & Upper Dining Rms*)
Smith's Gall.† WC2 *(Max*)*
700 Grosvenor Rms† NW2
(Grosvenor Suite*)
London Press Ctr† EC4
(Caxton Suite*)
Stoke Newington Town
Hall† N16 *(Max*)*
680 Browns Club† WC2 *(Max*)*
650 Royal Holloway Coll.†, Surrey
(Max*)
600 Chelsea Football Club† SW6
(Max*)
Mall Galls. SW1 *(Max*)*
New Connaught Rms† WC2
(Balmoral & Grand Hall*)
Porchester Ctr† W2 *(Ballroom*)*
Syon Pk (Banqueting)†, Middx
(Max*)

Private venues – standing

500	Blackheath Concert Halls† SE3 *(Gt Hall)*
	Boardwalk† W1 *(Max*)*
	Brass. Rocque† EC2 *(with Ter.*)*
	Cecil Sharp Hs† NW1 *(Kennedy Hall*)*
	Chelsea Gdner SW3 *(Max*)*
	Crazy Larry's† SW10 *(Max*)*
	Duke of York's HQ† SW3 *(Cadogan Hall)*
	Dulwich Coll.† SE21 *(Gt Hall)*
	Fulham Town Hall† SW6 *(Large Hall*)*
	Goldsmith's Coll.† SE14 *(Gt Hall*)*
	Hollyhedge Hs† SE3 *(Hall*)*
	Hon. Artillery Co† EC1 *(Albert Rm)*
	K Warehouse† E6 *(Cavern 1 or 2)*
	Mall Galls. SW1 *(Main Gall.)*
	Rose Gdn Rest.† W1 *(Max*)*
	Trafalgar Tav.† SE10 *(Nelson Suite*)*
	Westminster Boating Base† SW1 *(Total Facility with Marquee*)*
	Whitechapel Art Gall.† E1 *(Max*)*
	World Trade Ctr† E1 *(Max*)*
480	Chelsea Old Town Hall† SW3 *(Main Hall*)*
450	Hippodrome† WC2 *(Balcony – Rest.)*
	King's Coll.† WC2 *(Gt Hall)*
	Nat. Army Mus. SW3 *(Art & Uniform Galls.*)*
	Royal Green Jackets† W1 *(Hall*)*
400	Chelsea Football Club† SW6 *(Executive Club Rm)*
	Chelsea Gdner SW3 *(Shop)*
	City Livery Club EC4 *(Library*)*
	Cobden's Working Men's Club W10† *(Hall)*
	Congress Ctr† WC1 *(Congress Hall*)*
	Eatons† EC3 *(Max*)*
	Froebel Inst. Coll.† SW15 *(Max*)*
	Hubble & Co† EC1 *(Max*)*
	Le Gothique† SW18 *(with Acad. of Live & Recorded Arts*)*
	Little Ship Club† EC4 *(Max*)*
	London Press Ctr† EC4 *(Pepys Suite)*
	Naval & Military Club† W1 *(Coffee Rm)*
	Throgmorton's† EC2 *(Max*)*
360	Bishopsgate Inst.† EC2 *(Main Hall*)*
350	Clink† SE1 *(Max*)*
	Conway Hall† WC1 *(Large Hall*)*
	HMS President† EC4 *(Max*)*
	Jazz Café† NW1 *(Max*)*
	Legends† W1 *(Max*)*
	Royal Coll. of Art† SW7 *(Gulbenkian Upper Gall.*)*
	Royal Geographical Soc.† SW7 *(Max*)*
	Royal Holloway Coll.†, Surrey *(Founders Dining Hall)*
	Smith's Gall.† WC2 *(Rest.)*
	St Martin In Fields† WC2 *(Max*)*
300	Acad. of Live & Recorded Arts† SW18 *(Max*)*
	Baltic Exch.† EC3 *(Queen's Rm*)*
	Boat: Catamaran Cruisers† WC2 *(Naticia*)*
	Brass. Rocque† EC2 *(Inside)*
	Browns Club† WC2 *(Bar & Dance Fl or VIP Rm)*
	City Livery Club EC4 *(Dining Rm)*
	Grosvenor Rms† NW2 *(Executive Suite)*
	London Scottish† SW1 *(Hall*)*
	Mus. of Gdn History SE1 *(School*)*
	Naval & Military Club† W1 *(Smoking Rm)*
	New Connaught Rms† WC2 *(Edinburgh & Drawing Rm, Cornwall & Crown, or Brass.)*
	Royal Holloway Coll.†, Surrey *(Picture Gall.)*
	Royal Inst. of GB W1 *(Max*)*
	Royal Veterinary Coll.† NW1 *(Gdn*)*
	School of Pharmacy† WC1 *(Refectory*)*
	St Andrew Golf Club† EC4 *(Max*)*
	Strand Pal. Htl† WC2 *(Birley*)*
	Syon Pk (Banqueting), Middx *(Gdn Rm)*
	V&A Mus. Café† SW7 *(Max*)*
280	Syon Pk (Banqueting)†, Middx *(Lakeside Rm)*
275	Eatons† EC3 *(Banqueting Suite)*
	Viceroy† NW1 *(Max*)*
270	Boat: Catamaran Cruisers† WC2 *(Pridla)*
250	Boat: City Cruises† E14 *(Mayflower Gdn*)*
	Boat: Thames Leisure†, Kent *(Miyuki*)*
	Boat: Tidal Cruises† SE1 *(Royal Princess*)*
	Bramah Tea & Coffee Mus. SE1 *(Max*)*
	Clink† SE1 *(Winchester Hall)*
	Dulwich Coll.† SE21 *(Cricket Pavilion)*
	Footstool† SW1 *(Max*)*
	Fulham Hs† SW6 *(Main Hall*)*
	Fulham Town Hall† SW6 *(Concert Hall)*
	HMS President† EC4 *(Drill Hall)*
	Hon. Artillery Co† EC1 *(Long Rm)*
	Irish Club† SW1 *(Max*)*
	Old Refectory† W8 *(Max*)*
	Royal Veterinary Coll.† NW1 *(Gt Hall)*
	Smith's Gall.† WC2 *(Gall. 1)*
	St John's Hill† SW11 *(Drill Hall*)*
	St Peter's Hall† W11 *(Max*)*
	Westminster Boating Base† SW1 *(Total Facility)*
240	Dolphin Square† SW1 *(Rest.)*
210	Boat: Tidal Cruises† SE1 *(PV Viscountess)*
200	Bratts† SW7 *(Max*)*
	Broadgate Estates† EC2 *(Ice Rink*)*
	Café Greenwich Pk† SE10 *(inc Gdn)*
	Canal Brass.† W10 *(Max*)*
	Congress Ctr† WC1 *(Marble Hall)*
	Doggetts Coat & Badge† SE1 *(Max*)*
	Fulham Hs† SW6 *(Max)*
	Grosvenor Rms† NW2 *(Pearl Suite)*
	Hubble & Co† EC1 *(Wine Bar or Basement Rest.)*
	Lansdowne Club† W1 *(Ballroom*)*
	Legends† W1 *(Downstairs)*
	New Connaught Rms† WC2 *(York & Warwick & Kent)*

Private venues – standing

	Pentland Hs† SE3 *(Marquee / Lawn*)*
	Polish Hearth Club† SW7 *(First Fl*)*
	Porchester Ctr† W2 *(Baths)*
	Royal Coll. of Art† SW7 *(Entrance Gall. or Sitting Rm & Bar)*
	Royal Green Jackets† W1 *(St George's Club)*
	Royal Over-Seas League† SW1 *(Hall of India & Pakistan*)*
	St Peter's Hall† W11 *(North Hall)*
	Syon Pk (Banqueting)†, Middx *(Camellia Rm)*
	Throgmorton's† EC2 *(Oak Rm)*
	Westminster Boating Base† SW1 *(Edgson Rm & Buttery)*
195	Boat: Catamaran Cruisers† WC2 *(Chevening)*
190	George Inn SE1 *(Max*)*
180	All Saints - The Crypt† E14 *(Main Hall*)*
	Bankside Gall.† SE1 *(Max*)*
	Boat: Mainstream Leisure† SW15 *(Elizabethan*)*
	Boat: Tidal Cruises† SE1 *(Hurlingham)*
	Froebel Inst. Coll.† SW15 *(Main Common Rm)*
	Lauderdale Hs† N6 *(Lower Gall.*)*
	Ski Club of GB† SW1 *(Max*)*
175	Boat: City Cruises† E14 *(Eltham)*
	Leoni's Quo Vadis† W1 *(Private Rm*)*
	Stanley Hs† SW10 *(Max*)*
170	Blackheath Concert Halls† SE3 *(Recital Rm)*
160	Boat: Catamaran Cruisers† WC2 *(Abercorn or Valulla)*
150	Bakers' Hall EC3 *(Max*)*
	Boat: Thames Pleasure Craft Ltd† EC3 *(Golden Salamander*)*
	Boat: Turk Launches†, Surrey *(New Southern Belle*)*
	Café Greenwich Pk† SE10 *(Inside only)*
	Café St Pierre† EC1 *(Max*)*
	Canning Hs SW1 *(Max*)*
	Chelsea Old Town Hall† SW3 *(Small Hall or Cadogan Suite)*
	Church's† W8 *(Max*)*
	El-Cid† SW10 *(Max*)*
	Equinox at the Empire† WC2 *(Square Bar)*
	Guy's Hosp. Tower† SE1 *(Max*)*
	Irish Club† SW1 *(Munster Rm or Connaught Bar)*
	Le Gothique† SW18 *(Patio)*
	Mermaid Theatre EC4 *(River Rm*)*
	Old Operating Theatre Mus. & Herb Garret SE1 *(Max*)*
	Pentland Hs† SE3 *(Hall)*
	Photographers' Gall.† WC2 *(Max*)*
	Place Below EC2 *(Max*)*
	Royal Coll. of Art† SW7 *(Gulbenkian Lower Gall.)*
	Royal Geographical Soc.† SW7 *(New Map Rm)*
	Royal Inst. of GB W1 *(Anteroom or Long Library)*
	Royal Over-Seas League† SW1 *(St Andrew's Hall)*
	606 Club† SW10 *(Max*)*
	Smith's Gall.† WC2 *(Gall. 2)*
	Upper Refectory Suite SW6 *(Max*)*
	Westminster Boating Base† SW1 *(Edgson Rm)*
140	Cecil Sharp Hs† NW1 *(Trefusis Hall)*
130	Boat: Tidal Cruises† SE1 *(Old London)*
125	Boat: Turk Launches†, Surrey *(MV Yarmouth Belle)*
120	Anchor† SE1 *(Max*)*
	Boat: Crown River Cruises† EC4 *(Suerita*)*
	Chelsea Football Club† SW6 *(Trophy Rm)*
	Doggetts Coat & Badge† SE1 *(Rest.)*
	Dora Hs† SW7 *(Max*)*
	Dulwich Coll.† SE21 *(Lower Hall or North & South Cloisters)*
	French Inst. SW7 *(Café Club*)*
	Froebel Inst. Coll.† SW15 *(Ter. Rm)*
	Gunnersbury Pk† W3 *(Orangery or Small Mansion*)*
	Hippodrome† WC2 *(Star Bar)*
	HMS President† EC4 *(Wardroom)*
	Imp. Coll.† SW7 *(Council Rm*)*
	Little Ship Club† EC4 *(Dining Rm or Club Rm & Bar)*
	New Zealand Hs† SW1 *(Max*)*
	Royal Geographical Soc.† SW7 *(Main Hall)*
	St Peter's Hall† W11 *(Upper Hall)*
	Syon Pk (Banqueting)†, Middx *(Ter. Rm)*
	Coliseum WC2 *(Ter. Bar*)*
110	Boat: Maidenhead Steam Navigation† Berks *(Edwardian*)*
	Dickens Inn† E1 *(Nickleby Suite*)*
108	Bakers' Hall EC3 *(Livery Hall)*
100	Boat: Catamaran Cruisers† WC2 *(Viceroy)*
	Boat: City Cruises† E14 *(Westminster)*
	Boat: Floating Boater† W2 *(Prince Regent*)*
	Boat: Thames Leisure†, Kent *(Tideway)*
	Bratts† SW7 *(Top Fl or Middle bar)*
	Browns Club† WC2 *(Small VIP Rm)*
	Café Lazeez† SW7 *(Max*)*
	Chelsea Football Club† SW6 *(Sponsors Lounge)*
	City Livery Club EC4 *(Stanley Bell Rm)*
	Clink† SE1 *(Mus.)*
	Coliseum WC2 *(Dutch Bar)*
	The Conservatory SW11 *(Max*)*
	Conway Hall† WC1 *(Small Hall, Lobby or Bar Area)*
	Dolphin Square† SW1 *(Chichester Suite)*
	El Barco Latino† WC2 *(Max*)*
	Gunnersbury Pk† W3 *(Temple)*
	HMS President† EC4 *(Gun Rm or Quarter Deck)*
	Legends† W1 *(Mezz.)*
	Little Ship Club† EC4 *(Library)*
	London Scottish† SW1 *(Officers' Mess)*
	Mall Galls. SW1 *(East Gall.)*
	Mus. of Gdn History SE1 *(St Mary-at-Lambeth)*
	Nat. Army Mus. SW3 *(Templer Galls.)*
	Naval & Military Club† W1 *(Regimental Rm, Palmerston Rm or Egremont)*
	Opera Terazza! WC2 *(Ter.*)*

203

Private venues – standing

Royal Green Jackets† W1 *(Sergeants Mess)*
Smith's Gall.† WC2 *(Casbar or Wine Bar)*
St John's Hill† SW11 *(Officers or Sergeant's Mess)*
St Peter's Hall† W11 *(Lower Hall)*
Throgmorton's† EC2 *(Short Rm)*
90 Boat: Turk Launches†, Surrey *(Kingston Royale)*
Broadgate Estates† EC2 *(Exchange Square Marquee)*
Burgh Hs NW3 *(Max*)*
New Connaught Rms† WC2 *(Devon / Stafford)*
Rochester Htl† SW1 *(Wine Bar)*
Royal Veterinary Coll.† NW1 *(Northumberland Rm)*
80 Boat: Crown River Cruises† EC4 *(Spirit of London)*
Boat: Maidenhead Steam Navigation† Berks *(Bell)*
Anchor† SE1 *(Gdn or Adjoining Bar)*
Café Greenwich Pk† SE10 *(Upstairs Rm)*
Café St Pierre† EC1 *(Top Fl)*
Doggetts Coat & Badget† SE1 *(Ter. Bar)*
Dora Hs† SW7 *(Studio)*
Dr Johnsons' Hs EC4 *(Max*)*
Durrants Htl† W1 *(Edward VII Rm*)*
French Inst. SW7 *(Salon de Reception)*
King's Coll.† WC2 *(Council Rm)*
L'Express SW1 *(Max*)*
London Scottish† SW1 *(Queen Elizabeth Club)*
Mall Galls. SW1 *(North Gall.)*
Naval & Military Club† W1 *(Ctyard)*
Royal Veterinary Coll.† NW1 *(Clarence Rm)*
Ski Club of Gt Britain† SW1 *(Bistro or Arnold Lunn Rm)*
Smith's Gall.† WC2 *(Gall. 3)*
Throgmorton's† EC2 *(Long Rm)*
75 Boat: Jason's Trip† W9 *(Jason or Holland*)*
Boat: Thames Pleasure Craft Ltd† EC3 *(Captain James Cook)*
Boat: Turk Launches†, Surrey *(Empress of India)*
Blackheath Concert Halls† SE3 *(Webster Rm)*
Rose Gdn Rest.† W1 *(Prince Regent Rm)*
70 Antelope SW1 *(Upstairs*)*
Bar Escoba SW7 *(Private Rm*)*
Broadgate Estates† EC2 *(Raised Gdn Ter.)*
City Livery Club EC4 *(Members Rm)*
Hon. Artillery Co† EC1 *(Queen's Rm)*
Irish Club† SW1 *(Leinster Rm / Ulster Rm)*
Lansdowne Club† W1 *(Thirties Rm)*
London Press Ctr† EC4 *(Boswell Rm / Johnson Rm)*
Rochester Htl† SW1 *(Victoria Suite)*
60 Boat: Beric Sailing Barge† E1 *(Stationary*)*
Boat: Lady Daphne† SE1 *(Stationary*)*
Bakers' Hall EC3 *(Ct Rm)*
Café St Pierre† EC1 *(Ground or middle Fl)*
Coopers Arms SW3 *(Private Rm*)*

Duke of York's HQ† SW3 *(London Irish Mess)*
Durrants Htl W1 *(Oak Rm)*
Hon. Artillery Co† EC1 *(Medal Rm or Ct Rm)*
Lansdowne Club† W1 *(Blue Rm)*
Royal Geographical Soc.† SW7 *(Tea Rm)*
Royal Veterinary Coll.† NW1 *(Connaught Rm)*
Ski Club of GB† SW1 *(D'Egyers Bar)*
Syon Pk (Banqueting)†, Middx *(Conserv. Lounge)*
Trafalgar Tav.† SE10 *(Hawke & Howe Bar)*
V&A Mus. Café† SW7 *(Painted Rm)*
55 Royal Veterinary Coll.† NW1 *(Council Rm)*
50 Boat: Floating Boater† W2 *(Lapwing)*
Boat: Mainstream Leisure† SW15 *(Lady Rose of Regents)*
Boat: Turk Launches†, Surrey *(Richmond Royale)*
Chez Gerard W1 *(Private Rm*)*
Dickens' Hs Mus. WC1 *(Max*)*
Front Page SW3 *(Private Rm*)*
Henry J Beans SW3 *(Max*)*
Naval & Military Club† W1 *(Piccadilly)*
New Connaught Rms WC2 *(Penths, Oxford or Cambridge)*
Royal Inst. of GB W1 *(Council Rm)*
Royal Over-Seas League† SW1 *(Wrench)*
Royal Veterinary Coll. NW1 *(York or Cambridge Rm)*
Slug & Lettuce SW1 *(Max*)*
45 Royal Over-Seas League† SW1 *(Mountbatten Rutland)*
40 Boat: Beric Sailing Barge† E1 *(Afloat)*
Boat: Lady Daphne† SE1 *(Afloat)*
Crown & Goose NW1 *(Private Rm*)*
Dora Hs† SW7 *(Salon)*
Imp. Coll.† SW7 *(Solar)*
Nat. Army Mus. SW3 *(Council Chamber)*
Ski Club of GB† SW1 *(Landing)*
35 Viceroy† NW1 *(Private Rm*)*
30 Boat: City Cruises† E14 *(Halary)*
Boat: Jason's Trip† W9 *(Lace Plate)*
Doggetts Coat & Badge† SE1 *(Boardroom)*
Naval & Military Club† W1 *(Cowdray or Octagon)*
Rochester Htl† SW1 *(Rochester Suite)*
Royal Over-Seas League† SW1 *(Bennet-Clark)*
25 Durrants Htl W1 *(Armfield Rm)*
Coliseum WC2 *(Royal Retiring Rm)*
20 Coliseum WC2 *(Stoll Rm)*
Westminster Boating Base† SW1 *(Crow's Nest)*
15 Royal Over-Seas League† SW1 *(Park)*
12 Boat: Chas Newen Marine Co SW15 *(Panache, Majestic or Pomery*)*
Coliseum WC2 *(Arlen Rm)*

£B

2230 Le Hammersmith Palais† W6 *(Max*)*

Private venues – standing

2000	Café Club† SE1 *(Vaults*)*
1600	Astoria† WC2 *(Max*)*
1100	Electric Ballroom† NW1 *(Max*)*
	Fridge† SW2 *(Max*)*
	Ministry of Sound† SE1 *(Normal*)*
1000	Busby's† W1 *(Max*)*
	Queen's Ice Skating Club† W2 *(Max*)*
860	SW1 Club† SW1 *(Max*)*
850	Hammersmith Town Hall† W6 *(Max*)*
800	Rock Gdn† WC2 *(with Gdning Club*)*
	Wandsworth Civic Suite† SW18 *(Civic Suite*)*
750	Battersea Town Hall† SW11 *(Grand Hall*)*
	Polish Social & Cultural Assoc.† W6 *(Max*)*
700	Intl Students† W1 *(Max*)*
650	Subterania† W10 *(Max*)*
600	Maximus† W1 *(Max*)*
	Chariots† SW3 *(Max*)*
	Wag† W1 *(Max*)*
525	Café de Paris† W1 *(Max*)*
500	Iceni† W1 *(Max*)*
	Intl Students† W1 *(Theatre)*
	Le Scandale† W1 *(Max*)*
	Turnmills† EC1 *(Max*)*
475	Wandsworth Civic Suite† SW18 *(Civic Hall)*
450	RAW Club† WC1 *(Max*)*
400	Le Hammersmith Palais† W6 *(Balcony Bar)*
	Lundonia Hs† WC1 *(Max*)*
	Rock Gdn† WC2 *(Standalone)*
	Univ. of London Union† WC1 *(Manning Hall*)*
	Wandsworth Civic Suite† SW18 *(Banqueting Hall)*
350	Central Club (YWCA)† WC1 *(Queen Mary Hall*)*
	Hop Exch.† SE1 *(Max*)*
	HQ† NW1 *(Max*)*
330	Hop Cellars† SE1 *(Max*)*
300	Abbey Community Assoc.† SW1 *(Main Hall*)*
	Circa† W1 *(Max*)*
	Cittie of Yorke† WC1 *(Main Bar*)*
	Corney & Barrow† EC2 *(Max*)*
	Czech Club† NW6 *(Max*)*
	Davy's, Skinkers† SE1 *(Max*)*
	Holderness Hs† EC2 *(Hall*)*
	Horniman At Hay's† SE1 *(Max*)*
	Ministry of Sound† SE1 *(VIP)*
	Nôtre Dame Hall† WC2 *(Max*)*
	Polish Social & Cultural Assoc.† W6 *(Conf. Theatre)*
	Wag† W1 *(Either Fl)*
	Westminster Cathedral Hall† SW1 *(Max*)*
	WKD† NW1 *(Max*)*
280	St Etheldreda's Crypt† EC1 *(Max*)*
250	Brahms & Liszt† WC2 *(Max*)*
	Davy's, Bangers† EC2 *(Max*)*
	Davy's, City Flogger† EC3 *(Max*)*
	Davy's, Colonel Jaspers† EC1 *(Max*)*
	Davy's, Crown Passage Vaults† SW1 *(Max*)*
	Davy's, Chiv† W1 *(Max*)*
	Davy's, Vineyard† E1 *(Max*)*
	Holy Trinity Brompton Church Hall SW7 *(Max*)*
	Intl Students† W1 *(Marylebone Rm)*
	London Rowing Club† SW15 *(Max*)*
	Tattershall Castle† SW1 *(Steamers Discotheque*)*
	Vaults† EC1 *(Max*)*
	Univ. of London Boat Club† SW15 *(Outdoors*)*
	Univ. of London Union† WC1 *(Palms Wine Bar & Rest.)*
200	Balls Brothers† EC2 *(Max*)*
	Bar Industria† W1 *(Max*)*
	Battersea Town Hall† SW11 *(Lower Hall)*
	Chariots† SW3 *(Basement Club)*
	Clachan† W1 *(Highland Bar*)*
	Crown Tav. EC1 *(Max*)*
	Coates Karaoke Bar & Rest.† EC2 *(Max*)*
	Davy's, Bishop of Norwich† EC2 *(Max*)*
	Davy's, Burgundy's Ben's† EC1 *(Max*)*
	Davy's, Champagne Charlies† WC2 *(Max*)*
	Davy's, Chopper Lump† W1 *(Max*)*
	Davy's, City Boot† EC2 *(Max*)*
	Davy's, City Pipe† EC1 *(Max*)*
	Davy's, Davy's of Creed Ln† EC4 *(Max*)*
	Davy's, Guinea Butt† SE1 *(Max*)*
	Davy's, Lees Bag† W1 *(Max*)*
	Davy's, Habit† EC3 *(Max*)*
	Davy's, Truckles of Pied Bull Yard WC1 *(Max*)*
	Hash Eleven† W1 *(Max*)*
	Intl Student's Hs† W1 *(Rest.)*
	Le Scandale† W1 *(Front or Rear Bar)*
	London Welsh Ctr† WC1 *(Main Hall*)*
	Lundonia Hs† WC1 *(Ground Fl)*
	Polish Social & Cultural Assoc.† W6 *(Lowiczanka Rest. or Malinova Rm)*
	Ruby's† W1 *(Max*)*
	Southwark Tav. SE1 *(Max*)*
	Walkers of St James's† SW1 *(Max*)*
	Wessex Hs† SW11 *(Max*)*
	Westminster Coll. SW1 *(Rest.*)*
175	Circa† W1 *(Downstairs)*
	Iceni† W1 *(Ground Fl, First (dance) Fl or Second (bar) Fl)*
	St Bride Foundation Inst. EC4 *(Bridewell*)*
150	Africa Ctr† WC2 *(Main Hall*)*
	Balls Brothers† EC2 *(Weekday function)*
	Captain Kidd† E1 *(Max*)*
	Central Club (YWCA)† WC1 *(Martin Rm & Hampstead Rm)*
	Corney & Barrow† EC3 *(Max)*
	Crown & Greyhound† SE21 *(Max*)*
	Davy's, City FOB† EC3 *(Max*)*
	Davy's, Tapster† SW1 *(Max*)*
	Davy's, Cooperage† SE1 *(Max*)*
	Davy's, Mug Hs† SE1 *(Max*)*
	Davy's, Pulpit† EC2 *(Max*)*
	Davy's, Tumblers† W8 *(Max*)*
	Davy's, Udder Place Wine Rms† EC2 *(Max*)*
	Glassblower W1 *(Max*)*
	Hop Cellars† SE1 *(Malt Rm)*
	Intl Students† W1 *(Gulbenkian)*

Private venues – standing

      Le Hammersmith Palais† W6 *(VIP Bar)*
      Freemason's Arms WC2 *(Max*)*
      Gaslight† SW1 *(Max*)*
      Glasshouse Stores W1 *(Max*)*
      London Welsh Ctr† WC1 *(Lower Hall)*
      O-Bar† W1 *(Rest.*)*
      Old Thameside Inn† SE1 *(Cellar Bar*)*
      WKD† NW1 *(Ground Fl or Mezz.)*
      Ye Olde Cheshire Cheese† EC4 *(Cellar Bar*)*
140 Balls Brothers† SW1 *(Weekday function)*
130 Alma SW18 *(Private Rm*)*
      Balls Brothers† *(EC2 or EC4 Weekday function)*
      Vat's† WC1 *(Max*)*
125 Circa† W1 *(Upstairs)*
120 Abbey Community Assoc.† SW1 *(Annexe A & B & C)*
      Battersea Barge Bistro SW8 *(Max*)*
      Corney & Barrow EC4 *(Max)*
      Davy's, City Vaults† EC1 *(Max*)*
      Davy's, Dock Blida† W1 *(Max*)*
      Golden Lion SW1 *(Max*)*
      O-Bar† W1 *(Basement)*
      Shampers† W1 *(Max*)*
      St Moritz† W1 *(Max*)*
      Univ. of London Union† WC1 *(Wine Bar)*
      Upstairs At 58 W11 *(Max*)*
      WKD† NW1 *(Car Pk)*
100 Abbey Community Assoc.† SW1 *(Bar)*
      Balls Brothers† *(EC2 or EC3; Weekday function)*
      Barley Mow W1 *(Max*)*
      Britannia W8 *(Max*)*
      Café Club† SE1 *(Café Club)*
      Chariots† SW3 *(Bar or Gdn)*
      Coal Hole WC2 *(Max*)*
      Corney & Barrow† EC2 or EC4 *(Max)*
      Crown & Two Chairmen W1 *(Upstairs Bar*)*
      Davy's, Shotberries† EC4 *(Max*)*
      Davy's, Spittoon† EC1 *(Max*)*
      Duke of Clarence W11 *(Conserv.*)*
      Hollands W11 *(Max*)*
      Icen† W1 *(Ter.)*
      La Paquerette† EC2 *(Max*)*
      Larry's Wine Bar† WC2 *(Max*)*
      Maximus† W1 *(VIP)*
      Horniman At Hay's† SE1 *(Frederick John Horniman Rm)*
      Lamb Tav. EC3 *(Dining Rm or Dive*)*
      London Welsh Ctr† WC1 *(Bar)*
      Shuckburgh Arms SW3 *(Max*)*
      Univ. of London Boat Club† SW15 *(Indoors)*
      Vat's† WC1 *(Rest.)*
      Victoria Pump Hs† SW8 *(Max*)*
      White Horse SW6 *(Max*)*
90   Balls Brothers† EC2 *(Max)*
      Central Club (YWCA)† WC1 *(Swiss Parlour or Martin Rm)*
80   Africa Ctr† WC2 *(Rear Hall)*
      Balls Brothers† *(Weekday function)*
      Café Royal† W1 *(-1Cellars)*
      Catherine Wheel W8 *(Private Rm*)*
      Cittie of Yorke† WC1 *(Front or cellar bar)*
      Davy's, Chiv† W1 *(Dining Rm)*
      Glasshouse Stores W1 *(One side)*
      King of Diamonds EC1 *(Gdn or Cellar Bar*)*
      Minogue's Bar N1 *(Private Rm*)*
      Ye Olde Cheshire Cheese† EC4 *(Johnson's or Williams Rm)*
75   Betjeman's EC1 *(Max*)*
      Davy's, Bangers Too† EC3 *(Max*)*
      Hop Cellars† SE1 *(Porter Rm)*
      St Bride Foundation Inst. EC4 *(Farringdon Rm)*
70   Argyll Arms W1 *(Max*)*
      Central Club (YWCA)† WC1 *(Hampstead Rm)*
      Leadenhall Tapas Bar EC3 *(Max*)*
      Rochesters† SW1 *(Max*)*
      Shelleys W1 *(Max*)*
      Ye Olde Cheshire Cheese† EC4 *(Johnson's Bar)*
60   Balls Brothers† EC2 *(Weekday function)*
      Bill Bentley's EC2 *(Max*)*
      Café Royal† W1 *(5Tudor)*
      Calthorpe Arms WC1 *(Private Rm*)*
      Crown Tav. EC1 *(Upstairs Bar)*
      Kensington Conservative Assoc. W8 *(Max*)*
      Lundonia Hs† WC1 *(Top Fl Theatre)*
      Pitcher & Piano† SW10 *(Max*)*
      RAW Club† WC1 *(Gdning Rm)*
      Shampers† W1 *(Upstairs or Upstairs Bar)*
      Victoria Pump Hs† SW8 *(Two Fls)*
50   Balls Brothers† EC4 *(Weekday function)*
      Battersea Barge Bistro SW8 *(Upper Deck)*
      Café Royal† W1 *(1Lonsdale)*
      Central Club (YWCA)† WC1 *(Library Rm)*
      Corney & Barrow EC2 *(Max)*
      Phene Arms SW3 *(Upstairs Rm*)*
      Pimlico Wine Vaults SW1 *(Private Rm*)*
      Simpsons of Cornhill EC3 *(Amy's Bar or Wine Bar*)*
      Star Tav. SW1 *(Max*)*
      Two Chairmen SW1 *(Max*)*
      Westminster Coll. SW1 *(Escoffier)*
45   Plough WC2 *(Max*)*
40   Balls Brothers† EC2 *(Weekday function)*
      Battersea Town Hall† SW11 *(Mezz. Rm)*
      Café Royal† W1 *(3Club or 8Penths)*
      Davy's, Grapeshots† E1 *(Max*)*
      Duke of Albemarle W1 *(Max*)*
      Lundonia Hs† WC1 *(Space Biospheres Club)*
      Golden Lion SW1 *(Theatre Bar)*
      Ye Olde Cheshire Cheese† EC4 *(Snug Bar)*
35   Davy's, Skinkers† SE1 *(Boardroom)*
      Dog & Duck W1 *(Max*)*
30   Café Royal† W1 *(7-Trafalgar)*
      Shuckburgh Arms SW3 *(Gdn)*
      Tattershall Castle† SW1 *(Bridge)*
      Wandsworth Civic Suite† SW18 *(Reception Rm or Vip Lounge)*
25   Ye Olde Cheshire Cheese† EC4 *(Director's Rm)*
20   Davy's, Skinkers† SE1 *(Second private Rm)*

Private venues – seated

Venues listed by seated capacity

* largest entry for venue

£E

1000	Hampton Court Pal. *(Max*)*
450	Brit. Mus. WC1 *(Max*)*
300	Blenheim Pal., Oxon *(Max*)*
	V&A Mus. SW7 *(Dome, Medieval Treasury (& Pirelli Gdn)*)*
280	Hampton Court Pal. *(Gt Hall)*
250	Royal Acad. of Arts W1 *(Summer Exhib.*)*
200	Tate Gall. SW1 *(Pre Raphaelite & c18 Gall.*)*
190	V A Mus. SW7 *(Gamble Rm (inc Morris Rm))*
160	Cliveden, Berks *(Max*)*
150	Brocket Hall, Herts *(Max*)*
	Queen's Hs SE10 *(Henrietta Maria Suite*)*
	Syon Pk (Hs), Middx *(Max*)*
135	Queen's Hs SE10 *(Van De Velde Suite)*
120	Spencer Hs SW1 *(Max*)*
	Tate Gall. SW1 *(Sackler Octagon)*
110	Apsley Hs W1 *(Max*)*
100	Queen's Hs SE10 *(Gt Hall)*
	Royal Acad. of Arts W1 *(Private Rms)*
	Wallace Collection W1 *(Gt Gall.*)*
90	Tate Gall. SW1 *(Rex Whistler Rest.)*
80	Kenwood Hs NW3 *(Orangery*)*
70	Nat. Portrait Gall. WC2 *(Max*)*
60	Hampton Court Pal. *(Banqueting House)*
50	Cliveden, Berks *(French Dining Rm)*
40	Royal Acad. of Arts W1 *(General Assembly Rm)*
	V&A Mus. SW7 *(Morris Rm)*
35	Kenwood Hs NW3 *(Dining Rm)*
30	Queen's Hs SE10 *(Orangery Suite)*
	Sir John Soane's Mus. WC2 *(Max*)*
28	Cliveden, Berks *(Churchill Boardroom)*
24	Wallace Collection W1 *(Gall. 17)*
20	Annabel's W1 *(Private Rm*)*
	Chez Nico at Ninety Grosvenor Hs Htl W1 *(Private Rm*)*
14	Cliveden, Berks *(Mountbatten Rm)*
12	Suntory SW1 *(Tatami*)*
10	Tate Gall. SW1 *(Lodge)*
7	Suntory SW1 *(Teppan-Yaki)*

£M-E

2000	Royal Albert Hall SW7 *(Cabaret or Ball*)*
1500	Grosvenor Hs Htl W1 *(Gt Rm*)*
1000	Hilton on Pk Ln W1 *(Grand Ballroom)*
850	Inter-Continental W1 *(Grand Ballroom Suite*)*
800	London Zoo NW1 *(Marquee*)*
704	Guildhall EC2 *(Gt Hall*)*
600	Natural History Mus. SW7 *(Central Hall*)*
	Park Ln Htl W1 *(Ballroom*)*
550	Grosvenor Hs Htl W1 *(Ballroom)*
	Dorchester W1 *(Ballroom*)*
500	Savoy WC2 *(Lancaster Rm*)*
	Westway Studios W11 *(Studio 1*)*
400	Four Seasons Htl W1 *(Ballroom*)*
390	Westway Studios W11 *(Studio 2)*
380	Hilton on Pk Ln W1 *(Grand Ballroom - Section 1)*
375	Banqueting Hs SW1 *(Main Hall*)*
370	RAF Mus. NW9 *(Battle of Britain Hall*)*
360	Regent W1 *(Ballroom)*
	Royal Albert Hall SW7 *(Arena)*
350	Hilton on Pk Ln W1 *(Grand Ballroom - Section 2)*
330	Science Mus. SW7 *(East Hall*)*
320	Hyatt Carlton Tower SW1 *(Ballroom*)*
	Lincoln's Inn WC2 *(Gt Hall*)*
300	Guildhall EC2 *(Old Library)*
	Imp. War Mus. SE1 *(Exhib. Hall*)*
	London Dungeon SE1 *(Max*)*
	Mme Tussaud's NW1 *(Grand Hall*)*
	Middle Temple Hall EC4 *(Hall*)*
	Royal Albert Hall SW7 *(Gods)*
	Saatchi Gall. NW8 *(Max*)*
	Sotherby's W1 *(Max*)*
280	Merchant Taylors' Hall EC2 *(Gt Hall*)*
275	Hyde Pk Htl SW1 *(Ballroom*)*
250	Inner Temple Hall EC4 *(Hall*)*
	Inst. of Directors SW1 *(Nash*)*
	Le Meridien W1 *(Georgian*)*
	Royal Coll. of Music SW7 *(Concert Hall*)*
	South Bank Ctr SE1 *(Queen Elizabeth Hall Foyer*)*
240	Barbican Ctr EC2 *(Gdn Rm*)*
	Knebworth Hs, Herts *(Manor & Lodge Barns*)*
	Savoy WC2 *(Abraham Lincoln Rm & Manhattan Rm)*
	Serpentine Gall. W2 *(Max*)*
230	Banqueting Hs SW1 *(Undercroft)*
	Roof Gdns W8 *(Max*)*
224	Clothworkers' Hall EC3 *(Livery Hall*)*
210	Claridge's W1 *(Ballroom*)*
	Regent W1 *(Music Rm)*
205	Stationers' Hall EC4 *(Livery Hall*)*
200	Beaulieu, Hants *(Brabazon*)*
	Berkeley SW1 *(Ballroom*)*
	Christie's SW1 *(Max*)*
	Criterion W1 *(Max*)*
	Dulwich Picture Gall. SE21 *(Max*)*
	Goldsmiths' Hall EC2 *(Livery Hall*)*
	Guildhall EC2 *(East Crypt or Livery Hall)*
	Hilton on Pk Ln W1 *(Curzon Suite)*
	Imagination Gall. WC1 *(Gall.*)*
	Le Meridien W1 *(Edwardian)*
	London Zoo NW1 *(Regency Suite)*
	Mus. of London EC2 *(Max*)*
	Mus. of the Moving Image SE1 *(Festival Pavilion*)*
	Park Ln Htl W1 *(Tudor Rose Rm)*
	Royal Botanic Gdns, Surrey *(Temperate House*)*
	Science Mus. SW7 *(Flight Gall.)*
	Searcy's SW1 *(Max*)*
	Westway Studios W11 *(Studio 3)*
180	Guildhall EC2 *(West Crypt)*
	Leeds Castle, Kent *(Fairfax Hall*)*
	Natural History Mus. SW7 *(North Hall)*

207

Private venues – seated

170	Gray's Inn EC1 *(Hall*)*
	Skinners' Hall EC4 *(Max*)*
168	Boat: Woods River Svcs SE3 *(Silver Barracuda*)*
160	Arts Club W1 *(Dining Rm*)*
	Boat: Bateaux London WC2 *(Max*)*
	Dorchester W1 *(Orchid)*
	Hyde Pk Htl SW1 *(Knightsbridge Suite)*
	Royal Albert Hall SW7 *(Elgar Rm)*
	Regent W1 *(Drawing or Empire Rm)*
150	Barbican Ctr EC2 *(Conserv. Ter.)*
	Grocers' Hall EC2 *(Dining Rm*)*
	Hilton on Pk Ln W1 *(Harvest Rm)*
	Mirabelle W1 *(Max*)*
	Mus. of London EC2 *(Lord Mayor's Coach Gall.)*
	Natural History Mus. SW7 *(Gem Stone Fl)*
	Reform Club SW1 *(Library or Coffee Rm*)*
	South Bank Ctr SE1 *(Hong Kong & Chelsfield Rm)*
144	Inter-Continental W1 *(Pk Suite)*
140	Knebworth Hs, Herts *(Manor Barn)*
	Royal Albert Hall SW7 *(Picture Gall.)*
130	Apothecaries' Hall EC4 *(Hall*)*
	Hilton on Pk Ln W1 *(Crystal Pal. Rm)*
	Lincoln's Inn WC2 *(Old Hall)*
	Science Mus. SW7 *(Fellows' Rm)*
125	HQS Wellington WC2 *(Court Rm*)*
120	Beaulieu, Hants *(Domus)*
	Caledonian Club SW1 *(Members Dining Rm*)*
	Chelsea SW1 *(Sloane Suite*)*
	Grosvenor Hs Htl W1 *(Albemarle)*
	Monkey Island, Berks *(River Rm*)*
	Natural History Mus. SW7 *(Spencer Gall.)*
	Park Ln Htl W1 *(Gdn Rm)*
	Reform Club SW1 *(Max)*
	Ritz W1 *(Rest. or Palm Court & Marie Antoinette*)*
	Savoy WC2 *(River Rm)*
100	Four Seasons Htl W1 *(Gdn Rm)*
	Inst. of Materials SW1 *(Council Rm*)*
	Inter-Continental W1 *(Windsor Suite)*
	Knebworth Hs, Herts *(Lodge Barn)*
	Le Meridien W1 *(New Function Rms)*
	Leeds Castle, Kent *(Henry VIII Banqueting Hall)*
	London Zoo NW1 *(Raffles Bar & Rest.)*
	Mus. of Mankind W1 *(Max*)*
	Mus. of the Moving Image SE1 *(Max)*
	Orangery (Kensington Pal.) W8 *(Max*)*
	Phillips W1 *(Max*)*
	Royal Opera Hs WC2 *(Max*)*
	Westway Studios W11 *(Studio 4)*
92	Leighton Hs W14 *(Studio*)*
91	Innholders' Hall EC4 *(Hall*)*
90	Brighton Royal Pavilion, Sussex *(Banqueting Rm or Queen Adelaide Suite*)*
	Hilton on Pk Ln W1 *(Coronation Rm)*
	Inter-Continental W1 *(Byron Rm)*
	Ritz W1 *(Palm Court)*

81	Armourers' & Braisers' Hall EC2 *(Livery Hall*)*
80	Accademia Italiana SW7 *(Main Galls.)*
	Cannizaro Hs SW19 *(Viscount Melville, Earl of Mexborough & Lady Jane*)*
	Cutty Sark SE10 *(Tween Decks or Lower Hold*)*
	Four Seasons Htl W1 *(Oak Rm)*
	Halcyon Htl W11 *(Rest.*)*
	Hampshire Htl WC2 *(Penthouse*)*
	HQS Wellington WC2 *(Afterdeck)*
	Inner Temple Hall EC4 *(Parliament Chamber)*
	Inst. of Directors SW1 *(Burton)*
	Le Meridien W1 *(Adams / Regency)*
	Merchant Taylors' Hall EC2 *(Parlour)*
	Park Ln Htl W1 *(Oak Rm)*
	Ranger's Hs SE10 *(Max*)*
	Royal Albert Hall SW7 *(Victoria Rm)*
	Royal Botanic Gdns, Surrey *(Kew Gdns Gall.)*
	Stationers' Hall EC4 *(Court Rm)*
	Sanctuary WC2 *(Max*)*
75	Bank of Eng. Mus. EC2 *(Max*)*
	Halkin SW1 *(Max*)*
70	Brighton Royal Pavilion, Sussex *(William IV Rm)*
	Claridge's W1 *(Drawing Rm or French Salon or Mirror Rm)*
	Dorchester W1 *(Pk Suite)*
	Dukes Htl SW1 *(Marlborough Suite*)*
	Hever Castle, Kent *(Tudor Suite*)*
	Howard Htl WC2 *(Fitzalan*)*
	Hyde Pk Htl SW1 *(King Gustav Adolf Suite)*
	Inst. of Directors SW1 *(Waterloo)*
	Leeds Castle, Kent *(Gate-tower)*
	Mme Tussaud's NW1 *(Gdn Party)*
	Mostmann's Belfry SW1 *(Dining Rm*)*
	Theatre Mus. WC2 *(Paintings Gall.*)*
68	Boat: Woods River Svcs SE3 *(Silver Dolphin)*
65	Barbican Ctr EC2 *(Conserv.)*
60	Criterion W1 *(Ter.)*
	Hyde Pk Htl SW1 *(Pk Suite)*
	Inst. of Materials SW1 *(Library)*
	Leeds Castle, Kent *(State Dining Rm)*
	Mus. of London EC2 *(Eighteenth Century Gall.)*
	Rock Circus W1 *(Max*)*
	Lanesborough SW1 *(Wellington Rm*)*
	Ritz W1 *(Marie Antoinette Suite)*
	Savoy WC2 *(Beaufort)*
57	Dyers' Hall EC4 *(Max*)*
56	Middle Temple Hall EC4 *(Parliament Chamber)*
52	Caledonian Club SW1 *(Stuart)*
50	Berkeley SW1 *(Crystal Rm)*
	Cabinet War Rms SW1 *(Max*)*
	English Gdn SW3 *(Max*)*
	Grocers' Hall EC2 *(Piper Rm)*
	Hilton on Pk Ln W1 *(Pompeii Rm)*
	Howard Htl WC2 *(Arundel Suite)*
	Imp. War Mus. SE1 *(Boardroom 1)*
	Knebworth Hs, Herts *(House)*
	Lanesborough SW1 *(St George's Rm)*
	Marble Hill Hs TW1 *(Max*)*
	Mostmann's Belfry SW1 *(Harvey Nichols)*

208

Private venues – seated

	Natural History Mus. SW7 *(Lasting Impressions)*
	Raffles Dining Rm SW3 *(Max*)*
48	Hyatt Carlton Tower SW1 *(Drawing Rm)*
46	Stationers' Hall EC4 *(Stock Rm)*
42	Stafford SW1 *(Cellar*)*
40	Accademia Italiana SW7 *(Spazio Club)*
	Brighton Royal Pavilion, Sussex *(Gt Kitchen)*
	Cannizaro Hs SW19 *(Viscount Melville)*
	Dorchester W1 *(Holford or Pavilion)*
	Four Seasons Htl W1 *(Pine Rm)*
	Lanesborough SW1 *(Westminster Rm)*
	Leith's W11 *(Private Rm*)*
	Lincoln's Inn WC2 *(Drawing Rm)*
	Mosimann's Belfry SW1 *(Wedgewood)*
	Park Ln Htl W1 *(Orchard Suite or Mirror Rm)*
	Royal Coll. of Music SW7 *(Donaldson Rm)*
	Savoy WC2 *(Pinafore)*
	Sheraton Pk Tower *(Buckingham Rm)*
	Stafford SW1 *(Panel Rm & Sutherland Rm)*
36	Cannizaro Hs SW19 *(Queen Elizabeth Rm)*
	Dukes Htl SW1 *(Roof Ter.)*
	Hever Castle, Kent *(Dining Hall)*
	Hyde Pk Htl SW1 *(Loggia)*
	Temple Island, Oxon *(Inside*)*
35	Inst. of Directors SW1 *(Trafalgar II / St James)*
34	Green's SW1 *(Private Rm*)*
30	Arts Club W1 *(Drawing Rm)*
30	Berkeley SW1 *(Waterloo Rm)*
	Hampshire Htl WC2 *(Romsey or Burley)*
	HQS Wellington WC2 *(Model Rm & Library)*
	L'Incontro SW1 *(Private Rm*)*
	Lanesborough SW1 *(Wilkins Rm)*
	Leighton Hs W14 *(Dining Rm)*
	Mirabelle W1 *(Pine Rm)*
	Motcomb's SW1 *(McClue Suite*)*
	Raffles Dining Rm SW3 *(DiningRm)*
	Royal Albert Hall SW7 *(Prince of Wales)*
	Regent W1 *(Champagne Rm)*
	Ritz W1 *(Berkeley Dining Rm)*
28	Savoy WC2 *(Gondoliers)*
26	English Hs SW3 *(Max*)*
25	Berkeley SW1 *(Tattersall's Rm)*
	L'Etoile W1 *(Private Rm*)*
	Hampshire Htl WC2 *(Milton)*
	Innholders' Hall EC4 *(Court Rm)*
24	Caledonian Club SW1 *(Selkirk)*
	Cannizaro Hs SW19 *(Oak Rm)*
	Mitsukoshi SW1 *(Western Rm*)*
	Royal Coll. of Music SW7 *(Council Rm)*
	Savoy WC2 *(Patience)*
	Stafford SW1 *(Sutherland Rm)*
22	Apothecaries' Hall EC4 *(Court Rm or Parlour)*
	Capital SW3 *(Cadogan*)*
	Connaught W1 *(Regency Carlos Suite*)*
	Grosvenor Hs Htl W1 *(Boardroom)*
	Zen Central W1 *(Private Rm*)*
21	Boat: Interceptor Launch, Essex *(Max*)*
20	11 Hobart Place SW1 *(Edinburgh Rm or Gdn Rm*)*
	Armourers' & Braisers' Hall EC2 *(Court Rm)*
	Claridge's W1 *(Private Suite)*
	English Gdn SW3 *(Rm 1)*
	Le Gavroche W1 *(Private Rm*)*
	Halcyon Htl W1 *(Suite 34 or Halcyon Suite)*
	Imp. War Mus. SE1 *(Boardroom 2)*
	Inst. of Directors SW1 *(Trafalgar / Spears)*
	Middle Temple Hall EC4 *(Queen's Rm)*
	Neal St WC2 *(Private Rm*)*
	Park Ln Htl W1 *(Drawing Rm)*
	Regent W1 *(Boardroom)*
	Ritz W1 *(Trafalgar Suite or Berkeley Reception Rm)*
	Royal Albert Hall SW7 *(Henry Cole Rm)*
	Stationers' Hall EC4 *(Ante Rm)*
	South Bank Ctr SE1 *(Sunley Pavilion)*
18	Dorchester W1 *(Penthouse)*
	Howard Htl WC2 *(Westminster)*
	Inst. of Materials SW1 *(Bessemer Rm)*
	Savoy WC2 *(Mikado)*
16	Dukes Htl SW1 *(Double Suite)*
	Four Seasons Htl W1 *(Sitting & Dining Rms)*
	Hilton on Pk Ln W1 *(Serpentine Rm)*
	Monkey Island, Berks *(Boardroom)*
	Park Ln Htl W1 *(Boardroom)*
	Rib Rm Hyatt Carlton Tower Htl SW1 *(Boardroom*)*
	Wiltons SW1 *(Private Rm*)*
14	Caledonian Club SW1 *(Oval)*
	Claridge's W1 *(Orangery)*
	Lanesborough SW1 *(Wine Cellar)*
	Phillips W1 *(Private Dining Rm)*
	Stafford SW1 *(Argyll Rm)*
12	Boat: Chelsea Luxury Charters SW10 *(Max*)*
	Berkeley SW1 *(Billet)*
	Capital SW3 *(Eaton)*
	Connaught W1 *(Georgian Rm)*
	Cutty Sark SE10 *(Captain's Rm)*
	Dorchester W1 *(Boardroom)*
	Dukes Htl SW1 *(Batchelor Suite)*
	English Hs SW3 *(Front Rm)*
	Halkin SW1 *(Private Rm*)*
	Howard Htl WC2 *(Surrey)*
	Hyde Pk Htl SW1 *(19 Private Salons)*
	Mitsukoshi SW1 *(Tatami Rm)*
	Mosimann's Belfry SW1 *(Gucci)*
	Savoy WC2 *(Iolanthe)*
10	Cannizaro Hs SW19 *(Boardroom)*
	City Miyama EC4 *(Private Rm*)*
	English Gdn SW3 *(Rm 2)*
	Green's SW1 *(Private Rm)*
	Les Saveurs W1 *(Max*)*
	Mirabelle W1 *(Oak, Gdn & Teppan-Yaki Rms)*
	Mosimann's Belfry SW1 *(Alpha Romeo)*
	Stafford SW1 *(Panel Rm or Ping Rm)*
	Dukes Htl SW1 *(Single Suite)*
6	English Hs SW3 *(Blue Rm)*
	Mosimann's Belfry SW1 *(Baulthaup)*
	Savoy WC2 *(Sorcerer)*

Private venues – seated

£M

3000	Alexandra Pal. & Pk N22 *(Gt Hall*)*
2500	Sandown Pk, Surrey *(Tote Hall*)*
2000	Royal Lancaster W2 *(Nine King's Suite *)*
1500	Alexandra Pal. & Pk N22 *(West Hall)*
1120	Royal Lancaster W2 *(Westbourne Suite)*
800	Sandown Pk, Surrey *(Lower Tote Hall)*
750	Commonwealth Inst. W8 *(Comm. Galls.*)*
	Cumberland Htl W1 *(Production Box*)*
660	Brewery EC1 *(Max*)*
650	Café Royal W1 *(4Empire Napoleon*)*
	Hurlingham Club SW6 *(Max*)*
	Kempton Pk, Middx *(Max*)*
600	Royal Gdn Htl W8 *(Pal. Suite*)*
550	Forte Crest Regents Pk W1 *(Portland Suite*)*
	Sandown Pk, Surrey *(Claremont)*
500	London Marriott W1 *(Westminster Suite*)*
450	Jongleurs at Camden Lock NW1 *(Max*)*
	King David Suite W1 *(Main Rm*)*
420	Gloucester Htl SW7 *(Cotswold Suite *)*
	Waldorf Htl WC2 *(Adelphi Suite & Palm Court*)*
400	Bath – Pump Rm, Avon *(Max*)*
	Cabot Hall E14 *(Hall*)*
	Café Royal W1 *(6Dubarry)*
	Elizabeth Suite EC2 *(Spanish Rm*)*
	Kempton Pk, Middx *(Runnymede Suite)*
350	Brewery EC1 *(Porter Tun)*
	Cumberland Htl W1 *(Carlisle Suite)*
	Lloyd's of London EC3 *(Captains' Rm*)*
	Russell WC1 *(Warncliffe Suite or Woburn Suite*)*
300	Battersea Pk SW8 *(Riverside Ter.s*)*
	Brewery EC1 *(King George III)*
	Commonwealth Inst. W8 *(Art Gall.)*
	Inst. of Civil Engs SW1 *(Gt Hall*)*
	Jongleurs at the Cornet SW11 *(Max*)*
	Langham Hilton W1 *(Ballroom*)*
	London Transport Mus. WC2 *(Max*)*
	Mayfair W1 *(Crystal Rm*)*
	Mount Royal Htl W1 *(Edinburgh / Hyde Pk*)*
282	Selfridge Htl W1 *(Selfridge Suite*)*
280	Glaziers' Hall SE1 *(Hall*)*
	Waldorf Htl WC2 *(Charter 2)*
270	Café Royal W1 *(2Louis)*
	Kew Bridge Steam Mus., Middx *(Max*)*
260	Lord's NW8 *(Ballroom or Toynbee*)*
	Nat. Liberal Club SW1 *(Max*)*
250	Alexandra Pal. & Pk N22 *(Pal. Rest.)*
	Chartered Accountants' Hall EC2 *(Gt Hall*)*
	Ham Hs, Surrey *(Max*)*
	Hurlingham Club SW6 *(Quadrangle Suite)*
	Inst. of Civil Engs SW1 *(Rest.)*
	Sandown Pk, Surrey *(Wolsey or Ardross)*
	Syon Pk (Conserv.), Middx *(Max.*)*
	Tower Thistle E1 *(Tower Suite (York Rm & Lancaster Rm)*)*
240	Churchill W1 *(Chartwell Suite*)*
	Oval SE11 *(Banqueting Suite*)*
220	Bank of Eng. Club SW15 *(Max*)*
	Café Royal W1 *(1Elysee)*
	Chelsea Harbour Rms SW10 *(Turner & Corlyle Rms*)*
	Royal Majestic Suite NW6 *(Ground Fl*)*
	Law Soc. WC2 *(Common Rm*)*
210	Carpenters' Hall EC2 *(Livery Hall*)*
	Royal Inst. of Brit. Architects W1 *(Florence Hall*)*
	Insurance Hall EC2 *(Gt Hall*)*
200	BAFTA Ctr W1 *(Function Rm*)*
	Bath – Pump Rm, Avon *(Pump Rm)*
	Church Hs SW1 *(Harvey Goodwin Suite*)*
	Clandon, Surrey *(Rest.*)*
	Conrad Htl SW10 *(Henley Suite*)*
	Forte Crest Regents Pk W1 *(Albany)*
	Gloucester Htl SW7 *(Cotswold - 1/2)*
	ICA SW1 *(Max*)*
	Limelight W1 *(Gall. & Dome*)*
	Red Fort W1 *(Private Rm*)*
	Regent's Coll. NW1 *(Refectory)*
	Rembrandt Htl SW7 *(Edward & Charles & James & Princes (King Suite)*)*
	Sandown Pk, Surrey *(Tack & Saddle)*
	Stakis St Ermins SW1 *(Ballroom*)*
	Twickenham Banqueting Ctr TW1 *(Rose Rm*)*
190	St Bartholomew's Hosp. EC1 *(Gt Hall*)*
180	Clandon, Surrey *(Marble Hall)*
	Painters' Hall EC4 *(Livery Hall*)*
175	Twickenham Banqueting Ctr TW1 *(West Pavilion Suite)*
170	Basil Street Htl SW3 *(Parrot Club*)*
	Ironmongers' Hall EC2 *(Banqueting Hall*)*
	Kew Bridge Steam Mus., Middx *(Water Hall)*
	Royal Soc. of Arts WC2 *(All Vaults*)*
	RS Hispaniola WC2 *(Main Deck*)*
164	Butchers' Hall EC1 *(Gt Hall*)*
160	Kensington Pal. Thistle W8 *(Duchess*)*
	Langham Hilton W1 *(Memories of Empire*)*
	Simpsons- in-the-Strand WC2 *(Max*)*
154	Basil Street Htl SW3 *(Dining Rm)*
150	Amadeus Ctr W9 *(Upper Hall*)*
	Bath – Pump Rm, Avon *(Concert Rm)*
	Belvedere W8 *(Max*)*
	Bombay Brass. SW7 *(Max*)*
	Church Hs SW1 *(Hoare Memorial Hall)*
	Dartmouth Hs W1 *(Max*)*
	Forte Crest Regents Pk W1 *(Clarence)*
	Haberdashers' Hall EC2 *(Main Hall*)*

Private venues – seated

     Inst. of Mechanical
     Engs SW1 *(Marble Hall*)*
     Nat. Liberal Club SW1 *(Ter.)*
     Pinewood Studios, Bucks
     (Ballroom*)
     Queen's Eyot, Berks
     (Permanent Marquee*)
     Royal Nat. Theatre SE1
     (Ter. Café*)
     Theatre Royal WC2
     (Grand Salon*)
     Waldorf Htl WC2 *(Adelphi 3)*
145 Simpsons- in-the-Strand WC2
     (South Rm)
144 Churchill W1 *(Chartwell I)*
     HMS Belfast SE1
     (Ship Co's Dining Rm*)
140 Kempton Pk, Middx
     (Hampton Suite)
     Nat. Liberal Club SW1
     (David Lloyd George)
     Rubens Htl SW1
     (Old Masters Rest.*)
130 Alexandra Pal. & Pk N22
     (Loneborough Rm)
     Cavalry & Guards Club W1
     (Coffee Rm*)
     Feng Shang NW1 *(Max*)*
     Forte Crest Regents Pk W1
     (Devonshire)
     Winchester Hs Club SW15
     (Front Lawn*)
124 Nat. Liberal Club SW1
     (Dining Rm)
120 Barber-Surgeons' Hall EC2
     (Livery Hall*)
     Brewery EC1 *(Queen Charlotte)*
     Café Royal W1 *(6Dauphin, 5-Marquise or 2Pompadour)*
     Champenois EC2 *(Max*)*
     Church Hs SW1
     (Bishop Partridge Hall)
     City of London Club EC2
     (Main Dining Rm*)
     Conrad Htl SW10 *(Henley I)*
     Farmers' & Fletchers'
     Hall EC1 *(Max*)*
     Glaziers' Hall SE1 *(River Rm)*
     Grosvenor Htl SW1 *(Gall. Rm*)*
     Hamilton Suite W1 *(Max*)*
     Kempton Pk, Middx
     (Thames Suite or Paddock Suite)
     Royal Aeronautical Soc. W1
     (Argyll Rm & Hawker Rm*)
     Royal Gdn Htl W8 *(Balmoral Suite)*
     Royal Nat. Theatre SE1
     (Ovations and Olivier Stalls Foyer)
     Sandown Pk, Surrey *(Cavalry Bar)*
     St John's Gate EC1
     (Chapter Hall*)
     Staple Inn WC1 *(Hall*)*
     Trinity Hs EC3 *(Library*)*
110 Langham Hilton W1
     (Portland Suite)
     TS Queen Mary WC2
     (Queen Mary Suite*)
     Winchester Hs Club SW15
     (River Rm)
100 Bonham's SW7 *(Max*)*
     Brewery EC1
     (Smeaton's Vaults or Sugar Rms)
     Café Royal W1
     (1-Derby & Queensbury)
     Chartered Accountants'
     Hall EC2 *(Rest. & Wine Bar)*
     Chelsea Physic Gdn SW3
     (Private Rm*)
     Clandon, Surrey *(Salloon)*
     Conrad Htl SW10
     (Compass Rose or Thames)
     Cumberland Htl W1 *(Gloucester)*

     Dartmouth Hs W1
     (Long Drawing Rm)
     Glaziers' Hall SE1
     (Library / Court Rm)
     Hamilton Suite W1 *(Red Rm)*
     Hampton Court, Tiltyard,
     Surrey *(Max*)*
     Hurlingham Club SW6
     (Palm Court Suite)
     ICA SW1 *(Nash or Brandon)*
     Inst. of Civil Engs SW1 *(Smeaton Rm)*
     Kew Bridge Steam Mus.,
     Middx *(Steam Hall)*
     Law Soc. WC2 *(Members Dining Rm)*
     Mortons Club W1
     (Rest. & Bar*)
     Pal. Theatre W1 *(Stalls Bar*)*
     Pinewood Studios, Bucks
     (Gt Gatsby Rm)
     Royal Horseguards Thistle
     Htl SW1 *(Thames*)*
     St Stephens Constitutional
     Club SW1 *(Dining Rm*)*
     St Thomas's Hosp. SE1
     (Governors' Hall*)
     Stakis St Ermins SW1 *(Balcony)*
     TS Queen Mary WC2 *(Carvery)*
     Vanderbilt Htl SW7 *(Max*)*
     Washington Htl W1 *(Rest.*)*
     Westbury Htl W1
     (Mount Vernon Rm*)
     White Hs Htl NW1 *(Albany*)*
97 Tallow Chandlers' Hall EC4
     (Livery Hall*)
96 Churchill W1 *(Chartwell II)*
95 Royal Soc. of Arts WC2
     (Benjamin Franklin Rm)
90 Cavalry & Guards Club W1
     (Peninsula Rm)
     Chelsea Harbour Rms SW10
     (Turner Rm)
     Elizabeth Suite EC2
     (Golden Hind)
     Regent's Coll. NW1
     (Herringham Hall)
     Rembrandt Htl SW7 *(James)*
     RUSI Building SW1
     (Duke of Wellington Hall*)
     Spanish Club W1
     (Alfonso XIII Rm*)
     Waldorf Htl WC2 *(Charter 1)*
85 Royal Lancaster W2
     (Gloucester Suite)
80 Bank of Eng. Club SW15
     (Redgates Lodge)
     Brewers' Hall EC2 *(Livery Hall*)*
     Britannia Intercontinental W1
     (Manhattan*)
     Brown's Htl W1 *(Clarendon*)*
     Butchers' Hall EC1 *(Taurus Suite or Large Court Rm & Small Court Rm)*
     Canonbury Acad. N1
     (Long Gall. – there are 21 smaller Rms*)
     Commonwealth Inst. W8
     (Jehangir & Board Rms or Comm Brass.)
     Fulham Pal. SW6
     (Gt Hall or Drawing Rm*)
     Goring Htl SW1
     (Large Lounge (weekends only)*)
     Guards Mus. SW1 *(Max*)*
     Inst. of Civil Engs SW1
     (Brunel Rm or Council Rm)
     Inst. of Mechanical
     Engs SW1 *(Hinton)*
     Ironmongers' Hall EC2
     (Court Rm)
     Kensington Pal. Thistle W8
     (Marchioness)
     Limelight W1 *(Club VIP)*

Private venues – seated

Mayfair W1 *(Lansdowne Suite)*
Mountbatten WC2 *(Earl*)*
Pinewood Studios, Bucks *(Green Rm)*
Royal Gdn Htl W8 *(Kensington Suite)*
RS Hispaniola WC2 *(Top Deck)*
Sandown Pk, Surrey *(Lawn Suite)*
Trinity Hs EC3 *(Court Rm)*
Waldorf Htl WC2 *(Adelphi 1)*
Westbury Htl W1 *(Pine Rm)*

77 Kenwood Hs NW3 *(Old Kitchen*)*
75 Nº 1 Yacht Club WC2 *(Dining Rm*)*
Founders' Hall EC1 *(Livery Hall*)*
Insurance Hall EC2 *(Ostler Hall)*
Twickenham Banqueting Ctr TW1 *(Club Rm)*
72 Holiday Inn – Mayair W1 *(Stratton Suite *)*
Watermen & Lightermen's Hall EC3 *(Freemen's Rm*)*
70 41 Beak St W1 *(Max*)*
Belvedere W8 *(Lower level)*
Brown's Htl W1 *(Niagra & Roosevelt combined)*
Café Royal W1 *(1Domino, 3-Josephine, 5George or 3Nicols)*
Chelsea Harbour Rms SW10 *(Carlyle Rm)*
Downstairs At 190 SW7 *(Max*)*
Grosvenor Htl SW1 *(Bessborough Rm)*
Mus. of Childhood E2 *(Summerly Rm*)*
Orangery (Holland Pk) W8 *(Orangery*)*
Pewterers' Hall EC2 *(Livery Rm*)*
Royal Gdn Htl W8 *(Sandringham & Osborne Suite)*
Royal Majestic Suite NW6 *(First Fl)*
Tall Hs SE1 *(Max*)*
TS Queen Mary WC2 *(Captain's Suite)*
Westminster Conf. Ctr SW1 *(Rest.*)*
67 Basil Street Htl SW3 *(Brompton Rm)*
66 Brewery EC1 *(James Watt)*
65 Univ. Women's Club W1 *(Dining Rm*)*
60 Al Basha W8 *(Private Rm*)*
Amadeus Ctr W9 *(Lower Hall)*
Belvedere W8 *(Top level)*
Beotys WC2 *(Private Rm*)*
Cabot Hall E14 *(Sebastian Rm)*
Cadogan SW1 *(Rest.*)*
Chartered Accountants' Hall EC2 *(Main Reception Rm)*
Churchill W1 *(Library)*
Dartmouth Hs SW1 *(Ballroom)*
Forte Crest St James's SW1 *(Private dining Rm*)*
Ham Hs, Surrey *(Orangery)*
HMS Belfast SE1 *(Gun Rm)*
Ivy WC2 *(Private Rm*)*
Lloyd's of London EC3 *(Conf. Rm)*
London Metropole W2 *(Max*)*
London Television Ctr SE1 *(Westminster & St Pauls)*
Mountbatten WC2 *(Drawing Rm)*
Mus. of Childhood E2 *(Max)*
Oxford & Cambridge Club SW1 *(Marlborough*)*
Painters' Hall EC4 *(Court Rm)*

Queen's Eyot, Berks *(Max)*
Rembrandt Htl SW7 *(Edward)*
Royal Soc. of Arts WC2 *(Vault 1)*
RUSI Building SW1 *(McGarel-Groves Reading Rm)*
Sandown Pk, Surrey *(Persimmon)*
Soho Soho W1 *(Salon Privée*)*
Waldorf Htl WC2 *(Adelphi 2)*
Washington Htl W1 *(Richmond Suite)*
58 Haberdashers' Hall EC2 *(Court Rm)*
Rembrandt Htl SW7 *(Elizabeth & Victoria (Queen Suite))*
56 Bankers Club EC2 *(Dining Rm*)*
55 Au Jardin des Gourmets W1 *(Private Rm*)*
Cibo W14 *(Max*)*
Turners SW3 *(Max*)*
50 Alexandra Pal. & Pk N22 *(Palm Court 1-5)*
Brewery EC1 *(City Cellars)*
Café Royal W1 *(-1-Cellars)*
Cavalry & Guards Club W1 *(Balaclava Rm)*
City of London Club EC2 *(Gdn or Visitors Rm)*
Conrad Htl SW10 *(Harbour)*
Forte Crest Regents Pk W1 *(Chester Suite)*
Freud Mus. NW3 *(House & Gdn*)*
Goring Htl SW1 *(Ebury Rm)*
Hamilton Hs EC4 *(Max*)*
HMS Belfast SE1 *(Wardroom)*
Ironmongers' Hall EC2 *(Luncheon Rm)*
Knightsbridge Place SW1 *(Private Rm*)*
Nat. Liberal Club SW1 *(Lady Violet)*
Oxford & Cambridge Club SW1 *(Princess Marie Louise)*
Quayside E1 *(Private Rm*)*
Regent's Coll. NW1 *(Knapp Gall.)*
Royal Soc. of Arts WC2 *(Vault 4)*
Rubens Htl SW1 *(Rembrandt Rm)*
RUSI Building SW1 *(Library & McGarel-Groves Reading Rm)*
Russell WC1 *(Bedford or Grafton Suite)*
Sheraton Belgravia SW1 *(Dining Rm*)*
TS Queen Mary WC2 *(Wardroom Bistro)*
Univ. Women's Club W1 *(Drawing Rm or Library)*
Villandry Dining Rms W1 *(Max*)*
Waldorf Htl WC2 *(Somerset)*
West Wycombe Caves, Bucks *(Max*)*
48 Royal Soc. of Arts WC2 *(Tav. Rm)*
Rules WC2 *(Greene Rm*)*
Russell WC1 *(Ormond Suite)*
46 SB Lady Gwynfred E14 *(Max*)*
45 Brown's Htl W1 *(Roosevelt)*
Butchers' Hall EC1 *(Large Court Rm)*
Chartered Inst. of Public Finance & Accountancy WC2 *(Council Chamber*)*
Gloucester Htl SW7 *(Harrington / Stanhope)*
Inst. of Mechanical Engs SW1 *(Council)*
Julie's W11 *(Gothic Rm*)*
London Marriott W1 *(Hamilton Rm)*
Nosh Brothers SW6 *(Max*)*

Private venues – seated

Simpsons-in-the-Strand WC2 *(Smoking Rm)*
Waldorf Htl WC2 *(Aldwych)*
42 Mortons Club W1 *(Downstairs Rm)*
40 Ascot Racecourse, Berks *(King Edward VII*)*
Athenaeum Htl W1 *(Westminster Suite*)*
Bleeding Heart EC1 *(Champagne Rm*)*
Boyd's W8 *(Max*)*
Brown's Htl W1 *(Kipling or Niagara)*
Cabot Hall E14 *(St Lawrence Rm)*
Café Royal W1 *(1-Lonsdale)*
Chartered Inst. of Public Finance & Accountancy WC2 *(Committee Rm 4)*
Churchill W1 *(Edward or Victoria Suite)*
Conrad Htl SW10 *(Henley II or Henley III)*
L'Escargot W1 *(Barrell Vaulted Rm*)*
La Famiglia SW10 *(Private Rm*)*
Formula Veneta SW10 *(Private Rm*)*
Hamilton Suite W1 *(Conserv. Bar or Hamilton Rm)*
Langham Hilton W1 *(Ambassadors' Rm, Regent Rm, Welbeck Rm or Wimpole Rm)*
Law Soc. WC2 *(Grill Rm)*
Peacock Hs W14 *(Main Hall & Lounge*)*
Quaglino's SW1 *(Private Rm*)*
Rembrandt Htl SW7 *(Elizabeth)*
Royal Aeronautical Soc. W1 *(Handley Page or Council Rm & Bar)*
Royal Inst. of Brit. Architects W1 *(South Rm)*
Rules WC2 *(Charles Dickens Rm)*
Staple Inn WC1 *(Council Chamber)*
La Truffe Noir SE1 *(Upstairs Dining Rm*)*
Westbury Htl W1 *(Brighton Rm)*
Whittington's EC4 *(Rest.*)*
37 Watermen & Lightermen's Hall EC3 *(Court Rm)*
36 Dartmouth Hs W1 *(Small Drawing Rm)*
Empress Gdn W1 *(Private Rm*)*
Goring Htl SW1 *(Small Gdn Lounge)*
Royal Soc. of Arts WC2 *(Vault 2)*
35 Basil Street Htl SW3 *(Basil Rm)*
First Floor W11 *(Private Rm*)*
La Pomme d'Amour W11 *(Private Rm*)*
La Truffe Noir SE1 *(Downstairs Bistro)*
34 Drones SW1 *(Private Rm*)*
32 Ascot Racecourse, Berks *(Churchill)*
Cadogan SW1 *(Langtry Rm)*
Elizabeth Suite EC2 *(Library)*
Julie's W11 *(Gdn Rm)*
30 Bankers Club EC2 *(Private Dining Rms)*
Café Royal W1 *(3-Club)*
Chapter 11 SW10 *(Private Rm*)*
Chartered Accountants' Hall EC2 *(Members' Rm)*
Coopers' Hall EC2 *(Max*)*
Dan's SW3 *(Conserv.*)*
Fan Mus. SE10 *(Orangery*)*
Grosvenor Htl SW1 *(Warwick Rm)*
Insurance Hall EC2 *(Pipkin Rm)*
Kensington Pal. Thistle W8 *(Park)*

Launceston Place W8 *(Private Area)*
Law Soc. WC2 *(Old Council Chamber)*
Limelight W1 *(Study Bar)*
Lou Pescadou SW5 *(Private Rm*)*
Mayfair W1 *(Berkeley Suite or Curzon Suite)*
Mimmo d'Ischia SW1 *(Private Rm*)*
Mon Plaisir WC2 *(Private Rm*)*
Odette's NW1 *(Conserv.*)*
Royal Aeronautical Soc. W1 *(Sopwith Rm)*
Russell WC1 *(Guilford Suite)*
Sheekey's WC2 *(Section*)*
Shepherd's SW1 *(Max*)*
Stakis St Ermins SW1 *(York / Clarence)*
Le Suquet SW3 *(Private Rm*)*
Sweetings EC4 *(Max*)*
Tallow Chandlers' Hall EC4 *(Parlour)*
Washington Htl W1 *(Richmond 2)*
28 Brown's Htl W1 *(Hellenic)*
Fung Shing WC2 *(Private Rm*)*
La Dordogne W4 *(Private Section*)*
Royal Gdn Htl W8 *(Royal Suite)*
Scone E14 *(Max*)*
St Stephens Constitutional Club SW1 *(Gdn Rm)*
Trinity Hs EC3 *(Pepys Rm)*
26 Ascot Racecourse, Berks *(Brown Jack)*
Berkshire W1 *(Sonning Suite*)*
Frederick's N1 *(Clarence Rm*)*
Mao Tai SW6 *(Private Rm*)*
25 Au Jardin des Gourmets W1 *(Private Rm)*
Busabong Too SW10 *(Mezz.)*
Church Hs SW1 *(Smaller Rms)*
La Capannina W1 *(Private Rm*)*
London Marriott W1 *(John Adams Suite)*
Poissonnerie de l'Avenue SW3 *(Private Rm*)*
Rules WC2 *(King Edward VII Rm)*
Selfridge Htl W1 *(Drawing Rm)*
St John's Gate EC1 *(Council Chamber)*
Washington Htl W1 *(Richmond 1)*
ZeNW3 NW3 *(Private Rm*)*
24 Beauchamp Place SW3 *(Private Rm*)*
Butchers' Hall EC1 *(Small Court Rm)*
Café Royal W1 *(8-Penthouse)*
Cavalry & Guards Club W1 *(Waterloo Rm)*
Downstairs At 190 SW7 *(Private Rm)*
Julie's W11 *(Banqueting Rm)*
Le Mesurier EC1 *(Max*)*
Royal Soc. of Arts WC2 *(Vault 3)*
Tower Thistle E1 *(Raleigh or Spenser)*
Westminster Conf. Ctr SW1 *(Gloucester)*
22 L'Artiste Assoiffé W11 *(Private Rm*)*
Britannia Intercontinental W1 *(Grosvenor I)*
L'Escargot W1 *(Private Rm)*
Kaya Korean W1 *(Private Rm*)*
Rembrandt Htl SW7 *(Charles)*
Sheraton Belgravia SW1 *(Study & Library)*
St Bartholomew's Hosp. EC1 *(Guild Rm)*

Private venues – seated

Westminster Conf. Ctr SW1 *(Cambridge Rm)*
20 Ajimura WC2 *(Max*)*
Ascot Racecourse, Berks *(Hamilton)*
Bahn Thai W1 *(Private Rm*)*
Belvedere W8 *(Middle level)*
Berkshire W1 *(Sandhurst Suite)*
Brewers' Hall EC2 *(Court Rm)*
Dan's SW3 *(Private Rm)*
Forte Crest Regents Pk W1 *(1/2 Chester Suite)*
Founders' Hall EC1 *(Parlour)*
Freud Mus. NW3 *(House)*
Guinea W1 *(Boardroom*)*
Haberdashers' Hall EC2 *(Luncheon Rm)*
HMS Belfast SE1 *(Admiral's Quarters)*
Holiday Inn – Mayair W1 *(Presidential Suite &)*
Inst. of Civil Engs SW1 *(Old Members Rm)*
Insurance Hall EC2 *(Committee Rm 2)*
Ken Lo's Memories SW1 *(Private Rm*)*
Kensington Pal. Thistle W8 *(Countess Princess)*
Le Pont de la Tour SE1 *(Private Rm*)*
Leven is Strijd E14 *(Max*)*
Limelight W1 *(Annex)*
Lindsay Hs W1 *(Private Rm*)*
London Television Ctr SE1 *(Westminster / St Pauls)*
Oxford & Cambridge Club SW1 *(Edward VII)*
Royal Soc. of Arts WC2 *(Folkestone Rm)*
RSJ SE1 *(Private Rm*)*
RUSI Building SW1 *(Council Chamber)*
San Martino SW3 *(Max*)*
St Quentin SW3 *(Private Rm*)*
Stakis St Ermins SW1 *(Cameo)*
Theatre Royal WC2 *(Royal Retiring Rm or Board Rm)*
Trinity Hs EC3 *(Luncheon Rm)*
Vanderbilt Htl SW7 *(Vanderbilt)*
Waldorf Htl WC2 *(Kingsway)*
Westbury Htl W1 *(Regency Rm)*
Zen SW3 *(Private Rm*)*
18 Café Royal W1 *(5-Tudor or 7Trafalgar)*
Mountbatten WC2 *(Viceroy)*
St Bartholomew's Hosp. EC1 *(Treasurer's Rm)*
St Thomas's Hosp. SE1 *(Grand Committee Rm)*
17 Julie's W11 *(Conserv.)*
16 Al San Vincenzo W2 *(Private Rm*)*
Athenaeum Htl W1 *(Devonshire Suite)*
Cavalry & Guards Club W1 *(Double Bridal Rm)*
Grosvenor Htl SW1 *(Belgrave or Wilton Rm)*
Insurance Hall EC2 *(Morgan Owen Rm)*
Kensington Pal. Thistle W8 *(Baroness)*
Le Suquet SW3 *(Private Rm)*
Tall Hs SE1 *(Private Rm)*
La Truffe Noir SE1 *(Upstairs Bar)*
White Tower W1 *(Private Rm*)*
Winchester Hs Club SW15 *(Turner Rm)*
15 Benihana SW3 *(Private Rm*)*
London Marriott W1 *(Dukes Suite)*

Rembrandt Htl SW7 *(Victoria)*
Russell WC1 *(Library)*
14 L'Amico SW1 *(Private Rm*)*
Ascot Racecourse, Berks *(Crocker Bulteel or Gordon Carter)*
Au Jardin des Gourmets W1 *(Private Rm)*
Basil Street Htl SW3 *(Mezz. Rm)*
Churchill W1 *(Court Suite)*
La Dordogne W4 *(Private Rm)*
Goring Htl SW1 *(Drawing Rm)*
Hamilton Suite W1 *(Marble Rm)*
Insurance Hall EC2 *(Committee Rm 1)*
Julie's W11 *(Tomb (wbl))*
Launceston Place W8 *(Private Rm)*
Painters' Hall EC4 *(Painted Chamber)*
Royal Nat. Theatre SE1 *(Richardson Rm)*
Sheraton Belgravia SW1 *(Alcove in Dining Rm)*
St Bartholomew's Hosp. EC1 *(Peggy Turner Rm)*
Westminster Conf. Ctr SW1 *(Lancaster / Warwick)*
12 22 Jermyn St SW1 *(Max*)*
Basil Street Htl SW3 *(Room 246)*
Bentleys W1 *(Private Rm*)*
Britannia Intercontinental W1 *(Grosvenor II)*
Brown's Htl W1 *(Lord Byron or Albemarle)*
Cabot Hall E14 *(Cape Breton Rm)*
Le Carapace NW3 *(Private Rm*)*
Conrad Htl SW10 *(Nelson)*
Elizabeth Suite EC2 *(Willoughby Rm)*
Empress Gdn W1 *(Private Rm)*
Gay Hussar W1 *(Private Rm*)*
Hodgson's WC2 *(Private Rm*)*
Imp. City EC3 *(Private Vault*)*
Lindsay Hs W1 *(Private Rm)*
Mayfair W1 *(Stratton)*
Pomegranates SW1 *(Private Rm*)*
Royal Aeronautical Soc. W1 *(Hawker Rm or Brabazon)*
Royal Horseguards Thistle Htl SW1 *(Boardroom)*
Sheekey's WC2 *(Private Rm*)*
St Bartholomew's Hosp. EC1 *(Henry VIII Committee Rm)*
Waldorf Htl WC2 *(Westminster or Waterloo or Tavistock)*
10 L'Amico SW1 *(Private Rm*)*
Athenaeum Htl W1 *(Richmond Suite)*
Brewers' Hall EC2 *(Committee Rm)*
Bubb's EC1 *(Private Rm*)*
Empress Gdn W1 *(Private Rm)*
Julie's W11 *(Gall. (wbl))*
Langham Hilton W1 *(Cumberland Rm)*
Monkeys SW3 *(Private Rm*)*
Tatsuso EC2 *(Private Rm*)*
Rembrandt Htl SW7 *(Princes)*
9 Odette's NW1 *(Private Rm)*
8 Brown's Htl W1 *(Graham Bell)*
Cabot Hall E14 *(Nova Scotia Rm or Newfoundland Rm)*
Café Royal W1 *(7-Hepplewhite)*
Conrad Htl SW10 *(Wellington)*
Goring Htl SW1 *(Breakfast Rm)*
Holiday Inn – Mayair W1 *(Buckingham or Burlington)*
Insurance Hall EC2 *(President's Rm)*
Russell WC1 *(Boardroom)*

214

Private venues – seated

	Univ. Women's Club W1 *(Red Rm)*
	Westminster Conf. Ctr SW1 *(York Rm)*
6	Holiday Inn – Mayfair W1 *(Berkeley)*
4	Theatre Royal WC2 *(Duke of Bedford)*

£B-M

1200	Royal Horticultural Halls SW1 *(New Hall*)*
1000	Hon. Artillery Co EC1 *(Marquee*)*
	K Warehouse E6 *(Space 1*)*
700	Royal Coll. of Art SW7 *(Henry Moore Gall.*)*
600	Equinox at the Empire WC2 *(Max*)*
540	New Connaught Rms WC2 *(Balmoral & Grand Hall*)*
500	Cecil Sharp Hs NW1 *(Kennedy Hall*)*
	Duke of York's HQ SW3 *(Cadogan Hall with marquee*)*
	Grosvenor Rms NW2 *(Grosvenor Suite*)*
	Hollyhedge Hs SE3 *(Hall*)*
	K Warehouse E6 *(Cavern 1 or 2)*
	Porchester Ctr W2 *(Ballroom*)*
	Royal Horticultural Halls SW1 *(Old Hall)*
	Stoke Newington Town Hall N16 *(Max*)*
450	London Press Ctr EC4 *(Caxton Suite*)*
	Syon Pk (Banqueting), Middx *(Max*)*
440	Hippodrome WC2 *(Max*)*
400	Chelsea Old Town Hall SW3 *(Main Hall*)*
	Dulwich Coll. SE21 *(Christenson Hall & Upper Dining Rms*)*
350	Blackheath Concert Halls SE3 *(Gt Hall*)*
	Hon. Artillery Co EC1 *(Albert Rm)*
	World Trade Ctr E1 *(Max*)*
300	Equinox at the Empire WC2 *(Club)*
	Fulham Town Hall SW6 *(Large Hall*)*
	Jazz Café NW1 *(Max*)*
	London Press Ctr EC4 *(Pepys Suite)*
	Mall Galls. SW1 *(Main Gall.*)*
	Smith's Gall. WC2 *(Max*)*
260	New Connaught Rms WC2 *(Edinburgh & Drawing Rm / Cornwall & Crown)*
250	Acad. of Live & Recorded Arts SW18 *(Max*)*
	Congress Ctr WC1 *(Congress Hall*)*
	Dulwich Coll. SE21 *(Gt Hall)*
	Goldsmith's Coll. SE14 *(Gt Hall*)*
	Le Gothique SW18 *(with Acad. of Live & Recorded Arts*)*
	Smith's Gall. WC2 *(Rest.)*
	Trafalgar Tav. SE10 *(Nelson Suite*)*
240	Boat: Catamaran Cruisers WC2 *(Naticia*)*
230	Clink SE1 *(Max*)*
	Westminster Boating Base SW1 *(Total Facility with Marquee*)*
225	Strand Pal. Htl WC2 *(Birley*)*
220	Boat: Tidal Cruises SE1 *(Royal Princess*)*
	Chelsea Football Club SW6 *(Executive Club Rm*)*
	Hippodrome WC2 *(Auditorium)*
	King's Coll. WC2 *(Gt Hall*)*
200	Boardwalk W1 *(Max*)*
	Dolphin Square SW1 *(Rest.*)*
	Duke of York's HQ SW3 *(Cadogan Hall)*
	HMS President EC4 *(Drill Hall*)*
	Naval & Military Club W1 *(Coffee Rm*)*
	New Connaught Rms WC2 *(Brass.)*
	Pentland Hs SE3 *(Marquee / Lawn*)*
	Royal Coll. of Art SW7 *(Gulbenkian Upper Gall.)*
	Royal Over-Seas League SW1 *(Hall of India & Pakistan*)*
	Royal Holloway Coll., Surrey *(Founders Dining Hall*)*
	St Martin in the Fields WC2 *(Max*)*
	Viceroy NW1 *(Max*)*
180	Bishopsgate Inst. EC2 *(Main Hall*)*
	Grosvenor Rms NW2 *(Executive Suite)*
	Hon. Artillery Co EC1 *(Long Rm)*
	Royal Green Jackets W1 *(Hall*)*
175	Hippodrome WC2 *(Balcony - Rest.)*
160	City Livery Club EC4 *(Dining Rm*)*
	Clink SE1 *(Winchester Hall)*
	Conway Hall WC1 *(Large Hall*)*
	Eatons EC3 *(Banqueting Suite*)*
	London Scottish SW1 *(Hall*)*
150	Boat: Tidal Cruises SE1 *(PV Viscountess)*
	Chelsea Gdner SW3 *(Max*)*
	Congress Ctr WC1 *(Rest.)*
	Fulham Hs SW6 *(Main Hall*)*
	Fulham Town Hall SW6 *(Concert Hall)*
	Leoni's Quo Vadis W1 *(Private Rm*)*
	Royal Holloway Coll., Surrey *(Picture Gall.)*
	School of Pharmacy WC1 *(Assembley Hall*)*
	St Botolph's Hall EC2 *(Upper Hall*)*
	St John's Hill SW11 *(Drill Hall*)*
	606 Club SW10 *(Max*)*
	V&A Mus. Café SW7 *(Max*)*
148	Boat: Mainstream Leisure SW15 *(Elizabethan*)*
146	Syon Pk (Banqueting), Middx *(Gdn Rm)*
140	All Saints - The Crypt E14 *(Main Hall*)*
	Cecil Sharp Hs NW1 *(Trefusis Hall)*
	Froebel Inst. Coll. SW15 *(Main Common Rm*)*
	New Connaught Rms WC2 *(York & Warwick & Kent)*
	School of Pharmacy WC1 *(Refectory)*
132	Boat: Tidal Cruises SE1 *(Hurlingham)*
130	Baltic Exch. EC3 *(Queen's Rm*)*
	Blackheath Concert Halls SE3 *(Recital Rm)*
	Polish Hearth Club SW7 *(First Fl*)*
	Royal Veterinary Coll. NW1 *(Gt Hall*)*
	Syon Pk (Banqueting), Middx *(Lakeside Rm)*

Private venues – seated

120	Boat: Jason's Trip W9 *(Courtyard*)*
	Boat: Thames Leisure, Kent *(Miyuki*)*
	Brass. Rocque EC2 *(Inside*)*
	Footstool SW1 *(Max*)*
	Grosvenor Rms NW2 *(Pearl Suite)*
	Guy's Hosp. Tower SE1 *(Max*)*
	Hubble & Co EC1 *(Wine Bar or Basement Rest.*)*
	Old Refectory W8 *(Max*)*
	Royal Geographical Soc. SW7 *(Max*)*
	Smith's Gall. WC2 *(Gall. 1)*
	St Peter's Hall W11 *(North Hall*)*
	Westminster Boating Base SW1 *(Total Facility)*
110	Boat: City Cruises E14 *(Mayflower Gdn*)*
	Dickens Inn E1 *(Nickleby Suite*)*
	Syon Pk (Banqueting), Middx *(Camellia Rm)*
108	Boat: Catamaran Cruisers WC2 *(Pridla)*
106	Boat: Tidal Cruises SE1 *(Old London)*
100	Boat: Turk Launches, Surrey *(New Southern Belle*)*
	Chelsea Old Town Hall SW3 *(Small Hall)*
	Irish Club SW1 *(Munster Rm*)*
	Little Ship Club EC4 *(Max*)*
	Pentland Hs SE3 *(Hall)*
	Porchester Ctr W2 *(Baths)*
	Royal Geographical Soc. SW7 *(Main Hall)*
	Ski Club of GB SW1 *(Max*)*
	Stanley Hs SW10 *(Max*)*
	Throgmorton's EC2 *(Oak Rm*)*
90	Boat: City Cruises E14 *(Eltham)*
	Chelsea Gdner SW3 *(Conserv.)*
	Chelsea Old Town Hall SW3 *(Cadogan Suite)*
	Lansdowne Club W1 *(Ballroom*)*
	Little Ship Club EC4 *(Dining Rm)*
	Nat. Maritime Mus. SW3 *(Art & Uniform Galls.*)*
	Polish Hearth Club SW7 *(Rest.)*
80	Coliseum WC2 *(Ter. Bar*)*
	Jazz Café NW1 *(Balcony)*
	Lauderdale Hs N6 *(Lower Gall.*)*
	Mall Galls. SW1 *(East Gall.)*
	New Zealand Hs SW1 *(Max*)*
	Photographers' Gall. WC2 *(Max*)*
	Royal Coll. of Art SW7 *(Gulbenkian Lower Gall.)*
	Royal Over-Seas League SW1 *(St Andrew's Hall)*
	Smith's Gall. WC2 *(Gall. 2)*
	St Andrew Golf Club EC4 *(Max*)*
	St Peter's Hall W11 *(Upper Hall)*
	Syon Pk (Banqueting), Middx *(Ter. Rm)*
	Westminster Boating Base SW1 *(Edgson Rm & Buttery)*
75	Boat: Thames Pleasure Craft Ltd EC3 *(Captain James Cook*)*
	Upper Refectory Suite SW6 *(Max*)*
74	Bakers' Hall EC3 *(Livery Hall*)*
70	Anchor SE1 *(Upper Chart Rm*)*
	Boat: City Cruises E14 *(Westminster)*
	Borscht & Tears SW3 *(Private Rm*)*
	Canal Brass. W10 *(Max*)*

	Doggetts Coat & Badge SE1 *(Rest.*)*
	Dora Hs SW7 *(Studio*)*
	El Barco Latino WC2 *(Max*)*
	El-Cid SW10 *(Max*)*
	Froebel Inst. Coll. SW15 *(Ter. Rm)*
	Gunnersbury Pk W3 *(Orangery or Small Mansion*)*
	Mermaid Theatre EC4 *(River Rm*)*
	Mus. of Gdn History SE1 *(St Mary-at-Lambeth*)*
	Naval & Military Club W1 *(Regimental Rm)*
	Place Below EC2 *(Max*)*
	Royal Coll. of Art SW7 *(Senior Common Rm Dining Rm)*
	Royal Veterinary Coll. NW1 *(Clarence or Northumberland Rm)*
64	Burgh Hs NW3 *(Max*)*
60	Bankside Gall. SE1 *(Max*)*
	Blackheath Concert Halls SE3 *(Webster Rm)*
	Boat: Crown River Cruises EC4 *(Suerta*)*
	Chelsea Football Club SW6 *(Sponsors Lounge)*
	Clink SE1 *(Mus.)*
	Equinox at the Empire WC2 *(Square Bar)*
	George Inn SE1 *(Rest.*)*
	HMS President EC4 *(Wardroom)*
	Imp. Coll. SW7 *(Council Rm*)*
	Jakes SW10 *(Max*)*
	Le Gothique SW18 *(Rest. or Patio)*
	London Press Ctr EC4 *(Boswell Rm / Johnson Rm)*
	New Connaught Rms WC2 *(Devon / Stafford)*
	Smith's Gall. WC2 *(Casbar)*
	Westminster Boating Base SW1 *(Edgson Rm)*
	Whitechapel Art Gall. E1 *(Café)*
55	Dolphin Square SW1 *(Chichester Suite)*
	Durrants Htl W1 *(Edward VII Rm*)*
	George Inn SE1 *(George)*
54	Boat: Catamaran Cruisers WC2 *(Abercorn)*
50	Boat: Floating Boater W2 *(Prince Regent*)*
	Boat: Maidenhead Steam Navigation Berks *(Edwardian*)*
	Boat: Thames Pleasure Craft Ltd EC3 *(Golden Salamander)*
	Café Lazeez SW7 *(Max*)*
	City Livery Club EC4 *(Stanley Bell Rm)*
	Dulwich Coll. SE21 *(Old Library)*
	Fulham Hs SW6 *(Officers' Mess)*
	Gunnersbury Pk W3 *(Temple)*
	HMS President EC4 *(Gun Rm)*
	Hon. Artillery Co EC1 *(Queen's Rm)*
	Little Ship Club EC4 *(Library)*
	London Scottish SW1 *(Officers' Mess)*
	Mall Galls. SW1 *(North Gall.)*
	Nat. Army Mus. SW3 *(Templer Galls.)*
	Opera Terazza! WC2 *(Ter.*)*
	Rochester Htl SW1 *(Victoria Suite*)*
	Rose Gdn Rest. W1 *(Prince Regent Rm*)*
	Saigon W1 *(Max*)*
	Smith's Gall. WC2 *(Wine Bar)*
	Solange's WC2 *(Private Rm*)*
	St Peter's Hall W11 *(Lower Hall)*

Private venues – seated

48	Antelope SW1 *(Upstairs*)*
	Lansdowne Club W1 *(Thirties Rm)*
	Syon Pk (Banqueting), Middx *(Conserv. Lounge)*
45	Café St Pierre EC1 *(Top Fl*)*
	The Conservatory SW11 *(Max*)*
	St Botolph's Hall EC2 *(Lower Hall)*
	St John's Hill SW11 *(Sergeant's Mess)*
	Tuttons WC2 *(Larger Cellar*)*
42	Naval & Military Club W1 *(Palmerston Rm or Egremont)*
40	Bar Escoba SW7 *(Private Rm*)*
	Boat: Thames Leisure, Kent *(Tideway)*
	Boat: Turk Launches, Surrey *(Empress of India or MV Yarmouth Belle)*
	French Inst. SW7 *(Café Club*)*
	Hollyhedge Hs SE3 *(Officers Mess)*
	Hon. Artillery Co EC1 *(Medal Rm)*
	Imp. Coll. SW7 *(Dining Rm)*
	Irish Club SW1 *(Leinster Rm / Ulster Rm)*
	Mélange WC2 *(Private Rm*)*
	Mr Kong WC2 *(Private Basement*)*
	Now & Zen WC2 *(Private Rm*)*
	Royal Geographical Soc. SW7 *(Tea Rm)*
	Ski Club of GB SW1 *(Bistro or Arnold Lunn Rm)*
	Smith's Gall. WC2 *(Gall. 3)*
	St John's Hill SW11 *(Officers Mess)*
	V&A Mus. Café SW7 *(Painted Rm)*
36	Boat: Crown River Cruises EC4 *(Spirit of London)*
	Boat: Mainstream Leisure SW15 *(Lady Rose of Regents)*
35	Café St Pierre EC1 *(Ground or middle Fl)*
	Rochester Htl SW1 *(Bar & Rest.)*
	Royal Veterinary Coll. NW1 *(Council Rm)*
	Sun WC2 *(Max*)*
	Whitechapel Art Gall. E1 *(Meeting Rm)*
34	Foxtrot Oscar SW3 *(Max*)*
32	New Connaught Rms WC2 *(Penthouse)*
	Royal Over-Seas League SW1 *(Wrench or Mountbatten Rutland)*
30	Anchor SE1 *(Lower Chart Rm)*
	Boat: Maidenhead Steam Navigation Berks *(Bell)*
	Coopers Arms SW3 *(Private Rm*)*
	Duke of York's HQ SW3 *(London Irish Mess)*
	French Inst. SW7 *(Salon de Reception)*
	Hippodrome WC2 *(Star Bar)*
	HMS President EC4 *(Captain's Quarters)*
	Rochester Htl SW1 *(Rochester Suite)*
	Tank EC1 *(Max*)*
28	Ark W11 *(Private Rm*)*
26	Bakers' Hall EC3 *(Court Rm)*
	Boat: Lady Daphne SE1 *(Stationary or Afloat*)*
25	Anchor SE1 *(Shakespeare Rm)*
	Chez Gerard W1 *(Private Rm or Mezz.*)*
	George Inn SE1 *(Talbot)*
	Naval & Military Club W1 *(Piccadilly)*
	New Connaught Rms WC2 *(Oxford / Cambridge)*
	Slug & Lettuce SW1 *(Max*)*
	Tuttons WC2 *(Smaller Cellar)*
24	Baltic Exch. EC3 *(Directors' Dining Rm)*
	Boat: City Cruises E14 *(Halary)*
	Boat: Jason's Trip W9 *(Lace Plate)*
	Doggetts Coat & Badge SE1 *(Ter. Bar)*
	Durrants Htl W1 *(Oak Rm)*
	Fox & Anchor EC1 *(Private Rm*)*
	Lansdowne Club W1 *(Blue Rm)*
	Royal Geographical Soc. SW7 *(Council Rm)*
22	Boat: Beric Sailing Barge E1 *(Stationary or Afloat*)*
	Boat: Floating Boater W2 *(Lapwing)*
	Front Page SW3 *(Private Rm*)*
20	All Saints W10 *(Basement)*
	Congress Ctr WC1 *(Board Rm)*
	Crown & Goose NW1 *(Private Rm*)*
	Dora Hs SW7 *(Salon)*
	Gopal's of Soho W1 *(Private Rm*)*
	Ming W1 *(Private Rm*)*
	Nat. Army Mus. SW3 *(Council Chamber)*
	Naval & Military Club W1 *(Cowdray)*
	Paulo's W6 *(Max*)*
	Royal Veterinary Coll. NW1 *(Connaught Rm or Cambridge Rm)*
	Ski Club of GB SW1 *(Council Rm or Landing)*
	Viceroy NW1 *(Private Rm)*
18	Doggetts Coat & Badge SE1 *(Boardroom)*
	Westminster Boating Base SW1 *(Crow's Nest)*
16	Naval & Military Club W1 *(Octagon)*
	Royal Over-Seas League SW1 *(Bennet-Clark)*
14	Le Midi SW6 *(Private Rm*)*
	Royal Geographical Soc. SW7 *(Everest Rm)*
12	Boat: Chas Newen Marine Co SW15 *(Panache, Majestic or Pomery*)*
	Chelsea Football Club SW6 *(Box)*
	Church's W8 *(Private Rm*)*
	Coliseum WC2 *(Royal Retiring Rm or Stoll Rm)*
	Dickens' Hs Mus. WC1 *(Max*)*
	Durrants Htl W1 *(Armfield Rm)*
	Eatons SW1 *(Private Rm)*
	Ikkyu W1 *(Tatami Rm*)*
	London Press Ctr EC4 *(Milton Rm)*
	Royal Veterinary Coll. NW1 *(Coll. Principal's Suite)*
11	Royal Over-Seas League SW1 *(Park)*
10	Chiang Mai W1 *(Private Rm*)*
	Hubble & Co EC1 *(Private Rm)*
	Little Ship Club EC4 *(Chart Rm)*
	Naval & Military Club W1 *(Cambridge)*
	Royal Geographical Soc. SW7 *(Reading Rm)*
8	Coliseum WC2 *(Arlen Rm)*

£B

800	Wandsworth Civic Suite SW18 *(Max*)*

Private venues – seated

- 650 Le Hammersmith Palais W6 *(Max*)*
- 500 Chuen Cheng Ku W1 *(Max*)*
- 450 Hammersmith Town Hall W6 *(Max*)*
- 400 Battersea Town Hall SW11 *(Grand Hall*)*
  - Café Club SE1 *(Vaults*)*
  - Electric Ballroom NW1 *(Max*)*
  - SW1 Club SW1 *(Max*)*
- 300 Rock Gdn WC2 *(Max*)*
- 250 Davy's, Skinkers SE1 *(Max*)*
  - Hop Exchange SE1 *(Max*)*
- 200 Abbey Community Assoc. SW1 *(Main Hall*)*
  - Czech Club NW6 *(Max*)*
  - Davy's, Bangers EC2 *(Max*)*
  - Holy Trinity Brompton Church Hall SW7 *(Max*)*
  - Intl Students W1 *(Theatre*)*
  - London Welsh Ctr WC1 *(Main Hall*)*
  - Nôtre Dame Hall WC2 *(Max*)*
  - Polish Social & Cultural Assoc. W6 *(Malinova Rm or Conf. Theatre*)*
- 180 Central Club (YWCA) WC1 *(Queen Mary Hall*)*
  - Ley-Ons W1 *(Max*)*
  - St Etheldreda's Crypt EC1 *(Max*)*
- 150 Africa Ctr WC2 *(Main Hall*)*
  - Battersea Town Hall SW11 *(Lower Hall)*
  - Holderness Hs EC2 *(Hall*)*
  - Polish Social & Cultural Assoc. W6 *(Lowiczanka Rest.)*
  - Turnmills EC1 *(Max*)*
  - Walkers of St James's SW1 *(Max*)*
  - Westminster Coll. SW1 *(Rest.*)*
- 130 Intl Students W1 *(Marylebone Rm)*
- 120 Davy's, City Flogger EC3 *(Max*)*
  - Davy's, Colonel Jaspers EC1 *(Max*)*
  - Davy's, Crown Passage Vaults SW1 *(Max*)*
  - Kosher Luncheon Club E1 *(Max*)*
  - Vaults EC1 *(Max*)*
  - WKD NW1 *(Max*)*
- 100 Balls Brothers SE1 *(Max*)*
  - Captain Kidd E1 *(Max*)*
  - Coates Karaoke Bar & Rest. EC2 *(Max*)*
  - Davy's, Chopper Lump W1 *(Max*)*
  - Davy's, Davy's of Creed Ln EC4 *(Max*)*
  - Davy's, Lees Bag W1 *(Max*)*
  - Davy's, Habit EC3 *(Max*)*
  - Davy's, Pulpit EC2 *(Max*)*
  - Davy's, Vineyard E1 *(Max*)*
  - Davy's, Tumblers W8 *(Max*)*
  - Davy's, Udder Place Wine Rms EC2 *(Max*)*
  - London Rowing Club SW15 *(Max*)*
  - Tattershall Castle SW1 *(Steamers Discotheque*)*
  - Wessex Hs SW11 *(Max*)*
- 94 Balls Brothers SW1 *(Max)*
- 90 Cittie of Yorke WC1 *(Main Bar*)*
  - Hop Cellars SE1 *(Malt Rm*)*
  - Shampers W1 *(Max*)*
  - St Bride Foundation Inst. EC4 *(Bridewell Hall*)*
- 85 Davy's, Burgundy's Ben's EC1 *(Max*)*
  - Davy's, City Boot EC2 *(Max*)*
- 80 Africa Ctr WC2 *(Rear Hall)*
  - Crown & Greyhound SE21 *(Max*)*
  - Davy's, Bishop of Norwich EC2 *(Max*)*
  - Davy's, Chiv W1 *(Max*)*
  - Davy's, Truckles of Pied Bull Yard WC1 *(Max*)*
  - HQ NW1 *(Max*)*
  - London Welsh Ctr WC1 *(Lower Hall)*
  - Lundonia Hs WC1 *(Ground Fl*)*
  - Seafresh SW1 *(Private Rm*)*
- 75 Central Club (YWCA) WC1 *(Martin Rm & Hampstead Rm)*
  - Davy's, City FOB EC3 *(Max*)*
  - Davy's, Tapster SW1 *(Max*)*
- 74 Simpsons of Cornhill EC3 *(Rest.*)*
- 70 Corney & Barrow EC4 *(Max*)*
  - Davy's, Guinea Butt SE1 *(Max*)*
  - Larry's Wine Bar WC2 *(Max*)*
  - Horniman At Hay's SE1 *(Frederick John Horniman Rm*)*
  - Univ. of London Boat Club SW15 *(Indoors*)*
- 65 Cittie of Yorke WC1 *(Cellar Bar)*
  - Davy's, Dock Blida W1 *(Max*)*
  - Davy's, Mug Hs SE1 *(Max*)*
  - White Horse SW6 *(Max*)*
- 60 Abbey Community Assoc. SW1 *(Annexe A & B & C)*
  - Alma SW18 *(Private Rm*)*
  - Balls Brothers EC2, EC3 *(Weekday function)*
  - Chariots SW3 *(First Fl Rest.*)*
  - Circa W1 *(Either Fl*)*
  - Corney & Barrow EC2 *(Max)*
  - Crown & Two Chairmen W1 *(Upstairs Bar*)*
  - Davy's, Cooperage SE1 *(Max*)*
  - Gaslight SW1 *(Max*)*
  - Le Hammersmith Palais W6 *(VIP Bar)*
  - Hollands W11 *(Max*)*
  - Intl Students W1 *(Kennedy Rm)*
  - Jason's SW11 *(Max*)*
  - Kettners W1 *(Oak Rm*)*
  - La Paquerette EC2 *(Max*)*
  - Vat's WC1 *(Rest.*)*
  - WKD NW1 *(Mezz.)*
  - Ye Olde Cheshire Cheese EC4 *(Cellar Bar*)*
- 56 Glassblower W1 *(Max*)*
- 55 Ye Olde Cheshire Cheese EC4 *(Johnson's or Williams Rm)*
- 50 Abbey Community Assoc. SW1 *(Bar)*
  - Barley Mow W1 *(Max*)*
  - Chariots SW3 *(Bar or Gdn)*
  - Clachan W1 *(Highland Bar*)*
  - Corney & Barrow EC3 *(Max)*
  - Davy's, City Vaults EC1 *(Max*)*
  - Duke of Clarence W11 *(Conserv.*)*
  - Glasshouse Stores W1 *(Max*)*
  - Haandi NW1 *(Max*)*
  - Hop Cellars SE1 *(Porter Rm)*
  - King of Diamonds EC1 *(Gdn or Cellar Bar*)*
  - Lamb Tav. EC3 *(Dining Rm*)*
  - Simpsons of Cornhill EC3 *(Grill)*
  - Spaghetti Hs W1 *(Private Section*)*

Private venues – dinner dance

45 Balzac W12 *(Max*)*
Central Club (YWCA) WC1
(Swiss Parlour or Martin Rm)
Davy's, Shotberries EC4 *(Max*)*
Davy's, Spitoon EC1 *(Max*)*
Freemason's Arms WC2 *(Max*)*
Leadenhall Tapas Bar EC3 *(Max*)*
Shampers W1
(Upstairs or Downstairs)

40 Balls Brothers EC4
(Weekday function)
Bill Bentley's EC2 *(Max*)*
Café Club SE1 *(Café Club)*
Cittie of Yorke WC1 *(Front Bar)*
Davy's, Chiv W1 *(Dining Rm)*
Hollands W11 *(Conserv.)*
Pizzeria Condotti W1 *(Private Rm*)*
Rodos WC2 *(Private Rm*)*
Shelleys W1 *(Max*)*
St Bride Foundation
Inst. EC4 *(Farringdon Rm)*

38 Pimlico Wine Vaults SW1 *(Private Rm*)*

36 Calthorpe Arms WC1 *(Private Rm*)*

35 Betjeman's EC1 *(Max*)*
Britannia W8 *(Max*)*
Central Club (YWCA) WC1
(Hampstead Rm)

32 Westminster Coll. SW1 *(Escoffler)*

30 Corney & Barrow EC2 or EC4 *(Max)*
Crown Tav. EC1 *(Upstairs Bar)*
Davy's, Bishop's Parlour EC2 *(Max*)*
Davy's, Gyngleboy W2 *(Max*)*
Kensington Conservative
Assoc. W8 *(Max*)*
Kettners W1 *(Blue Rm)*
Minogue's Bar N1 *(Private Rm*)*
Phene Arms SW3 *(Upstairs Rm*)*
Plough WC2 *(Max*)*

28 Corney & Barrow EC2 *(Max)*
Pitcher & Piano SW10 *(Max*)*

26 Pigeon SW6 *(Private Rm*)*

25 Central Club (YWCA) WC1 *(Library Rm)*
Catherine Wheel W8 *(Private Rm*)*

24 Mekong SW1 *(Private Rm*)*
Walton's SW3 *(Private Rm*)*

22 Two Chairmen SW1 *(Max*)*

20 Davy's, Skinkers SE1 *(Boardroom)*
Duke of Albemarle W1 *(Max*)*
Golden Lion SW1 *(Theatre Bar*)*
Holderness Hs EC2 *(Rifleman's Bar)*

18 Davy's, City Pipe EC1 *(Boardroom*)*

16 Kettners W1 *(Soho Rm)*

12 Balls Brothers SE1 *(Private Rm 2)*
Battersea Barge Bistro SW8 *(Captain's Cabin*)*
Costa's Grill W8 *(Private Rm*)*
Davy's, Skinkers SE1 *(Second private rm)*

10 Lundonia Hs WC1 *(Space Biospheres Club)*
Wynkyn de Worde EC4 *(Private Rm*)*
Ye Olde Cheshire Cheese EC4 *(Director's Rm)*

8 Balls Brothers SW1 *(Private Rm 1 or 2)*

Venues listed by dinner-dance capacity

* largest entry for venue

£E

300 Blenheim Pal., Oxon *(Max*)*
160 Cliveden, Berks *(Max*)*
150 Brocket Hall, Herts *(Max*)*
Queen's Hs SE10 *(Max*)*
120 Spencer Hs SW1 *(Max*)*

£M-E

1500 Grosvenor Hs Htl W1 *(Gt Rm*)*
1300 Royal Albert Hall SW7 *(Cabaret or Ball*)*
1000 Hilton on Pk Ln W1 *(Grand Ballroom*)*
700 Inter-Continental W1 *(Grand Ballroom Suite*)*
550 Park Ln Htl W1 *(Ballroom*)*
500 Grosvenor Hs Htl W1 *(Ballroom)*
Reform Club SW1 *(Max*)*
Westway Studios W11 *(Max*)*
450 Dorchester W1 *(Ballroom*)*
Natural History Mus. SW7 *(Central Hall*)*
400 Savoy WC2 *(Lancaster Rm*)*
375 Banqueting Hs SW1 *(Max*)*
370 RAF Mus. NW9 *(Battle of Britain Hall*)*
350 Knebworth Hs, Herts *(Manor & Lodge Barns*)*
Royal Albert Hall SW7 *(Arena)*
325 Four Seasons Htl W1 *(Ballroom*)*
310 Regent W1 *(Ballroom*)*
300 Hyatt Carlton Tower SW1 *(Ballroom*)*
Imp. War Mus. SE1 *(Max*)*
Middle Temple Hall EC4 *(Max*)*
Mme Tussaud's NW1 *(Max*)*
250 Inner Temple Hall EC4 *(Max*)*
Lincoln's Inn WC2 *(Gt Hall*)*
Mme Tussaud's NW1 *(Grand Hall)*
240 Barbican Ctr EC2 *(Gdn Rm*)*
London Zoo NW1 *(Regency Suite*)*
230 Hyde Pk Htl SW1 *(Ballroom*)*
210 Le Meridien W1 *(Georgian*)*
200 Mus. of London EC2 *(Max*)*
Royal Coll. of Music SW7 *(Concert Hall*)*
190 Knebworth Hs, Herts *(Manor Barn)*
180 Berkeley SW1 *(Ballroom*)*
Claridge's W1 *(Ballroom*)*
Imagination Gall. WC1 *(Max*)*
Middle Temple Hall EC4 *(Hall)*
Searcy's SW1 *(Max*)*
Roof Gdns W8 *(Max*)*
Savoy WC2 *(Abraham Lincoln Rm & Manhattan Rm)*
175 Stationers' Hall EC4 *(Livery Hall*)*
170 Gray's Inn EC1 *(Max*)*
Science Mus. SW7 *(Flight Gall.*)*
Serpentine Gall. W2 *(Max*)*
Skinners' Hall EC4 *(Max*)*
168 Boat: Woods River Svcs SE3 *(Silver Barracuda*)*
160 Beaulieu, Hants *(Brabazon*)*
Leeds Castle, Kent *(Fairfax Hall*)*

Private venues – dinner dance

150	Hilton on Pk Ln W1 *(Curzon Suite)*
	Inst. of Directors SW1 *(Nash*)*
	London Dungeon SE1 *(Max*)*
	Le Meridien W1 *(Edwardian)*
	Natural History Mus. SW7 *(North Hall)*
140	Park Ln Htl W1 *(Tudor Rose Rm)*
	Regent W1 *(Music Rm)*
120	Arts Club W1 *(Dining Rm*)*
	Caledonian Club SW1 *(Max*)*
	Chelsea SW1 *(Sloane Suite*)*
	Dorchester W1 *(Orchid)*
	Inter-Continental W1 *(Pk Suite)*
	Ritz W1 *(Palm Court & Marie Antoinette*)*
	Savoy WC2 *(River Rm)*
110	Regent W1 *(Drawing or Empire Rm)*
100	Hilton on Pk Ln W1 *(Crystal Pal. Rm)*
	Inst. of Materials SW1 *(Max*)*
	Inter-Continental W1 *(Windsor Suite)*
	Knebworth Hs, Herts *(Lodge Barn)*
	Mirabelle W1 *(Max*)*
	Monkey Island, Berks *(River Rm*)*
	Mus. of the Moving Image SE1 *(Max*)*
	Park Ln Htl W1 *(Gdn Rm)*
80	Beaulieu, Hants *(Domus)*
	Four Seasons Htl W1 *(Gdn Rm)*
	Grosvenor Hs Htl W1 *(Albemarle)*
70	Halcyon Htl W11 *(Rest.*)*
68	Boat: Woods River Svcs SE3 *(Silver Dolphin)*
60	Caledonian Club SW1 *(Members Dining Rm)*
	Dorchester W1 *(Pk Suite)*
	Four Seasons Htl W1 *(Oak Rm)*
	Hampshire Htl WC2 *(Penthouse*)*
	Hilton on Pk Ln W1 *(Coronation Rm)*
	Rock Circus W1 *(Max*)*
50	Berkeley SW1 *(Crystal Rm)*
	Cabinet War Rms SW1 *(Max*)*
	Dukes Htl SW1 *(Marlborough Suite*)*
	Park Ln Htl W1 *(Oak Rm)*
	Raffles Dining Rm SW3 *(Max*)*
	Sanctuary WC2 *(Max*)*
40	Hyde Pk Htl SW1 *(Pk Suite)*
	Inter-Continental W1 *(Byron Rm)*
30	Lanesborough SW1 *(Wilkins Rm*)*

£M

2750	Alexandra Pal. & Pk N22 *(Gt Hall*)*
2000	Sandown Pk, Surrey *(Tote Hall*)*
1400	Alexandra Pal. & Pk N22 *(West Hall)*
1300	Royal Lancaster W2 *(Nine King's Suite*)*
750	Commonwealth Inst. W8 *(Comm Galls.*)*
660	Brewery EC1 *(Max*)*
650	Hurlingham Club SW6 *(Max*)*
	Kempton Pk, Middx *(Max*)*
600	Royal Lancaster W2 *(Westbourne Suite)*
	Sandown Pk, Surrey *(Lower Tote Hall)*
570	Cumberland Htl W1 *(Production Box*)*
550	Café Royal W1 *(4Empire Napoleon*)*
	Royal Gdn Htl W8 *(Pal. Suite*)*
500	Forte Crest Regents Pk W1 *(Portland Suite*)*
	London Marriott W1 *(Westminster Suite*)*
450	Jongleurs at Camden Lock NW1 *(Max*)*
420	Waldorf Htl WC2 *(Max*)*
400	Bath – Pump Rm, Avon *(Max*)*
	Sandown Pk, Surrey *(Claremont)*
380	King David Suite W1 *(Main Rm*)*
360	Waldorf Htl WC2 *(Adelphi Suite & Palm Court)*
350	Brewery EC1 *(Porter Tun)*
	Cabot Hall E14 *(Hall*)*
	Elizabeth Suite EC2 *(Spanish Rm*)*
	Gloucester Htl SW7 *(Cotswold Suite*)*
	Kempton Pk, Middx *(Runnymede Suite)*
325	Cumberland Htl W1 *(Carlisle Suite)*
300	Brewery EC1 *(King George III)*
	Café Royal W1 *(6Dubarry)*
	Jongleurs at the Cornet SW11 *(Max*)*
	Russell WC1 *(Warncliffe or Woburn Suite*)*
260	Lord's NW8 *(Max*)*
	Nat. Liberal Club SW1 *(Max*)*
250	Commonwealth Inst. W8 *(Art Gall.)*
	Inst. of Civil Engs SW1 *(Gt Hall*)*
	Lloyd's of London EC3 *(Captains' Rm*)*
	Mount Royal Htl W1 *(Edinburgh / Hyde Pk*)*
240	Mayfair W1 *(Crystal Rm*)*
230	Waldorf Htl WC2 *(Charter 2)*
228	Selfridge Htl W1 *(Selfridge Suite*)*
225	Tower Thistle E1 *(Tower Suite (York Rm & Lancaster Rm)*)*
220	Langham Hilton W1 *(Ballroom*)*
200	Alexandra Pal. & Pk N22 *(Pal. Rest.)*
	BAFTA Ctr W1 *(Max*)*
	Café Royal W1 *(2Louis)*
	Chartered Accountants' Hall EC2 *(Max*)*
	Chelsea Harbour Rms SW10 *(Turner & Carlyle Rms*)*
	Glaziers' Hall SE1 *(Hall*)*
	Limelight W1 *(Gall. & Dome*)*
	Regent's Coll. NW1 *(Refectory*)*
	Royal Majestic Suite NW6 *(Ground Fl*)*
	Sandown Pk, Surrey *(Wolsey)*
	Stakis St Ermins SW1 *(Ballroom*)*
	Syon Pk (Conserv.), Middx *(Max*)*
	Twickenham Banqueting Ctr TW1 *(Max*)*
180	Bank of Eng. Club SW15 *(Max*)*
	Churchill W1 *(Chartwell Suite*)*
	Oval SE11 *(Banqueting Suite*)*
	Sandown Pk, Surrey *(Ardross)*
	Rembrandt Htl SW7 *(Edward & Charles & James & Princes (King Suite)*)*
	Winchester Hs Club SW15 *(River Lawn*)*
170	Kew Bridge Steam Mus., Middx *(Max*)*
	Lord's NW8 *(Ballroom)*
	RS Hispaniola WC2 *(Max*)*
164	Butchers' Hall EC1 *(Max*)*
160	Bath – Pump Rm, Avon *(Pump Rm)*
	Café Royal W1 *(1Elysee)*
	Church Hs SW1 *(Harvey Goodwin Suite*)*
	Clandon, Surrey *(Rest.*)*

Private venues – dinner dance

	Conrad Htl SW10 *(Henley Suite*)*
150	Amadeus Ctr W9 *(Max*)*
	Barbarella 1 SW6 *(Max*)*
	Dartmouth Hs W1 *(Max*)*
	Law Soc. WC2 *(Common Rm*)*
	Lord's NW8 *(Toynbee)*
	Pinewood Studios, Bucks *(Max*)*
	Royal Inst. of Brit. Architects W1 *(Florence Hall*)*
	Royal Soc. of Arts WC2 *(All Vaults*)*
	Sandown Pk, Surrey *(Tack & Saddle)*
140	Barbarella 2 SW7 *(Max*)*
130	Gloucester Htl SW7 *(Cotswold - 1/2)*
	Kensington Pal. Thistle W8 *(Duchess*)*
120	Basil Street Htl SW3 *(Parrot Club*)*
	Hamilton Suite W1 *(Max*)*
	Royal Aeronautical Soc. W1 *(Max*)*
	Brewery EC1 *(Queen Charlotte)*
	Trinity Hs EC3 *(Max*)*
110	Bath – Pump Rm, Avon *(Concert Rm)*
	Champenois EC2 *(Max*)*
	TS Queen Mary WC2 *(Queen Mary Suite*)*
100	Alexandra Pal. & Pk N22 *(Loneborough Rm)*
	Brewery EC1 *(Smeaton's Vaults or Sugar Rms)*
	Grosvenor Htl SW1 *(Gall. Rm*)*
	ICA SW1 *(Max*)*
	Mortons Club W1 *(Rest. & Bar*)*
	Simpsons- in-the-Strand WC2 *(South Rm*)*
	St Stephens Constitutional Club SW1 *(Max*)*
	Vanderbilt Htl SW7 *(Max*)*
96	City of London Club EC2 *(Main Dining Rm*)*
	HMS Belfast SE1 *(Ship Co's Dining Rm*)*
90	Royal Gdn Htl W8 *(Balmoral Suite)*
	White Hs Htl NW1 *(Albany*)*
80	Britannia Intercontinental W1 *(Max*)*
	Café Royal W1 *(5Marquise or 2Pompadour)*
	Churchill W1 *(Chartwell I)*
	Conrad Htl SW10 *(Compass Rose or Thames)*
	Fulham Pal. SW6 *(Max*)*
	Guards Mus. SW1 *(Max*)*
	Law Soc. WC2 *(Members Dining Rm)*
	Limelight W1 *(Club VIP)*
	Royal Gdn Htl W8 *(Kensington Suite)*
	Sandown Pk, Surrey *(Cavalry Bar)*
	Washington Htl W1 *(Rest. *)*
	Westbury Htl W1 *(Mount Vernon Rm*)*
75	Hampton Court, Tiltyard, Surrey *(Max*)*
	Nº 1 Yacht Club WC2 *(Max*)*
70	41 Beak St W1 *(Max*)*
	Café Royal W1 *(1-Derby & Queensbury)*
	Royal Lancaster W2 *(Gloucester Suite)*
	Royal Majestic Suite NW6 *(First Fl)*
	Winchester Hs Club SW15 *(River Rm)*
66	Brewery EC1 *(James Watt)*
60	Chelsea Harbour Rms SW10 *(Carlyle Rm)*
	HMS Belfast SE1 *(Gun Rm)*
	Elizabeth Suite EC2 *(Golden Hind)*
	Kensington Pal. Thistle W8 *(Marchioness)*
	Mayfair W1 *(Lansdowne Suite)*
	Oxford & Cambridge Club SW1 *(Max*)*
	Royal Horseguards Thistle Htl SW1 *(Thames*)*
	Royal Soc. of Arts WC2 *(Benjamin Franklin Rm)*
	Westbury Htl W1 *(Pine Rm)*
50	Brown's Htl W1 *(Clarendon*)*
	Café Royal W1 *(1Domino)*
	Founders' Hall EC1 *(Livery Hall*)*
	Grosvenor Htl SW1 *(Bessborough Rm)*
	HMS Belfast SE1 *(Wardroom)*
	Mountbatten WC2 *(Earl*)*
	Royal Gdn Htl W8 *(Sandringham & Osborne Suite)*
	West Wycombe Caves, Bucks *(Max*)*
45	Washington Htl W1 *(Richmond Suite)*
40	Athenaeum Htl W1 *(Max*)*
	Brewery EC1 *(City Cellars)*
	Café Royal W1 *(1Lonsdale)*
	Churchill W1 *(Chartwell II)*
	Sandown Pk, Surrey *(Lawn Suite)*
38	Rembrandt Htl SW7 *(Elizabeth & Victoria (Queen Suite))*
36	SB Lady Gwynfred E14 *(Max*)*

£B-M

1000	K Warehouse E6 *(Space 1*)*
	Royal Horticultural Halls SW1 *(New Hall*)*
700	Royal Coll. of Art SW7 *(Henry Moore Gall.*)*
600	Equinox at the Empire WC2 *(Max*)*
500	Duke of York's HQ SW3 *(Cadogan Hall with marquee*)*
	K Warehouse E6 *(Cavern 1 or 2)*
450	Stoke Newington Town Hall N16 *(Max*)*
440	Hippodrome WC2 *(Max*)*
420	Grosvenor Rms NW2 *(Grosvenor Suite*)*
400	New Connaught Rms WC2 *(Balmoral & Grand Hall*)*
	Porchester Ctr W2 *(Ballroom)*
	Royal Horticultural Halls SW1 *(Old Hall)*
350	Blackheath Concert Halls SE3 *(Max*)*
	London Press Ctr EC4 *(Caxton Suite*)*
	Syon Pk (Banqueting), Middx *(Max*)*
300	Cecil Sharp Hs NW1 *(Kennedy Hall*)*
	Dulwich Coll. SE21 *(Christenson Hall & Upper Dining Rms*)*
	Hollyhedge Hs SE3 *(Hall*)*
	Hon. Artillery Co EC1 *(Albert Rm*)*
280	World Trade Ctr E1 *(Max*)*
270	Jazz Café NW1 *(Max*)*
250	Blackheath Concert Halls SE3 *(Gt Hall)*
	Chelsea Old Town Hall SW3 *(Main Hall*)*
	Duke of York's HQ SW3 *(Cadogan Hall)*
	Smith's Gall. WC2 *(Max*)*

Private venues – dinner dance

240	Boat: Catamaran Cruisers WC2 *(Naticia*)*
230	Fulham Town Hall SW6 *(Large Hall*)*
220	Boat: Tidal Cruises SE1 *(Royal Princess*)*
	Chelsea Football Club SW6 *(Max*)*
	Hippodrome WC2 *(Auditorium)*
200	Acad. of Live & Recorded Arts W6 *(Max*)*
	Boardwalk W1 *(Max*)*
	Congress Ctr WC1 *(Congress Hall*)*
	Dulwich Coll. SE21 *(Gt Hall)*
	Goldsmith's Coll. SE14 *(Gt Hall*)*
	Le Gothique SW18 *(with Acad. of Live & Recorded Arts*)*
	Naval & Military Club W1 *(Max*)*
	Pentland Hs SE3 *(Max*)*
	Trafalgar Tav. SE10 *(Nelson Suite*)*
180	Grosvenor Rms NW2 *(Executive Suite)*
	New Connaught Rms WC2 *(Brass.)*
	Strand Pal. Htl WC2 *(Birley*)*
175	Hippodrome WC2 *(Balcony – Rest.)*
170	New Connaught Rms WC2 *(Edinburgh & Drawing Rm / Cornwall & Crown)*
	Royal Holloway Coll., Surrey *(Founders Dining Hall*)*
	Westminster Boating Base SW1 *(Max*)*
160	Clink SE1 *(Max*)*
	HMS President EC4 *(Drill Hall*)*
	King's Coll. WC2 *(Gt Hall*)*
150	Boat: Tidal Cruises SE1 *(PV Viscountess)*
	Eatons EC3 *(Banqueting Suite*)*
	Fulham Hs SW6 *(Main Hall*)*
	London Press Ctr EC4 *(Pepys Suite)*
	St John's Hill SW11 *(Drill Hall*)*
	St Martin in the Fields WC2 *(Max*)*
	Viceroy NW1 *(Max*)*
148	Boat: Mainstream Leisure SW15 *(Elizabethan*)*
140	All Saints – The Crypt E14 *(Main Hall*)*
	Conway Hall WC1 *(Large Hall*)*
	Froebel Inst. Coll. SW15 *(Max*)*
132	Boat: Tidal Cruises SE1 *(Hurlingham)*
130	Baltic Exchange EC3 *(Max*)*
	Bishopsgate Inst. EC2 *(Main Hall*)*
	Naval & Military Club W1 *(Coffee Rm)*
125	Dolphin Square SW1 *(Rest.*)*
120	Boat: Thames Leisure, Kent *(Miyuki*)*
	Grosvenor Rms NW2 *(Pearl Suite)*
	Lansdowne Club W1 *(Max*)*
	London Scottish SW1 *(Hall*)*
	New Connaught Rms WC2 *(York & Warwick & Kent)*
	Royal Geographical Soc. SW7 *(Max*)*
	Royal Green Jackets W1 *(Hall*)*
	V&A Mus. Café SW7 *(Max*)*
110	Boat: City Cruises E14 *(Mayflower Gdn*)*
	Clink SE1 *(Winchester Hall)*
	Dickens Inn E1 *(Nickleby Suite*)*
	Royal Veterinary Coll. NW1 *(Gt Hall*)*
106	Boat: Tidal Cruises SE1 *(Old London)*
100	Blackheath Concert Halls SE3 *(Recital Rm)*
	Cecil Sharp Hs NW1 *(Trefusis Hall)*
	Fulham Town Hall SW6 *(Concert Hall)*
	Guy's Hosp. Tower SE1 *(Max*)*
	Irish Club SW1 *(Munster Rm*)*
	Little Ship Club EC4 *(Max*)*
	Royal Over-Seas League SW1 *(Hall of India & Pakistan*)*
	Ski Club of GB SW1 *(Max*)*
	Throgmorton's EC2 *(Oak Rm*)*
90	Boat: City Cruises E14 *(Eltham)*
	Brass. Rocque EC2 *(Inside*)*
	Footstool SW1 *(Max*)*
80	Hubble & Co EC1 *(Wine Bar or Basement Rest.*)*
	New Zealand Hs SW1 *(Max*)*
	Old Refectory W8 *(Max*)*
	Photographers' Gall. WC2 *(Max*)*
	St Andrew Golf Club EC4 *(Max*)*
	Stanley Hs SW10 *(Max*)*
70	Boat: City Cruises E14 *(Westminster)*
	El-Cid SW10 *(Max*)*
60	Boat: Crown River Cruises EC4 *(Suertta*)*
	Boat: Turk Launches, Surrey *(New Southern Belle*)*
	Equinox at the Empire WC2 *(Square Bar)*
	Royal Over-Seas League SW1 *(St Andrew's Hall)*
	Whitechapel Art Gall. E1 *(Max*)*
50	Boat: Thames Pleasure Craft Ltd EC3 *(Golden Salamander*)*
	Rochester Htl SW1 *(Max*)*
45	Café St Pierre EC1 *(Max*)*
40	Boat: Floating Boater W2 *(Prince Regent*)*
	Boat: Thames Leisure, Kent *(Tideway)*
36	Boat: Crown River Cruises EC4 *(Spirit of London)*
	Boat: Mainstream Leisure SW15 *(Lady Rose of Regents)*
30	Hippodrome WC2 *(Star Bar)*
24	Boat: Jason's Trip W9 *(Lace Plate*)*

£B

650	Le Hammersmith Palais W6 *(Max*)*
550	Wandsworth Civic Suite SW18 *(Max*)*
400	Café Club SE1 *(Vaults*)*
	Electric Ballroom NW1 *(Max*)*
350	Battersea Town Hall SW11 *(Grand Hall*)*
330	SW1 Club SW1 *(Max*)*
300	Hammersmith Town Hall W6 *(Max*)*
220	Hop Exchange SE1 *(Max*)*
200	Abbey Community Assoc. SW1 *(Main Hall*)*
	Davy's, Skinkers SE1 *(Max*)*
	Davy's, Chiv W1 *(Max*)*
	Polish Social & Cultural Assoc. W6 *(Malinova Rm*)*
160	Nôtre Dame Hall WC2 *(Max*)*
	Polish Social & Cultural Assoc. W6 *(Conf. Theatre)*
150	Central Club (YWCA) WC1 *(Queen Mary Hall*)*
	Holderness Hs EC2 *(Hall*)*

Private venues – dinner dance

130	St Etheldreda's Crypt EC1 *(Max*)*
120	Vaults EC1 *(Max*)*
110	Battersea Town Hall SW11 *(Lower Hall)*
	Polish Social & Cultural Assoc. W6 *(Lowiczanka Rest.)*
100	Balls Brothers SE1 *(Max*)*
	Coates Karaoke Bar & Rest. EC2 *(Max*)*
	London Welsh Ctr WC1 *(Main Hall*)*
	Tattershall Castle SW1 *(Steamers Discotheque*)*
90	Cittie of Yorke WC1 *(Main Bar*)*
	Hop Cellars SE1 *(Max*)*
70	Corney & Barrow EC4 *(Max*)*
	Hop Cellars SE1 *(Malt Rm)*
	Larry's Wine Bar WC2 *(Max*)*
	Univ. of London Boat Club SW15 *(Indoors*)*
65	Davy's, Mug Hs SE1 *(Max*)*
60	Circa W1 *(Downstairs*)*
	Davy's, Cooperage SE1 *(Max*)*
	Lundonia Hs WC1 *(Ground Fl*)*
	WKD NW1 *(Mezz.*)*
50	Captain Kidd E1 *(Max*)*
	Crown & Greyhound SE21 *(Max*)*
45	Shampers W1 *(Max*)*
40	Cittie of Yorke WC1 *(Cellar Bar)*
	Vat's WC1 *(Rest.*)*
28	Pitcher & Piano SW10 *(Max*)*

Alphabetical index

Aardvark, 175
Abbey Acoustics, 166
Abbey Comm. Ctr, 18
Above the Salt, 148
Acad. Costumes, 175
Acad. of Live &
  Recorded Arts, 18
Accademia Italiana, 18
Accidental Prodns
  (Murder by Accident), 164
Ace Speedy Ice, 157
Acker's Int.
  Jazz Agency, 160
The Admirable
  Crichton, 148, 155, 158
Africa Ctr, 18
Ajimura, 18
Al Basha, 19
Al San Vincenzo, 19
Albero & Grana, 135
Jean Alexander
  Food Flair, 148
Alexandra Pal. & Pk, 19
All Saints, 19
All Saints - The Crypt, 19
Alma, 19
Altarmobiles
  (MJ Ellard), 174
Alternative Arts, 161
Alternative Corp Ents, 158
AM & PM Catering, 148
Amadeus Ctr, 19
American Bar
  at the Savoy, 132
American Classic
  Hire Co, 174
L'Amico, 19
Anchor, 20
Andrew Edmunds, 143
Anemos, 143
Angels & Bermans, 175
Anglia Fireworks, 167
Anna's Pl, 135
Annabel's, 20
Anne Fayrer
  Cakes & Flowers, 154
Antelope, 20
Apothecaries' Hall, 20
Apsley Hs, 20
Aquila Press, 181
The Argyll Arms, 20
The Ark, 20
John Armit, 156
Armourers' &
  Braisers' Hall, 21
L'Artiste Assoiffé, 21
Arts Club, 21
Ascot Racecourse,
  Berks, 21
Jane Asher, 154
Astoria, 21
At Your Service, 155
Athenaeum Htl, 21
Au Jardin
  des Gourmets, 22
Audio & Acoustics, 172
John Austin
  Organisation, 161
Austin Reed, 176
The AV Co, 172
AVE, 172

BAFTA Ctr, 22
Bahn Thai, 22
Paul Bailey Agency, 161

Bailey Carr, 158
Bakers' Hall, 22
The Balloon and
  Kite Emporium, 171
Balloon Factory, 171
The Balloon Printery,171
The Balloon Works, 171
Balloonland, 171
Balloons and
  Parties Today, 171
Balloons Inc, 171
Balloons World Wide, 171
Balls Bros., 22
Baltic Exchange, 23
Balzac, 23
Banana Split, 158, 165
Bangers, 45
Bangers Too, 45
Bank of Eng. Club, 23
Bank of Eng. Mus., 23
The Bankers Club, 23
Bankside Gall., 23
Banqueting Hs, 24
Bar Escoba, 24
Bar Industria, 24
Bar Madrid (inc Viva
  Brazil), 143
Barbarella, 24, 135
Barber-Surgeons' Hall,24
Barbican Ctr, 24
El Barco Latino, 24
Barkers Marquees, 168
The Barley Mow, 25
Barn Dance Agency, 161
Barnum's, 177
William
  Bartholomew, 158, 165
Basil Street Htl, 25
Basildon Marquee
  Hire, 168
Bateaux London,124,132
Bath – Pump Room, 25
The Battersea
  Barge Bistro, 25
Battersea Pk, 25
Battersea Town Hall, 25
Beach Blanket
  Babylon, 135
Beauchamp Pl, 25
Beaulieu, 26
Beeton Rumford, 148
HMS Belfast, 26
Belgo, 135
Belgrave & Portman
  Press Bur, 178
Belvedere, 26, 135
Ben's Thai, 143
Benihana, 26, 135
Bentalls, 156
Bentley's, 158
Bentleys, 26
Beotys, 26
The Berkeley, 26
The Berkshire, 27
Berry Bros & Rudd, 156
Betjeman's, 27
Bibendum, 132
Big Easy, 143
Bill Bentley's, 27
Bishop of Norwich, 45
Bishop's Parlour, 45
Bishopsgate Inst., 27
Black & Edgington, 168
Black & Edgington
  Flags, 172

Blackheath
  Concert Halls, 27
Blakes, 132
Bleeding Heart, 27
Blenheim Pal., 27
Blooming Marvellous, 169
Blue Elephant, 132
Blue Moon Casino, 165
Blue Print Café, 136
Blue Ribbon
  Catering Svcs, 148
Blues & Royals, 164
Boardwalk, 28, 136
BOC Gases, 171
Bojolly's & BJ Hire, 159
Bombay Brass., 28, 132
Bon Ton Roulet, 143
Bond Enterprises, 174
Bonham's, 28
Borscht & Tears, 28
Bottlescrue, 45
Le Bouchon
  Lyonnais, 136
Boyd's, 28
Martin Bradley
  Lighting & Sound, 172
Brahms & Liszt, 28
Bramah Tea &
  Coffee Mus., 28
Brandon Hire, 154
Brass. Rocque, 28
Bratts, 29
Brazilian Party Co, 149
Brewers' Hall, 29
The Brewery, 29
Brighton Royal
  Pavilion, 29
Britannia, 29
Britannia
  Intercontinental Htl, 29
British Mus., 30
Brixtonian, 136
Brixtonian Backyard, 136
Broadgate Estates, 30
Brocket Hall, 30
Brown's Htl, 30
Browns Club, 30
Bubb's, 30
Buckmore Pk, 128
Alfred Bull & Co, 168
Bung Hole, 45
Burgh Hs, 31
Burgundy's Ben's, 45
Busabong Too, 31
Busby's, 31
Busy Lizzie, 171
Butchers' Hall, 31
Mark Butler
  Associates, 159
Butlers Catering, 149
Buzkash, 136
Buzz Prodns, 159
By Word of Mouth, 149

**Cabaret Casino
  Associates, 165**
Cabinet War Rms, 31
Cabot Hall, 31
The Cadogan, 32
Café Club, 32
Café de Paris, 32
Café du Marché, 136
Café Greenwich Pk, 32
Café Lazeez, 32, 136
Café Météor, 143
Café Pacifico, 136
Café Royal, 33

Alphabetical index

Café St Pierre, 33
Café Suze, 149
Cahill Ent, 161
The Caledonian Club, 33
Caledonian Enterprises, 161
Calthorpe Arms, 33
Camelot Barthropp, 174
Canal Brass., 33
Canapé Direct, 149
Canning Hs, 34
Cannizaro Hs, 34
Canonbury Acad., 34
The Canteen, 137
La Capannina, 34
The Capital, 34
Le Caprice, 132
Captain Kidd, 34
Le Carapace, 34
Caravan Serai, 137
Carnival Promotions, 165
Caroline's Kitchen, 149
Carpenters' Hall, 35
John M Carter, 168
Dennis Carter, 174
Le Casino, 143
Casino Ent Svcs, 165
Caspers, 137
Castle Catering Svcs, 149
Catamaran Cruisers, 124
The Catherine Wheel, 35
Cavalry & Guards Club, 35
The Cavern, 175
Caves de la Madeleine, 156
CB Helicopters, 175
CBM Svcs, 175
Cecil Sharp Hs, 35
Central Club (YWCA), 35
Le Champenois, 35
Chance, 159, 163
A Chance to Dance, 177
Chapter 11, 35
The Chariots, 36
Chariots of Fire, 149
Chartered Inst. of Pub. Finance & Accountancy, 36
Chartered Accountants' Hall, 36
Chas Newen Marine Co, 124
The Chelsea, 36
Chelsea Catering Co, 149
Chelsea Football Club, 36
The Chelsea Gardener, 36
Chelsea Luxury Charters, 124
Chelsea Physic Garden, 37
Chelsea Harbour Rms, 37
Chelsea Old Town Hall, 37
Chez Gerard, 37
Chez Nico at Ninety Grosvenor Hs Htl, 37
Chiang Mai, 37
China Jazz, 132
Chiswick Hs, 38
The Chiv, 45
Chopper Lump, 45
Christie's, 38
Chuen Cheng Ku, 38
Church Hs, 38
Church's, 38

Churchill, 38
Cibo, 38
Circa, 39
Circus Circus, 177
Cittie of Yorke, 39
City Boot, 45
City Cruises, 125
City Dress Arcade, 175
City Flogger, 45
City FOB, 45
City Livery Club, 39
City Miyama, 39
City of London Club, 39
City Pipe, 45
City Vaults, 45
The Clachan, 39
Clandon, 40
Claridge's, 40
Classic Lighting, 172
Classical Cuisine, 149
The Clink, 40
Cliveden, 40
Clothworkers' Hall, 40
The Coal Hole, 40
Coates Karaoke Bar & Rest., 41
Cobden's Working Men's Club & Inst., 41
The Coliseum, 41
Colonel Jaspers, 45
Nicki Colwyn, 159
Comedy Store, 137
Commonwealth Inst., 41
Concorde, 126
Congress Ctr, 41
The Connaught, 42, 132
Conrad Htl, 42
The Conservatory, 42
Contemporary Wardrobe, 176
Conway Hall, 42
The Cooperage, 45
Coopers Arms, 42
Coopers' Hall, 42
Laurence Corner, 176
Corney & Barrow, 43, 156
Corps of Commissionaires, 181
The Tessa Corr Catering Co, 149
Costa's Grill, 43
The Costume Studio, 176
Cottons Atrium, 43
Courtauld Inst., 43
Crazy Larry's, 43
Crêchendo, 164
The Criterion, 43, 137
Crown Passage Vaults, 45
Crowd Pullers, 161
Crown & Goose, 44
Crown & Greyhound, 44
The Crown and Two Chairmen, 44
Crown Catering, 149
Crown Ents, 161
Crown River Cruises, 125
The Crown Tav., 44
Cuba, 137
Cuba Libre, 137
Culinary Arts, 150
Culture Vultures, 176
Cumberland Htl, 44
Andrea Cunningham, 178
Cutty Sark, 44

Czech Club, 44

Da Mario, 143
Dan's, 45
Danish Catering, 150
Daphne's, 137
Dark Blues Managment, 161
Dartmouth Hs, 45
Davenports, 177
Davy's of Creed Lane, 45
DCS Fairs, 154
Pattie de Clifford, 169
Charles Dean, 168
Dell'Ugo, 138
Design Mus., 46
Dickens Inn, 46
The Dickens' Hs Mus., 46
Caroline Dickenson, 169
Dinner Jackets Catering, 150
Diorama, 46
Disco-Tech, 166
Dock Blida, 45
The Dog & Duck, 46
Dog Hs, 138
Doggetts Coat & Badge, 47
Dolphin Square, 47
Dora Hs, 47
The Dorchester, 47
La Dordogne, 47
Dover Street WB, 138
Down Mexico Way, 144
Downstairs At 190, 47
Dr Johnsons' Hs, 48
Drapers' Hall, 48
The Draycott, 48
Drones, 48, 138
Duke of Albemarle, 48
Duke of Clarence, 48
Duke of York's HQ, 48
Dukes Htl, 49
Dulwich Coll., 49
Dulwich Picture Gall., 49
Durrants Htl, 49
Dyas Marquees, 168
Dyers' Hall, 49

East India Club, 49
Eatons, 50
Eatons, 150
Ecando Systems, 173
Efes Kebab Hs 1 and 2, 144
El-Cid, 50
Electric Ballroom, 50
Electrowerkz Two, 129
11 Hobart Pl, 50
Elite Staff Svcs, 155
The Elizabeth Suite, 50
Empress Garden, 50
English Garden, 51
English Hs, 51
Equinox at the Empire, 51
Escapade, 176
L'Escargot, 51
L'Etoile, 51
Event Playcare Mgt, 164
Exclusive Discos, 165
L'Expr, 51

Fait Accompli, 159
Fakhreldine, 138

225

Alphabetical index

La Famiglia, 51, 138
Fan Mus., 52
Fantastic Fireworks, 167
Farmers' & Fletchers' Hall, 52
Feathers, 150
Feng Shang, 52
Fêtes, 159
Final Touch, 154
The Finishing Touch Entertaiments Co, 159
The Firework Co, 167
First Floor, 52, 138
Fisher Lighting, 173
Fishmongers' Hall, 52
Fleetwood Classic Limos, 174
Floating Boater, 125
Florians, 138
Footstool, 52
Formula 1, 128
Formula Fun, 128
Formula Veneta, 52, 138
Forte Crest St James's, 53
Forte Crest Regents Pk, 53
Fortnum & Mason, 156
41 Beak St, 53
The Founders' Hall, 53
Four Seasons Htl, 53
Fox, 161
Fox & Anchor, 53
Fox Fireworks, 167
Foxtrot Oscar, 53
Frederick's, 54, 139
The Freemason's Arms, 54
French Inst., 54
Freud Mus., 54
The Fridge, 54
Frock Around the Clock, 177
Froebel Inst. Coll., 54
Frog Frolics, 177
Front Page, 54
Annie Fryer Catering, 150
Fulham Hs, 55
Fulham Pal., 55
Fulham Town Hall, 55
Fung Shing, 55

The Gaslight, 55
Gasworks, 139
Le Gavroche, 55
Gay Hussar, 55
Gemini Ents, 161
Gemini Prodns, 173
George Inn, 56
Glaisters, 139
Glassblower, 56
The Glasshouse Stores, 56
Glaziers' Hall, 56
Glenby's, 173
Gloucester Htl, 56
The Golden Lion, 56
Goldsmith's Coll., 56
Goldsmiths' Hall, 57
Edward Goodyear, 169
Gopal's of Soho, 57
Gorgeous Gourmets, 150, 154
Goring Htl, 57
Le Gothique, 57
Gourmet Diner, 144

Grapeshots, 45
Gray's Inn, 57
Green's, 57
Greenhill, 175
Grenadier Guards, 164
Grocers' Hall, 58
Grosvenor Htl, 58
Grosvenor Prodns, 162
Grosvenor Rms, 58
Grosvenor Hs Htl, 58
Group 4, 181
The Richard Groves Catering Co, 150
Guards Mus., 58
Guildhall, 59
The Guinea, 59
Guinea Butt, 45
Gunnersbury Pk, 59
Guy's Hospital Tower, 59
Gyngleboy, 45

Haandi, 59
Haberdashers' Hall, 59
The Habit, 45
Halcyon Htl, 60
The Halkin, 60
Ham Hs, 60
Duncan Hamilton, 170
Hamilton Hs, 60
Hamilton Suite, 60
Hamiltons Gall., 60
Hamlin's of Kensington, 150
Hammersmith Palais, 60
Hammersmith Town Hall, 61
Hampshire Htl, 61
Hampton Court Pal., 61
Hampton Court, Tiltyard, 61
Sophie Hanna Flowers, 170
Hard Rock Café, 144
Harrods, 156
Harvey's Café, 144
Hash Eleven, 61
Hayward Gall., 61
Toni & Herman Heller, 153
Henry J Beans, 61
Hever Castle, 62
The Highland Gathering, 162
Hilton on Pk Lane, 62
The Hippodrome, 62
RS Hispaniola, 62
Hodgson's, 62
Holderness Hs, 62
Holiday Inn – Mayair, 63
Hollands, 63
Hollyhedge Hs, 63
Holy Trinity Brompton Church Hall, 63
Honourable Artillery Co, 63
Hop Cellars, 63
Hop Exchange, 64
The Horniman At Hay's, 64
Howard Htl, 64
HQ, 64
Hs on Rosslyn Hill, 144
HSS Hire Shops, 173
Hubble & Co, 64
Hurlingham Club, 64
Huxley Car Hire Co, 174
Hyatt Carlton Tower, 65

Hyde Pk Htl, 65

ICA, 65
Iceni, 65
Ikkyu, 65
The Imagination Gall., 65
Imp. City, 66
Imp. Coll., 66
Imp. War Mus., 66
L'Incontro, 66, 133
Initiative Unlimited, 164
Inner Temple Hall, 66
Innholders' Hall, 67
Inst. of Directors, 67
Inst. of Materials, 67
Inst. of Civ.Engineers, 67
Inst. of Mech. Engineers, 67
The Insurance Hall, 68
Insurex, 181
Inter-Continental, 68
Interceptor Launch, 125
Int. Students Hs, 68
Invitation 2000, 181
Irish Club, 68
Irish Guards, 164
Ironmongers' Hall, 68
Ivy, 69, 133

Jakes, 69
Jason's, 69
Jason's Trip, 125
Michael Jay The Freelance Chef, 150
Jazz Café, 69, 139
Joe Allen, 139
Joe's Brass's, 144
Joffins, 165
John (Personal Svcs), 155
Jones, 154
RG Jones (Morden), 173
David Jones and Noel Minett, 170
Jongleurs at Camden Lock, 69, 139
Jongleurs at The Cornet, 69, 139
Jukebox Junction, 173
Juliana's, 159, 165
Julie's, 133
Julie's Rest. & WB, 69
Just Balloons, 172
Just Hire, 154
Justerini & Brooks, 156

K & M Caterers, 150
K Warehouse, 69
Kalamaras Micro, 144
Kaya Korean, 70
Kempton Pk, 70
Ken Lo's Memories, 70
Kennys, 139
Kensington Conservative Assn, 70
Kensington Pl, 139
Kensington Pal. Thistle, 70
Kenwood Hs, 70
Kenwood Hs, Old Kitchen, 70
Kettners, 70, 144
Kew Bridge Steam Mus., 71
Khan's, 145
King David Suite, 71
King of Diamonds, 71

Alphabetical index

King's Coll., 71
Kite & Balloon Co, 172
Knebworth Hs, 71
Knightsbridge Pl, 71
The Kosher
  Luncheon Club, 72

The Lady Daphne, 125
SB Lady Gwynfred, 72
The Lamb Tav., 72
The Lanesborough, 72
Langan's Brass., 133
Langham Hilton, 72
Lansdowne Club, 72
Larry's WB, 73
Laser Creations Int., 167
Laser Dynamics, 168
Laser Grafix, 168
Lauderdale Hs, 73
Launceston Pl, 73, 133
The Law Soc, 73
Lawson Ross Mgt, 162
Lay & Wheeler, 156
Le Cap Ent, 162
Le Maitre Fireworks, 167
Lea & Sandeman, 156
Leadenhall Tapas Bar, 73
Jeremy Lee
  Associates, 162
Leeds Castle, 73
Lees Bag, 45
Legends, 74
Leighton Hs, 74
Leith's, 74
Leith's Good Food, 151
Lemonia, 145
Leoni's Quo Vadis, 74
Leslie & Godwin, 181
Letherby &
  Christopher, 151
Leven is Strijd, 74
Ley-Ons, 74
Life Guards, 164
Limelight, 74
Lincoln's Inn, 75
Lindsay Hs, 75
Lipman & Sons, 176
The Little Ship Club, 75
Lively Sounds, 162
Lloyd's of London, 75
London Carriage Co, 175
London Coaches, 175
The London Dungeon, 75
London Limousine
  Co, 174
The London
  Marquee Co, 169
London Marriott, 75
London Metropole, 76
London
  Music Agency, 162
London Palladium, 76
London Press Ctr, 76
London Rowing Club, 76
London Scottish, 76
The London
  Television Ctr, 76
London Transport
  Mus., 77
London Zoo, 77
The London Welsh
  Centre, 77
Lord's, 77
Lou Pescadou, 77
The Lumsden Twins, 151
Lundonia Hs, 77

M&B Marquees, 169
MacQuisten Mitchell, 151
Madame Jo Jos, 140
Madame Tussaud's, 78
Magnum Marketing, 159
Maidenhead
  Steam Navigation, 125
Mainstream
  Leisure, 126, 140
Mall Galleries, 78
Mange Tout, 151
Mao Tai, 78
Marble Hill Hs, 78
Margaret's Cakes
  of Distinction, 154
Marine Ices, 145
Maroush, 133
Marquees over
  London, 169
Massey's Agency, 155
Maximus, 78
Maxwell Car Svcs, 174
The Mayfair, 78
Mekong, 78
Mélange, 79
Mercers' Hall, 79
Merchant Taylors'
  Hall, 79
Le Meridien, 79
Mermaid Thtr, 79
Le Mesurier, 79
Middle Temple Hall, 80
Le Midi, 80, 140
Midnight Design, 173
Mimmo d'Ischia, 80
Ming, 80
The Ministry
  of Sound, 80
Minogue's Bar, 80
Mirabelle, 80
Mitchell Linen Hire, 155
Mitsukoshi, 81
Mobi-Deque, 166
Mon Plaisir, 81
Monkey Island, 81
Monkeys, 81
Philip Moore, 151
More Balls
  Than Most, 162
Mortons Club, 81
Mosimann's, 151
Mosimann's Belfry, 81
Moss Bros, 176
Motcomb's, 81, 140
Mount Royal Htl, 82
The Mountbatten, 82
Moveable Feasts, 151
Moving Venue, 151
Moyses Stevens, 170
Mr Kong, 82
Mr Wing, 140
The Mug Hs, 45
Murder my Lord?, 164
Norman Murray
  & Anne Chudleigh, 162
Mus. of Childhood, 82
Mus. of
  Garden History, 82
Mus. of London, 83
Mus. of Mankind, 83
Mus. of
  the Moving Image, 83
Music Mgt, 162
Mustard Caterers, 151
Muzic Non Stop
  Soundz, 166

Nacho's, 145
Nam Long, 140
Nat. Assn of
  Toastmasters, 162
Nat. Army Mus., 83
Nat. Liberal Club, 83
Nat. Portrait Gall., 84
Nat. Westminster
  Hall, 84
Natural History Mus., 84
Naval & Military
  Club, 84
Neal St, 84
Neptunus, 169
New Connaught Rms, 85
New Quebec Quisine, 151
New World, 145
New Zealand Hs, 85
Nikita's, 140
Non-stop Party Shop, 177
Nosh Bros., 85, 140
Nostalgia
  Amusements, 173
Nôtre Dame Hall, 85
Now & Zen, 85
Nº 1 Yacht Club, 85

The O-Bar, 85
Oberlander, 153
Occasions, 152
Oddbins, 157
Odette's, 86, 133
The Old Operating Thtr
  Mus. & Herb Garret, 86
Old Refectory, 86
Old Royal
  Observatory, 86
The Old Thameside
  Inn, 86
One Night Stand, 177
Opera Terazza!, 86
Orangery
  (Holland Pk), 87
Orangery
  (Kensington Pal.), 87
Orient Expr, 124
Orso, 140
Oscar's Den, 177
Osteria Basilico, 145
Oval, 87
Owen Bros. Catering, 152
Owen Brown, 169
Owens & Monteith, 152
Oxford & Cambridge
  Club, 87

PA Music, 166
Jane Packer, 170
Tony Page, 153
Pains Fireworks, 167
The Paintball Co, 129
Painters' Hall, 87
Pal. Thtr, 87
Palio, 141
Palm Brokers, 170
Palms-on-the-Hill, 145
Palookaville, 141
La Paquerette, 87
Pk Lane Htl, 88
Party
  Ingredients, 152, 155
Party Jazz, 162
Party Planners, 159
Party Professionals, 160
Paulo's, 88
Payne & Gunter, 152
Peacock Hs, 88

Alphabetical index

Penguins Ent, 162, 166
Pentland Hs, 88
Jo Peters, 163
Pewterers' Hall, 88
Phene Arms, 88
Phillips, 88
Detta Phillips, 170
Photographers' Gall., 89
Michael Pickworth, 170
Nic Picot, 163
Pigeon, 89
Pimlico Wine Vaults, 89
Pinewood Studios, 89
Pitcher & Piano, 89
Pizza on the Pk, 145
Pizza Pomodoro, 145
Pizzeria Condotti, 89
PJ's, 141
The Pl Below, 89
Plaisterers' Hall, 90
Planet Hollywood, 141
Planner Catering
 (Equip. Hire), 155
Platters, 152
Players Thtr, 141
Playscape
 Pro Racing, 128
The Plough, 90
Poissonnerie
 de l'Avenue, 90
Polish Hearth Club, 90
Polish Social &
 Cultural Assn, 90
Pomegranates, 90
La Pomme d'Amour, 90
Pont de la Tour, 90, 133
Porchester Ctr, 91
Prelude, 163
HMS President, 91
Alison Price, 152
Prime Performers, 163
Princes, 152
Puddleduck, 164
Pulbrook & Gould, 170
The Pulpit, 45
Punters, 91
The Puppet Ctr
 Trust, 163
Puttin' on the Glitz, 177

Quaglino's, 91, 141
Quasar, 130
Quayside, 91
TS Queen Mary, 91
Queen's Eyot, 91
Queen's Hs, 92
Queen's
 Ice Skating Club, 92

**Raffles
 Dining Room, 92**
Ranger's Hs, 92
The RAW Club, 92
Rayner's Catering &
 Equip. Hire, 155
Rebato's, 141
Red Fort, 92
Reform Club, 93
The Regent, 93
Regent's Coll., 93
The Rembrandt Htl, 93
Rent-a-Loo, 173
Rib Room Hyatt
 Carlton Tower Htl, 93
Richmond Caterers, 152
Ring & Brymer, 152
The Ritz, 94, 134

The River Café, 134
Robersons, 157
Rochester Htl, 94
Rochesters, 94
Rock Circus, 94
Rock Garden, 94
Rodos, 94
Ronnie Scots, 141
The Roof
 Gardens, 95, 133
Rose Garden Rest., 95
Royal Acad. of Arts, 95
Royal
 Aeronautical Soc, 95
Royal Air Force Mus., 95
Royal Albert Hall, 96
Royal
 Botanic Gardens, 96
Royal Coll. of Art, 96
Royal Coll. of Music, 96
Royal Garden Htl, 97
Royal Green Jackets, 97
Royal Inst.
 of British Architects,
 98
Royal Inst. of GB, 98
Royal Lancaster, 98
Royal Majestic Suite, 98
Royal Nat. Thtr
 Costume Hire Dept,
 176
Royal Nat. Thtr, 99
Royal Opera Hs, 99
Royal Over-Seas
 League, 99
Royal Parks
 Executive Agency, 99
Royal Soc of Arts, 99
Royal Veterinary
 Coll., 100
Royal Geographical
 Soc, 97
Royal Holloway Coll., 97
Royal Horseguards
 Thistle Htl, 97
Royal
 Horticultural Halls, 98
RSJ, 100
Rubens Htl, 100
Ruby in the Dust, 146
Ruby's, 100
La Rueda, 141
Rules, 100
Rumours, 146
RUSI Building, 100
Russell, 101

Saatchi Gall., 101
Saddlers' Hall, 101
Saigon, 101
St Andrew Golf Club,101
St Bartholomew's
 Hospital, 101
St Botolph's Hall, 101
St Bride
 Foundation Inst., 102
St Etheldreda's
 Crypt, 102
St John's Gate, 102
St John's Hill, 102
St Martin
 In The Fields, 102
St Moritz, 102
St Peter's Hall, 102
St Quentin, 102
St Thomas's
 Hospital, 103

Salters' Hall, 103
San Lorenzo, 134
San Martino, 103
The Sanctuary, 103
Sandown Park
 Racecourse, 104
Sandrini, 141
Les Saveurs, 104
The Savoy, 104
Savoy Grill, 134
Savoy River Room, 134
Le Scandale, 104
Schaverien, 153
School Dinners Rest.,142
School of Pharmacy, 104
Science Mus., 104
Scone, 105
Seafresh, 105
Searcy's, 105, 152
The Jonathan Seaward
 Organisation, 160
Selfridge Htl, 105
Selfridges, 157
Serpentine Gall., 105
Shampers, 105
Sheekey's, 106
Shell Shock, 167
Shelleys, 106
Shepherd's, 106
Sheraton Belgravia, 106
Sheraton Park Tower,106
Shotberries, 45
Shuckburgh Arms, 106
Simply Delicious, 153
Simpsons of Cornhill,106
Simpsons-
 in-the-Strand, 107
Sir John Soane's
 Mus., 107
606 Club, 107
Ski Club of GB, 107
Skinners' Hall, 107
Skinkers, 45
Skirmish, 129
Slug & Lettuce, 108
Smith's Gall., 108
Smollensky's
 Balloon, 142
Smollensky's on the
 Strand, 142
Smythsons, 181
Snows on the Green, 142
Soc of London
 Toastmasters, 163
Sofra, 142
Soho Soho, 108
Soho Wine Supply, 157
Solange's, 108
Sotherby's, 108
Sounds Good to Me, 166
The South Bank
 Center, 108
Southwark Tav., 108
Spaceworks
 Furniture Hire, 173
Spaghetti Hs, 108
Spanish Club, 109
Spencer Hs, 109
Spitting Image Mus.,109
Splitting Images
 Lookalike Agency, 163
The Spitoon, 45
Sproule Ents, 163
St Stephens
 Const. Club, 103
The Stafford, 109
Stakis St Ermins, 109

Alphabetical index

Standard Fireworks 167
Stanley Hs, 109
Staple Inn, 110
Star Expr Limos, 174
Star of India, 146
Star Tavern, 110
Starlight, 174
Stationers' Hall, 110
Sternberg-Clarke, 163
Stitches, 169
Stoke Newington Town Hall, 110
Stoll-Moss Thtrs VIP Service, 134
Strand Pal. Htl, 110
Streatham Mega Bowl, 110
Subterania, 110
The Sun, 111
Suntory, 111
Le Suquet, 111
Survival Game, 130
SW1 Club, 111
Sweetings, 111
Syon Park (Banqueting), 111
Syon Park (Conservatory), 111
Syon Park (House), 112

The Talent Corpn UK, 163
Tall House, 112
Tallow Chandlers' Hall, 112
The Tank, 112
Tapster, 45
Tastefully Yours, 153
Tate Gall., 112
Tatsuso, 112
The Tattershall Castle, 113
Taylor's Hire, 155
Team Daytona, 128
Temple Island, 113
Texas Lone Star, 146
Thames Leisure, 126
Thames Pleasure Craft, 126
Thtr Mus., 113
Thtr Royal, 113
The Theatre Zoo, 176
The Theme Makers, 160
Theme Traders, 160
Thierry's, 113
Thresher, 157
Throgmorton's, 113
Tidal Cruises Ltd & Jackson Bros. (River Svcs), 126
Tiroler Hut, 142
TKO Mobile Nightclub, 166
Top Nosh, 153
Top Tier Catering, 153
Tower Bridge, 114
Tower Thistle, 114
Town & Country Flowers, 170
Town & County, 153
Trafalgar Tav., 114
Trinity Hs, 114
Truckles of Pied Bull Yard, 45
La Truffe Noir, 114
Tumblers, 45
Turk Launches, 126

Kenneth Turner, 170
Turners, 114
Turnmills, 115
Turtle & Pearce, 172
Tuttons, 115
20th Century Frox, 177
22 Jermyn St, 115
Twickenham Banqueting Ctr, 115
The Two Chairmen, 115

Ubique, 160
Udder Pl Wine Rms, 46
Ultimate Experience, 160
Uncommon Cooks, 153
Univ of London Boat Club, 115
Univ of London Union, 115
Univ Women's Club, 116
Upper Refectory Suite, 116
Upstairs At 58, 116

Vanderbilt Htl, 116
Vat's, 116
The Vaults, 116
The Viceroy, 116
V&A Mus., 116
V&A Mus. Café, 116
Victoria Pump Hs, 116
Villandry Dining Rms, 116
The Vineyard, 46
The Vintage Hs, 157

Wag, 116
Waldorf Htl, 118
Walkers of St James's, 118
Wallace Collection, 118
Walton's, 118
Wandsworth Civic Suite, 118
Washington Htl, 118
Water Sculpture, 174
Watermen & Lightermen's Hall, 119
Wedding Plan, 181
HQS Wellington, 119
Welsh Guards, 164
Wembley Grehound Stadium, 143
Wessex Hs, 119
West Side Balloons, 172
West Wycombe Caves, 119
Westbury Htl, 119
Westminster Boating Base, 119
Westminster Cathedral Hall, 120
Westminster Coll., 120
Westminster Conference Ctr, 120
Westway Studios, 120
The White Horse, 120
White Hs Htl, 120
White Tower, 121
Whitechapel Art Gall., 121
Whittington's, 121
Wilson's, 121
Wiltons, 121
Wimbledon Greyhound Stad., 142

Winchester Hs Club, 121
Windows on the World Hilton Htl, 134
Wine Gallery, 146
Lorna Wing, 153
WKD, 122
Wódka, 142
Woods River Svcs, 126
World Trade Ctr, 122
The Wren Press, 181
Wynkyn de Worde, 122

Xenon, 122

Ye Olde Cheshire Cheese, 122
Young's, 166, 176
Your Ent Svcs, 163

Zen, 122
Zen Central, 122, 134
ZeNW3, 122
Zinos, 166
Zona Virtual Reality, 165

Notes

Also from Harden's Guides ...

Harden's London Restaurants

The only annual London restaurant guide written on the basis of personal inspections by the editors of each establishment listed and a detailed annual survey of regular London restaurant-goers.

Published every November

"User-friendly in price, size and outlook"
Nicholas Lander, *Financial Times*

"A brilliant little listings guide"
Lindsey Bareham, LBC

"Impressively reliable"
Louise Nicholson, *Fodor's London Companion*